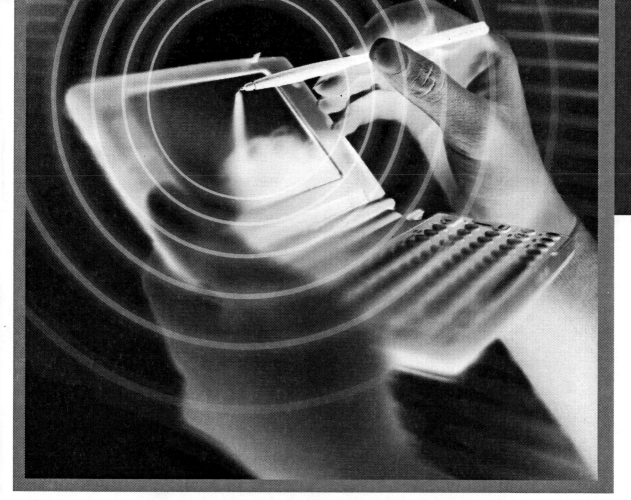

(((cwna™ Certified Wireless Network Administrator

Official CWNA Study Guide

D1307259

WestNet Learning Technologies

www.westnetinc.com

CREDITS

Author and Development Editor: Devin Akin, Planet3 Wireless

Editorial and Production Manager: Marilee E. Aust

Book Design and Composition: D. Kari Luraas, Clairvoyance Design

Illustrator: Lynn Siefken

Illustrations marked Copyright Young Design, Inc. reprinted with permission by Michael Young, www.ydi.com

Technical Writer and Editor: David M. Watts

Indexer: Amy Casey

Copy Editor: Mara Gaiser Chance

Cover Design: David Jones

Proofreader: Larry Beckett

Certified Wireless Network Administrator: Official Certification Guide
656 pp., includes illustrations and index

1. Introduction to Wireless LANs 2. RF Fundamentals 3. Spread Spectrum Technology 4. Wireless LAN Infrastructure Devices 5. Antennas and Accessories 6. Wireless LAN Organizations and Standards 7. The 802.11 Network Architecture 8. Physical Layers 9. Troubleshooting Wireless LAN Installations 10. Wireless LAN Security 11. Site Survey Fundamentals

VPS71.0

For instructor-led training, self-paced courses,
turn-key curricula solutions, or more information contact:

WestNet Learning Technologies (dba: WestNet Inc.)
5420 Ward Road, Suite 150, Arvada, CO 80002 USA
E-mail: Info@westnetinc.com

To access the WestNet student resource site, go to
http://www.westnetinc.com/student

Preface

Who Should Study This Course

This course introduces wireless LAN technology and instructs students to install, configure, and troubleshoot wireless LAN networks. It provides vendor-neutral information that will prepare you for the Certified Wireless Network Administrator (CWNA) exam. You can use this course to help in your preparation to become CWNA certified, or if you simply want to obtain knowledge and skills for administering wireless networks.

The CWNA certification is appropriate for:

- Systems and Network Administrators
- Systems and Network Engineers
- Systems and Network Analysts
- Technical Support and Implementation Engineers
- Technical Consultants
- Network Architects

Prerequisites

To fully benefit from the material presented in this course, it is recommended that students possess a level of networking knowledge similar to that tested by Network+, CCNA, CNE, or MSCE certification exams.

Important Notes About CWNA Certification

This course has been developed to meet the 2002 objectives of the CWNA credential examination (Exam# PWO-100), the first step toward the Certified Wireless Network Engineer (CWNE) certification. Certification is a worthwhile goal, and is probably the reason that you bought this course. However, this is not an "exam cram" study guide that guarantees that you will pass the test with a minimum of effort.

Our goal is to prepare you to be a productive member of a wireless LAN networking staff. Therefore, this course teaches the technical concepts and principles that you will use regularly throughout your networking or computing career. If you study this material diligently, you will gain the knowledge that you need to be successful in the wireless LAN networking industry. That same knowledge will also help you to pass the certification test.

Exam Objectives

The table below lists the CWNA credential exam objectives, by subject area, that were published at the time of this writing (for the latest details, visit **www.cwne.com**).

Subject Area	% of Exam
Radio Frequency (RF) Technologies	24%
Wireless LAN Technologies	17%
Wireless LAN Implementation and Management	30%
Wireless LAN Security	16%
Wireless LAN Industry and Standards	13%
Total	100%

Features

Several unique features are included in this text to enhance your understanding of the materials and ability to apply concepts. Throughout the course, emphasis is placed on applying concepts to real-world scenarios through end-of-lesson activities, extended activities, and other exercises and examples.

Learning Objectives, Unit Summaries, Discussion Questions, and Activities/Exercises

Learning objectives, unit summaries, discussion questions, and activities/exercises are designed to function as integrated study tools. Learning objectives reflect what you should be able to accomplish after completing each unit. Unit summaries highlight the key concepts you should master. The discussion questions help guide critical thinking about those key concepts, and the activities/exercises provide you with opportunities to practice important techniques.

Key Terms

The wireless industry includes many unique terms that are critical to creating a workable language when combined with the world of business. Definitions of key terms are provided in alphabetical order at the beginning of each unit of the textbook and in a glossary at the end of the book.

Resources Available in Instructor-led Settings

An Instructor's Resource Tool Kit accompanies this course when it used in an academic or instructor-led setting. The online-based kit includes an Instructor's Guide with the answers to activities/exercises, unit quizzes, and the end-of-course exam. It also includes PowerPoint presentations organized by lesson, unit, and course.

WestNet Learning Technologies' cutting edge Administrative tools offer a unique online Windows®-based exam software. The Instructor's Resource Web site also includes sample syllabi, discussion topics, puzzles, cryptograms, and up-to-the-minute supplements to the textbooks and course materials. The online course exam engine includes hundreds of lesson, unit, and course questions. These exams can be accessed by individual students and are presented in random order, ensuring that student never get the same question in the same order. This feature allows instructors to create printed and online pretests, practice tests, and actual examinations.

Why Choose WestNet?

WestNet Learning Technologies offers comprehensive information technologies (IT) educational and certification programs and curricula to secondary schools, colleges and universities, as well as corporations, resellers, and individual participants around the globe. These programs provide participants with the skills necessary to further their technical knowledge and obtain hands-on experience.

This unique program, which is vendor neutral, helps prepare participants to pursue IT careers, earn secondary and post-secondary educational degrees, and/or obtain industry certification.

WestNet Learning Technologies' programs are currently provided to more than 1,000 institutions around the world. Its programs are also offered internationally in more than a dozen countries and in five languages.

Contents

INTRODUCTION

The Certified Wireless Network Administrator (CWNA) course is designed for students who want to obtain a broad range of skills and knowledge for administering wireless LANs and those who plan to take the CWNA exam (Exam # PWO-100). This course provides the information an IT professional needs to successfully install, configure, and maintain wireless LANs. The vendor-neutral material covered in this course comprehensively teaches wireless LAN technology, instead of focusing on a specific vendor's product line. By learning vendor-neutral information, students are able to apply their knowledge to any vendor's product line.

KEY TOPICS

- Wireless LAN Organizations, Standards, and Competing Technologies
- Radio Frequency (RF) Behaviors
- Frequency Hopping Spread Spectrum (FHSS)
- Direct Sequence Spread Spectrum (DSSS)
- Wireless LAN Infrastructure Devices
- Antenna Categories, Concepts, and Installation
- 802.11 Network Architecture
- Interframe Spacing, RTS/CTS, and Modulation
- Wired Equivalent Privacy (WEP) and Wireless LAN Security
- RF Site Survey Fundamentals

COURSE OBJECTIVES

- Define and apply the basic concepts of RF technology, including how spread spectrum technologies apply to wireless LANs

- Explain the fundamental principles and concepts behind installing, configuring, and maintaining wireless LANs

- Describe the organizations and regulations that govern wireless LANs

- Demonstrate the necessary knowledge for complying with regulations that apply to setting up and maintaining a wireless LAN

- Install, set up, and maintain a wireless network using various hardware devices, such as access points, bridges, gateways, and antennas

- Analyze and troubleshoot the problems that can occur with wireless LAN data transmission, including multipath, hidden nodes, and interference

- Perform a basic site survey for the installation of a wireless LAN, and explain factors to be considered

- Secure the transmission of data over a wireless LAN, and identify the different types of attacks that can occur from hackers

COURSE OVERVIEW

Unit 1, "Introduction to Wireless LANs," discusses the wireless LAN market, presenting an overview of the past, present, and future of wireless LANs, and an introduction to the standards that govern wireless LANs. We discuss some of the appropriate applications of wireless LANs and introduce you to the various organizations that guide the evolution and development of wireless LANs.

Unit 2, "RF Fundamentals," discusses the properties of RF radiation and its effect on wireless LANs' performance. We explain key antenna concepts, including antenna gain, intentional radiator, and equivalent isotropically radiated power (EIRP). You will learn the mathematical relationships that exist in RF circuits and how to perform necessary RF math calculations.

Unit 3 defines and describes spread spectrum technology and discusses how it is used according to FCC guidelines. The two main spread spectrum technologies, FHSS and DSSS are differentiated, compared, and discussed in depth. This unit also explains how spread spectrum technology is implemented in wireless LANs.

Unit 4 covers the different categories of wireless network infrastructure equipment and some of the variations within each category. The hardware items within each category are the physical building blocks of every wireless LAN. As you read this unit, you will become more versed in the implementation of wireless LANs by learning how to configure and install each type of hardware.

In Unit 5, "Antennas and Accessories," we discuss a basic element of the devices that make access points, bridges, PC cards, and other wireless devices communicate: antennas. We describe the many different items that connect antennas to other wireless LAN hardware. Antennas are most often used to increase the range of wireless LAN systems, but proper antenna selection can also enhance the security of a wireless LAN. All wireless LAN antennas fall into three general categories: omnidirectional, semidirectional, and highly directional. You will learn the attributes of each of these groups and the proper methods for installing each kind of antenna.

We describe the following wireless LAN accessories: RF amplifiers, RF attenuators, and lightening arrestors. Knowing these devices' uses, specifications, and effects on RF signal strength is essential for building a functional wireless LAN. We also discuss Power over Ethernet (PoE), an important technology in today's wireless networks that has spawned new product lines and new standards.

In Unit 6, "Wireless LAN Organizations and Standards," we discuss the Federal Communications Commission (FCC)'s role in defining and enforcing the regulations governing wireless communication, and the role of the Institute of Electrical and Electronics Engineers (IEEE) in creating standards that allow wireless devices to work together. We cover the different frequency bands on which wireless LANs operate, and examine the IEEE 802.11 family of standards. We cover three major organizations that contribute to growth and education in the wireless LAN marketplace: Wireless Ethernet Compatibility Alliance (WECA), European Telecommunications Standards Institute (ETSI), and Wireless LAN Association (WLANA). Finally, this unit covers some of the emerging technologies and standards that compete with the 802.11 family of standards and drive enterprise spending, including HomeRF, Bluetooth, Infrared, and OpenAir.

By understanding the regulations and the standards that govern and guide wireless LAN technology, you will be able to ensure that any wireless system you implement will be interoperable and comply with the regulation.

Unit 7 covers some of the key concepts found in the 802.11 network architecture. Most of the topics in this unit are defined directly in the 802.11 standard, and are required for implementation of 802.11-compliant hardware. We examine the process by which clients connect to an access point, the terms used for organizing wireless LANs, and how power management is accomplished in wireless LAN client devices.

In Unit 8, "Physical Layers," we discuss some of the media access control (MAC) and Physical Layer characteristics of wireless LANs that are common to all wireless LAN products, regardless of the manufacturer. We explain the difference between Ethernet and wireless LAN frames and how wireless LANs avoid collisions. We also describe how wireless LAN stations communicate with one another under normal circumstances, and how collision handling occurs in a wireless LAN.

In Unit 9, we discuss the more common obstacles to successful implementation of a wireless LAN, and how to troubleshoot them. There are different methods of discovering when these challenges exist, and each of the challenges discussed has its remedies and workarounds. Many consider the challenges to implementing any wireless LAN to be "textbook" problems that can commonly occur and, therefore, can be avoided by careful planning.

Unit 10 explains the key to making a wireless LAN secure: educating those who implement and manage the wireless LAN about preventing security breaches. We discuss the much-maligned 802.11 security solution known as Wired Equivalent Privacy (WEP). You will learn why WEP alone will not keep a hacker out of a wireless LAN, and how to use WEP with some level of effectiveness.

To prepare you as an administrator to prevent security problems, we explain the various methods that can be used to attack a wireless LAN. We discuss some of the emerging security solutions that are available, but not yet specified by any of the 802.11 standards. Finally, we offer some recommendations for maintaining wireless LAN security and discuss corporate security policy as it pertains specifically to wireless LANs.

In Unit 11, we discuss the process of conducting a site survey, also known as a "facilities analysis." Concepts such as throughput needs, power accessibility, extendibility, application requirements, budget requirements, and signal range are all key components as you conduct a site survey. We further discuss the ramifications of a weak site survey and no site survey at all. Our discussion covers a checklist of tasks that you need to accomplish and equipment you will use. We will apply those checklists to several hypothetical examples.

Unit 1
Introduction to Wireless LANs

Wireless LANs were once considered expensive and slow solutions to certain network connectivity issues. Wireless LAN sales are now exploding. A recent industry publication stated that wireless network sales are the only part of an otherwise depressed network solution market actually increasing in market share. Enterprise solution vendors such as Cisco Systems and Avaya Communications, and small office/home office (SOHO) vendors, such as Linksys and D-Link, all offer some type of wireless network solution.

Wireless networks are finding their way into large enterprises, such as banks and hospitals, where they help solve network connectivity challenges such as extremely long distances between network nodes and mobile user communications. Small and mid-sized businesses can expand their existing networks quickly and inexpensively and can have a new network up and running in less than a day. Law enforcement, fire and rescue teams, ambulatory services, and other government agencies are finding wireless LANs useful in a Wireless Metropolitan Area Network (WMAN) configuration. Finally, home users who want to share a broadband connection no longer have to pull wires or use the home electrical wiring as a networking medium.

This unit discusses the wireless LAN market, presenting an overview of the past, present, and future of wireless LANs, and provides an introduction to the standards that govern wireless LANs. We discuss some of the appropriate applications of wireless LANs and introduce you to the various organizations that guide the evolution and development of wireless LANs.

The knowledge of the history and evolution of wireless LAN technology is an essential part of the foundational principles of wireless LANs. A thorough understanding of the origins of wireless LANs and the organizations and applications that helped the technology mature enables you to better apply wireless LAN technologies to meet your organization's or client's needs.

Lessons

1. The Wireless LAN Market
2. Wireless LAN Applications

Terms

100BaseT—The group of proposed IEEE 802.3 Physical Layer specifications for 100-Mbps Ethernet (fast Ethernet) over various wiring specifications is referred to as 100BaseT. Fast Ethernet and the 100BaseT standard are synonymous. 100BaseT is the specification for twisted pair wiring in a Fast Ethernet environment.

802.11—802.11 is the IEEE standard that specifies medium access and Physical Layer specifications for 1 Mbps and 2 Mbps wireless connectivity between fixed, portable, and moving stations within a local area.

802.11a—802.11a, a revision to the IEEE standard, operates in the unlicensed 5 GHz band. Most 802.11a products have data rates up to 54 Mbps and must support 6, 12, and 24 Mbps.

802.11b—802.11b is a revision to the IEEE standard for direct sequence wireless LANs. Most 802.11b products have data rates of up to 11 Mbps, even though the standard does not specify the techniques for achieving these data rates.

802.11g—IEEE 802.11g is a proposed wireless network standard designed to provide the bandwidth of 802.11a networks while maintaining backward compatibility with 802.11b networks. 802.11g operates in the 2.4-GHz ISM band.

access layer—The access layer provides client devices access to the network in a three-layer hierarchy network design.

access point—An access point is a Layer 2 (Data Link Layer) device that serves as an interface between the wireless network and a wired network and can control medium access using RTS/CTS. Access points combined with a distribution system (Ethernet, for example) support the creation of multiple radio cells (also called basic service sets [BSSs]) that enable roaming throughout a facility.

Asymmetric Digital Subscriber Line (ADSL)—ADSL is a relatively new technology used to deliver high-speed digital communications across the local loop over standard local loop copper wire. ADSL data rates range from 128 Kbps to over 1.5 Mbps downstream, and 64 Kbps to over 640 Kbps upstream.

Asynchronous Transfer Mode (ATM)—ATM is connection-oriented cell relay technology based on (53-byte) cells. An ATM network consists of ATM switches that form multiple virtual circuits to carry groups of cells from source to destination. ATM can provides high-speed transport services for audio, data, and video.

basic service set (BSS)—BSS is a set of 802.11-compliant stations and an access point that operates as a fully connected wireless network.

beamwidth—Beamwidth is the measure of the horizontal and vertical lobes of an antenna signal. An omnidirectional antenna has a 360-degree horizontal beamwidth, while a semidirectional antenna may only have a 30-degree beamwidth.

Carrier Sense Multiple Access with Collision Detection (CSMA/CD)—CSMA/CD is the technique Ethernet uses for controlling access to the shared transmission medium (the bus). In CSMA/CD, a node may not transmit unless the medium is idle (carrier sense). If the transmitting node detects (collision detection) that another station (multiple access) has begun to transmit at the same time, both nodes stop, then wait a random time interval before attempting to retransmit.

Category 5 UTP data cable—Category 5 cabling is certified for data rates up to 100 Mbps, which facilitates 802.3 100BaseT (Ethernet) networks.

core layer—In a three-layer hierarchy network design, the core layer provides access to external networks, and routes packets between distribution layers. The core layer should be fast, versatile, stable, and redundant.

distribution layer—In a three-layer hierarchy network design, the distribution layer moves packets between the access layers, and passes information up to the core layer.

Ethernet—Ethernet technology, originally developed in the 1970s by Xerox Corporation in conjunction with Intel and DEC, is now the primary medium for LANs. The original Ethernet has 10-Mbps throughput and uses the CSMA/CD method to access the physical media. Fast Ethernet (100-Mbps Ethernet) and Gigabit Ethernet (1,000-Mbps Ethernet) are also used.

Federal Communications Commission (FCC)—The FCC is an independent U.S. government agency, directly responsible to Congress. The FCC was established by the Communications Act of 1934 and is charged with regulating interstate and international communications by radio, television, wire, satellite, and cable. The FCC's jurisdiction covers the 50 states, the District of Columbia, and U.S. possessions.

frame relay—Frame relay is a packet switching technology designed to move data across a WAN. Frame relay normally operates at speeds of 56 Kbps to 45 Mbps.

Gigahertz (GHz)—A GHz is one billion cycles per second (hertz).

highly directional antenna—A highly directional antenna is one that tightly focuses the horizontal and vertical RF beamwidths to maximize the distance the propagated wave can travel.

Institute of Electrical and Electronic Engineers (IEEE)—IEEE is a United States-based standards organization participating in the development of standards for data transmission systems. IEEE has made significant progress in the establishment of standards for LANs, in particular, the IEEE 802 series of standards.

last mile—Last mile is a term used to describe the local loop. A local loop is the pair of copper wires that connects a customer's telephone to the telephone company's CO switching system.

megabits per second (Mbps)—Mbps identifies the rate at which information travels down a physical medium or through space (wireless). Mbps is equivalent to 1,000,000 bits per second. 1.544 Mbps is equivalent to 1,544,000 bits per second.

omnidirectional antenna—An omnidirectional (omni) antenna is one that has a 360-degree horizontal beamwidth and a variable vertical beamwidth. Omni antennas propagate the RF signal equally in all horizontal directions.

personal digital assistant (PDA)—PDAs are small, handheld devices that provide a subset of the operations of a typical PC. They are used for scheduling, electronic notepads, and small database applications.

point-to-point (PtP)—A PtP connection provides dedicated communications between two, and only two, endpoints.

point-to-multipoint (PtMP)—A PtMP connection connects a single point to multiple outlying points. Also known as hub-and-spoke, the hub is the focal point for communications between several adjacent networks. All communications center on the hub.

Request to Send/Clear to Send (RTS/CTS)—RTS/CTS is a virtual carrier sense protocol used on WLANs. When RTS/CTS is enabled on a wireless LAN, a station wishing to communicate effectively reserves the medium for a period of time. All other stations then must wait for the communications to end before they can use the medium.

semidirectional antenna—A semidirectional antenna is one where the antenna focuses most of the radio signal energy in one direction, while creating several smaller lobes around the edges of the major signal. Semidirectional antennas are well suited for short to medium range bridging between buildings, but can also be used indoors to better direct the radio signal down halls or around obstacles.

small office/home office (SOHO)—SOHO is a term used to describe data and voice communications workers who either work from their home, or work in a small office of 50 or fewer workers.

Token Ring—Token Ring is the IEEE 802.5-specified, ring-based, token-passing LAN topology. Each node on the ring acts as a repeater, passing the token from node to node as the token travels around the entire ring. Each node must wait its turn to transmit data and may only transmit when it controls the token.

Unlicensed National Information Infrastructure (UNII) bands—A segment of RF frequencies allocated by the FCC for unlicensed data communications, used by IEEE 802.11a, 802.11h, and HyperLAN2 wireless LANs; the three bands are: 5.15 to 5.25 GHz, 5.25 to 5.35 GHz, and 5.725 to 5.825 GHz.

Wireless Ethernet Compatibility Alliance (WECA)—WECA's mission is to certify interoperability of Wi-Fi™ (IEEE 802.11) products and to promote Wi-Fi as the global wireless LAN standard across all market segments.

Wireless Fidelity™ (Wi-Fi™)—Wi-Fi™ is the WECA certification standard signifying interoperability among 802.11b products.

Wireless Internet Service Provider (WISP)—A WISP is an Internet service provider (ISP) that provides customers with access to the Internet over wireless networks. WISPs often operate in rural areas where the wired infrastructure is inadequate for providing anything but dialup Internet access.

Wireless LAN Association (WLANA)—The Wireless LAN Association (WLANA) is a nonprofit educational trade association, comprised of the leaders and technology innovators in the local area wireless technology industry. Through sponsor and affiliate members' knowledge and experience, WLANA provides a clearinghouse of information about wireless local area applications, issues, and trends. In addition, WLANA serves as an industry resource regarding wireless LAN and PAN products, as well as to industry press and analysts.

xDSL—xDSL is a generic term used to describe different types of Digital Subscriber Line services.

Lesson 1—The Wireless LAN Market

The market for wireless local area networks (WLANs) seems to be evolving similarly to the networking industry as a whole, starting with the early adopters using whatever technology was available. The market has moved into a rapid growth stage, for which popular standards are providing the catalyst. The big difference between the networking market as a whole and the wireless LAN market is the rate of growth. The flexible implementation of wireless LANs makes it clear why they are outpacing every other market sector.

Objectives

At the end of this lesson you will be able to:

- Explain the general history of wireless LANs
- Identify standards specific to today's wireless LANs

 **Key Point**

Today's wireless LAN standards evolved from the military's need for simple and secure data communications in a combat environment.

History of Wireless LANs

Spread spectrum wireless networks, like many technologies, came of age under the military's guidance. The military needed a simple, easily implemented, and secure method of exchanging data in a combat environment.

As the cost of wireless technology decreased and the quality increased, it became cost-effective for enterprise companies to integrate wireless segments into their network. Wireless technology offered a relatively inexpensive way for corporate campuses to connect buildings to one another without laying copper or fiber cabling. Today, the cost of wireless technology enables most businesses to implement wireless segments on their network. Many companies have converted completely to wireless networks, saving time and money while allowing the flexibility of roaming.

Households are also benefiting from the low cost and subsequent availability of wireless LAN hardware. Many people are now installing cost-effective wireless networks that take advantage of the convenience of mobility and creating home offices or wireless gaming stations.

As wireless LAN technology improves, the cost of manufacturing (and therefore purchasing and implementing) the hardware continues to fall, and the number of installed wireless LANs continues to increase. The standards that govern wireless LAN operation increasingly stress interoperability and compatibility. As the number of users grows, lack of compatibility may render a network useless, and the lack of interoperability may interfere with the proper operation of other networks.

Today's Wireless LAN Standards

Because wireless LANs transmit using radio frequencies, the same types of regulations that govern such things as AM/FM radios regulate wireless LANs. The Federal Communications Commission (FCC) regulates the use of wireless LAN devices. In the current wireless LAN market, several accepted operational standards and drafts in the United States are created and maintained by the Institute of Electrical and Electronic Engineers (IEEE).

Groups of people that represent many different organizations, including academics, business, military, and the government create these standards. Because IEEE standards can have a significant impact on the development of technology, the standards can take many years to be created and agreed upon. You may even have an opportunity to comment on these standards at certain times during the creation process.

Wireless LAN Specific Standards

The standards specific to wireless LANs are covered in greater detail in further reading on wireless LAN organizations and standards. Because these standards are the basis upon which the latest wireless LANs are built, a brief overview is provided here:

- **IEEE 802.11**—the original wireless LAN standard that specifies the slowest data transfer rates in both spread spectrum RF and infrared transmission technologies.

- **IEEE 802.11b**—describes data transfer rates faster than 802.11 and a more restrictive scope of transmission technologies, using only Direct Sequence Spread Spectrum (DSSS) technology. This standard is also widely promoted as Wi-Fi™ by the Wireless Ethernet Compatibility Alliance, or WECA.

- **IEEE 802.11a**—describes much faster data transfer rate than IEEE 802.11b (but lacks backwards compatibility), and uses the 5 GHz UNII frequency bands.

- **IEEE 802.11g**—the most recent draft based on the 802.11 series of standards that describes data transfer rates equally as fast as IEEE 802.11a, and boasts the backward compatibility to 802.11b required to make inexpensive upgrades possible.

Emerging technologies will require standards that describe and define their proper behavior. The challenge for manufacturers and standards makers alike will be bringing their resources to bear on the difficulties of interoperability and compatibility.

Activities

1. Which of the following reasons explain why wireless LANs have recently grown in popularity? (Choose three.)

   a. They provide increased speed over wired network solutions.

   b. They provide an inexpensive way to connect buildings on a corporate campus.

   c. They enable users to build home networks without installing network cables.

   d. They save time and money when building new network segments.

2. Which of the following wireless LAN standards specifies the lowest data transfer rate?

   a. 802.11

   b. 802.11a

   c. 802.11b

   d. 802.11g

3. Which of the following organizations creates and maintains the U.S. wireless LAN standards?

   a. FCC

   b. WECA

   c. IEEE

   d. IETF

4. Which of the following wireless LAN standards specifies data rates higher than, but remains backward compatible with, 802.11b?

   a. 802.11

   b. 802.11a

   c. 802.11f

   d. 802.11g

5. Which of the following organizations promotes 802.11b as Wi-Fi?

   a. FAA

   b. WECA

   c. IEEE

   d. IETF

Extended Activities

1. Research the history of spread spectrum wireless LANs, from their military origins to their current applications. How do the military applications differ from today's use of the technology? How are they the same?

   _____

   _____

   _____

   _____

2. Visit several wireless LAN vendor sites and compare their products. How do their products differ in features such as security, manageability, and utilities? Which vendor do you think offers the most features for the money? Which are better suited to enterprise versus home use, and vice versa?

   _____

   _____

   _____

   _____

Lesson 2—Wireless LAN Applications

When computers were first built, only large universities and corporations could afford them. Today you may find three or four personal computers in your neighbor's house. Wireless LANs have taken a similar path, first used by large enterprises, and now available to us all at affordable prices. Because of the many advantages they offer to a variety of situations, wireless LANs have been adopted very quickly. In this section, we will discuss some of the most common and appropriate uses of wireless LANs.

Objectives

At the end of this lesson you will be able to:

* Identify appropriate applications of wireless LAN technologies

* Compare the advantages and disadvantages that each wireless LAN application offers

 **Key Point**

Wireless LAN technologies address a wide range of network access needs.

Roles of Wireless LANs

Today's wireless LAN technologies meet a variety of network connectivity needs. From the home or small office network to last-mile data delivery, wireless networks are quite versatile in their applications.

Access Role

Wireless LANs are usually deployed in an access capacity, meaning that they are used as an entry point into a wired network. In the past, access has been defined as dial-up, ADSL, cable, cellular, Ethernet, Token Ring, frame relay, ATM, and so forth. Wireless is simply another method for users to access a network. Wireless LANs are Data Link Layer networks, like all of the access methods just listed. Due to a lack of speed and resiliency, wireless networks are not typically implemented in distribution or core roles in networks. Of course, in small networks, there may be no differentiation between the core, distribution, or access layers of a three-layer hierarchical network model. The core layer of a network should be very fast and stable, able to handle a tremendous amount of traffic with little difficulty, and experience no down time. The distribution layer of a network should be fast, flexible, and reliable. Wireless LANs do not typically meet these requirements. The Access Role of a Wireless LAN Diagram illustrates mobile clients gaining access to a wired network through a connection device (access point).

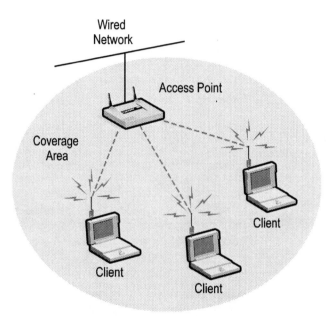

Access Role of a Wireless LAN

Wireless LANs offer a specific solution to a difficult problem: mobility. Without a doubt, wireless LANs solve a host of problems for corporations and home users alike, but all of these problems point to the need for freedom from data cabling. Cellular solutions have been available for quite some time, offering users the ability to roam while staying connected, but at slow speeds and very high prices. Wireless LANs offer the same flexibility without the disadvantages. Wireless LANs are fast, inexpensive, and they can be located almost anywhere.

When considering wireless LANs for use in your network, keep in mind that using them for their intended purpose will provide the best results. To avoid having to remove them later, administrators implementing wireless LANs in a core or distribution role should understand exactly what performance to expect before implementing them in this fashion. The only distribution role in a corporate network that is definitely appropriate for wireless LANs is that of building-to-building bridging. In this scenario, wireless could be considered as playing a distribution role; however, it will always depend on how the wireless bridging segments are used in the network.

Some Wireless Internet Service Providers (WISPs) use licensed wireless frequencies in a distribution role, but in this role they very rarely use unlicensed frequencies such as the ones discussed at length in this book. It is common to see WISPs deploy 802.11-based technologies in an access role, but due to the possibility of losing large amounts of customers at a time when significant interference occurs, it is common for the distribution links to be licensed frequencies.

Network Extension

Wireless networks can serve as an extension to a wired network. There may be cases where extending the network requires installing additional cabling that is cost prohibitive. You may discover that hiring cable installers and electricians to build out a new section of office space for the network is going to cost tens of thousands of dollars. Or, in the case of a large warehouse, the distances may be too great to use Category 5 (Cat5) cable for the Ethernet network. Fiber might have to be installed, requiring an even greater investment of time and resources. Installing fiber might involve upgrades to existing edge switches.

Wireless LANs can be easily implemented to provide seamless connectivity to remote areas within a building, as illustrated by the floor plan image on the Network Extension Diagram. Because little wiring is necessary to install a wireless LAN, the costs of hiring installers and purchasing Ethernet cable might be drastically reduced.

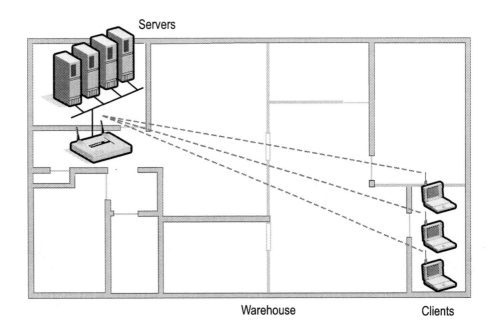

Servers

Warehouse   Clients

Network Extension

Building-to-Building Connectivity

In a campus environment or an environment with as few as two adjacent buildings, there may be a need to provide the network users in each of the different buildings direct access to the same computer network. In the past, this type of access and connectivity was accomplished by running cables underground from one building to another or by renting expensive, leased lines from a local telephone company.

Using wireless LAN technology, equipment can be installed quickly and easily to allow two or more buildings to be part of the same network without the expense of leased lines or the need to dig up the ground between buildings. With the proper wireless antennas, any number of buildings can be linked together on the same network. Certainly there are limitations to using wireless LAN technology; every data-connectivity solution comes with limitations. However, the flexibility, speed, and cost savings that wireless LANs introduce to the network administrator make them indispensable.

15

There are two different types of building-to-building connectivity. The first is point-to-point (PtP), and the second is point-to-multipoint (PtMP). Point-to-point links are wireless connections between only two buildings, as illustrated on the Building-to-Building Connectivity Diagram. PtP connections almost always use semidirectional or highly directional antennas at each end of the link. The low gain provided by omnidirectional antennas restricts the PtP link power to a value much lower than the maximum the FCC allows.

Building-to-Building Connectivity

Point-to-multipoint links are wireless connections between three or more buildings, typically implemented in a hub-and-spoke fashion, in which one building is the focal point of the network design. An example of how wireless LANs are deployed in a distribution role in a network follows:

- The central building houses the core network, Internet connectivity, and the server farm.

- Point-to-multipoint links between buildings typically use omnidirectional antennas in the central "hub" building and semidirectional antennas on each of the outlying "spoke" buildings.

There are many ways to implement these two basic types of connectivity, as you will undoubtedly see over the course of your career as a wireless LAN administrator or consultant.

Last Mile Data Delivery

Wireless Internet Service Providers (WISPs) are now taking advantage of recent advancements in wireless technology to offer last mile data delivery service to their customers. "Last mile" refers to the communication infrastructure—wired or wireless—that exists between the central office of the telecommunications company (telco) or cable company and the end user. Currently, the telcos and cable companies own their last mile infrastructure, but with the broadening interest in wireless technology, WISPs are now creating their own wireless last mile delivery service, as illustrated in the Last Mile Service Diagram.

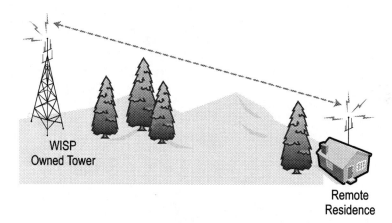

WISP Owned Tower

Remote Residence

Last Mile Service

Consider the case where both the cable companies and telecommunications companies (telcos) are encountering difficulties expanding their networks to offer broadband connections to more households or businesses. If you live in a rural area, chances are you do not have access to a broadband connection (cable modem or xDSL), and probably will not for quite some time. It is much more cost effective for WISPs to offer wireless access to these remote locations because WISPs will not encounter the same costs a cable or telco would incur in order to install the necessary equipment.

WISPs have their own unique set of challenges. Just as xDSL providers have problems going further than 18,000 feet from the central office and cable providers have issues with the cable being a shared medium to users, WISPs have problems with rooftop access, trees, mountains, lightning, towers, and many other obstacles to connectivity. Although WISPs do not have a fail-proof solution, they do have the capability to offer broadband access to users that other, more conventional technologies cannot reach.

Mobility

As an access layer solution, wireless LANs cannot replace wired LANs in terms of data rates (100BaseT at 100Mbps versus IEEE 802.11a at 54Mbps). A wireless environment uses intermittent connections and has higher error rates over what is usually a narrower bandwidth. As a result, applications and messaging protocols designed for the wired world sometimes operate poorly in a wireless environment. The wireless expectations of end users and IT managers are set by the performance and behaviors of their wired networks. What wireless LANs do offer is increased mobility as a trade-off for speed and quality of service. The Mobile Wireless Access Diagram illustrates a wireless mobility solution.

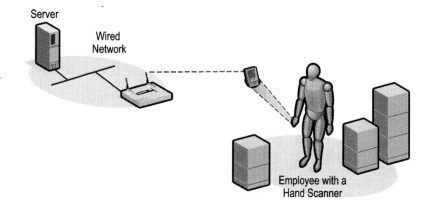

Server
Wired
Network
Employee with a
Hand Scanner

Mobile Wireless Access

For example, a parcel delivery company uses wireless technology to update parcel-tracking data immediately upon the arrival of a delivery vehicle. As a driver parks at the dock, the driver's computer has already logged onto the network and transferred the day's delivery data to the central network.

In warehousing facilities, wireless networks are used to track the storage locations and disposition of products. This data is then synchronized in a central computer for the purchasing and shipping departments. Handheld wireless scanners are becoming commonplace in organizations with employees that move around within their facility while processing orders and inventory.

In each of these cases, wireless networks have created the ability to transfer data without requiring the time and manpower to input the data manually at a wired terminal. Wireless connectivity has also eliminated the need for such user devices to be connected using wires that would otherwise get in the way of the users.

Some of the newest wireless technology allows users to roam, or move physically from one area of wireless coverage to another, without losing connectivity, just as a mobile telephone customer is able to roam between cellular coverage areas. In larger organizations, where wireless coverage spans large areas, roaming capability has significantly increased the productivity of these organizations, simply because users remain connected to the network when they are away from their main workstations.

SO/HO

As an Information Technology (IT) professional or student, you may have more than one computer at your home. And if you do, you may have networked these computers together so you can share files, a printer, or a broadband connection.

This type of configuration is also utilized by many businesses that have only a few employees. These businesses have the need for the sharing of information between users and a single Internet connection for efficiency and greater productivity.

For applications such as a small office/home office (SOHO), a wireless LAN is a very simple and effective solution. The SOHO Wireless LAN Diagram illustrates a typical SOHO wireless LAN solution. Wireless SOHO devices are especially beneficial when office workers want to share a single Internet connection. The alternative, of course, is running wires throughout the office to interconnect all of the workstations. Many small offices are not outfitted with pre-installed Ethernet ports, and only a very small number of houses are wired for Ethernet networks. Trying to retrofit these places with Cat 5 cabling usually results in creating unsightly holes in the walls and ceilings. With a wireless LAN, users can be interconnected easily and neatly.

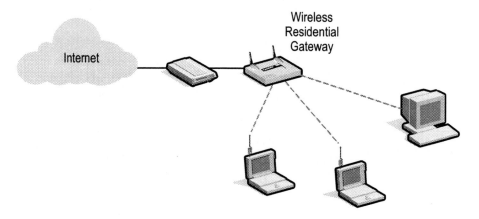

SOHO Wireless LAN

Mobile Offices

Mobile offices or classrooms allow users to pack up their computer equipment quickly and move to another location. Due to overcrowded classrooms, many schools now use mobile classrooms. These classrooms usually consist of large, movable trailers that are used while more permanent structures are built. In order to extend the computer network to these temporary buildings, aerial or underground cabling would have to be installed at great expense. Wireless LAN connections from the main school building to the mobile classrooms allow for flexible configurations at a fraction of the cost of alternative cabling. A simplistic example of connecting mobile classrooms using wireless LAN connectivity is illustrated in the School with Mobile Classrooms Diagram.

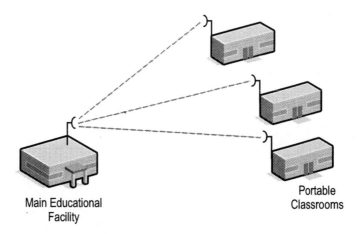

Main Educational
Facility

Portable
Classrooms

School with Mobile Classrooms

Temporary office spaces also benefit from being networked with wireless LANs. As companies grow, they often experience a shortage of office space, and need to move some workers to a nearby location, such as an adjacent office or an office on another floor of the same building. Installing Cat5 or fiber cabling for these short periods of time is not cost-effective, and usually the owners of the building do not allow for the installed cables to be removed. With a wireless network, the network components can be packed up and moved to the next location quickly and easily.

Many organizations can benefit from using movable networks. Some of these include the Superbowl, the Olympics, circuses, carnivals, fairs, festivals, and construction companies. Wireless LANs are well suited to these types of environments.

Hospitals and other healthcare facilities also benefit greatly from wireless LANs. Some valuable uses of wireless LANs within these facilities include wireless PDAs that doctors use to connect to networks, and mobile diagnostic carts that nurses can move from room to room to connect to networks. Wireless networks allow doctors and nurses to perform their jobs more efficiently using these new devices and associated software.

Industrial facilities, such as warehouses and manufacturing facilities, utilize wireless networks in various ways. A good example of an industrial wireless LAN application is shipping companies whose trucks pull into the dock and automatically connect to a wireless network. This type of networking allows shipping companies to become automated and more efficient at handling the uploading of data onto the central servers.

Activities

1. Which statement best describes a wireless LAN used in an access role?

    a. Access points connect mobile clients to shared network resources.

    b. Several building networks communicate through roof mounted antennas.

    c. The wireless network creates a high-speed network backbone.

    d. Clients connect to the wired network from great distances.

2. A ski resort obtains high-speed Internet access through a WISP. In which role is the wireless network operating?

    a. Access role

    b. Last mile data delivery

    c. Building-to-building connectivity

    d. Network extension

3. A manufacturing company needs to connect two networks in buildings located across the street from each other. Which type of building-to-building connectivity is this?

    a. Point-to-point

    b. Peer-to-peer

    c. Spoke-to-hub

    d. Point-to-multipoint

4. A university campus consists of five buildings: a centrally located administration building and four adjacent buildings housing classrooms, labs, and so forth. A wired network serving the building's users is in each building. The administration building network is the campus backbone. It uses wireless links to connect each adjacent building's network to the campus backbone. Which type of antenna would typically be located on the administration building?

    a. semidirectional

    b. omnidirectional

    c. multidirectional

    d. unidirectional

5. In which one of the following applications might you deploy a wireless LAN in a distribution layer role?

   a. As a building-to-building bridge linking corporate network segments

   b. When the network requires speed, flexibility, and reliability

   c. When the distribution layer must handle large amounts of network traffic

   d. As a replacement for a 100Mbps wired network backbone

Extended Activities

1. Several network equipment vendors market enterprise level wireless products. Form focus groups of three or four members and have each group research a different vendor's products. Using the lesson diagrams as a guide, sketch out a point-to-multipoint wireless network connecting three corporate campus buildings to another central building. Label each wireless component with the vendor's model number. Include the appropriate antenna types on each building. Present your solution to the other groups, and be prepared to defend your component choices.

2. While still in your focus groups, choose a different vendor and sketch out a home wireless network solution for connecting three PCs to a broadband Internet connection. Label each component, present your solution, and be prepared to defend your choices.

Summary

This unit discussed the wireless LAN market by presenting an overview of the past, present, and future of wireless LANs and introducing the standards that govern this technology. Wireless LANs, once used only by large enterprises, are now available to all at affordable prices. The big difference between the networking market as a whole and the wireless LAN market is the rate of growth. Due to the flexible implementation of wireless LANs, they are outpacing every other market sector.

Unit 1 also described some of the appropriate applications of wireless LANs. This unit included essential information about antenna principles required by wireless network administrators. Because wireless administrators must know how to calculate the RF signal power at the intentional radiator (IR) and equivalent isotropically radiated power (EIRP), the RF mathematic fundamentals important to wireless network administration were also covered.

Unit 1 Quiz

1. Which one of the following does wireless LAN technology provide that wired technology does not?

   a. Mobility

   b. Centralized security

   c. Reliability

   d. VPN security

2. Which one of the following would NOT be an appropriate use of wireless LAN technologies?

   a. Connecting two buildings together that are on opposite sides of the street

   b. Connecting two computers together in a small office so they can share a printer

   c. Connecting a remote home to a WISP for Internet access

   d. Connecting two rack-mounted computers together

3. Why is a wireless LAN a good choice for extending a network? (Choose three.)

   a. It reduces the cost of cables required for installation.

   b. It can be installed faster than a wired network.

   c. The hardware is considerably less expensive than wired LAN hardware.

   d. It eliminates a significant portion of the labor charges for installation.

4. Wireless ISPs provide which one of the following services?

   a. Small office/home office services

   b. Connectivity for large enterprises

   c. Last mile data delivery

   d. Building-to-building connectivity

5. Wireless LANs are primarily deployed in which one of the following roles?

   a. Backbone

   b. Access

   c. Application

   d. Core

6. Why would a mobile office be a good choice for using a wireless LAN? (Choose two.)

    a. Wireless LANs take less time to setup than wired LANs.

    b. Wireless LAN equipment could be easily removed if the office moves.

    c. Wireless LANs do not require administration.

    d. Wireless LANs take a more centralized approach than wired LANs.

7. Which one of the following is the IEEE family of standards for wireless LANs?

    a. 802.3

    b. 803.5

    c. 802.11

    d. 802.1x

8. As a consultant, you have taken a job creating a wireless LAN for an office complex that will connect together five buildings in close vicinity. Given only this information, which one of the following wireless LAN implementations would be most appropriate for this scenario?

    a. Last-mile data service from a WISP

    b. Point-to-point bridge links between all buildings

    c. Point-to-multipoint bridge link from a central building to all remote buildings

    d. One central antenna at the main building only

9. Which of the following are challenges WISPs face that telephone companies and cable companies do not? (Choose two.)

    a. Customers located more than 18,000 feet (5.7 km) from a central office

    b. High costs of installing telephone lines or copper cabling

    c. Trees as line of sight obstructions

    d. Rooftop access for antenna installation

10. In what organization did the use of spread spectrum wireless for data transfer originate?

    a. WECA

    b. WLANA

    c. FCC

    d. U.S. Military

11. Which one of the following IEEE wireless LAN standards is NOT compatible with the standard currently known as Wi-Fi?

    a. 802.11

    b. 802.11g

    c. 802.11a

    d. 802.11b

12. Which one of the following IEEE 802.11 standards for wireless LANs utilizes the 5 GHz UNII bands for its radio signal transmissions?

    a. 802.11

    b. Bluetooth

    c. 802.11b

    d. 802.11g

    e. 802.11a

13. A WISP would take advantage of which one of the following applications for wireless LANs?

    a. Last mile data delivery

    b. Building-to-building bridging

    c. Classroom connectivity

    d. Home network connectivity

14. Which organization makes the regulations that govern the technical requirements, licensing, and usage of wireless LANs in the United States?

    a. IEEE

    b. WECA

    c. FCC

    d. FAA

Unit 2
RF Fundamentals

To a wireless LAN administrator, an understanding of radio frequency (RF) concepts is essential to the implementation, expansion, maintenance, and troubleshooting of a wireless network. In order to understand a wireless LAN's use of radio waves as its transmission medium, an administrator must have a solid foundation in the fundamentals of radio frequency theory. This unit discusses the properties of RF radiation and how its behavior can affect the performance of a wireless LAN. We introduce the uses and properties of antennas. We explain the mathematical relationships that exist in RF circuits and why they are important, as well as how to perform the necessary RF math calculations.

Lessons

1. RF
2. VSWR
3. Principles of Antennas
4. RF Mathematics

Terms

alternating current (AC)—AC is the alternatively positive and negative polarity current supplied to homes and businesses by the local utility company. U.S. AC power changes polarity 60 times per second; each cycle is called a "hertz." Hence, U.S. AC current is known as 60-Hz power. Other countries in Europe and the Far East use 240-volt AC (VAC) at 50 Hz.

amplitude—Amplitude is the height of a wave, or how far from the center it swings.

antenna diversity—Antenna diversity is the use of multiple antennas on wireless APs or client radios to allow the device to sample the received signals and choose the antenna with the best reception.

decibel (dB)—A decibel is a logarithmic relational measure of a change in power in watts or milliwatts. Decibels allow us to represent very small or very large power levels in an easily read form. Power gain and loss (positive or negative changes) are measured in dBs.

decibels isotropic (dBi)—dBi is the unit of measure of an antenna's gain. One dBi gain equals 1 dBi.

decibels referenced to one milliwatt (dBm)—A dBm is an absolute measure of signal power, defined as the relationship of the dB scale to the watt scale with a reference point of 1mW. On this scale, 1mW equates to 0dBm.

diffraction—Diffraction occurs when a surface with sharp irregularities or a rough surface obstructs an RF signal's path. The RF wavefront bends around the obstruction, changing the signal's path.

equivalent isotropically radiated power (EIRP)—EIRP is the power actually radiated by the antenna element. This concept is important because the FCC regulates EIRP, and EIRP is used in calculating whether or not a wireless link is viable. EIRP takes into account the gain of the antenna.

Fresnel Zone—The Fresnel Zone is the conical area around an RF transmission path extending out from an antenna in the direction the signal is traveling.

gain—Gain or amplification is the ratio of the strength of an output signal to that of an input signal. The output signal strength will be greater than the input.

horizontal polarization—In reference to antennas, horizontal polarization is the electrical field that is parallel to the surface of the earth.

impedance—Impedance is a component's resistance to AC current flow.

logarithm—A logarithm is a mathematical function; it is the exponent that indicates the power to which a number is raised to produce a given number. For example, 10 squared = 100; thus, 10 raised to the second power equals 100.

loss—Loss is a ratio of the strength of an output signal to that of an input signal, where the output signal strength will be smaller than the input.

milliwatt—A milliwatt is one thousandth of a watt. It is used as a reference point for signal levels at a given point in a circuit.

multipath—Multipath refers to the routes taken by RF energy between a transmitter and a receiver. At a given transmitter, one signal is transmitted. However, after the signal hits many reflection points along the path from the transmitter to a receiver, many signals can result. Signals can cancel themselves out, decrease in amplitude, increase in amplitude, or become corrupted.

noise—Noise is any condition, such as electrical interference, that destroys signal integrity. Noise can be caused by many electromagnetic sources, such as radio transmissions, electrical cables, electric motors, lighting dimmers, or bad cable connections. See interference.

phase—RF signals cycle over a period of 360 degrees. A signal's phase refers to its relationship to its horizontal axis, typically represented on a graph as a horizontal line. A signal at its peak amplitude is considered at a phase of 90 degrees, while at its lowest amplitude its phase it 270 degrees. When a signal is phase modulated, each phase of the signal presents a certain digital bit pattern.

radio frequency (RF)—RF is any frequency within the electromagnetic spectrum normally associated with radio wave propagation.

reflection—Reflection occurs when RF signals contact a large surface through which they cannot pass. The signal's path is modified from that of the main signal's, causing signal loss and scattering.

refraction—Refraction is the tendency of a light ray, or electromagnetic signal, to be deflected from a straight path when it passes obliquely from one medium into another medium that has a different index of refraction.

resistance—Resistance refers to the opposition of current flow in a conductor. Different conductors present different resistance characteristics.

RF attenuator—An RF attenuator is a component installed in the path of an RF signal for the purpose of introducing loss. The attenuator is placed between the radio output and the antenna input.

RF line of sight (LOS)—RF LOS is the clear radio signal path from the transmitting node to the receiver. An RF device can see an RF LOS based on both the visual line of sight and a clear Fresnel Zone.

scattering—Scattering is the diffusion of an RF signal caused by the signal coming in contact with uneven yet reflective surfaces or by travelling through a medium containing heavy particle content. The scattered signal is simultaneously dispersed in many directions; resulting signals do not have enough power to reach the intended receiver.

sensitivity threshold—A wireless radio's sensitivity threshold is the point at which the radio can clearly distinguish a signal from the background noise.

visual line of sight (LOS)—Visual LOS is the apparently "straight" line from the object in site to the observer's eye.

Voltage Standing Wave Ratio (VSWR)—VSWR is the ratio of forward RF signal power to the reverse power. Reverse power occurs when there is an impedance mismatch in the RF circuit.

watt—A watt is the unit of electricity consumption that represents the product of amperage and voltage. The power requirement of a device is listed in watts; thus, you can find the ampere requirement by dividing the wattage by the voltage (for example, 1,200 watts divided by 120 volts, equals 10 amps).

Lesson 1—RF

RFs are high frequency, alternating current (AC) signals that are passed along a copper conductor and then radiated into the air by means of an antenna. An antenna converts an electrical signal in the wire to a wirelessly radiated signal and vice versa. When the high frequency AC signal is radiated into the air, it forms radio waves. These radio waves propagate (move) away from the source (the antenna) in a straight line in all directions at once.

Objectives

At the end of this lesson you will be able to:

- Explain and apply the basic concepts of RF behavior
- Describe the difference between signal gain and loss
- Explain how reflection, refraction, diffraction, and scattering affect the operation of wireless LANs

 **Key Point**

Radio waves travel in patterns similar to ripples in a pond.

RF Behaviors

If you can imagine dropping a rock into a still pond and watching the concentric ripples flow away from the point where the rock hit the water, then you have an idea of how RF behaves as it is propagated from an antenna. The Rock into a Pond Diagram illustrates this effect.

Rock into a Pond

Understanding the behavior of these propagated RF waves is an important part of understanding why and how wireless LANs function. Without this base of knowledge, an administrator would be unable to locate proper installation locations of equipment and would not understand how to troubleshoot a problematic wireless LAN.

RF is sometimes referred to as "smoke and mirrors" because RF seems to act erratically and inconsistently under given circumstances. Things as small as a loose connector or a slight line impedance mismatch can cause erratic behavior and undesirable results. The following sections describe these types of behaviors and what can happen to radio waves as they are transmitted.

Gain

Gain is the term used to describe an increase in an RF signal's amplitude. The Power Gain Diagram shows this process. Gain is usually an active process; meaning that an external power source, such as an RF amplifier, is used to amplify the signal. However, gain can also be passive. For example, a high-gain antenna is used to focus the beam width of a signal to increase its signal amplitude, and reflected RF signals can combine with the main signal to increase the main signal's strength.

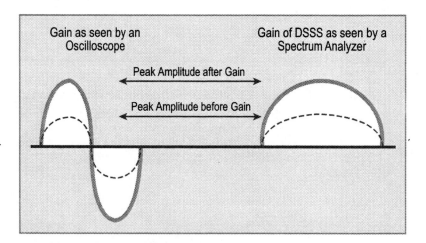

Power Gain

Increasing the RF signal's strength may have a positive or a negative result. Typically, more power is better, but in some cases, such as when a transmitter is radiating power very close to the legal power output limit, added power poses a legal problem.

Loss

Loss describes a decrease in signal strength, as shown on the Power Loss Diagram. Many things can cause RF signal loss, both while the signal is still in the cable as a high frequency AC electrical signal and when the signal is propagated as radio waves through the air by the antenna. Resistance of cables and connectors causes loss due to the conversion of AC signals to heat. Impedance mismatches in the cables and connectors can cause power to be reflected back toward the source, which can cause signal degradation. Objects directly in the propagated wave's transmission path can absorb, reflect, or scatter RF signals. Loss can be intentionally injected into a circuit with an RF attenuator. RF attenuators are accurate resistors that convert high frequency AC to heat in order to reduce signal amplitude at that point in the circuit.

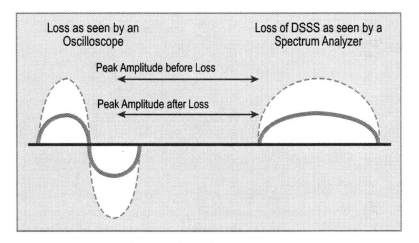

Power Loss

Note: Many things can affect an RF signal between the transmitter and receiver. In order for gains or losses to be relevant to the implementation of wireless LANs, they must be quantifiable. The section in this chapter about RF mathematics will discuss quantifiable loss and gain and how to calculate and compensate for them.

The ability to measure and compensate for loss in an RF connection or circuit is important because radios have a receive sensitivity threshold. A sensitivity threshold is defined as the point at which a radio can clearly distinguish a signal from background noise. Since a receiver's sensitivity is finite, the transmitting station must transmit a signal with enough amplitude to be recognizable at the receiver. If losses are great enough to prevent signal reception from occurring between the transmitter and receiver, the problem must be corrected either by removing the objects causing loss or by increasing the transmission power.

Reflection

Reflection, as illustrated on the Reflection Diagram, occurs when a propagating electromagnetic wave impinges upon an object that has very large dimensions compared to the wavelength of the propagating wave. Reflections occur from the surface of the earth, buildings, walls, and many other obstacles. If the surface is smooth, the reflected signal may remain intact, although some loss occurs, due to absorption and scattering of the signal.

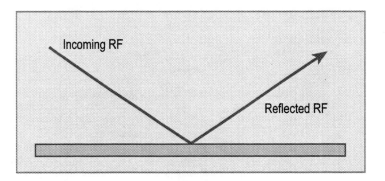

Reflection

RF signal reflection can cause serious problems for wireless LANs. This reflecting of the main signal from many objects in the area of the transmission is referred to as multipath. Multipath can have severe adverse affects on a wireless LAN, such as degrading or canceling the main signal and causing holes or gaps in the RF coverage area. Surfaces such as lakes, metal roofs, metal blinds, metal doors, and others can cause severe reflection, creating multipath.

Reflection of this magnitude is never desirable and typically requires special compensating functionality, such as antenna diversity within wireless LAN hardware. Both multipath and antenna diversity are discussed in further reading on troubleshooting.

Refraction

Refraction describes the bending of a radio wave as it passes through a medium of different density. As an RF wave passes into a denser medium, such as a pool of cold air lying in a valley, the wave will be bent such that its direction changes. When passing through such a medium, some of the wave will be reflected away from the intended signal path, and some will be bent through the medium in another direction, as illustrated on the Refraction Diagram.

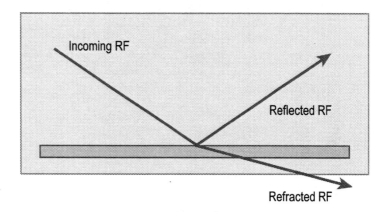

Refraction

Refraction can become a problem for long distance RF links. As atmospheric conditions change, the RF waves may change direction, diverting the signal away from the intended target.

Diffraction

Diffraction occurs when a surface with sharp irregularities or some sort of rough surface obstructs the radio path between a transmitter and receiver. At high frequencies, diffraction, like reflection, depends on the geometry of the obstructing object and the amplitude, phase, and polarization of the incident wave at the point of diffraction.

Diffraction is commonly confused with and improperly used interchangeably with refraction. Care should be taken not to confuse these terms. Diffraction describes a wave bending around an obstacle as shown on the Diffraction Diagram, whereas refraction describes a wave bending through a medium. Taking the rock in the pond example, now consider a small twig sticking up through the surface of the water near where the rock hit the water. As the ripples hit the stick, they would be blocked to a small degree, but to a larger degree, the ripples would bend around the twig. This illustration shows how diffraction acts with obstacles in its path, depending on the makeup of the obstacle. If the object was large or jagged enough, the wave might not bend, but rather might be blocked.

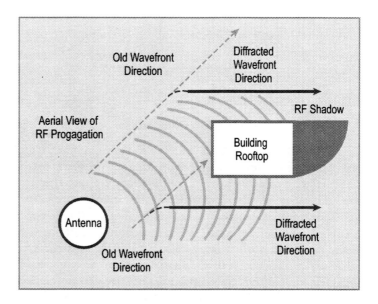

Diffraction

Diffraction is the slowing of the wave front at the point where the wave front strikes an obstacle, while the rest of the wave front maintains the same speed of propagation. Diffraction is the effect of waves turning, or bending, around the obstacle. As another example, consider a machine blowing a steady stream of smoke. The smoke would flow straight until an obstacle entered its path. Introducing a large wooden block into the smoke stream would cause the smoke to curl around the corners of the block causing a noticeable degradation in the smoke's velocity and a significant change in direction.

Scattering

Scattering occurs when the medium through which a wave travels consists of objects with dimensions that are small compared to the wavelength of the signal, and the number of obstacles per unit volume is large. Rough surfaces, small objects, and other irregularities in the signal path scatter waves, as can be seen on the Scattering Diagram.

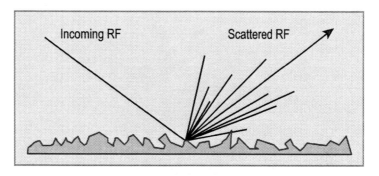

Scattering

Some outdoor examples of objects that can cause scattering in a mobile communications system include foliage, street signs, and lampposts. Scattering can take place in two primary ways:

- **Scattering can occur when a wave strikes an uneven surface and is reflected in many directions simultaneously.** Scattering of this type yields many small amplitude reflections and destroys the main RF signal. Dissipation of an RF signal may occur when an RF wave is reflected off sand, rocks, or other jagged surfaces. When scattered in this manner, RF signal degradation can be significant to the point of intermittently disrupting communications or causing complete signal loss.

- **Scattering can occur as a signal wave travels through particles, such as heavy dust content, in a medium.** In this case, rather than being reflected off an uneven surface, the RF waves are individually reflected on a very small scale off tiny particles.

Absorption

As shown on the Absorption Diagram, absorption occurs when an RF signal strikes an object and is absorbed into the material of the object in such a manner that it does not pass through, reflect off, or bend around the object.

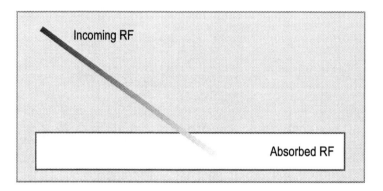

Absorption

Examples of objects that absorb RF signals are concrete, cement, pavement, wood and trees.

Activities

1. Which statement best describes gain in an RF signal?

    a. The propagation of a wave from the source in a straight line in all directions at once

    b. The reduction of the signal's amplitude as it approaches the source

    c. The increase of the RF signal's amplitude caused by an external power source

    d. The change in an RF signal's direction caused by reflecting off of an object

2. You are troubleshooting a multipath problem on a building-to-building bridge link. By inspecting the area between the buildings, you notice that the southwest side of the buildings have metal roll down shades on all the windows. The multipath problem only occurs in the afternoon and early evening. You raise the shades, and the problem subsides. This is an example of what type of RF signal behavior?

    a. Reflection

    b. Refraction

    c. Diffraction

    d. Scattering

3. You are performing a site survey for a point-to-point wireless bridge link. The geographical area is quite dry and windy, and susceptible to frequent dust storms. Which type of RF behavior might the signal display during these dust storms?

    a. Reflection

    b. Refraction

    c. Diffraction

    d. Scattering

4. Which RF behavior occurs when RF signals traverse changing atmospheric conditions over long distances?

    a. Reflection

    b. Refraction

    c. Diffraction

    d. Scattering

5. How might you compensate for loss on an RF link? (Choose three.)

   a. Increase the transmitter power

   b. Increase the receiver gain

   c. Remove the cause of the loss

   d. Increase the receiver's sensitivity threshold

Extended Activities

1. Assume you are building a wireless link from your home or office to a remote location three miles away. What local conditions could cause a change in the RF signal's behavior over the course of this link? What RF behavior(s) would the signal exhibit in response to each cause? How could you resolve them?

   _____

   _____

   _____

   _____

2. Visit both enterprise and home office wireless product vendors' Web sites. Review the product specifications and determine which vendors' products allow you to adjust the transmitter's output RF signal power level to compensate for noise and loss. In which category do these products fall, enterprise or home office? At about what price point do these features appear?

   _____

   _____

   _____

   _____

Lesson 2—VSWR

Voltage Standing Wave Ratio (VSWR) is the ratio of forward power to reverse power. Reverse power occurs when there is mismatched impedance (resistance to current flow, measured in ohms) between devices in an RF system. An RF signal reflected at a point of impedance mismatch in the signal path causes a high VSWR. Reflected power causes return loss, which is the loss of forward energy through a system because of some of the power being reflected back toward the transmitter. If the impedances of the ends of a connection do not match, the maximum amount of the transmitted power will not be received at the antenna, which serves as the circuit's load. When part of the RF signal is reflected back toward the transmitter, the signal level on the line varies instead of being steady. This variance is an indicator of high VSWR.

Objectives

At the end of this lesson you will be able to:

* Describe VSWR measurements

* Explain the effects of VSWR

* Explain solutions to VSWR

 **Key Point**

VSWR is a measure of how impedance mismatches affect RF signal strength.

VSWR

To understand VSWR, imagine water flowing through two garden hoses. As long as the two hoses are the same diameter, water flows through them seamlessly. If the hose connected to the faucet were significantly larger than the next hose down the line, backpressure would occur on the faucet and even at the connection between the two hoses. This standing backpressure illustrates VSWR, as shown in the VSWR Diagram. In this example, you can see that backpressure can cause negative effects, and not nearly as much water is transferred to the second hose as would have with matching hoses screwed together properly.

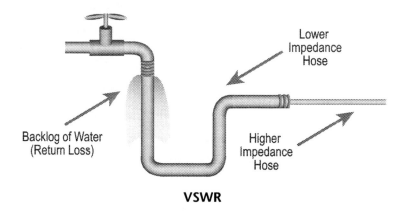

VSWR

VSWR Measurements

VSWR is a ratio; therefore, it is expressed as a relationship between two numbers. A typical VSWR value is 1.5:1. The two numbers relate the ratio of forward power to reverse power. The second number is always 1, representing 100 percent power delivery into the load. The first number varies depending on reflected power. The lower the first number (closer to 1), the better impedance matching your system has, and the less reflected power that will result. For example, a VSWR of 1.1:1 is better than 1.4:1. A VSWR measurement of 1:1 would denote a perfect impedance match, and no voltage standing wave would be present in the signal path.

Effects of VSWR

Excessive VSWR can cause serious problems in an RF circuit. Most of the time, the result is a marked decrease in the amplitude and stability of the transmitted RF signal. However, because some transmitters are not protected against power that is applied (or returned) to the transmitter output circuit, the reflected power can burn out the electronics of the transmitter. VSWR's effects are evident when transmitter circuits burn out, power output levels are unstable, and the power observed is significantly different from the expected power. The methods of changing VSWR in a circuit include proper use of proper equipment. Tight connections between cables and connectors, use of impedance-matched hardware throughout, and use of high-quality equipment with calibration reports where necessary are all good preventative measures against VSWR. High-accuracy instrumentation, such as SWR meters, can measure VSWR, but this measurement is beyond the scope of this text and the job tasks of a network administrator.

Solutions to VSWR

To prevent the negative effects of VSWR, it is imperative that all cables, connectors, and devices have impedances that match as closely as possible to each other. Never use 75-ohm cable with 50-ohm devices, for example. Most of today's wireless LAN devices have an impedance of 50 Ohms, but it is still recommended that you check each device before implementation, just to be sure. Every device from the transmitter to the antenna must have impedances matching as closely as possible, including cables, connectors, antennas, amplifiers, attenuators, the transmitter output circuit, and the receiver input circuit.

Activities

1. Which of the following are possible effects VSWR can have on RF circuits? (Choose three.)

   a. Damaged transmitter circuits

   b. Signal refraction

   c. Unstable output power

   d. Changes in signal power

2. VSWR is the result of what condition in an RF circuit?

   a. Power mismatch

   b. Impedance mismatch

   c. Signal mismatch

   d. Current mismatch

3. Which statement best describes return loss in an RF circuit?

   a. The loss of the signal returned to the transmitter from the receiver.

   b. The loss of the feedback circuit in the RF signal generator.

   c. Atmospheric conditions cause the reflection of the RF signal back toward the source.

   d. The loss of signal energy caused by reflection in the signal's path.

4. Which of the following are methods we could use to change VSWR in a circuit? (Choose three.)

   a. Use impedance-matched cables and connectors

   b. Use high quality, calibrated equipment

   c. Use larger connectors on the antenna side of the cable

   d. Use good quality, tight-fitting connectors

5. To avoid VSWR, which of the following wireless LAN devices must have matching impedances? (Choose two.)

   a. The power supply

   b. The antenna connector

   c. The network connection

   d. The amplifier circuit

Extended Activity

Visit the Cisco Systems Web site at **http://www.cisco.com/warp/ public/cc/pd/witc/ao350ap/prodlit/agder_rg.htm**, and research antenna VSWR ratings. Which is nearest to the perfect VSWR? Which is the farthest?

Lesson 3—Principles of Antennas

This course does not provide advanced instruction on antenna theory. Instead, this course explains some very basic antenna principals that directly relate to use of wireless LANs. It is not necessary for a wireless LAN administrator to thoroughly understand antenna design in order to administer the network. However, a wireless network administrator must have a basic understanding of antenna principles as they apply to wireless LANs.

Objectives

At the end of this lesson you will be able to:

- Explain the difference between Visual Line of Sight and RF Line of Sight

- Describe the Fresnel Zone and its importance to wireless LAN communications

- Explain key RF antenna concepts including antenna gain, intentional radiator (IR), and Equivalent Isotropically Radiated Power (EIRP)

 **Key Point**

Wireless LAN antennas must have RF Line of Sight for communications to occur.

Wireless LAN Antenna Principles

Wireless vendors make little noise about antenna performance. Although it is of less importance in a home or small office environment, antenna performance and operation are critical when connecting enterprise network segments with wireless access points (APs) or bridges.

Two key points that are important to understand about antennas are:

- Antennas convert electrical energy into RF waves in the case of a transmitting antenna, or RF waves into electrical energy in the case of a receiving antenna.

- The physical dimensions of an antenna, such as its length, are directly related to the frequency at which the antenna can propagate waves or receive propagated waves.

The following sections discuss some essential points of understanding in administering license-free wireless LANs.

LOS

With visible light, visual line of sight (LOS) is defined as the apparently straight line from the object in sight (the transmitter) to the observer's eye (the receiver). The LOS is an apparently straight line because light waves are subject to changes in direction due to refraction, diffraction, and reflection in the same way as RF frequencies. The LoS Diagram illustrates visual LOS.

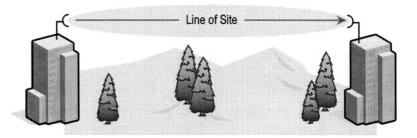

LoS

RF works very much the same way as visible light within wireless LAN frequencies, with one major exception: RF LOS can also be affected by blockage of the Fresnel Zone. Imagine that you are looking through a 2-foot long piece of pipe. Imagine further that an obstruction is blocking part of the inside of the pipe. Obviously, this obstruction would block your view of the objects at the other end of the pipe. This simple illustration shows how RF works when objects block the Fresnel Zone (discussed in the next section), except that, with the pipe scenario, you can still see the other end to some degree. With RF, that same limited ability to see translates into a broken or corrupted connection. RF LOS is important because RF does not behave in exactly the same manner as visible light.

Fresnel Zone

A consideration when planning or troubleshooting an RF link is the Fresnel (pronounced "fra-NEL") Zone. The Fresnel Zone occupies a series of concentric ellipsoid-shaped areas around the LOS path, as shown on the Fresnel Zone Diagram. The Fresnel Zone is important to the integrity of the RF link because it defines an area around the LOS that can introduce RF signal interference if blocked. Objects in the Fresnel Zone such as trees, hilltops, and buildings can diffract or reflect the main signal away from the receiver, changing the RF LOS. These same objects can absorb or scatter the main RF signal, causing degradation or complete signal loss.

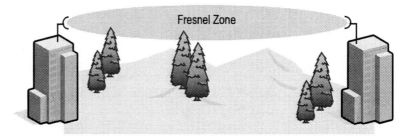

Fresnel Zone

The radius of the Fresnel Zone at its widest point can be calculated using the following formula:

$$r = 43.3 \times \sqrt{\frac{d}{4f}}$$

where *d* is the link distance in miles, *f* is the frequency in GHz, and the answer, *r*, is in feet. For example, suppose a 2.4000 GHz link is 5 miles (8.35 km) in length. The resulting Fresnel Zone would have a radius of 31.25 feet (9.52 m).

Note: Fresnel Zone calculations are not part of the CWNA exam. The formula is provided to you for your administrative tasks.

Obstructions

Considering the importance of Fresnel Zone clearance, it is also important to quantify the degree to which the Fresnel Zone can be blocked. Since an RF signal, when partially blocked, will bend around the obstacle to some degree, some blockage of the Fresnel Zone can occur without significant link disruption. Typically, 20 percent to 40 percent Fresnel Zone blockage introduces little to no interference into the link. It is always suggested to err on the conservative side, allowing no more than 20 percent blockage of the Fresnel Zone. Obviously, if trees or other growing objects are the source of the blockage, consider designing the link based on 0% blockage.

If the Fresnel Zone of a proposed RF link is more than 20 percent blocked, or if new construction or tree growth blocks an active link, raising the height of the antennas will usually alleviate the problem.

A question commonly asked about the Fresnel Zone when using indoor wireless LAN equipment, such as PC cards and access points, is how blockage of the Fresnel Zone affects indoor installations. In most indoor installations, RF signals pass through, reflect off, and refract around walls, furniture, and other obstructions. The Fresnel Zone is not encroached upon unless the signal is partially or fully blocked. This is sometimes the case, but is rarely noticed due to most wireless users being mobile. In a mobile environment, the Fresnel Zone is constantly changing; thus, users normally dismiss it, because they assume that the coverage is simply "bad" where they are located—without giving thought to why the coverage is bad.

Antenna Gain

An antenna—without its typically associated amplifiers and filters —is a passive device. There is no conditioning, amplifying, or manipulating of the signal by the antenna itself. The antenna can create the effect of amplification by virtue of its physical shape. Signal amplification in an antenna results from focusing the RF radiation into a tighter beam, just as the bulb of a flashlight can be focused into a tighter beam, which creates a seemingly brighter light source that sends the light farther. Beamwidths, which are measured in horizontal and vertical degrees, measure the focusing of radiation. For example, an omnidirectional antenna has a 360-degree horizontal beamwidth. By limiting the 360-degree beamwidth into a more focused beam of, say, 30 degrees, at the same power, the RF waves will be radiated farther. This is how patch, panel, and Yagi antennas (all of which are semidirectional antennas) are designed. Highly directional antennas take this theory a step farther by very tightly focusing both horizontal and vertical beamwidths to maximize distance of the propagated wave at low power.

IR

As defined by the Federal Communication Commission (FCC), an IR is an RF device specifically designed to generate and radiate RF signals. In terms of hardware, an IR includes an RF device and all cabling and connectors up to (but not including) the antenna, as illustrated on the IR Diagram.

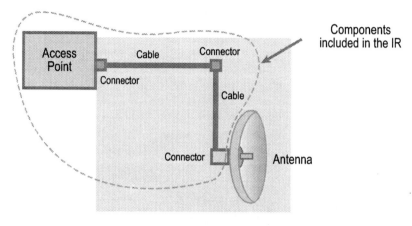

IR

Any reference to "power output of the IR" refers to the power output at the end of the last cable or connector before the antenna. For example, consider a 30-milliwatt transmitter that loses 15 milliwatts of power in the cable and another 5 milliwatts from the connector at the antenna. The power at the IR would be 10 milliwatts. As an administrator, it is your responsibility to understand the FCC rules relating to IRs and their power output. This course covers how power output is measured, how much power is allowed, and how to calculate these. FCC regulations concerning output power at the IR and EIRP are found in Part 47 of the Code of Federal Regulations (CFR), Chapter 1, Section 15.247, dated October 1, 2000.

EIRP

Equivalent Isotropically Radiated Power (EIRP) is the power actually radiated by the antenna element, as shown in the EIRP Diagram. This concept is important because it is regulated by the FCC and because it is used in calculating whether or not a wireless link is viable. EIRP takes into account the gain of the antenna.

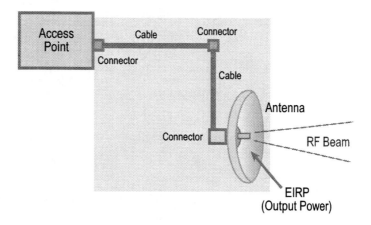

EIRP

Suppose a transmitting station uses a 10-dBi antenna, which amplifies the signal 10-fold, and is fed by 100 milliwatts from the IR. The EIRP is 1000 mW, or 1 Watt. The FCC has rules defining the power output at both the IR and the antenna element.

Note: Failure to comply with FCC rules regarding power output can subject the administrator or the organization (or both) to legal action, RF system shutdown, and fines.

Activities

1. A wireless link connects two nodes across a large warehouse. Blocking as much as 50 percent of the Fresnel Zone between the two node antennas are metal shelves, light fixtures, and other obstructions. In this situation, which one of the following statements is true?

   a. Communications will occur between the nodes as long as the visual LOS remains unobstructed.

   b. RF signals will not be affected because the Fresnel Zone is 20 to 40 percent clear of obstructions.

   c. These objects may obstruct visual LOS, but RF LOS is still acceptable.

   d. Although visual LOS may be clear, RF LOS is obstructed.

2. How does an antenna create gain in the received RF signal?

   a. The antenna's amplifier circuit increases the received signal's amplitude.

   b. The antenna's shape focuses the received signal into a tighter beam.

   c. The antenna regenerates the signal and filters out the background noise.

   d. The antenna bends the signal around any obstructions between the sender and receiver.

3. Consider a cable connecting a wireless access point to an antenna. The cable connects the transmitter to an amplifier. The amplifier connects to another section of cable, which then attaches to the antenna. Using an RF power meter, you wish to measure the IR. Where would you take this measurement?

   a. At the antenna's input

   b. At the transmitter's output

   c. At the input to the amplifier

   d. At the amplifier's output

4. Consider a cable connecting a wireless access point to an antenna. The cable connects the transmitter to an amplifier. The amplifier connects to another section of cable, which then attaches to the antenna. You wish to measure the EIRP. Where would you take this measurement?

    a. At the cable's antenna connector

    b. At the transmitter's output

    c. At the antenna element

    d. At the amplifier's output

5. A transmitter outputs 100mW. An antenna cable connects the transmitter to an amplifier, and the power into the amplifier's input measures 50mW. The amplifier amplifies the signal to the original power level and sends the signal to the antenna. The antenna receives the signal at 75mW, and transmits at 150mW. What is the IR's power level in this RF circuit?

    a. 50mW

    b. 75mW

    c. 100mW

    d. 150mW

Extended Activities

1. Think of and list as many ways as you can that an antenna could have visual LOS but not RF LOS. Next, list ways it could have RF LOS but not visual LOS.

   _____

   _____

   _____

   _____

2. Consider other radio-based communications devices you use everyday, such as the car radio, your cell phone, or your pager. Notice where these devices lose signal strength, or lose the signal altogether. How might a wireless LAN behave in these same areas?

   _____

   _____

   _____

   _____

Lesson 4—RF Mathematics

When designing and installing a wireless LAN, one must be aware of the FCC imposed power limits on wireless transmitters. Although manufacturers often list their products' maximum power output levels, when antennas, RF cables, and connectors are introduced onto the output circuit, the manufacturer's transmitter specifications no longer reflect the circuit's RF signal power level. Hence, wireless administrators must know how to calculate the RF signal power at the IR and EIRP. This lesson discusses RF mathematics fundamentals important to wireless network administration.

Objectives

At the end of this lesson you will be able to:

- Explain key RF power terms, including dB, dBi, dBm, watts, and milliwatts

- Apply the basic concepts of RF mathematics in determining output RF power

 **Key Point**

Basic RF mathematics skills help you ensure that your wireless LAN's RF output meets FCC rules, ensuring proper operation and an accurate design.

RF Power Calculations

The four important areas of power calculation in a wireless LAN are as follows:

- Power at the transmitting device

- Loss and gain of connectivity devices between the antenna and transmitting devices, such as cables, connectors, amplifiers, attenuators, and splitters

- Power at the last connector before the RF signal enters the antenna (IR)

- Power at the antenna element (EIRP)

These areas will be discussed in calculation examples in forthcoming sections. Each of these areas will help determine whether RF links are viable, without overstepping power limitations set by the FCC. Each of these factors must be taken into account when planning a wireless LAN, and all of these factors are related mathematically. The following sections explain the units of measurement and formulas used to calculate power output when configuring wireless LAN devices.

Units of RF Power Measurement

There are a few standard units of measure that a wireless network administrator should become familiar with in order to be effective in implementing and troubleshooting wireless LANs. We will discuss them all in detail, giving examples of their usage. We will then put them to use in some sample math problems so that you have a solid grasp of what some of a CWNA's job tasks require.

Watts

The basic unit of power is a watt (W). A watt is defined as one ampere (A) of current at one volt (V). As an example of what these units mean, think of a garden hose that has water flowing through it. The pressure on the water line would represent the voltage in an electrical circuit. The water flow would represent the amperes (current) flowing through the garden hose. Think of a watt as the result of a given amount of pressure and a given amount of water in the garden hose. One watt is equal to 1 ampere multiplied by 1 volt.

A typical 120-volt plug-in night-light uses about 7 W of power. On a clear night this 7-watt light may be seen 50 miles away in all directions, and, if we could somehow encode information, such as with Morse code, we would have a wireless link established. Remember, we are only interested in sending and receiving data, not illuminating the receiver with RF energy as we would illuminate a room with light. You can see that relatively little power is required to form an RF link of great distance. The FCC allows only 4 watts of power to be radiated from an antenna in a point-to-multipoint wireless LAN connection using unlicensed, 2.4 GHz spread spectrum equipment. Four watts might not seem like much power, but it is enough to send a clear RF data signal for miles.

Milliwatt

When implementing wireless LANs, power levels as low as 1 milliwatt (1/1000 watt, abbreviated as "mW") can be used for a small area, and power levels on a single wireless LAN segment are rarely above 100 mW. These levels of power are enough to communicate up to a half mile (0.83 km) in optimum conditions. Access points generally have the ability to radiate 30 to 100 mW of power, depending on the manufacturer. It is only in the case of point-to-point outdoor connections between buildings that power levels above 100 mW are used. Most of the power levels referred to by administrators will be in mW or decibels referenced to a milliwatt (dBm). These two industry-standard units of measurement represent an absolute amount of power.

Decibels

When a receiver is very sensitive to RF signals, it may be able to pick up signals as small as 0.000000001 Watts. Other than its obvious numerical meaning, this tiny number has little intuitive meaning to a layperson and will likely be ignored or misread. Decibels allow us to represent these numbers by making them more manageable and understandable. Decibels are based on a logarithmic relationship to the previously explained linear measurement of power-- watts. Concerning RF, a logarithm is the exponent to which the number 10 must be raised to reach some given value.

If we are given the number 1000 and asked to find the logarithm (log), we find that log 1000 = 3 because 10^3 = 1000. Notice that our logarithm, 3, is the exponent. An important thing to note about logarithms is that the logarithm of a negative number or zero does not exist:

Log (-100) = undefined!

Log (0) = undefined!

On the linear watt scale we can plot points of absolute power. Absolute power measurement refers to the measurement of power in relation to some fixed reference. On most linear scales (watts, degrees Kelvin, miles per hour), the reference is fixed at zero, which usually describes the absence of the thing measured: zero watts = no power, zero degrees Kelvin = no thermal energy, zero MPH = no movement. On a logarithmic scale, the reference cannot be zero because the log of zero does not exist. Decibels are a relative measurement unit, unlike the absolute measurement of milliwatts.

Gain and Loss Measurements

Power gain and loss are measured in decibels, not in watts, because gain and loss are relative concepts and a decibel is a relative measurement. Gain or loss in an RF system may be referred to by absolute power measurement (10 watts of power, for example) or by a relative power measurement (half of its power, for example). Losing half of the power in a system corresponds to losing 3 decibels. If a system loses half of its power (-3 dB), then loses half again (another -3 dB), the total system loss is three quarters of the original power: one-half first, then one-quarter (one-half of one-half). Clearly, no absolute measurement of watts can quantify this asymmetrical loss in a meaningful way, but decibels do just that.

As a quick and easy reference, there are some numbers related to gain and loss with which an administrator should be familiar. These numbers are:

-3 dB = half the power in mW

+3 dB = double the power in mW

-10 dB = one tenth the power in mW

+10 dB = ten times the power in mW

We refer to these quick references as the 10s and 3s of RF math. When calculating power gain and loss, one can almost always divide an amount of gain or loss by 10 or 3, or both. These values give an administrator the ability to quickly and easily calculate RF loss and gain with a fair amount of accuracy without the use of a calculator. In the case where use of this method is not possible, conversion formulas, shown below, can be used for these calculations.

The following is the general equation for converting mW to dBm:

$$P_{dbm} = 10 \log_{PmW}$$

This equation can be manipulated to reverse the conversion, now converting dBm to mW:

$$Pmw = \log^{-1}\left(\frac{P_{dbm}}{10}\right)$$

$\log^{-1}$ denotes the inverse logarithm (inverse log)

Note: You will not be tested on logarithmic functions using these formulas as part of the CWNA exam. These formulas are provided only for your reference in case they are needed during your administrative tasks. Calculators are not needed on the CWNA exam.

Another important point is that gains and losses are additive. If an access point is connected to a cable whose loss is -2 dB and then to a connector whose loss is -1 dB, the loss measurements are additive and yield a total of -3 dB of loss. We will perform the steps of some RF calculations in the coming sections to give you a better idea of how to relate these numbers to actual scenarios.

dBm

The reference point that relates the logarithmic dB scale to the linear watt scale is:

1 mW = 0 dBm

The "m" in dBm refers simply to the fact that the reference is 1 milliwatt (1 mW). Therefore, a dBm measurement is a measurement of absolute power.

The relationship between the decibels scale and the watt scale can be estimated using the following rules of thumb:

* +3 dB will double the watt value:
  (10 mW + 3dB ˜ 20 mW)

* -3 dB will halve the watt value:
  (100 mW - 3dB ˜ 50 mW)

* +10 dB will increase the watt value by ten-fold:
  (10 mW + 10dB ˜ 100 mW)

* -10 dB will decrease the watt value to one tenth of that value:
  (300 mW - 10dB ˜ 30 mW)

These rules will allow a quick calculation of milliwatt power levels when given power levels, gains, and losses in dBm and dB. The Power Level Chart Diagram shows that the reference point is always the same, but power levels can move in either direction from the reference point, depending on whether they represent a power gain or loss.

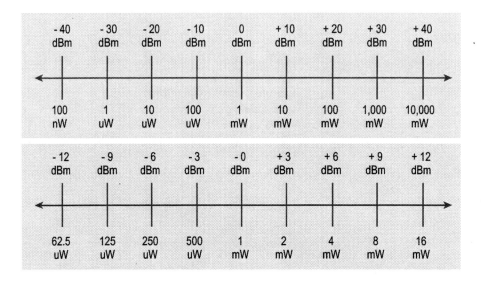

Power Level Chart

In the top chart, gains and losses of 10 dB are shown at each increment. Notice that a gain of +10 dB from the reference point of 1 mW moves the power to +10 dBm (10 mW). Conversely, notice that a loss of -10 dB moves the power to -10 dBm (100 microwatts). On the bottom chart, the same principal applies. These charts both represent the same thing, except that one is incremented in gains and losses of 3 dB and the other for gains and losses of 10 dB. Using these charts, one can easily convert dBm and mW power levels.

Examples

+43 dBm divided into 10s and 3s would equal +10 +10 +10 +10 +3. From the reference point, the charts show you to multiply the milliwatt value (starting at the reference point) times a factor of 10 four times, then times a factor of 2 one time, yielding the following:

1 mW x **10** = 10 mW

10 mW x **10** = 100 mW

100 mW x **10** = 1,000 mW

1,000 mW x **10** = 10,000 mW

10,000 mW x **2** = 20,000 mW = 20 watts

Thus, we now see that +43 dBm equals 20 watts of power.

Another example that takes into consideration measurement negative from the reference point would be -26 dBm. In this example, we see that -26 dBm equals -10 -10 -3 -3. From the reference point, the charts show you to divide the milliwatt value (starting at the reference point) by a factor of 10 twice, then by a factor of 3 twice yielding the following:

1 mW / **10** = 100 uW

100 uW / **10** = 10 uW

10 uW / **2** = 5 uW

5 uW / **2** = 2.5 uW

Thus, we now see that -26 dBm equals 2.5 microwatts of power.

dBi

As discussed previously, gain and loss are measured in decibels. When quantifying the gain of an antenna, the decibel units are represented by decibels isotropic (dBi). The unit of measurement dBi refers only to the gain of an antenna. The "i" stands for "isotropic," which means that the change in power is referenced against an isotropic radiator. An isotropic radiator is a theoretical ideal transmitter that produces useful electromagnetic field output in all directions with equal intensity, and at 100-percent efficiency, in three-dimensional space. One example of an isotropic radiator is the sun. Think of dBi as being referenced against perfection. The dBi measurement is used in RF calculations in the same manner as dB. Units of dBi are relative.

Consider a 10 dBi antenna with 1 watt of power applied. What is the EIRP (output power at the antenna element)?

1 W + 10 dBi (a ten-fold increase) = 10 W

This calculation works in the same fashion as showing gain measured in dB. A gain of 10 dBi multiplies the input power of the antenna by a factor of ten. Unless they are malfunctioning, antennas do not degrade the signal. Thus, the dBi value is always positive. Like dB, dBi is a relative unit of measure and can be added to or subtracted from other decibel units. For example, if an RF signal is reduced by 3 dB as it runs through a copper cable, and is then transmitted by an antenna with a gain of 5 dBi, the result is an overall gain of +2 dB.

Example

Given the RF circuit shown in the Sample Wireless LAN Configuration Diagram, determine the power at all marked points in milliwatts. (See the Measurements Taken at Key Points Table.)

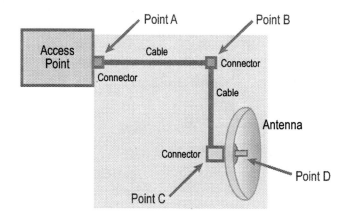

Sample Wireless LAN Configuration

Measurements Taken at Key Points

Access Point 100 mW	Point A −3 dB (÷2)	Point B −3 dB (÷2)	Point C −3 dB (÷2)	Point D +12 dBi *
÷2	50mW			
÷2		25mW		
÷2			12.5mW	
x16				200mW
*(x2 x2 x2 x2 or x16)				

**Accurate
Measurements**

Although these techniques are helpful and expedient in some situations, at times rounded or even numbers may not be available. When this occurs, the formula is the best method of doing RF calculations. Because the decibel is a unit of relative power measurement, a change in power level is implied. If the power level is given in dBm, the change in dB is simple to calculate:

Initial power = 20 dBm

Final power = 33 dBm

Change in power, ΔP, = 33 – 20 = +13 dB. (The value is positive, indicating an increase in power.)

If the power levels are given in milliwatts, the process can become more complicated:

Initial power = 130 mW

Final power = 5.2 W

To calculate the change in power:

$$\Delta P = 10 \log\left(\frac{P_f}{P_i}\right)$$

$$= 10 \log\left(\frac{5.2W}{130mW}\right)$$

$$= 10 \log 40$$

$$= 10 * 1.6$$

$$= 16dB$$

Note: You will not be tested on logarithmic functions using these formulas as part of the CWNA exam, but your understanding of power calculations using the 10s and 3s will be tested. These formulas are provided only for your reference in case they are needed during your administrative tasks. Calculators are not needed on the CWNA exam.

Activities

1. An access point transmits at 75 mW. It connects to a 6 dBi gain omnidirectional antenna by means of a cable with -3dB of loss. What is the EIRP in mW?

   a.   37.5 mW

   b.   75 mW

   c.   150 mW

   d.   300 mW

2. Gain and loss are measured with which units of measure? (Choose two.)

   a.   dB

   b.   dBi

   c.   dBm

   d.   mW

3. One milliwatt is equal to which of the following? (Choose two.)

   a.   0 dBm

   b.   10 dBm

   c.   1/100 watt

   d.   1/1000 watt

4. A wireless network adapter transmits at 100 mW. An external 9 dBi gain Yagi antenna with a –3 dB loss cable is attached. What is the IR power output?

   a.   3 dBm

   b.   7 dBm

   c.   9 mW

   d.   17 dBm

5. Which of the following statements is true concerning gain and loss measurements on a wireless network?

   a. The signal strength in mW triples for each 3 dB of gain.

   b. The signal strength in mW drops by one tenth for each dB of loss.

   c. The signal strength in mW increases tenfold for each 10 dB of gain.

   d. The signal strength in mW drops in half for each 10 dB of loss.

Extended Activities

1. Read the paper "RF in Perspective.doc," written by Michael F. Young of Young Design, Inc. The paper is located in the West-Net Learning Technologies, Inc. Student Resources site at **http://www.westnetinc.com**. You will need to register and log in to the site to access the paper.

2. Visit a wireless vendor's Web site, and gather as much information as possible concerning access point power output, antenna gain, cable loss, amplifier gain, and so forth. Using this information, sketch out several different configurations, staying within FCC rules for point-to-multipoint link power limits. Build a system with omnidirectional, semidirectional, and highly directional antennas. How long a cable can you use with each antenna while still meeting the access point's receive sensitivity threshold? What does this tell you about antenna positioning in relation to the access point?

Summary

This unit discussed the properties of RF radiation and its effect on wireless LAN performance. RFs are high-frequency AC signals that are passed along a copper conductor and then radiated into the air by means of an antenna. Key antenna concepts, including antenna gain, IR, and EIRP, were covered in this unit. This unit also discussed VSWR, which is the ratio of forward power to reverse power. Reverse power occurs when mismatched impedance (resistance to current flow, measured in Ohms) is present between devices in an RF system. An RF signal reflected at a point of impedance mismatch in the signal path causes a high VSWR.

When designing and installing a wireless LAN, it is important to be aware of the FCC-imposed power limits on wireless transmitters. Wireless administrators must know how to calculate the RF signal power at the IR and EIRP. This unit explained the mathematic relationships that exist in RF circuits and how to perform necessary RF calculations.

Unit 2 Quiz

1. When visual LOS is present, RF LOS will also always be present.

    a. This statement is always true.

    b. This statement is always false.

    c. This statement depends on the configuration of the antenna.

2. When RF LOS is present, visual LOS will also always be present.

    a. This statement is always true.

    b. This statement is always false.

    c. It depends on the specific factors.

3. Which units of measure are used to quantify the power gain or loss of an RF signal? (Choose two.)

    a. dBi

    b. dBm

    c. Watts

    d. dB

4. Which of the following will reduce the likelihood of VSWR? (Choose two.)

    a. Cables and connectors that all have an impedance of 50 Ohms

    b. Cables with a 50 ohm impedance and connectors with 75 ohm impedance

    c. Cables and connectors that all have an impedance of 75 Ohms

    d. Cables with 75 ohm impedance and connectors with 50 ohm impedance

5. What is the IR defined as in an RF circuit?

    a. The output of the transmitting device

    b. The output of the last connector before the signal enters the antenna

    c. The output as measured after the antenna

    d. The output after the first length of cable attached to the transmitting device

6. dBi is a relative measurement of decibels to which one of the following?

   a. Internal receiver

   b. IR

   c. Isotropic radiator

   d. Isotropic radio

7. Which one of the following is considered impedance in an RF circuit?

   a. The inability to transmit RF signals

   b. The pressure that causes current flow

   c. Resistance to current flow, measured in Ohms

   d. The frequency on which an RF transmitter sends signals

8. In RF mathematics, what measurement does 1 watt equal in dBm?

   a. 10

   b. 30

   c. 100

   d. 300

9. Which one of the following RF behaviors is defined as "the bending of a wave as it passes through a medium of different density"?

   a. Diffraction

   b. Reflection

   c. Refraction

   d. Distraction

10. A year ago, while working for your current organization, you installed a wireless link between two buildings. Recently you have received reports that the throughput of the link has decreased. After investigating the connection problems, you discover there is a tree within the Fresnel Zone of the link causing 25 percent blockage of the connection. Which of the following statements are true? (Choose two.)

    a. The tree cannot be the problem, because only 25 percent of the connection is blocked.

    b. The tree might be the problem, because up to 40 percent of the Fresnel Zone can be blocked without causing severe problems.

    c. If the tree is the problem, raising the heights of both antennas will fix the problem.

    d. If the tree is the problem, increasing the power at the transmitters at each end of the link will fix the problem.

11. Given an access point with 100 mW of output power connected through a 50-foot cable with 3 dB of loss to an antenna with 10 dBi of gain, what is the EIRP at the antenna in mW?

    a. 100 mW

    b. 250 mW

    c. 500 mW

    d. 1 W

12. Given a wireless bridge with 200 mW of output power connected through a 100 foot cable with 6 dB of loss to an antenna with 9 dBi of gain, what is the EIRP at the antenna in dBm?

    a. 20 dBm

    b. 26 dBm

    c. 30 dBm

    d. 36 dBm

13. Given an access point with an output power of 100 mW connected through a cable with a loss of 2 dB to an antenna with a gain of 11 dBi, what is the EIRP in mW?

    a. 200 mW

    b. 400 mW

    c. 800 mW

    d. 1 W

14. Given an access point with an output power of 20 dBm, connected through a cable with a loss of 6 dB to an amplifier with a 10 dB gain, and then through a cable with 3 dB of loss to an antenna with 6 dBi of gain, what is the EIRP in dBm?

    a.   18 dBm

    b.   23 dBm

    c.   25 dBm

    d.   27 dBm

15. What is the net gain or loss of a circuit if it is using two cables with 3 dB loss each, one amplifier with a 12 dB gain, one antenna with 9 dBi gain, and an attenuator with a loss of 5 dB?

    a.   5 dB

    b.   10 dB

    c.   15 dB

    d.   20 dB

16. Which of the following is a cause of VSWR?

    a.   Mismatched impedances between wireless LAN connectors

    b.   Too much power radiated from the antenna element

    c.   The incorrect type of antenna used to transmit a signal

    d.   Use of the incorrect RF frequency band

17. In what manner do radio waves propagate (move) away from the source (antenna)?

    a.   In a straight line in all directions at once within the vertical and horizontal beamwidths

    b.   In circles spiraling away from the antenna

    c.   In spherical, concentric circles within the horizontal beamwidth

    d.   Up and down across the area of coverage

18. Why is the Fresnel Zone important to the integrity of the RF link?

    a. The Fresnel Zone defines the area of coverage in a typical RF coverage cell.

    b. For a wireless LAN to operate properly, the Fresnel Zone must always be 100 percent clear of blockage.

    c. The Fresnel Zone defines an area around the RF LOS that can introduce RF signal interference if blocked.

    d. The Fresnel Zone does not change with the length of the RF link

19. The FCC allows how many watts of power to be radiated from an antenna in a point-to-multipoint wireless LAN connection using unlicensed 2.4 GHz spread spectrum equipment?

    a. 1 watt

    b. 2 watts

    c. 3 watts

    d. 4 watts

20. In regards to gain and loss measurements in wireless LANs, the statement that gains and losses are additive is:

    a. Always true

    b. Always false

    c. Sometimes true

    d. Sometimes false

    e. It depends on the equipment manufacturer

Unit 3
Spread Spectrum Technology

In order to administer and troubleshoot wireless LANs effectively, a solid understanding of spread spectrum technology and its implementation is required. This unit defines and describes spread spectrum technology and discusses how it is used according to FCC guidelines. The two main spread spectrum technologies, Frequency Hopping Spread Spectrum (FHSS) and Direct Sequence Spread Spectrum (DSSS) are differentiated, compared, and discussed in depth. This unit also explains how spread spectrum technology is implemented in wireless LANs.

Lessons

1. Introducing Spread Spectrum
2. FHSS
3. DSSS
4. Comparing FHSS and DSSS

Terms

802.15 Bluetooth—Bluetooth is a close-range, frequency hopping technology that operates in the 2.4-GHz ISM band and hops at a rate of 1600 hops per second. Bluetooth devices create all-band interference with other 2.4-GHz ISM band devices. Bluetooth is considered Wireless Personal Area Network (WPAN) technology and does not directly compete against Wi-Fi devices in the market.

beacon—See beacon management frame.

beacon management frame—Beacon management frames are short frames sent from the access point to the stations in infrastructure mode or from station-to-station in adhoc mode. They are used to organize and synchronize wireless LAN communications.

channel—In wireless networks, a channel is a set of frequencies used between two or more communicating devices.

chipping code—The chipping code represents how the data bits sent on a set of RF carrier frequencies are spread across the frequencies. The wider the spreading is, the higher the resistance to narrowband interference. Also, the wider the bit spreading is, the higher the processing gain.

chips—Chips are a set of bits used in wireless LANs to indicate a single bit of digital data. It may take 10 or 11 chips (0s or 1s) to equal one data bit.

Code Division Multiple Access (CDMA)—CDMA is a form of cellular communications that uses spread spectrum technologies.

co-location—Co-location is the arrangement of multiple access points (APs) within the same physical area. When co-located, APs can interfere with one another, or if properly configured, provide additional bandwidth, throughput, and failover capabilities.

Direct Sequence Spread Spectrum (DSSS)—DSSS combines a data signal at the sending station with a higher data rate bit sequence, which many refer to as a chip sequence (directly related to processing gain). A high processing gain increases a signal's resistance to interference. The minimum processing gain that the FCC allows is 10, and most products operate under 20.

dwell time—The dwell time is the amount of time a frequency-hopping device remains on a single carrier frequency.

encoding—Encoding is the process of translating binary data (1s and 0s) into signals to be transmitted across a physical link. The most common signaling forms are electrical signals, light signals, and radio signals.

European Telecommunications Standards Institute (ETSI)—ETSI is a nonprofit organization whose mission is to produce the telecommunications standards that will be used throughout Europe, including HiperLAN/1 and HiperLAN/2.

Frequency Hopping Spread Spectrum (FHSS)—FHSS takes the data signal and modulates it with a carrier signal that hops from frequency to frequency as a function of time over a wide band of frequencies. For example, a frequency-hopping radio will hop on individual carrier frequencies over the 2.4-GHz Industrial Scientific Medical (ISM) band between 2.402 GHz and 2.480 GHz. A hopping sequence called a "channel" determines the frequencies on which it will transmit and in which order. To properly receive the signal, the receiver must be set to the same channel and listen to the incoming signal at the right time at the correct frequency.

Global Positioning System (GPS)—GPS is a system that determines a position on the Earth's surface by triangulating signals from several satellites through a receiver on Earth.

HomeRF—Founded in March 1998, this organization's charter is to establish the mass deployment of interoperable wireless networking access devices; products utilize the 2.4-GHz ISM band, FHSS technology, and a proprietary access protocol called Simple Workflow Access Protocol (SWAP) to achieve data rates of up to 10 Mbps.

hop time—The hop time is the amount of time it takes for a frequency hopping device to hop to a new frequency.

Industrial, Scientific, and Medical (ISM) bands—ISM bands are radio frequency bands that the Federal Communications Commission (FCC) authorized for wireless LANs. The ISM bands are located at 915+/-13 MHz, 2450+/-50 MHz, and 5800+/-75 MHz.

megahertz (MHz)—Radio signals are measured in cycles per second, or Hertz (Hz). One Hz is 1 cycle per second; 1,000 cycles per second is 1 kHz; 1 million cycles per second is 1 MHz; and 1 billion cycles per second is 1 GHz.

microsecond—A microsecond is one millionth of a second.

modulation—Modulation is the process of modifying the form of a carrier wave (electrical signal) so that it can carry intelligent information on a communications medium.

narrowband—Narrowband is a form of radio transmission that uses only a small portion of the RF spectrum. In the context of wireless LANs, a narrowband signal is one that uses only as much of the frequency spectrum as is needed to carry the data signal.

noise floor—Noise floor is the level of RF that is inherently present in the surrounding environment. This noise is generated by a number of sources and is typically between -70 and -100 dBm in most environments. For a data signal to be effectively communicated, it must be significantly higher than the noise floor, which is high enough for the receiver to clearly distinguish between the RF data signal and the background noise.

OpenAir—OpenAir is an FHSS standard, developed by the Wireless LAN Interoperability Forum, that specifies data rates of 800 Kbps or 1.6 Mbps.

personal area network (PAN)—A PAN is a short-distance wireless network that connects a user's personal electronic devices, such as a cell phone, PDA, and headphones. It is also called a WPAN.

Personal Communications System (PCS)—PCS is a set of digital cellular services popular in the United States. PCS phones communicate digitally in the 1.9 GHz frequency band.

processing gain—Processing gain is the ratio of the chip rate to the data rate of a direct sequence signal. A higher-processing gain is better and increases a signal's interference immunity. Also see chipping code.

Shared Wireless Access Protocol (SWAP)—SWAP is a wireless protocol used in HomeRF networks that combines CSMA and TDMA technologies for wireless voice and data networking.

throughput—Throughput describes the overall capacity of a network to perform useful work. While bandwidth measurements focus on the raw number of bits a network can carry, throughput measurements express the actual or effective data rates of a network. Throughput is most often used to describe the overall performance of a network. It is measured in pulses per second (PPS) or bits per second (bps).

wide area network (WAN)—WANs are essentially interconnected local area networks (LANs) or metropolitan area networks (MANs). They can be homogeneous, interconnecting similar networks, but are often heterogeneous, interconnecting LANs or MANs that have been built using different technologies. A WAN can span campuses, cities, states, or even continents.

wireless metropolitan area network (WMAN)—A wireless MAN provides communications links between buildings, avoiding the costly installation of cabling or leasing fees and the down time associated with system failures.

wireless personal area network (WPAN)—A wireless PAN uses RF technology to create a short range, personal communications network.

wireless wide area network (WWAN)—A wireless WAN is a wireless network that connects LANs across large geographic areas, such as between sites in different cities or states.

Lesson 1—Introducing Spread Spectrum

Spread spectrum is a communications technique characterized by wide bandwidth and low peak power. Spread spectrum communication uses various modulation techniques in wireless LANs and possesses many advantages over its precursor, narrowband communication. Spread spectrum signals are noise-like, hard to detect, and even harder to intercept or demodulate without the proper equipment. Jamming and interference have less of an effect on spread spectrum communications than on narrowband communications. For these reasons, spread spectrum has long been a favorite communications technique of the military. To explain spread spectrum, we must first establish a reference by discussing the concept of narrowband transmission.

Objectives

At the end of this lesson you will be able to:

- Describe different uses for spread spectrum technologies, such as wireless LANs (WLANs), wireless personal area network (WPAN), and wireless wide area network (WWAN)

- Explain why you would choose one spread spectrum technology over another

 **Key Point**

Today's wireless LANs most often use either FHSS or DSSS spread spectrum technologies.

Narrowband Transmission

A narrowband transmission is a communications technology that uses only enough of the frequency spectrum to carry a data signal, and no more. It has always been the mission of the Federal Communications Commission (FCC) to conserve frequency usage as much as possible, handing out only what is absolutely necessary to "get the job done." Spread spectrum opposes that mission because it uses much wider frequency bands than are necessary to transmit information. This brings us to the first requirement for a signal to be considered spread spectrum: a signal is a spread spectrum signal when the bandwidth is much wider than what is required to send the information.

The Narrowband vs. Spread Spectrum on a Frequency Domain Diagram illustrates the difference between narrowband and spread spectrum transmissions. Notice that one of the characteristics of narrowband is high peak power. More power is required to send a transmission when using a smaller frequency range. In order for narrowband signals to be received, they must stand out above the environment's inherent level of RF noise, called the noise floor, by a significant amount. Because its band is so narrow, a high peak power ensures error-free reception of a narrowband signal.

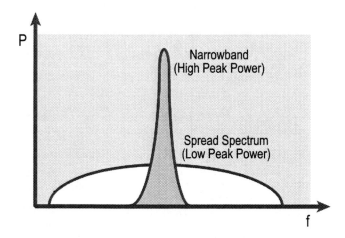

Narrowband vs. Spread Spectrum on a Frequency Domain

A compelling argument against narrowband transmission, other than the high peak power required to send it, is that narrowband signals can be jammed or experience interference very easily. Jamming is the intentional overpowering of a transmission using unwanted signals transmitted on the same band. Because its band is so narrow, other narrowband signals, such as noise, can completely eliminate the information by overpowering a narrowband transmission--much like a passing train overpowers a quiet conversation.

Spread Spectrum Technology

Spread spectrum technology allows us to take the same amount of information that we previously would have sent using a narrowband carrier signal, and spread it out over a much larger frequency range. For example, we may use 1 MHz at 10 Watts with narrowband, but 20 MHz at 100 mW with spread spectrum. By using a wider frequency spectrum, we reduce the probability that a narrowband transmission will corrupt or jam the data. A narrowband jamming attempt on a spread spectrum signal would likely be thwarted by virtue of only a small part of the information falling into the narrowband signal's frequency range. Most of the digital data would be received error-free. Today's spread spectrum RF radios can retransmit any small amount of data loss due to narrowband interference.

While the spread spectrum band is relatively wide, the peak power of the signal is quite low. This is the second requirement for a signal to be considered spread spectrum: for a signal to be considered spread spectrum, it must use low power.

These two characteristics of spread spectrum (use of a wide band of frequencies and very low power) make a spread spectrum signal look like a noise signal to most receivers. Noise is a wide band, low power signal, but the difference is that noise is unwanted. Furthermore, because most radio receivers view the spread spectrum signal as noise, these receivers will not attempt to demodulate or interpret it, creating a slightly more secure communication.

Uses of Spread Spectrum

This inherent security in spread spectrum technology is what interested the military in the 1950s and 1960s. Because of its noise-like characteristics, spread spectrum signals could be sent under the noses of enemies using classic communication techniques. Security was all but guaranteed. Naturally, this perceived communication security was only valid as long as no one else used the technology. If another group used the same technology, these spread spectrum communications could be discovered, and possibly intercepted and decoded.

In the 1980s, the FCC implemented a set of rules making spread spectrum technology available to the public and encouraging research and investigation into the commercialization of spread spectrum technology. Though at first glance it may seem that the military lost its advantage, it had not. The bands used by the military are different from the bands used by the public. Also, the military uses very different modulation and encoding techniques to ensure that its spread spectrum communications are far more difficult to intercept than those of the general public.

Since the 1980s, when research began in earnest, spread spectrum technologies have been used in cordless phones, global positioning systems (GPS), digital cellular telephony (code division multiple access [CDMA]), personal communications system (PCS), and now wireless local area networks (wireless LANs). Amateur radio enthusiasts are now beginning to experiment with spread spectrum technologies for many of the reasons we have discussed.

In addition to wireless LANs (WLANs), the following networks are also taking advantage of spread spectrum technologies: wireless personal area network (WPAN), wireless metropolitan area network (WMAN), and wireless wide area network (WWAN). WPAN use Bluetooth technology to take advantage of very low power requirements to allow wireless networking within a very short range. WWAN and WMAN can use highly directional, high-gain antennas to establish long-distance, high-speed RF links with relatively low power.

Wireless LANs

Wireless LANs, WMAN, and WWAN use the same spread spectrum technologies in different ways. For example, a wireless LAN might be used within a building to provide connectivity for mobile users, or bridges might be used to provide building-to-building connectivity across a campus. These are specific uses of spread spectrum technology that fit within the description of a LAN.

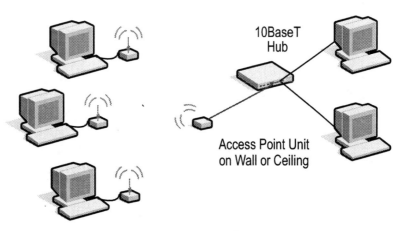

Radio-based Wireless LANs

The most common uses of spread spectrum technology today lie in a combination of wireless 802.11-compliant LANs and 802.15-compliant Bluetooth devices. These two technologies have captured a tremendous market share. Ironically, the two function much differently, play within the same FCC rules, and yet interfere with each other greatly. Considerable research, time, and resources have gone into making these two technologies coexist peacefully.

WPANs

Bluetooth, the most popular of WPAN technologies, is specified by the IEEE 802.15 standard. The FCC regulations regarding spread spectrum use are broad, allowing for differing types of spread spectrum implementations. Some forms of spread spectrum introduce the concept of frequency-hopping, meaning that the transmitting and receiving systems hop from frequency to frequency within a frequency band, and transmit data as they go. For example, Bluetooth hops approximately 1600 times per second, while HomeRF 2.0 technology (a wide-band wireless LAN technology) hops approximately 50 times per second. Both of these technologies vary greatly from the standard 802.11 wireless LAN, which typically hops 5-10 times per second.

Each of these technologies has different uses in the marketplace, but all fall within the FCC regulations. For example, a typical 802.11 frequency hopping wireless LAN might be implemented as an enterprise wireless networking solution, while HomeRF 2.0 is only implemented in home environments, due to lower output power restrictions by the FCC.

WMANs

Other spread spectrum uses, such as wireless links that span an entire city using high-power point-to-point links to create a network, fall into the category known as Wireless Metropolitan Area Network (WMAN). A network formed from many meshed, point-to-point wireless connections across a very large geographical area is considered a WMAN, but it still uses the same transmission technologies as a wireless LAN.

The difference between a wireless LAN and a WMAN is that in many cases, WMAN use licensed frequencies instead of the unlicensed frequencies typically used with WLANs. The reason for this difference is that an organization implementing the network will have control of the frequency range where the WMAN is implemented, and will not have to worry about the chance of someone else implementing an interfering network. The same factors apply to WWAN.

FCC Specifications

Although there are many different implementations of spread spectrum technology, the FCC has, until recently, only specified two types: Direct Sequencing and Frequency Hopping. The FCC specifies spread spectrum devices in Title 47, a collection of regulations passed by Congress and adopted by the FCC under the heading "Telegraphs, Telephones, and Radiotelegraphs." These provide the basis for implementation and regulation by the FCC.

Note: The FCC regulations can be found in the Codes of Federal Regulation (CFR), volume 47 (the regulations are found in the CFR volume with the same number as the Title), part 15. Wireless LAN devices described in these regulations are sometimes called "part 15 devices."

Activities

1. Which statement best describes narrowband transmission?

   a. It is more secure than spread spectrum technology.

   b. It is less expensive than spread spectrum technology.

   c. It is not susceptible to jamming, which can block the signal.

   d. It is susceptible to noise, which can overpower the signal.

2. Bluetooth technology, which is included as part of IEEE 802.15, is an example of which use of spread spectrum technology?

   a. Wireless LAN

   b. WMAN

   c. WPAN

   d. WWAN

3. Which two of the following spread spectrum technologies does the FCC describe for use in the license free 2.4 GHz ISM band? (Choose two.)

   a. DFHSS

   b. DSSS

   c. FHSS

   d. FSSS

4. How does DSSS reduce the probability that a signal will be jammed?

   a. By transmitting over a wider frequency spectrum

   b. By transmitting an anti-jamming signal along with the intelligence

   c. By spreading the signal over a range of narrow frequency bands

   d. By using low power transmitters

5. Which of the following is a characteristic of a spread spectrum system?

   a. Low input power

   b. Low output power

   c. High output power

   d. Narrow frequency bands

Extended Activities

1. Research wireless WAN applications. What are the advantages and disadvantages of this technology?

   _____

   _____

   _____

   _____

2. How might an enterprise use wireless PANs to increase worker mobility and productivity?

   _____

   _____

   _____

   _____

Lesson 2—FHSS

Frequency-hopping spread spectrum (FHSS) is a spread spectrum technique that uses frequency agility to spread the data over a minimum of 75 and a maximum of 79 carrier frequencies in the 2.4 GHz Industrial Scientific Medical (ISM) band. Frequency agility refers to a radio's ability to change transmission frequency abruptly within the usable RF frequency band. In the case of frequency-hopping wireless LANs, the usable portion of the 2.4 GHz ISM band is 83.5 MHz wide per FCC regulation and the IEEE 802.11 standard.

Objectives

At the end of this lesson you will be able to:

- Describe how FHSS systems operate

- Explain how narrowband interference affects FHSS communications

- Describe the FCC rules that govern FHSS-based wireless networks

 **Key Point**

FHSS systems spread transmitted intelligence across a set of carrier frequencies using a pseudo-random hoping pattern.

How FHSS Works

In frequency-hopping systems, a carrier changes frequency, or hops, according to a pseudo-random sequence. The pseudo-random sequence is a list of several frequencies to which the carrier will hop at specified time intervals before repeating the pattern. The transmitter uses this hop sequence to select its transmission frequencies. The carrier will remain at a certain frequency for a specified time (called the "dwell time"), and then use a small amount of time to hop to the next frequency (called "hop time"). When the list of frequencies has been exhausted, the transmitter repeats the sequence.

The Single Frequency-Hopping System Diagram shows a frequency-hopping system using a hop sequence of five frequencies over a 5 MHz band. In this example, the sequence is:

1. 2.449 GHz

2. 2.452 GHz

3. 2.448 GHz

4. 2.450 GHz

5. 2.451 GHz

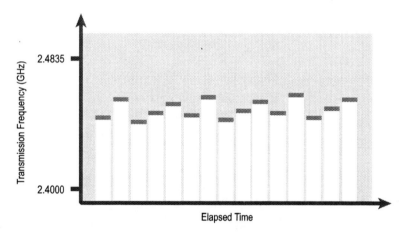

Single Frequency-Hopping System

Once the radio has transmitted the information on the 2.451-GHz carrier, the radio repeats the hop sequence, starting again at 2.449 GHz. The process of repeating the sequence continues until the information is received completely.

The receiver radio is synchronized to the transmitting radio's hop sequence in order to receive on the proper frequency at the proper time. The signal is then demodulated and used by the receiving computer.

Effects of Narrowband Interference

Frequency-hopping is a method of sending data where the transmission and receiving systems hop together along a repeatable pattern of frequencies. As is the case with all spread spectrum technologies, frequency-hopping systems are resistant—but not immune—to narrowband interference. On the Single Frequency Hopping System Diagram, if a signal interfered with the frequency-hopping signal on 2.451 GHz, only that portion of the spread spectrum signal would be lost. The rest of the spread spectrum signal would remain intact, and the lost data would be retransmitted.

In reality, an interfering narrowband signal may occupy several megahertz of bandwidth. Because a frequency-hopping band is over 83 MHz wide, even the interfering signal on 2.451 GHz will cause little degradation of the spread spectrum signal.

Frequency-Hopping Systems

It is the IEEE's job to create standards of operation within the confines of the regulations created by the FCC. The IEEE and OpenAir standards regarding FHSS systems describe:

- What frequency bands may be used ·
- Dwell times
- Hop sequences (channels)
- Carrier frequency bandwidth
- Power output levels
- Data rates

The IEEE 802.11 standard specifies data rates of 1 Mbps and 2 Mbps, and OpenAir, a standard created by the now defunct Wireless LAN Interoperability Forum, specifies data rates of 800 kbps and 1.6 Mbps. In order for a frequency-hopping system to be 802.11, or OpenAir-compliant, it must operate in the 2.4 GHz ISM band, which is defined by the FCC as being from 2.4000 GHz to 2.5000 GHz. Both standards allow operation in the range of 2.4000 GHz to 2.4835 GHz.

Note: Because the Wireless LAN Interoperability Forum (WLIF) no longer supports the OpenAir standard, IEEE-compliant systems will be the main focus for FHSS systems in this course.

Channels

A frequency-hopping system operates using a specified hopping pattern called a "channel." Frequency-hopping systems typically use the FCC's 26 standard hop patterns or a subset thereof. Some frequency-hopping systems allow custom hop patterns to be created, and others even allow synchronization between systems to completely eliminate collisions in a co-located environment.

Although it is possible to have as many as 79 synchronized, co-located access points, as shown on the Co-located Frequency-Hopping Systems Diagram, this number of systems requires that each frequency-hopping radio be precisely synchronized with all of the others. This synchronization ensures that each access point will not interfere with (transmit on the same frequency as) another frequency-hopping radio in the area. The cost of such a set of systems is prohibitive and is usually not considered an option. If synchronized radios are used, the expense tends to dictate 12 co-located systems as the maximum.

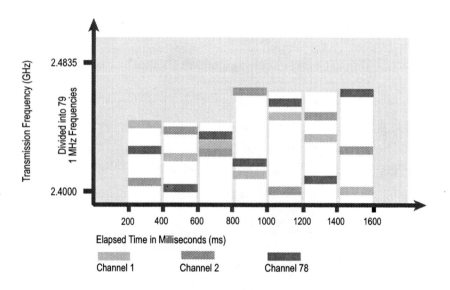

Co-located Frequency-Hopping Systems

If nonsynchronized radios will be used, 26 systems can be co-located in a wireless LAN; this number is considered to be the maximum in a medium-traffic wireless LAN. Increasing the traffic significantly or routinely transferring large files limits the practical number of co-located systems to about 15. More than 15 co-located frequency-hopping systems in this environment will interfere with each other to an extent that collisions will begin to reduce the aggregate throughput of the wireless LAN.

Dwell Time

When discussing frequency-hopping systems, we are identifying systems that must transmit on a specified frequency for a time, and then hop to a different frequency to continue transmitting. When a frequency-hopping system transmits on a frequency, it must do so for a specified amount of time, called the "dwell time." Once the configured dwell time has expired, the system will switch to a different frequency and begin to transmit again.

Suppose a frequency-hopping system transmits on only two frequencies, 2.401 GHz and 2.402 GHz. The system will transmit (dwell) on the 2.401 GHz frequency for the duration of the dwell time—100 milliseconds (ms), for example. After 100ms, the radio must change its transmitter frequency to 2.402 GHz and send information at that frequency for 100ms. Because, in our example, the radio is only using 2.401 and 2.402 GHz, the radio will hop back to 2.401 GHz and begin the process over again.

Hop Time

Dwell time is only one issue when considering the hopping action of a frequency-hopping radio. When a frequency-hopping radio jumps from frequency A to frequency B, it must change the transmit frequency in one of two ways. It either must switch to a different circuit tuned to the new frequency, or it must change some element of the current circuit in order to tune to the new frequency. In either case, the process of changing to the new frequency must be complete before transmission can resume, and this change takes time due to electrical latencies inherent in the circuitry. There is a small amount of time, called the "hop time," during this frequency change when the radio does not transmit. The hop time is measured in microseconds, and with relatively long dwell times of around 100–200 ms, the hop time is insignificant. A typical 802.11 FHSS system hops between channels in 200–300 microseconds.

With very short dwell times of 500–600 microseconds, like those used in some frequency-hopping systems, such as Bluetooth, hop time can become very significant. If we look at the effect of hop time in terms of data throughput, we discover that the longer the hop time is in relation to the dwell time, the slower the data rate will be of transmitted bits. This translates roughly to "longer dwell time = greater throughput."

Dwell Time Limits

The FCC defines the maximum dwell time of a frequency-hopping spread spectrum system at 400 ms per carrier frequency in any 30-second time period. For example, if a transmitter uses a frequency for 100 ms, and then hops through the entire sequence of 75 hops (each hop having the same 100 ms dwell time) returning to the original frequency, it has expended slightly over 7.5 seconds in this hopping sequence. The reason it is not exactly 7.5 seconds is due to hop time. Hopping through the hop sequence four consecutive times would yield 400 ms on each of the carrier frequencies during this timeframe of just barely over 30 seconds (7.5 seconds x 4 passes through the hop sequence), which is allowable by FCC rules. Other examples of how an FHSS system might stay within the FCC rules are a dwell time of 200 ms passing through the hop sequence only twice in 30 seconds, or a dwell time of 400 ms passing through the hop sequence only once in 30 seconds. Any of these scenarios are perfectly fine for a manufacturer to implement. The major difference between each of these scenarios is how hop time affects throughput. Using a dwell time of 100 ms, four times as many hops must be made as when using a 400 ms dwell time. This additional hopping time decreases system throughput.

Normally, frequency-hopping radios are not programmed to operate at the legal limit; but instead provide some room between the legal limit and the actual operating range in order to provide the operator with the flexibility of adjustment. By adjusting the dwell time, an administrator can optimize the FHSS network for areas where there is either considerable interference or very little interference. In an area where there is little interference, longer dwell time, and therefore greater throughput, is desirable. Conversely, in an area where considerable interference and many retransmissions are likely the result of corrupted data packets, shorter dwell times are desirable.

FCC Rules Governing FHSS Systems

On August 31, 2000, the FCC changed the rules governing how FHSS can be implemented. The rule changes allowed frequency-hopping systems to be more flexible and more robust. The rules are typically divided into "pre- 8/31/2000" rules and "post- 8/31/2000" rules, but the FCC allows the manufacturer or the implementer some decision making. If a manufacturer creates a frequency-hopping system today, the manufacturer may use either the "pre- 8/31/2000" rules or the "post- 8/31/2000" rules, depending on the company's needs. If the manufacturer uses the "post- 8/31/2000" rules, the manufacturer is bound by all of these rules. Conversely, if using the "pre- 8/31/2000" rules, the manufacturer is bound by that set of rules. A manufacturer cannot use some provisions from the "pre- 8/31/2000" rules and mix them with other provisions of the "post- 8/31/2000" rules.

Prior to August 31, 2000, the FCC (and the IEEE) mandated FHSS systems to use at least 75 of the possible 79 carrier frequencies in a frequency hop set at a maximum output power of 1 Watt at the intentional radiator. Each carrier frequency is a multiple of 1 MHz between 2.402 GHz and 2.480 GHz. This rule states that the system must hop on 75 of the 79 frequencies before repeating the pattern.

This rule was amended on August 31, 2000 to state that only 15 hops in a set were required, but other changes ensued as well. For example, the maximum output power of a system complying with these new rules is 125 mW and can have a maximum of 5 MHz of carrier frequency bandwidth. Remember, with an increase in bandwidth for the same information, less peak power is required. As further explanation of this rule change, although not exactly in the same wording used by the FCC regulation, the number of hops multiplied times the bandwidth of the carrier was required to equal a total span of at least 75 MHz. For example, if 25 hops are used, a carrier frequency only 3 MHz wide is required, or if 15 hops are used, a carrier frequency 5 MHz wide (the maximum) must be used. It is important to note that systems may comply with either the pre- 8/31/00 rule or the post- 8/31/00 rule, but no mixing or matching of pieces of each rule is allowed.

Note: The IEEE did not change the 802.11 standard to reflect the post-8/31/00 rules. Rather, HomeRF is the only organization to adopt these changes into any sort of technical standard.

No overlapping frequencies are allowed under either rule. If the minimum 75 MHz of used bandwidth within the frequency spectrum were cut into pieces as wide as the carrier frequency bandwidth in use, the pieces would have to sit side-by-side throughout the spectrum with no overlap. This regulation translates into a minimum of 75 nonoverlapping carrier frequencies under the pre- 8/31/00 rules and 15 to 74 nonoverlapping carrier frequencies under the post-8/31/00 rules.

The IEEE states in the 802.11 standard that FHSS systems will have at least 6 MHz of carrier frequency separation between hops. Therefore, an FHSS system transmitting on 2.410 GHz must hop to at least 2.404 if decreasing in frequency, or 2.416 if increasing in frequency. This requirement was left unchanged by the IEEE after the FCC change on August 31, 2000.

The pre-8/31/00 FCC rules concerning FHSS systems allowed a maximum of 2 Mbps by today's technology. By increasing the maximum carrier bandwidth from 1 MHz to 5 MHz, the maximum data rate was increased to 10 Mbps.

Activities

1. Which statement best describes FHSS's use of frequency agility?

   a. It spreads the data across a single frequency band.

   b. It changes frequencies often across the available RF band.

   c. It varies the radio frequency from 900 MHz to 2.4G Hz.

   d. It spreads the data across three nonoverlapping channels.

2. Assume that an FHSS system hops data across the following set frequency sequence: 2.410, 2.412, 2.422, 2.431, and 2.411 GHz. What will the radio do after it has completed transmission on the last carrier band and has more information to send?

   a. Stop transmitting

   b. Choose the next frequency at random

   c. Start from the beginning

   d. Choose a new set of frequencies

3. Assume that an FHSS system hops data across the following set frequency sequence: 2.410, 2.412, 2.422, 2.431, and 2.411 GHz. If the system experiences interference on the 2.422 GHz band, what will most likely happen to the data?

   a. The data on that band will be lost.

   b. The radio will choose another frequency sequence.

   c. The entire data transmission will fail.

   d. The data will be retransmitted on the next dwell.

4. Which of the following data rates does the OpenAir standard specify? (Choose two.)

   a. 800 kbps

   b. 1 Mbps

   c. 1.6 Mbps

   d. 2 Mbps

5. What is the maximum practical number of synchronized, co-located radios that can be used with an FHSS system?

   a. 12

   b. 15

   c. 26

   d. 79

6. Which statement best describes dwell time in an FHSS system?

   a. The time it takes the radio to hop to the next channel

   b. The time it takes to transmit a frame between nodes

   c. The time a radio transmits on a specific frequency

   d. The time a radio spends communicating with a specific node

Extended Activities

1. Explain the effect short dwell times have on a wireless network's throughput. Give some examples to defend your conclusions.

2. Using the IEEE standard for minimum carrier frequency separation between hops, determine the minimum upper and lower next hop frequencies for the following:

Frequency	Lower next hop frequency	Upper next hop frequency
2.415 GHz		
2.450 GHz		
2.466 GHz		
2.407 GHz		

Lesson 3—DSSS

Direct sequence spread spectrum (DSSS) is very widely known and the most used of the spread spectrum types, owing most of its popularity to its ease of implementation and high data rates. The majority of wireless LAN equipment on the market today uses DSSS technology. DSSS is a method of sending data in which the transmitting and receiving systems are both on a 22 MHz-wide set of frequencies. The wide channel enables devices to transmit more information at a higher data rate than current FHSS systems.

Objectives

At the end of this lesson you will be able to:

- Describe how DSSS systems operate

- Explain the effects of narrowband interference on DSSS systems

- Describe the FCC rules that govern DSSS-based wireless networks

 **Key Point**

DSSS systems spread transmitted intelligence over an adjacent set of 22 MHz carrier frequencies.

How DSSS Works

DSSS combines a data signal at the sending station with a higher data rate bit sequence, which is referred to as a chipping code. A set of bits that represents a single data bit increases a signal's resistance to interference because if one or more chips are interfered with, the receiving station can still reconstruct the signal. The ratio of chips to data bits is called the "processing gain." Over the last couple of years, the Federal Communications Commission (FCC) required a minimum linear processing gain of at least 10, and most commercial products operate under 20. The FCC recently removed this requirement from Part 15 rules, citing a lack of need due to the industry's self-regulation in this area. The IEEE 802.11 working group has set their minimum processing gain requirements at 11.

The process of direct sequence begins with a carrier being modulated with a code sequence. The number of chips in the code will determine how much spreading occurs, the number of chips per bit, and the speed of the code (in chips per second) will determine the data rate.

Direct Sequence Systems

In the 2.4 GHz ISM band, the IEEE specifies the use of DSSS at a data rate of 1 or 2 Mbps under the 802.11 standard. Under the 802.11b standard, sometimes called high-rate wireless, data rates of 5.5 and 11 Mbps are specified.

IEEE 802.11b devices operating at 5.5 or 11 Mbps are able to communicate with 802.11 DSSS devices operating at 1 or 2 Mbps because the 802.11b standard provides for backward compatibility. Users employing 802.11 DSSS devices do not need to upgrade their entire wireless LAN in order to use 802.11b devices on their network.

Until recently, 11 Mbps was the most bandwidth available to 802.11 DSSS networks. However, the 802.11g draft specifies direct sequence systems operating in the 2.4 GHz ISM band that can deliver up to 54 Mbps data rate. The 802.11g technology is the first 54 Mbps technology that was backward compatible with 802.11 and 802.11b devices, but is not presently available.

Note: As of this writing, the first draft of the 802.11g standard has been approved as a future standard, but the specifications of this new standard are still in draft form. More information about 802.11g can be found at http://standards.ieee.org/cgi-bin/status?wireless.

Channels

Unlike frequency-hopping systems that use hop sequences to define the channels, direct sequence systems use a more conventional definition of channels. Each channel is a contiguous band of frequencies 22 MHz wide, and 1 MHz carrier frequencies are used just as with FHSS. Channel 1, for example, operates from 2.401 GHz to 2.423 GHz (2.412 GHz ± 11 MHz); channel 2 operates from 2.406 to 2.429 GHz (2.417 ± 11 MHz), and so forth. The DSSS Channel Allocation and Spectral Relationship Diagram illustrates this point.

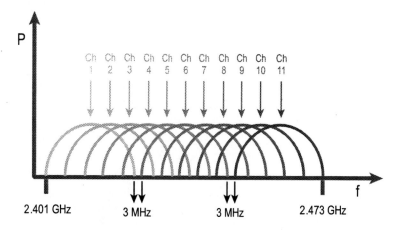

DSSS Channel Allocation and Spectral Relationship

The DSSS Channel Frequency Assignments Table has a complete list of channels used in the United States and Europe (ETSI). The FCC specifies only 11 channels for nonlicensed use in the United States. We can see that channels 1 and 2 overlap by a significant amount. Each of the frequencies listed in this chart are considered center frequencies. From this center frequency, 11 MHz is added and subtracted to get the useable 22-MHz-wide channel. It is easy to see that adjacent channels (channels directly next to each other) would overlap significantly.

DSSS Channel Frequency Assignments

Channel ID	FCC Channel Frequencies GHz	ETSI Channel Frequencies GHz
1	2.412	N/A
2	2.417	N/A
3	2.422	2.422
4	2.427	2.427
5	2.432	2.432
6	2.437	2.437
7	2.442	2.442
8	2.447	2.447
9	2.452	2.452
10	2.457	2.457
11	2.462	2.462

To use DSSS systems with overlapping channels in the same physical space would cause interference between the systems. DSSS systems with overlapping channels should not be co-located because a drastic or complete reduction in throughput will almost always occur. Because the center frequencies are 5 MHz apart, and the channels are 22 MHz wide, channels should be co-located only if the channel numbers are at least five apart: channels 1 and 6 do not overlap, channels 2 and 7 do not overlap, and so forth. A maximum of three co-located direct sequence systems are possible because channels 1, 6, and 11 are the only theoretically nonoverlapping channels. The three nonoverlapping channels are illustrated on the DSSS Nonoverlapping Channels Diagram.

Note: The word "theoretically" is used here because, as we will discus in further reading on troubleshooting, channel 6 can in fact overlap (depending on the output power and distance between systems) with channels 1 and 11, causing degradation of the wireless LAN connection and speed.

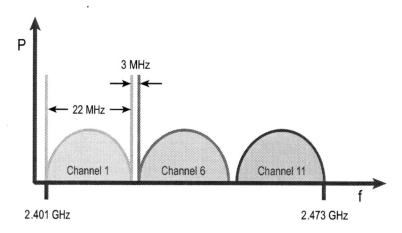

DSSS Nonoverlapping Channels

Effects of Narrowband Interference

Like frequency-hopping systems, direct sequence systems are also resistant to narrowband interference, due to their spread spectrum characteristics. A DSSS signal is more susceptible to narrowband interference than FHSS because the DSSS band is much smaller (22 MHz wide instead of the 79 MHz wide band used by FHSS) and the information is transmitted along the entire band simultaneously instead of one frequency at a time. With FHSS, frequency agility and a wide frequency band ensures that the interference is only influential for a small amount of time, corrupting only a small portion of the data.

FCC Rules Affecting DSSS

Just as with FHSS systems, the FCC has regulated that DSSS systems use a maximum of 1 watt of transmit power in point-to-multipoint configurations. The maximum output power is independent of the channel selection, which means that regardless of the channel used, the same power output maximum applies. This regulation applies to spread spectrum in both the 2.4 GHz ISM band and the upper 5 GHz UNII bands.

Activities

1. The ratio of the chipping code to data bits for a DSSS signal is called which of the following?

    a. Overhead

    b. Data integrity threshold

    c. Compression algorithm

    d. Processing gain

2. The IEEE specifies the use of DSSS in the 2.4 GHz ISM band with which of the following standards?

    a. 802.11

    b. 802.11a

    c. 802.11b

    d. 802.11f

3. Which IEEE draft or standard was the first to introduce technology capable of providing 54 Mbps bandwidth while remaining backward compatible with 11 Mbps DSSS systems?

    a. 802.11

    b. 802.11a

    c. 802.11f

    d. 802.11g

4. Which of the following 802.11b channels do NOT overlap?

    a. Channels 1 and 4

    b. Channels 2 and 7

    c. Channels 3 and 6

    d. Channels 7 and 11

5. You are designing a DSSS wireless LAN. How many co-located access points can you have in an area without overlapping channels?

    a. 2

    b. 3

    c. 12

    d. 15

6. Why would a DSSS system be more susceptible to narrowband interference than an FHSS system?

    a. DSSS systems transmit across many narrow frequency bands, any of which could be jammed easily.

    b. DSSS systems transmit across the entire ISM band rather than hopping across channels.

    c. DSSS systems transmit at much lower power levels; therefore, signals are hard to differentiate from noise.

    d. DSSS systems transmit over a single, smaller frequency band for the duration of the communications session.

Extended Activities

1. Draw a chart showing each of the 11 U.S. DSSS channel frequency ranges. Indicate the low and high frequencies for each channel, as well as the carrier frequencies.

2. What is the 802.11g draft's status in the approval (ratification) process? What are some barriers to its acceptance? Do you think it has a chance against existing standards such as 802.11a?

_____

_____

_____

_____

Lesson 4—Comparing FHSS and DSSS

Both FHSS and DSSS technologies have advantages and disadvantages, and it is incumbent on the wireless LAN administrator to give each its due consideration when deciding how to implement a wireless LAN. This lesson covers some of the factors to discuss when determining which technology is appropriate for your organization.

Objectives

At the end of this lesson you will be able to:

- Explain determining factors important to consider when deciding which spread spectrum technology is appropriate for your application

- Describe the advantages and disadvantages of each spread spectrum technology

 **Key Point**

The wireless LAN application and environment dictates the spread spectrum technology to use.

Determining Factors Driving Spread Spectrum Technology Choices

When an administrator must choose between FHSS and DSSS technologies, it is recommended that he or she consider the following factors:

- Narrowband interference present in the environment

- Co-location for failover, load balancing, or added capacity

- Cost of FHSS and DSSS systems

- Equipment compatibility and availability

- Data rate and throughput

- Security

- Standards support

The following sections discuss each of these factors.

Narrowband Interference Present in the Environment

The advantages of FHSS include a greater resistance to narrowband interference. DSSS systems may be affected by narrowband interference more than FHSS because they use 22 MHz wide contiguous bands instead of the 79 MHz used by FHSS. This fact may be a serious consideration if the proposed wireless LAN site is in an environment that has narrowband interference present.

Cost of FHSS and DSSS Systems

When implementing a wireless LAN on a tight budget, the advantages of DSSS may be more compelling than those of FHSS systems. The cost of implementing a direct sequence system is far less than that of a frequency-hopping system. DSSS equipment is widely available in today's marketplace, and its rapid adoption has helped drive down the costs. A few short years ago, only enterprise customers could afford the equipment. Today, very good quality 802.11b-compliant PC cards can be purchased for under $100. FHSS cards complying with either the 802.11 or OpenAir standards typically run between $150 and $350 in today's market, depending on the manufacturer and the standards to which the cards adhere.

Co-location for Failover, Load Balancing, and Added Capacity

An advantage of FHSS over DSSS is the ability for many more frequency-hopping systems to be co-located than direct sequence systems. Because frequency-hopping systems are "frequency agile" and make use of 79 discrete carrier frequencies, FHSS systems can be more densely co-located than DSSS systems, which have a maximum co-location of three access points. The Co-location Comparison Diagram illustrates this.

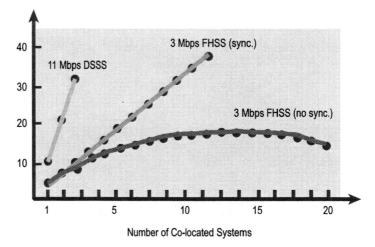

Co-location Comparison

However, when calculating the hardware costs of an FHSS system in order to obtain the same throughput as a DSSS system, the "advantage" of higher density co-location quickly disappears. Because DSSS can have three co-located access points, the maximum raw bandwidth for this configuration is:

3 access points x 11 Mbps = 33 Mbps

At roughly 50 percent of rated bandwidth, the DSSS system throughput would be approximately:

33 Mbps / 2 = 16.5 Mbps

To achieve roughly the same rated system bandwidth using an IEEE 802.1-compliant FHSS system would require:

16 access points x 2 Mbps = 32 Mbps

At roughly 50 percent of rated bandwidth, the FHSS system throughput would be approximately:

32 Mbps / 2 = 16 Mbps

In this configuration, an FHSS system would require purchasing 13 additional access points to get the same throughput as the DSSS system. Also, additional installation services for these units, cables, connectors, and antennas would all need to be purchased.

There are advantages to co-location for each type of system. If the objectives are low cost and high throughput, clearly DSSS technology wins out. If keeping users segmented using different access points in a dense co-location environment is the objective, FHSS might be a viable alternative.

Equipment Compatibility and Availability

The Wireless Ethernet Compatibility Alliance (WECA) tests 802.11b-compliant DSSS wireless LAN equipment to ensure that such equipment will operate in the presence of, and interoperate with, other 802.11b DSSS devices. The interoperability standard that WECA created and now uses is called "Wireless Fidelity," or "Wi-Fi™," and those devices that pass the tests for interoperability are called "Wi-Fi-compliant" devices. Wi-Fi-compliant devices are allowed to affix the Wi-Fi logo on the related marketing material and devices themselves, showing that they have been tested and interoperate with other Wi-Fi-compliant devices.

There are no such compatibility tests for FHSS equipment. Standards such as 802.11 and OpenAir exist, but no organization has stepped forward to do the same kind of compatibility testing for FHSS as WECA does for DSSS.

Due to the immense popularity of 802.11b-compliant radios, it is much easier to obtain these units. The demand seems to be growing only for the Wi-Fi-compliant radios, while the demand for FHSS radios has remained fairly steady, even decreasing to some degree over the past year.

Data Rate and Throughput

The latest frequency-hopping systems are slower than the latest DSSS systems, mainly because their maximum data rate is only 2 Mbps. Although some FHSS systems operate at 3 Mbps or higher, these systems are not 802.11 compliant and may not interoperate with other FHSS systems. FHSS and DSSS systems have a throughput (data actually sent) of only about half of the data rate. When testing the throughput of a new wireless LAN installation, achieving 5 to 6 Mbps on the 11 Mbps setting for DSSS or 1 Mbps on the 2 Mbps setting for FHSS is common.

Note: HomeRF 2.0 uses wide-band frequency-hopping technology to achieve 10-Mbps data rates, which in turn achieve approximately 5 Mbps of actual throughput. HomeRF 2.0 and 802.11, however, are significantly different. One difference is HomeRF's limited power output (125 mW) as compared to that of 802.11 systems (1 watt) in point-to-multipoint circuits.

When wireless frames are transmitted, there are pauses, called "interframe spacing," between data frames for control signals and other overhead tasks. With frequency-hopping systems, interframe spacing is longer than that used by direct sequence systems, causing additional network overhead that reduces throughput. Additionally, when the FHSS system is in the process of changing the transmit frequency, no data is sent. This translates to even more lost throughput, although it is only a minor amount. Some wireless LAN systems use proprietary Physical Layer protocols to increase throughput. These methods work, yielding throughputs as high as 80 percent of the data rate, but in so doing, sacrifice interoperability.

Security

A widely touted myth concerning frequency-hopping systems is that they are inherently more secure than direct sequence systems. The fact that only a minimal number of manufacturers produce FHSS radios disproves this myth. Of this small list of manufacturers, all adhere to standards such as 802.11 or OpenAir in order to sell their products effectively. Also, each of these manufacturers uses a standard set of hop sequences that generally comply with a predetermined list produced by the standards body, such as IEEE or WLIF. These two facts combined make breaking the code of hop sequences relatively simple.

Other reasons that make finding the hop sequence quite simple is that the radio broadcasts the channel number in the clear with each beacon. A beacon is a short frame sent by the access point to the wireless clients to organize and synchronize wireless LAN communications. Also, the MAC address of the transmitting access point can be seen with each beacon. Each MAC address contains a component that indicates the manufacturer of the radio. Some manufacturers allow administrators the flexibility of defining custom hopping patterns. However, even this custom capability provides no level of security, because fairly unsophisticated devices, such as spectrum analyzers and a standard laptop computer, can be used to track the hopping pattern of an FHSS radio in a matter of seconds.

Standards Support

As previously discussed, DSSS has gained wide acceptance because of its low cost and high speed, WECA's Wi-Fi interoperability standards, and many other factors. This market acceptance will only accelerate due to the industry moving toward newer, faster DSSS systems, such as the new 802.11g-compliant wireless LAN hardware. WECA's new Wi-Fi interoperability standard for 5 GHz DSSS systems operating in the UNII bands will help move the industry along even faster in the same direction it is already headed. The new standards for FHSS systems include HomeRF 2.0 and 802.15 (in support of WPAN, such as Bluetooth), but none for advancing FHSS systems in the enterprise. All of these standards and technologies will be discussed in further reading.

Activities

1. Why is HomeRF 2.0 NOT a good alternative to 802.11 networks in an enterprise environment? (Choose two.)

   a. It uses only frequency-hopping technologies.

   b. It is limited to a lower radio power output.

   c. It lacks large-scale management features.

   d. It achieves only 2 Mbps of throughput.

2. Which component of an FHSS system creates more overhead than that found in a DSSS system?

   a. The frame size

   b. The maximum data rate

   c. The noise floor

   d. The interframe spacing

3. Which are reasons why FHSS systems are no more secure than DSSS systems? (Choose three.)

   a. FHSS systems are produced by a limited number of manufacturers.

   b. FHSS system manufacturers use a standard set of hop sequences.

   c. FHSS systems transmit the channel number in beacon frames.

   d. FHSS systems use chipping code for data security.

4. With six nonoverlapping FHSS access points (APs) operating at 2 Mbps, approximately how much system throughput will this 802.11 wireless network provide?

   a. 3 Mbps

   b. 6 Mbps

   c. 12 Mbps

   d. 32 Mbps

5. Which of the following are standards defined for FHSS systems? (Choose two.)

    a. OpenAir

    b. HomeRF 2.0

    c. Wi-Fi

    d. WECA

Extended Activities

1. Research and compare the HomeRF 2.0, OpenAir, and 802.11 FHSS standards. How are they similar and how do they differ? Which do you think is the best choice for building an FHSS wireless LAN? Why?

    _____

    _____

    _____

    _____

2. Research the IEEE 802.15 Wireless PAN standard. How does this differ from the 802.11 Wireless LAN standard?

    _____

    _____

    _____

    _____

Summary

This unit defined and described spread spectrum technology and detailed how it is implemented in wireless LANs according to FCC guidelines. Spread spectrum is a communications technique characterized by wide bandwidth and low peak power. Spread spectrum communication uses various modulation techniques in wireless LANs and offers many advantages over its precursor, narrow band communication.

Within this unit, the two main spread spectrum technologies, FHSS and DSSS, were compared. FHSS is a spread spectrum technique that uses frequency agility to spread the data over 75 to 79 carrier frequencies in the 2.4-GHz ISM band. DSSS is a method of sending data in which the transmitting and receiving systems are both on a 22-MHz-wide set of frequencies. The wide channel enables devices to transmit more information at a higher data rate than current FHSS systems.

Both FHSS and DSSS technologies have advantages and disadvantages, and it is incumbent on a wireless LAN administrator to consider both when deciding how to implement a wireless LAN.

Unit 3 Quiz

1. Increasing the dwell time for an FHSS system will increase the throughput.

    a. This statement is always true

    b. This statement is always false

    c. It depends on the manufacturer of the equipment

2. Which one of the following dwell times will result in the greatest throughput over a 30-second period in an FHSS system and will still be within FCC regulations?

    a. 100 ms

    b. 200 ms

    c. 300 ms

    d. 400 ms

3. An 802.11b-compliant wireless LAN configuration using DSSS can have a maximum of how many nonoverlapping, co-located access points?

    a. 3

    b. 15

    c. 26

    d. 79

4. Consider the following two wireless LAN configurations:

    System 1—IEEE 802.11-compliant FHSS system, six co-located access points running at maximum data rate.

    System 2—IEEE 802.11b-compliant DSSS system, three co-located access points running at 50% of maximum data rate.

    Which of the following statements is true? (Choose two.)

    a. System 1 provides greater throughput.

    b. System 2 provides greater throughput.

    c. System 1 provides more bandwidth.

    d. System 2 provides more bandwidth.

5. How wide is each channel on an 802.11b-compliant DSSS system?

    a. 5Mhz

    b. 20MHz

    c. 22MHz

    d. 83MHz

6. Which of the following are advantages of 802.11b DSSS over 802.11 FHSS? (Choose two.)

    a. Cost

    b. Throughput

    c. Security

    d. Resistance to narrowband interference

7. If having compatible equipment from different manufactures is an important factor when purchasing wireless LAN equipment, which of the following spread spectrum technologies is the best choice?

    a. FHSS

    b. DSSS

    c. FSSS

    d. DHSS

8. The FCC has two sets of rules regarding FHSS that are sometimes known as "old" and "new" rules. The change in FCC rules was made on which of the following dates?

    a. June 30, 2000

    b. August 31, 1999

    c. August 31, 2000

    d. August 31, 2001

9. The latest published FCC rules regarding power output for FHSS states a maximum output of which one of the following?

    a. 100 mW

    b. 125 mW

    c. 200 mW

    d. 1 W

10. How many channels does the FCC specify can be used in the 2.4 GHz ISM band for DSSS in the United States?

    a. 3

    b. 6

    c. 9

    d. 11

11. You have been hired as a consultant to increase the capacity of an existing FHSS wireless LAN. After your research is completed, you recommend a replacement system based on DSSS. Which of the following arguments could you use to defend your position? (Choose two.)

    a. The DSSS devices will cost less and provide greater throughput.

    b. The DSSS devices will cost more, but provide greater throughput.

    c. Additional new FHSS devices may not be compatible with the older devices.

    d. DSSS is more secure than FHSS.

12. Which of the following statements concerning 802.11b wireless LAN devices is true?

    a. 802.11b FHSS devices are backward compatible with 802.11 FHSS devices.

    b. 802.11b DSSS devices are backward compatible with 802.11 DSSS devices.

    c. 802.11b devices cannot communicate with 802.11 devices.

    d. 802.11b DSSS devices are backward compatible with 802.11 FHSS devices.

13. If nonsynchronized radios are to be used, what is the maximum number of co-located FHSS access points in a wireless LAN considered to be?

    a. 3

    b. 16

    c. 20

    d. 26

14. In frequency-hopping wireless LAN systems, the term "hopping" refers to which one of the following?

    a. Switching between throughput speeds from 11 Mbps to 5.5 Mbps

    b. The same result as when the carrier frequency is changed

    c. The change that occurs as a result of the RF signal getting weaker

    d. Changing technologies from FHSS to DSSS

15. Which of the following makes a DSSS channel more susceptible to narrowband interference than an FHSS channel? (Choose three.)

    a. The DSSS channel is much smaller (22 MHz wide instead of the 75-79 MHz wide band used by FHSS).

    b. The information is transmitted simultaneously along the entire band instead of one frequency at a time.

    c. FHSS systems simply avoid the frequency on which the narrowband interference is located.

    d. FHSS systems only use one frequency at a time; thus, the narrowband interference must be on the same exact frequency at the same time.

16. Which one of the following statements defines noise floor?

    a. The general level of RF noise in the environment around the wireless LAN

    b. The noise that is generated as a result of foot traffic

    c. A fixed level of -100 dBm

    d. The level of noise at which a wireless LAN starts working

17. Which one of the following is NOT described by the IEEE and OpenAir standards regarding FHSS systems?

    a. What frequency bands may be used

    b. Hop sequences

    c. Allowable levels of interference

    d. Dwell times

    e. Data rates

18. An RF signal is considered spread spectrum when which one of the following statements are true?

    a. The system sending the signal is using infrared technology.

    b. The power required to send the information is significantly greater than is necessary.

    c. The bandwidth used is much wider than what is required to send the information.

    d. The bandwidth used is much less than what is used to send the information.

19. Some 2.4 GHz FHSS systems operate at 3 Mbps or more. Which of the following is true regarding these systems?

    a. They are always IEEE 802.11 compliant.

    b. They may not interoperate with other FHSS systems.

    c. They are always OpenAir compliant.

    d. They are backwards compatible with 900 MHz systems.

20. Until recently, how many different types of implementations of spread spectrum technology has the FCC specified for the 2.4 GHz ISM band?

    a. 1

    b. 2

    c. 3

    d. 4

Unit 4
Wireless LAN Infrastructure Devices

This unit covers the different categories of wireless network infrastructure equipment and some of the variations within each category. From reading this unit alone, you will become more versed in the implementation of wireless LANs, simply by familiarizing yourself with the variety of wireless LAN equipment at your disposal when you begin to create or add to a wireless network. These hardware items are the physical building blocks for any wireless LAN.

For each type of hardware covered in this lesson, we cover the following topics:

- Definition and role of the hardware on the network

- Common options that might be included with the hardware

- How to install and configure the hardware

This section of the course introduces all the types of hardware that are available for the variety of wireless LAN configurations you will encounter as a wireless LAN administrator. Antennas and wireless LAN accessories are covered in further reading.

Lessons

1. Access Points
2. Wireless Bridges
3. Wireless Workgroup Bridges
4. Wireless LAN Client Devices
5. Wireless Residential Gateways
6. Enterprise Wireless Gateways

Terms

10BaseTX—10BaseTX is the IEEE standard for 10 Mbps baseband Ethernet over twisted-pair wire.

100BaseFX—100BaseFX is the IEEE standard for 100 Mbps baseband Ethernet over optical fiber.

100BaseTX—100BaseTX is the IEEE standard for a 100 Mbps baseband Ethernet over twisted-pair wire.

802.1x—IEEE 802.1x is a recently approved IEEE standard for port-based access control. It is used to control access to a network access device (switch, access point, etc.).

802.5—See Token Ring.

Ad Hoc network—An ad hoc network is a wireless network composed of only stations and no access point.

association table—An association table is a list of wireless client devices associated with the access point. The association table shows the client connection status, including the connection state.

bridge mode—A bridge is a network component that provides internetworking functionality at the data link layer. A wireless access point operating in bridge mode serves to wirelessly bridge multiple wired segments.

cable modem—A cable modem is a device located in a cable television subscriber's home that provides broadband Internet access over a cable television provider's network.

cell—In wireless networking terminology, a cell is the coverage area created by the radio signal transmitted by a single access point.

Command Line Interface (CLI)—A CLI is a method of managing network devices from a terminal–like interface, where the administrator inputs commands in a textual format.

compact flash (CF)—CF is a small form factor (1.7" x 1.4" x .13" thick) expansion card, designed initially in 1994 by the SanDisk Corporation as nonvolatile storage. CF devices now provide input/output functionality (modems, networking) for palmtop PCs and personal digital devices (PDAs).

Dynamic Host Configuration Protocol (DHCP)—DHCP issues IP addresses automatically within a specified range to devices such as PCs when they are first powered on. The device retains the use of the IP address for a specific license period that the system administrator can define. DHCP is available as part of many operating systems including Microsoft Windows, NT Server, and UNIX.

Ethernet switch—An Ethernet switch is a connectivity device that is more intelligent than a hub, having the ability to connect the sending station directly to the receiving station in a full duplex configuration. Additionally, it has filtering and learning capabilities.

Extensible Authentication Protocol (EAP)—EAP is a general protocol for Point-to-Point Protocol (PPP) authentication that supports multiple authentication mechanisms. EAP does not select a specific authentication mechanism at link control phase, but rather postpones this step until the authentication phase. This allows the authenticator to request more information before determining the specific authentication mechanism. This also permits the use of a "back-end" server, which actually implements the various mechanisms while the PPP authenticator merely passes through the authentication exchange. EAP serves as a flexible replacement for CHAP and/or PAP.

failover routing—Failover routing is a feature built into network devices that allows them to fail over to an alternative link if the primary connection fails.

firewall—A firewall is a device that interfaces the network to the outside world and shields the network from unauthorized users. The firewall does this by blocking certain types of traffic. For example, some firewalls permit only electronic mail traffic to enter the network from elsewhere. This helps protect the network against attacks made on other network resources, such as sensitive files, databases, and applications.

Hypertext Transfer Protocol (HTTP)—HTTP is the Application Layer protocol used to request and transmit HTML documents. HTTP is the underlying protocol of the World Wide Web.

Hypertext Transfer Protocol Secure (HTTPS)—HTTPS secures Internet connections using Secure Socket Layer (SSL) technology to encrypt the client/server transactions. Also see Secure Sockets Layer.

Infrastructure mode—Infrastructure mode is a wireless network operating mode that requires an access point through which all wireless traffic is passed. Client-to-client transmissions are not allowed in infrastructure mode.

Industry Standard Architecture (ISA)—ISA is an older PC bus technology used in IBM XT and AT computers.

Lightweight Directory Access Protocol (LDAP)—LDAP is a set of protocols for accessing information directories conforming to the X.500 standard.

media access control layer (MAC Layer)—The MAC Layer, one of the two sublayers that make up the Data Link Layer of the Open Systems Interconnection (OSI) model, provides medium-access services for IEEE 802 LANs.

Mobile Internet Protocol (IP)—Mobile IP is a protocol developed by the Internet Engineering Task Force (IETF) to enable users to roam to parts of the network associated with a different IP address than what is loaded in the user's appliance. It is an extension to IP that provides mobile clients a single IP address, no matter where they are connected to the home network. Mobile nodes connect to the local network by means of home agents, which are routers that track the mobile nodes' location; or if away, by means of foreign agents, which are routers on foreign networks that can relay packets from the home agent to the mobile node. Wherever located, the mobile keeps its home IP address and subnet, using a second IP address supplied by the foreign agent when on the foreign network.

National Electrical Manufacturers Association (NEMA)—NEMA is an organization established in 1926 to "support the standardization of electrical equipment, enabling consumers to select a range of safe, effective, and compatible electrical products." Learn more about NEMA at **http://www.nema.org**.

Network Address Translation (NAT)—NAT is an Internet standard that enables a local-area network (LAN) to use one set of IP addresses for internal traffic and a second set of addresses for external traffic. The four types of IP addresses are: static, dynamic, overloading, and overlapping.

open system authentication—Open system authentication is the IEEE 802.11 default authentication method, which is a very simple, two-step process. First the station wanting to authenticate with another station sends an authentication management frame containing the sending station's identification. The receiving station then sends back a frame alerting whether it recognizes the identity of the authenticating station.

packet queuing—A generic term used to describe the segregation of outbound packets at a network device's port, arranging them and putting them in line for transmission based on some Quality of Service (QoS) characteristic.

Peripheral Component Interconnect (PCI)—PCI is a local bus that provides a high-speed connection between peripherals and a CPU. It includes buffers that allow relatively slow peripherals to operate asynchronously and can be used with other buses such as ISA or EISA.

Personal Computer Memory Card International Association (PCMCIA)—The PCMCIA slot in a laptop was designed for PC memory expansion. Network interface cards (NICs) and modems can attach to a laptop through the PCMCIA slot.

Plug and play (PnP)—PnP is a standard that gives computers the ability to automatically recognize a newly installed device, without a complex process of user configuration.

Point-to-Point Protocol over Ethernet (PPPoE)—RFC 2516 describes PPPoE as an extension to the PPP protocol for use over shared network connections. A service provider can assign login credentials to each user of the shared connection, require them to log in to the carrier network to use the connection, and thus bill each user individually.

Port Address Translation (PAT)—PAT is a NAT technique where the local network host source address is converted by the NAT device to a single public address shared by many local hosts. This single source IP address and a unique source port address, again assigned by the NAT device, identify each outbound connection. This eliminates the need for the NAT device to maintain a one-to-one mapping of local host addresses to public host addresses.

portal—A portal is a logical point where MAC Service Data Units (MSDUs) from a nonIEEE 802.11 LAN enter the distribution system of an extended service set wireless network.

Power over Ethernet (PoE)—PoE is the method of injecting DC current over the unused pairs in Cat5 cabling to power access points in remote locations; it reduces difficulty in access point installation in terms of power installation.

print serving—Print serving occurs when several network devices need to share a single printer, and a print server is used. A print server is a LAN-based computer or device that provides users on a network access to the shared printer.

profile—In general, a profile is a set of characteristics that identify a certain user, capability, or component. On a wireless device, a profile is used to identify a connection's characteristics, such as the encryption level, SSID, and so forth. By using profiles, one can easily change a client's configuration to match a particular network configuration.

Quality of Service (QoS)—QoS defines the type of service a communications link can provide. QoS can specify factors such as delay, throughput, error rate, and loss.

Rate limiting—Rate limiting is a technique of controlling how much of the available link bandwidth each connection is supplied.

reassociation service—Reassociation service enables an IEEE 802.11 station to change its association with different access points as the station moves throughout the facility without reauthentication.

Remote Authentication Dial-In User Service (RADIUS)—RADIUS is an authentication service specified by the IETF that utilizes a computer-based database (RADIUS server) to compare usernames and passwords to allow access to a network.

repeater mode—When operating in repeater mode, an access point relays wireless signals between remote access points or access points and clients. This serves to extend the reach of a wireless network, but takes a toll on throughput.

roaming—The process of moving from one access point to another without having to reauthenticate to the wireless network.

Role-based access control (RBAC)—RBAC allows a network administrator to assign a certain level of wireless network access to a person based on their role in the organization. This allows the administrator to control network resource usage while allowing easy user moves, adds, and changes.

root mode—When operating in root mode, an access point is connected to the host wired network segment, and is able to communicate with other root mode APs over the wired segment. Clients and APs operating in repeater mode connect over wireless links to a root mode access point.

Secure Sockets Layer (SSL)—SSL is an application of both public-key and single-key encryption that secures an Internet connection between browser and server. Web-page URLs that use SSL begin with "https://."

Service Set Identifier (SSID)—The SSID is a unique, case-sensitive, alphanumeric network name used to identify a wireless LAN. The SSID can be used to segment wireless networks, but is only a rudimentary security measure. Access points broadcast SSIDs in their beacon frames; therefore, SSIDs can be easily intercepted.

shared key authentication—Shared key authentication is a type of authentication that assumes each station has received a secret shared key through a secure channel that is independent from an 802.11 network. Stations authenticate through shared knowledge of the secret key. Use of shared key authentication requires implementation of the 802.11 Wireless Equivalent Privacy (WEP) algorithm.

Simple Network Management Protocol (SNMP)—SNMP is a network management protocol that defines the transfer of information between Management Information Bases (MIBs). Most high-end network monitoring stations require the implementation of SNMP on each of the components the organization wishes to monitor.

Spanning Tree Protocol (STP)—STP is a link management protocol that is part of the IEEE 802.1 standard (802.1d) for media access control bridges. Using the spanning tree algorithm, STP provides path redundancy while preventing undesirable loops in a network that are created by multiple active paths between stations. Loops occur when there are alternate routes between hosts. To establish path redundancy, STP creates a tree that spans all of the switches in an extended network, forcing redundant paths into a standby, or blocked, state. STP allows only one active path at a time between any two network devices (this prevents the loops) but establishes the redundant links as a backup if the initial link should fail.

Token Ring—Token Ring is a network architecture that uses a ring topology and a token passing strategy to control network access. The IEEE 802.5 standard defines the token ring architecture and how it operates at the OSI model Physical and Data Link Layers.

Universal Serial Bus (USB)—USB is an external bus that can transfer up to 12 Mbps. Up to 127 peripheral devices can be connected to a single USB port. A USB adapter is a PC expansion device that conforms to the USB standard. USB device examples include network interface cards (NICs), modems, scanners, and CD-ROM drives.

Unlicensed National Information Infrastructure (UNII)—The UNII bands are the three FCC mandated nonlicensed radio frequency bands located in the 5- to 6- GHz range. 802.11a networks operate in one of the three UNII bands.

User tracking—User tracking enables the network administrator to locate and track hosts on the network.

variable output—Variable output is a feature built into a wireless access point that allows the administrator to control the radio output by means of software, rather than inserting attenuators in the RF signal path.

Virtual Private Network (VPN)—A VPN is a connection over a shared network that behaves like a dedicated link. VPNs are created using a technique called "tunneling," which transmits data packets across a public network, such as the Internet or other commercially available network, in a private "tunnel" that simulates a point-to-point connection. The tunnels of a VPN can be encrypted for additional security.

virtual server—A wireless gateway can act as a virtual network server, accepting connection requests for a specific service, such as HTTP or FTP, and forwarding the request to a local host. To the requesting node, the connection appears to terminate at the gateway, when in fact the gateway forwards the request to the local server. The local server is not accessible directly from the outside network.

Wired Equivalent Privacy (WEP)—WEP is an optional IEEE 802.11 function that offers frame transmission privacy similar to a wired network. WEP generates secret shared encryption keys that both source and destination stations can use to alter frame bits to avoid disclosure to eavesdroppers.

Lesson 1—Access Points

Second only to the basic wireless PC card, the access point is probably the most common wireless LAN device with which you will work as a wireless LAN administrator. As its name suggests, the access point provides clients with a point of access into a network. This lesson introduces wireless access points, their features, and management tools.

Objectives

At the end of this lesson you will be able to:

- Describe basic features of wireless access points
- Explain and apply wireless access point communication modes
- Describe common wireless access point options
- Describe common access point configuration and management tools

 **Key Point**

Wireless access points provide wireless clients a central point of access to the wired network.

What Is a Wireless Access Point?

An access point is a half-duplex device with intelligence equivalent to that of a sophisticated Ethernet switch. The Sample Access Point Diagram shows an example of an access point, and the Access Point Installed on a Network Diagram illustrates where an access point is used on a wireless LAN.

Sample Access Point

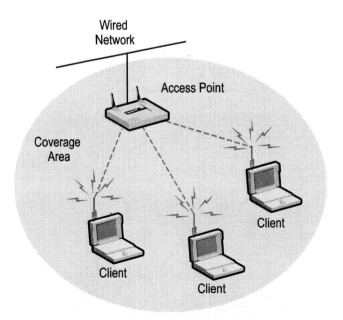

Access Point Installed on a Network

Access Point Modes

Access points communicate with their wireless clients, with the wired network, and with other access points. An access point can be configured in three modes:

- Root Mode
- Repeater Mode
- Bridge Mode

Each of these modes is described in the following sections.

Root Mode

Root Mode is used when the access point is connected to a wired backbone through its wired (usually Ethernet) interface. Most access points that support modes other than root mode are configured in root mode by default according to the 802.11 standard. When an access point is connected to the wired segment through its Ethernet port, it will most often be configured for root mode. Access points in root mode that are connected to the same wired distribution system can talk to each other over the wired segment. Access points talk to each other to coordinate roaming functionality, such as reassociation. Wireless clients can communicate with other wireless clients who are located in different cells through their respective access points across the wired segment, as shown on the Access Point in Root Mode Diagram.

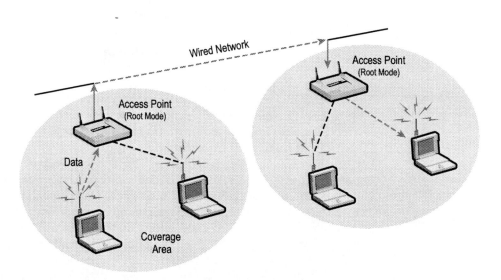

Access Point in Root Mode

Bridge Mode

In bridge mode, access points act exactly like wireless bridges, which are wireless devices used to interconnect wired segments. In fact, they become wireless bridges while configured in this manner. We will discuss wireless bridges in more detail later. Only a small number of access points on the market provide bridge functionality, which typically adds significant cost to the equipment. We will explain shortly how wireless bridges function, but you can see from the Access Point in Bridge Mode Diagram that clients do not associate to bridges, but rather bridges are used to link two or more wired segments together wirelessly.

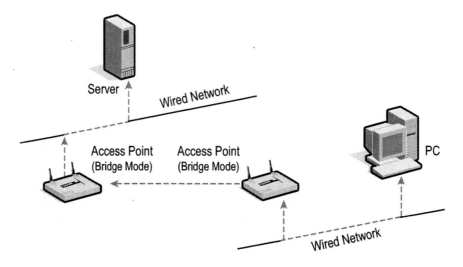

Access Point in Bridge Mode

Repeater Mode

In repeater mode, access points have the ability to provide a wireless upstream link into the wired network, rather than the normal wired link. As you can see in the Access Point in Repeater Mode Diagram, one access point serves as the root access point, and the other serves as a wireless repeater. The access point in repeater mode connects to clients as an access point and connects to the upstream root access point as a client itself. Using an access point in repeater mode is not suggested unless absolutely necessary because cells around each access point in this scenario must overlap by a minimum of 50 percent. This configuration drastically reduces the range at which clients can connect to the repeater access point. Additionally, the repeater access point communicates with the clients, as well as the upstream access point over the same half-duplex wireless link, reducing throughput on the wireless segment. Users attached to the repeater access point will likely experience low throughput and high latencies in this scenario. It is typical for the wired Ethernet port to be disabled while in repeater mode.

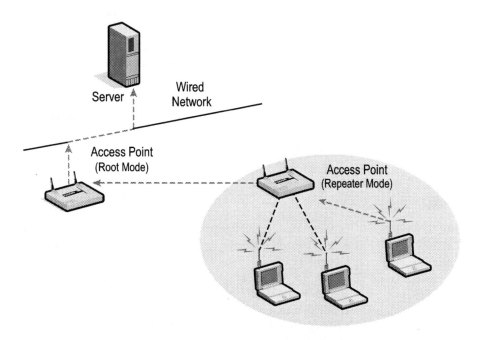

Access Point in Repeater Mode

Common Access Point Options

An access point is considered a portal because it allows client connectivity from an 802.11 network to an 802.3 or an 802.5 network. Access points are available with many different hardware and software options. The most common of these options are:

- Fixed or Detachable Antennas
- Advanced Filtering Capabilities
- Removable (Modular) Radio Cards
- Variable Output Power
- Varied Types of Wired Connectivity

Fixed or Detachable Antennas

Depending on your organization's or client's needs, you will need to choose between having an access point with fixed (meaning nonremovable) antennas or detachable antennas. An access point with detachable antennas gives you the ability to attach a different antenna to the access point using whatever length of cable you require. For example, if you needed to mount the access point indoors, and give outdoor users access to the network, you could attach a cable and an outdoor antenna directly to the access point and mount only the antenna outside.

Access points may be shipped with or without diversity antennas. Wireless LAN antenna diversity is the use of multiple antennas with multiple inputs on a single receiver in order to sample signals arriving through each antenna. The point of sampling two antennas is to pick the input signal of whichever antenna has the best reception. The two antennas might have different signal reception because of a phenomenon called multipath, which will be discussed in detail in a later chapter.

Advanced Filtering Capabilities

MAC or protocol filtering functionality may be included on an access point. Filtering is typically used to screen out intruders on a wireless LAN or to authorize particular users. As a basic security provision, an access point can be configured to filter out devices that are not listed in the access point's MAC filter list, which the administrator controls. In reverse, an access point can be configured to specifically allow particular MAC addresses onto the network and disallow all others.

Protocol filtering allows an administrator to decide and control which protocols are used across a wireless link. For example, if the administrator only wishes to provide http access across the wireless link to enable users to browse the Web and check their Web-based email, setting up an http protocol filter would prevent all other types of protocol access to that segment of the network.

Removable (Modular) Radio Cards

Some manufacturers allow you to add and remove radios to and from built-in Personal Computer Memory Card International Association (PCMCIA) slots on access points without removing a cover. Some access points may have two PCMCIA slots for special functionality. Having two radio slots in an access point allows one radio card to act as an access point while the other radio card acts as a bridge (in most cases a wireless backbone). Another somewhat dissimilar use is to set up each radio card as an independent access point. By configuring each card to act as an independent access point, an administrator can accommodate twice as many users in the same physical space without purchasing a second access point, further reducing costs. When the access point is configured in this manner, each radio card should be configured on a nonoverlapping channel, ideally channels 1 and 11, respectively. Additionally, when configured as a dual access point, it is important to use external antennas to separate the RF emissions as far apart as is feasible in the network design. This will result in the best throughput and will avoid significant adjacent channel interference.

Variable Output Power

Variable output power allows an administrator to control the power (in milliwatts) that an access point uses to send its data. Controlling the power output may become necessary in some situations where distant nodes cannot locate the access point. It may also simply be a luxury that allows an administrator to control the area of coverage for the access point. As the power output is increased on the access point, clients will be able to move farther away from the access point without losing connectivity. Keep in mind that client/access point connectivity is a two-way street. Each of the two must transmit with enough power to reach the other. A variable output power feature can also increase security by allowing proper sizing of RF cells, preventing intruders from connecting to the network from outside the building's walls.

The alternative to using the variable output power feature is to use fixed output access points. With a fixed output from the access point, creative measures such as amplifiers, attenuators, long cables, or high-gain antennas may have to be implemented. To operate within FCC guidelines, controlling output power both from the access point and the antenna is also required.

Varied Types of Wired Connectivity

Connectivity options for an access point can include a link for 10baseTX, 10/100baseTX, 100baseTX, 100baseFX, or Token Ring. Because an access point is typically the device through which clients communicate with the wired network backbone, an administrator must understand how to properly connect the access point into the wired network. Proper network design and connectivity will help prevent the access point from being a bottleneck and result in reduced problems caused by malfunctioning equipment.

If you use an off-the-shelf access point in an enterprise wireless LAN, and the access point is located 150 meters from the nearest wiring closet, running a category 5 (Cat5) Ethernet cable to the access point probably would not work. This scenario would be a problem because Ethernet over Cat5 cable is only specified to 100 meters. In this case, purchasing an access point with a 100baseFX connector, and running fiber from the wiring closet to the access point mounting location ahead of time would allow this configuration to function properly and more easily.

Access Point Configuration and Management

The method or methods used to configure and manage access points vary with each manufacturer. Most brands offer at least console, telnet, universal serial bus (USB), or a built-in Web server for browser access. Some access points have custom configuration and management software. The manufacturer assigns an IP address to the access point during the initial configuration. If an administrator needs to reset the device to factory defaults, a hardware reset button is usually provided on the outside of the unit for this purpose.

Features found in access points vary. However, one thing is constant: the more features an access point has, the more the access point costs. For example, some small office/home office (SOHO) access points have Wired Equivalent Privacy (WEP), media access control (MAC) filters, and even a built-in Web server. If features such as viewing the association table, 802.1x/EAP support, virtual private network (VPN) support, routing functionality, Inter-access point protocol, and RADIUS support are required, expect to pay several times as much for an enterprise-level access point.

Even features that are standard on Wi-Fi compliant access points sometimes vary in their implementation. For example, two different brands of a SOHO access point may offer MAC filters, but only one of them may offer MAC filtering that enables you to explicitly permit and deny stations, rather than select only one or the other. Some access points support full-duplex 10/100 wired connectivity, whereas others offer only 10baseT half duplex connectivity on the wired side.

Understanding what features to expect on small office/home office (SOHO)s, mid-range, and enterprise-level access points is an important part of being a wireless network administrator. The following is a list of features to look for in SOHO and enterprise categories. This listing is by no means comprehensive because manufacturers frequently release new features at each level. This list provides an idea of where to start looking for an appropriate access point. These lists build upon each other beginning with the SOHO level access point, meaning that each consecutive level includes the features of the layer below it.

- SOHO
  - MAC filters
  - WEP (64- or 128-bit)
  - USB or console configuration interface
  - Simple built-in Web server configuration interface
  - Simple custom configuration application

- Enterprise
  - Advanced custom configuration application
  - Advanced built-in web server configuration interface
  - Telnet access
  - SNMP management
  - 802.1x/EAP
  - RADIUS client
  - VPN client and server
  - Routing (static/dynamic)
  - Repeater functions
  - Bridging functions

Using manufacturers' manuals and quick start guides will provide more specific information for each brand. Some of these functions, such as those related to RADIUS security and VPN support, will be discussed in later sections. Other functions are prerequisites to this course, such as telnet, USB, and Web-servers. Other topics, such as static and dynamic routing, are beyond the scope of this course.

As a wireless LAN administrator, you should know your environment, look for products that fit your deployment and security needs, and then compare features among three or four vendors that make products for that particular market segment. This evaluation process will undoubtedly take a substantial amount of time, but time spent learning about the different products on the market is worthwhile. The best possible resource for learning about each of the competing brands in a particular market is each manufacturer's Web site. When choosing an access point, be sure to take into account manufacturer support, in addition to features and price.

Mounting

Some things to keep in mind when mounting access points are:

- Use heavy duty zip ties to mount access points to columns or beams.

- Do not cover access point lights when mounting access points with zip ties.

- Mount access points upside down so that indicator lights can be seen from the floor.

- Label access points.

- When column mounting, it is possible to use a 2 x 4 beam as a base for the access point. Mount the 2 x 4 to the column, and then mount the access point to the 2 x 4.

- When beam mounting, you may use zip ties directly or perhaps a 2 x 4 mounted to the beam with beam clamps with the access point mounted to it. Remember to mount the antenna the same way as is specified in the site survey.

- Some access points come with slide mount holes, and others may have a separate mounting kit or frame. Some do not, by design, allow for mounting.

The Mounting Access Points Diagram shows some examples of mounting access points.

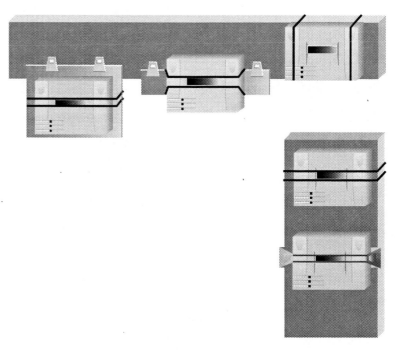

Mounting Access Points

Activities

1. Which of the following management options might you expect to find in a SOHO wireless access point? (Choose three.)

   a. Web-based

   b. Console

   c. USB

   d. SNMP

2. Which statement best describes wireless antenna diversity?

   a. The antenna supports any vendor's wireless clients

   b. The antenna switches between receivers depending on received signal strength

   c. The radio can receive multiple radio signals simultaneously

   d. The radio uses multiple antennas and chooses the one with the best reception

3. Which of the following statements is true concerning a wireless access point operating in repeater mode?

   a. Wireless throughput is doubled by the use of two APs, one on each of the radio links.

   b. The repeater access point acts as a client, connecting to the root access point on behalf of the remote clients.

   c. The root access point connects to the remote clients and passes data traffic upstream to the repeater access point.

   d. The repeater access point will experience low latency and high throughput by aggregating the multiple radio signals.

4. In which operating mode do APs come configured by default?

   a. Root

   b. Repeater

   c. Bridging

   d. Client

5. You are building a wireless network segment for your customer. You need to install an access point to provide wireless
   connectivity for users who move from office to office. The
   wireless users will always be within the access point's RF cell.
   In which mode should the access point be installed?

   a. Bridge

   b. Peer

   c. Root

   d. Repeater

Extended Activities

1. You are designing a wireless network for your employer or
   school. The network will span several floors of a building.
   Only the first floor is wired for Ethernet; the other three floors
   are not. Draw a diagram showing where you would place the
   APs to provide network connectivity for each floor, and label
   the APs with their operating modes. You will not install any
   cable in the top three floors. Do not concern yourself with cell
   coverage at this time; assume instead that a single access
   point will be adequate to cover each floor.

2. You are designing a wireless network for your employer or
   school. The network will span several floors of a building. All
   four floors are wired for Ethernet. Draw a diagram showing
   where you would place the APs on each floor, and label the
   APs with their operating modes. Do not concern yourself with
   cell coverage at this time; assume instead that a single access
   point will be adequate to cover each floor.

Lesson 2—Wireless Bridges

A wireless bridge provides connectivity between two wired LAN segments, and is used in point-to-point or point-to-multipoint configurations. For example, you would use a wireless bridge to connect networks located in office buildings separated by obstacles such as a street, railroad, or river. The lesson discusses wireless bridges, their features and options, and their applications.

Objectives

At the end of this lesson you will be able to:

- Describe basic wireless bridge features
- Explain wireless bridge communication modes
- Describe wireless bridge options
- Describe common wireless bridge configuration and management tools

 **Key Point**

Wireless bridges wirelessly connect wired network segments over short or long distances.

What Is a Wireless Bridge?

A wireless bridge is a half-duplex device capable of layer 2 wireless connectivity only. The Sample Wireless Bridge Diagram shows an example of a wireless bridge, while the Point-to-Point Wireless Bridge Link Diagram illustrates where a wireless bridge is used on a wireless LAN.

Sample Wireless Bridge

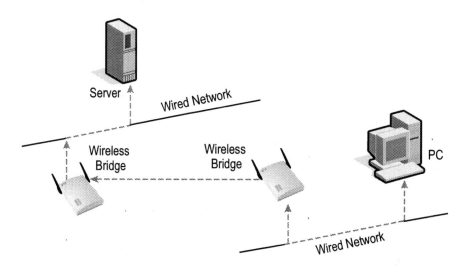

Point-to-Point Wireless Bridge Link

Wireless Bridge Modes

Wireless bridges communicate with other wireless bridges in one of four modes:

- Root Mode
- Nonroot Mode
- Access Point Mode
- Repeater Mode

The following sections discuss each of these modes.

Root Mode

One bridge in each group of bridges must be set as the root bridge. A root bridge can only communicate with nonroot bridges and other client devices (in special circumstances) and cannot associate with another root bridge. The Root Bridge Communicating with Nonroot Bridges Diagram illustrates a root bridge communicating with nonroot bridges.

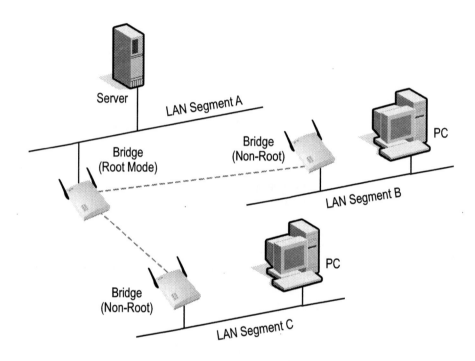

Root Bridge Communicating with Nonroot Bridges

Nonroot Mode

Wireless bridges in nonroot mode attach, wirelessly, to wireless bridges that are in root mode. Some manufacturers' wireless bridges support client connectivity to nonroot mode bridges while operating in bridging mode. This is a special functionality in which the bridge acts simultaneously as an access point and a bridge. Client devices associate to access points (or bridges in access point mode), and bridges talk to bridges. When using Spanning Tree Protocol (STP), all nonroot bridges must have connectivity to the root bridge.

Access Point Mode

Some manufacturers give administrators the ability to allow clients to connect to their bridges by giving bridges access point functionality. In many cases, the bridge has an access point mode that converts the bridge into an access point entirely.

Repeater Mode

Wireless bridges can also be configured as repeaters, as shown on the Wireless Bridge in Repeater Mode Diagram. In repeater configuration, a bridge is positioned between two other bridges for the purpose of extending the length of the wireless bridged segment. While using a wireless bridge, this configuration has the advantage of extending the link. It has the disadvantage of decreased throughput because the repeater bridge must repeat all frames using the same half-duplex radio. Repeater bridges are nonroot bridges, and many times the wired port is disabled while the bridge is in repeater mode.

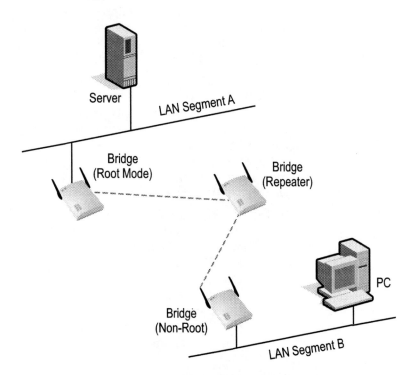

Wireless Bridge in Repeater Mode

Common Bridge Options

The hardware and software options of a wireless bridge are similar to those of an access point and perform many of the same functions:

- Fixed or Detachable Antennas
- Advanced Filtering Capabilities
- Removable (Modular) Radio Cards
- Variable Output Power
- Varied Types of Wired Connectivity

Fixed or Detachable Antennas

Wireless bridge antennas may be fixed or detachable and may come with or without diversity. It is often unnecessary for administrators to consider diversity when configuring a wireless bridge because both bridges (one at each end of the link) are static, and the environment around wireless bridges very rarely changes. For these reasons, multipath is usually only taken into consideration during bridge installation and is not as much of a concern as it is with access points and mobile users.

Detachable antennas are a useful feature with wireless bridges because they provide the ability to mount the bridge indoors and run a cable outdoors to connect to the antenna. In many cases, semidirectional or directional antennas are used with wireless bridges. The alternative to connecting a detachable antenna to a wireless bridge and mounting the bridge indoors is mounting the wireless bridge outdoors in a NEMA-compliant weatherproof enclosure.

Note: In 1926, the Electric Power Club and the Associated Manufacturers of Electrical Supplies merged their operations to form the National Electrical Manufacturers Association (NEMA). NEMA has always focused on standardization of electrical equipment, advocacy on behalf of the industry, and economic analysis. Among other things, NEMA specifies standards for enclosures (used in every industry) that protect the contents of the enclosure from the negative effects of adverse weather conditions.

Advanced Filtering Capabilities

Media access control (MAC) or protocol filters may be built into a wireless bridge. As a basic security provision, an administrator may configure a wireless bridge to allow or disallow client network access based on MAC addresses.

Most wireless bridges offer protocol filtering. Protocol filtering typically uses layer 4 ports to filter layer 7 applications. For example, by filtering TCP port 80, we could specifically allow or deny HTTP traffic. Protocol filters are useful for limiting the use of wireless LANs. For example, an administrator may prevent a group of users from using bandwidth-intensive applications based on the port or protocol used by the application.

Removable (Modular) Radio Cards

The ability to form a wireless backbone using one of the two radio card slots found in some bridges reduces the number of devices from four to two when providing client connectivity and bridging functionality. These functions would typically require an access point and a bridge on both ends of the link. Some wireless bridges perform these same functions using a single radio. While still performing the same tasks, this configuration allows for much less throughput than when separate sets of radios are used for the access point and bridging functions.

Variable Output Power

The variable output power feature allows an administrator to control the power (in milliwatts) that a bridge uses to send its RF signal. This functionality is especially useful when performing an outdoor site survey because it allows the site surveyor the flexibility to control the output power without adding and subtracting amplifiers, attenuators, and lengths of cable from the circuit during testing. Used in conjunction with amplifiers, variable output in the bridge on long-distance links can reduce the amount of time it takes to fine-tune the output power, such that the power is high enough to create a viable link and low enough to stay within FCC regulations.

Varied Types of Wired Connectivity

Connectivity options for a wireless bridge can include the following: 10baseTX, 10/100baseTX, 100baseTX, or 100baseFX. 100BaseFX connectivity ensures that the bridge can be located well beyond the 100-meter physical segment length limit that the IEEE specifies for UTP Ethernet network segments. Always attempt to establish a full-duplex connection to the wired segment in order to maximize the throughput of the wireless bridge. When preparing to purchase a wireless bridge, it is important to take note of certain issues, such as the distance from the nearest wiring closet, for the purpose of specifying wired connectivity options for wireless bridges.

Configuration and Management

Wireless bridges have much the same configuration accessibility as do access points: console, telnet, HTTP (Web-based), SNMP, or custom configuration and management software. Many bridges support Power over Ethernet (PoE) as well. Once wireless bridges are implemented, throughput checks should be done regularly to ensure that the link has not degraded because a piece of the equipment was moved or the antenna shifted.

Wireless bridges usually come with a factory default IP address and can be accessed by means of the methods mentioned above for initial configuration. A hardware reset button is almost always located on the outside of a unit for resetting the unit back to factory defaults.

Activities

1. Which statement best describes protocol filtering implemented in a wireless bridge?

   a. Allowing or denying wireless traffic by MAC address

   b. Allowing or denying wireless access by username and password

   c. Allowing or denying wireless traffic by wired network segment protocol

   d. Allowing or denying wireless traffic by layer 4 ports and layer 7 applications

2. You are performing a site survey for a point-to-multipoint wireless link. You notice that the central bridge's RF cell range extends well beyond the adjacent buildings. You are concerned that this makes the radio signal easy to intercept from outside the corporate campus. What wireless bridge feature will allow you to reduce the cell size without adding cables, antennas, and attenuators to the transmitter output?

   a. Variable antenna power

   b. Variable output power

   c. Advanced filtering capabilities

   d. Removable radio cards

3. You are researching a wireless bridge. Your bridge will be located about 130 meters from the nearest wired network segment. Which type of wired connectivity should the bridge provide?

   a. 10BaseT

   b. 10BaseTX

   c. 100BaseFX

   d. 10/100BaseTX

4. In most cases, which antenna types are used with wireless bridges? (Choose two.)

   a. omnidirectional

   b. bidirectional

   c. semidirectional

   d. directional

5. Why is multipath not as great a concern with wireless bridges as it is with APs?

   a. Bridged nodes do not move as much as client nodes.

   b. Bridges support more diverse antennas than do APs or clients.

   c. Bridge radio receivers are more sensitive than are access point or client radios.

   d. Bridge transmitter power can be adjusted to suit the environment.

Extended Activities

1. You are planning a point-to-multipoint wireless campus network. The campus consists of five buildings: a central hub building and four outlying buildings. Draw the campus network, showing the buildings and bridges. Use only one bridge per building. Label the bridges by their operating mode. Label the type of antenna (directional, semidirectional, etc.) used on each building.

2. You are planning a point-to-point wireless link between two buildings separated by a river. Draw the link, showing the buildings and bridges. Use only one bridge per building. Label the bridges by their operating mode. Label the type of antenna (directional, semidirectional, etc.) used on each building.

Lesson 3—Wireless Workgroup Bridges

Wireless workgroup bridges (WGBs) are similar to and often confused with wireless bridges. A WGB provides wired client connectivity to the wireless network. This lesson discusses WGBs, their options, and management capabilities.

Objectives

At the end of this lesson you will be able to:

- Describe wireless workgroup bridge options

- Explain common wireless workgroup bridge configuration and management tools

 **Key Point**

Wireless workgroup bridges connect wired clients to wireless network segments as a single collective client.

What Is a Wireless Workgroup Bridge?

The biggest difference between a bridge and a workgroup bridge is that a workgroup bridge is a client device. A wireless workgroup bridge is capable of aggregating multiple wired LAN client devices into one collective wireless LAN client.

In the association table on an access point, a workgroup bridge will appear in the table as a single client device. An association table is a list of wireless client connection statuses associated with, or connected to, a wireless access point or bridge. The media access control (MAC) addresses of devices behind the workgroup bridge will not be seen on the access point. Workgroup bridges are especially useful in environments with mobile classrooms, mobile offices, or even remote campus buildings where a small group of users need access into the main network. Bridges can be used for this type of functionality, but if an access point rather than a bridge is in place at the central site, using a workgroup bridge prevents the administrator from having to buy an additional bridge for the central site. The Sample Wireless Workgroup Bridge Diagram shows an example of a wireless workgroup bridge, while the Wireless Workgroup Bridge Installed on a Network Diagram illustrates where it is used on a wireless LAN.

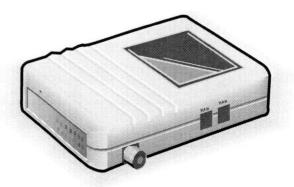

Sample Wireless Workgroup Bridge

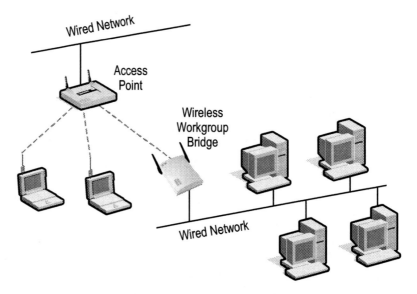

Wireless Workgroup Bridge Installed on a Network

In an indoor environment in which a small group of wired users is physically separated from the main body of network users, a workgroup bridge can be ideal for wirelessly connecting the entire group back into the main network. Additionally, workgroup bridges may have protocol filtering capabilities allowing administrators to control traffic across the wireless links.

Common Options

Because a wireless workgroup bridge is a type of bridge, many of the options that you will find in a bridge – MAC and protocol filtering, fixed or detachable antennas, variable power output, and varied types of wired connectivity – are also found in a workgroup bridge. A limited number of stations may use the workgroup bridge from the wired segment. Depending on the manufacturer, this number ranges between 8 and 128. Using more than about 20 clients over the wireless segment is likely to cause throughput to drop to a point at which users might feel that the wireless link is simply too slow to adequately perform tasks.

Configuration and Management

The methods used to access, configure, and manage a wireless workgroup bridge are similar to those of a wireless bridge: console, telnet, HTTP, SNMP support, and custom configuration and management software. Workgroup bridges are configured for a default IP address assigned by the manufacturer, but can be changed either by accessing the unit by means of a console port, Web browser, telnet, or custom software application. An administrator can reset the device to factory defaults by using the hardware reset button on the device.

Activities

1. At what point will wireless WGB-attached clients find that network throughput is unacceptable?

   a. When the client count reaches more than 128 wireless nodes.

   b. When the client count reaches more than 20 wired nodes.

   c. When the client count reaches more than 128 wired nodes.

   d. When the client count reaches more than 8 wireless nodes.

2. Which statement best describes a network application to which a wireless workgroup bridge is the best suited?

   a. When remote buildings house small groups of wireless clients needing network access

   b. When mobile buildings house large groups of wired clients needing access to the wireless network

   c. When remote buildings house a large group of wireless clients needing access to the wired network

   d. When remote buildings house small groups of wired clients needing network access

3. Which WGB feature allows an administrator to control network access by application type?

   a. Protocol filtering

   b. MAC filtering

   c. Variable power output

   d. Wired topology filtering

4. Which of the following are management options found in wireless workgroup bridges? (Choose three.)

   a. Console

   b. Restricted

   c. Telnet

   d. SNMP

Extended Activities

1. You need to connect ten wired clients located in a single-story, temporary building to the central, main wired network. Since the temporary building is on site only for the duration of the building remodel project, you choose not to run cable to it. Draw the site layout, showing the wireless devices you would use to connect the two buildings. Label the antenna types used and the appropriate wireless device operating modes.

2. How could a wireless WGB simplify connecting network nodes in your office? Would you save time and money using this sort of device instead of a traditional wired network solution?

Lesson 4—Wireless LAN Client Devices

Wireless LAN clients are end-user nodes such as desktop, laptop, or personal digital assistant (PDA) computers that need wireless connectivity into the wireless network infrastructure. Wireless LAN client devices provide connectivity for wireless LAN clients. This lesson discusses LAN client devices, their features and applications, configuration and management, and common utilities included with each.

Objectives

At the end of this lesson you will be able to:

- Choose a wireless client device appropriate for the client node type

- Explain common wireless client configuration and management tools

- Determine which wireless client devices require drivers installed on the client node

- Describe utilities included with wireless client devices

 **Key Point**

Wireless LAN client devices connect client nodes to access points, bridges, and other wireless clients.

Types of Wireless Client Devices

It is important to understand that manufacturers currently make radio cards in only two physical formats: Personal Computer Memory Card International Association (PCMCIA) and Compact Flash (CF). All radio card manufacturers build their products into these card formats and then connect them to adapters such as Peripheral Component Interconnect (PCI), Industry Standard Architecture (ISA), Universal Serial Bus (USB), and so forth.

For purposes of this discussion, the term "client devices" covers several wireless LAN devices that an access point would recognize as a client on a wireless network. These devices include:

- PCMCIA and Compact Flash Radio Cards
- Ethernet and Serial Converters
- USB Adapters
- PCI and ISA Adapters

PCMCIA and Compact Flash Radio Cards

The most common wireless client device is the PCMCIA card. More commonly known as "PC cards," these devices are used in notebook (laptop) computers and PDAs. The PC card is the component that provides the connection between a client device and the network. The PC card also serves as a modular radio in access points, bridges, workgroup bridges, USB adapters, PCI and ISA adapters, and even print servers. The Sample PCMCIA Card Diagram shows an example of a PCMCIA card.

Sample PCMCIA Card

Antennas on PC cards vary with each manufacturer. You might notice that several manufacturers use the same antenna, while others use radically different designs. Some are small and flat, such as the one shown on the Sample PCMCIA Card Diagram, while others are detachable and connected to the PC card by means of a short cable. Some PC cards are shipped with multiple antennas and even include accessories for mounting detachable antennas to the laptop or desktop case with Velcro.

Note: The two major manufacturers of radio chipsets that make up the heart of the very popular 802.11b PC and compact flash (CF) cards are: Agere Systems (formerly Lucent Technologies) and Intersil. Atheros was the first to mass produce chip sets for the 802.11a standard that uses the 5 GHz UNII frequency bands. These manufacturers sell their chipsets to the PC and CF radio card manufacturers (the wireless LAN hardware manufacturing companies) who use the radios in their product lines.

CF cards provide the same functionality as wireless PC cards, but CF cards are much smaller and typically used in PDAs. Wireless CF cards draw very little power and are about the size of a matchbook.

Wireless Ethernet and Serial Converters

Ethernet and serial converters are used with any device providing Ethernet or legacy 9-pin serial ports for the purpose of converting those wired connections into wireless LAN connections. When you use a wireless Ethernet converter, you use a Category 5 cable to externally connect the Ethernet converter box (which houses a wireless LAN radio) to the computer's Ethernet network interface card (NIC). Wireless Ethernet converters are commonly used to connect an Ethernet-based print server to a wireless network.

Serial devices are considered legacy devices and are rarely used to network personal computers. Serial converters are typically used on old equipment that uses legacy 25-pin or 9-pin serial ports for network connectivity, such as terminals, telemetry equipment, and serial printers. Manufacturers frequently sell client devices that include both a serial and Ethernet converter in the same enclosure.

These Ethernet and serial converter devices do not normally include a PC card radio. Instead, the radio must be purchased separately and installed in the converter enclosure's PC card slot. Ethernet converters in particular allow administrators to convert a large number of wired nodes to wireless network in a short period of time.

Configuration of Ethernet and serial converters varies. In most cases, a 9-pin legacy serial port provides console access, or custom configuration and management software is provided with the unit. The software is run from a desktop computer while the converter is attached. The Sample Ethernet and Serial Converter Diagram shows an example of a combined Ethernet and serial converter.

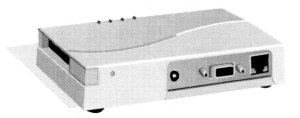

Sample Ethernet and Serial Converter

USB Adapters

USB clients are becoming very popular due to their simple connectivity. USB client devices support plug and play (PnP), and require no additional power other than that delivered through a computer's USB port. Some USB clients utilize modular, easily removable radio cards, and others have a fixed internal card that cannot be removed without opening the case. When purchasing a USB client device, be sure you understand whether or not the USB adapter includes the PC card radio. In cases of a USB adapter that requires a PC card, it is recommended, although not always required, that you use the same vendor's equipment for both the adapter and the PC card. The Sample USB Client Diagram shows an example of a USB client.

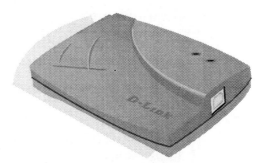

Sample USB Client

PCI and ISA Adapters

Wireless PCI and ISA adapters are installed inside a desktop computer. Wireless PCI devices are PnP compatible, but they may also only come as "empty" PCI cards, which require a radio card to be inserted into the PCMCIA slot after the PCI card is installed into the computer. Wireless ISA cards are not usually PnP compatible and require manual configuration both by means of a DOS-based software utility and configuration of the operating system. Because an operating system cannot automatically configure ISA devices that are incompatible with PnP, the administrator must make sure the adapter's setting and those of the operating system match. Manufacturers typically have separate drivers for the PCI or ISA adapters and the PC card that will be inserted into each. As with USB adapters, it is recommended that you use the same vendor's equipment for the PCI/ISA adapters and the PC card. The Sample PCI Adapter Diagram shows an example of a PCI adapter with a PC card inserted.

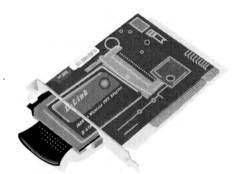

Sample PCI Adapter

Configuration and Management

The two steps to installing wireless LAN client devices are:

1. Install the drivers
2. Install manufacturer's wireless utilities

Driver Installation

The drivers included for cards are installed the same way drivers for any other type of PC hardware would be. Most devices (other than ISA adapters) are PnP compatible, which means that when the client device is first installed, the OS prompts the user to insert the CD or disks containing the driver software into a drive. Specific steps for device installation will vary by manufacturer. Be sure to follow the instruction manuals for your specific brand of hardware.

Note: When purchasing client devices, make sure the drivers are included for the specific operating system in which you will be installing the hardware.

Serial and Ethernet converters require no special drivers to work; however, wireless LAN client utilities can still be installed and utilized. The configuration software, if required, must be used to initially configure the converter.

Manufacturer Utilities

Some manufacturers offer a full suite of utilities and others simply provide users with the most basic means of connectivity. A robust set of utilities might include:

- Site Survey tools

- Spectrum Analyzer

- Power and speed monitoring tools

- Profile configuration utilities

- Link status monitor with link testing functionality

Site Survey Tools

Site survey tools can include many different items that allow the user to find networks, identify media access control (MAC) addresses of access points (APs), quantify signal strengths and signal-to-noise ratios, and see interfering access points all at the same time during a site survey. Site survey tools and procedures are discussed in more detail in further reading.

Spectrum Analyzer

Spectrum analyzer software has many practical uses, including finding interference sources and overlapping wireless LAN channels in the immediate area around a wireless LAN.

Power and Speed Monitoring Tools

Power output and speed configuration utilities and monitors are useful for knowing what a wireless link is capable of doing at any particular time. For example, a user who plans on transferring a large amount of data from a server to a laptop may not want to start the transfer until the wireless connection to the network is 11 Mbps, instead of 1 Mbps. Knowing the location at which throughput increases/decreases is valuable for increasing user productivity.

Profile Configuration Utilities

Profile configuration utilities ease administration tasks considerably when changing from one wireless network to another. Instead of manually reconfiguring all of a wireless client's settings each time you change networks, you can configure profiles for each wireless network during the initial configuration of the client device to save time later.

Link Status Monitor with Link Testing Functionality

Link status monitor utilities allow users to view packet errors, successful transmissions, connection speed, link viability, and many other valuable parameters. A utility for doing real-time link connectivity tests is usually included. This utility enables an administrator, for example, to determine how stable a wireless link is while in the presence of heavy RF interference or signal blockage. This type of utility typically works only between a single manufacturer's client and access point.

Common Utility Functionality

The functionality of manufacturers' utilities varies greatly, but share a common set of configurable parameters. Each of the following parameters is discussed in detail later in further reading:

- Infrastructure mode/Ad Hoc mode
- Service Set Indentifier (SSID), or Network Name
- Channel (if in ad hoc mode)
- Wired Equivalent Privacy (WEP) Keys
- Authentication type (Open System, Shared Key)

Activities

1. Which of the following wireless client devices requires you to install drivers on the client node? (Choose two.)

   a. ISA client

   b. Serial converter

   c. Ethernet converter

   d. USB client

2. Which statement concerning a USB wireless client is true?

   a. It may not include the radio card.

   b. It requires a serial converter to connect to the client node.

   c. It requires manual configuration on the client node.

   d. It requires an external power source.

3. Which of the following functions does a serial converter in a wireless network perform?

   a. Connecting a laptop computer to the wireless network

   b. Connecting a desktop PC to the wireless network

   c. Connecting a desktop PC to the wired network

   d. Connecting a mainframe terminal to the wireless network

4. Which of the following are tasks you would likely need to perform to install and configure a wireless ISA adapter? (Choose three.)

   a. Set the serial port's data rate to match the card

   b. Configure the OS and adapter settings

   c. Load drivers for the adapter

   d. Load drivers for the radio card

5. Which wireless client utility allows you to locate interference sources and overlapping wireless channels in the immediate area around the wireless LAN?

   a. Site survey tools

   b. Power monitoring tools

   c. Spectrum analyzer

   d. Link status monitor

6. Which wireless client utility allows a network administrator to view packet errors, connection speed, and link viability?

   a. Site survey tools

   b. Power monitoring tools

   c. Spectrum analyzer

   d. Link status monitor

Extended Activities

1. The USB 1.1 standard specifies theoretical data rates up to 12 Mbps, shared between up to 127 devices. On a client node connecting to several USB devices, what effect do you think this shared bandwidth limitation would have on a client's wireless network throughput? Would USB 2.0 improve this situation?

   _____

   _____

   _____

   _____

2. One tool available for capturing information on a wireless network is called NetStumbler, available for download from **http://www.netstumbler.com**. The utility only supports cards with a certain wireless chipset. Research the utility and determine on which chipset NetStumbler runs. Then, research wireless clients that use this chipset.

   _____

   _____

   _____

   _____

Lesson 5—Wireless Residential Gateways

A gateway is a network device that provides a path to a remote network segment, such as a network router that connects the local network to the Internet. The client nodes forward Internet traffic to the gateway, which in turn forwards the client traffic to the remote network. Wireless network equipment manufacturers have begun combining the roles of access points and gateways into a single device, called a Wireless Residential Gateway. This lesson discusses wireless residential gateways, their applications, common options, and configuration and management tools.

Objectives

At the end of this lesson you will be able to:

*   Describe the WAN connection types wireless residential gateways support

*   Describe common options found in wireless residential gateways

*   Explain common wireless residential gateway configuration and management tools

 **Key Point**

> *Wireless residential gateways provide a quick and easy means to connect several wireless client nodes to a shared, broadband connection.*

What Is a Wireless Residential Gateway?

A wireless residential gateway is a device designed to connect a small number of wireless nodes to a single device for Layer 2 (wired and wireless) and Layer 3 connectivity to the Internet or to another network segment. Wireless residential gateways usually include a built-in hub or switch, as well as a fully configurable, Wi-Fi-compliant access point. The WAN port on a wireless residential gateway is the Internet-facing Ethernet port that may be connected to the Internet through one of the following:

*   Cable modem

*   xDSL modem

*   Analog modem

*   Satellite modem

The Sample Wireless Residential Gateway Diagram shows an example of a wireless residential gateway, and the Wireless Residential Gateway Installed on a Network Diagram illustrates where a wireless residential gateway is used on a wireless LAN.

Sample Wireless Residential Gateway

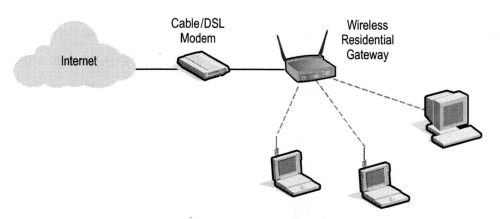

Wireless Residential Gateway Installed on a Network

Common Options

Because wireless residential gateways are becoming increasingly popular in small businesses and homes of telecommuters, manufacturers have begun adding more features to these devices to aid in productivity and security. Common options that most wireless residential gateways include are:

- Point-to-Point Protocol over Ethernet (PPPoE)
- Network Address Translation (NAT)
- Port Address Translation (PAT)
- Ethernet switching
- Virtual servers (a.k.a. Port Forwarding)
- Print serving
- Fail-over routing
- Virtual Private Networks (VPNs)
- Dynamic Host Configuration Protocol (DHCP) server and client
- Configurable firewall

This diverse array of functionality allows home and small office users to afford an all-in-one single device solution that is easily configurable and meets most business needs. Residential gateways have been around for quite some time, but recently, with the extreme popularity of 802.11b compliant wireless devices, wireless was added as a feature. Wireless residential gateways have all of the expected small office/home office (SOHO)-class access point configuration selections, such as Wired Equivalent Privacy (WEP), media access control (MAC) filters, channel selection, and service set ID (SSID).

Configuration and Management

Configuring and installing wireless residential gateways generally consists of browsing to the built-in HTTP server by means of one of the built-in Ethernet ports and changing the user-configurable settings to meet your particular needs. This configuration may include changing ISP, LAN, or virtual private network (VPN) settings. Configuration and monitoring are done in similar fashion through the browser interface. Some wireless residential gateway units support console, telnet, and USB connectivity for management and configuration. The console port and telnet sessions typically provide text-based menus that are less user-friendly than the browser interface, but adequate for configuration. Statistics that can be monitored may include items such as up time, dynamic IP addresses, and VPN connectivity. These settings are usually well marked or explained for nontechnical home or home office users.

Note: When you choose to install a wireless residential gateway at your home or business, be aware that your ISP will not provide technical support for connecting your unit to the Internet unless it specifically states that it will. ISPs usually only support the hardware that you have purchased from them or that they have installed. This incomplete service can be especially frustrating to a nontechnical user who must configure the correct IP addresses and settings in the gateway unit to get Internet access. The best source of support for installing these devices is the manual provided with the device or someone who has already successfully installed similar units. Because wireless residential gateways are so common now, many individuals who consider themselves nontechnical have gained significant experience installing and configuring them.

Activities

1. Which of the following technologies are common options found in wireless residential gateways? (Choose two.)

   a. RADIUS

   b. NAT

   c. VLAN

   d. PPPoE

2. Which of the following are SOHO-class access point configuration options also found on wireless residential gateways? (Choose three.)

   a. WEP

   b. Protocol filters

   c. MAC filters

   d. SSID

3. You purchased a wireless residential gateway to share your broadband connection with your spouse and children. Your spouse's PC uses a compatible wireless client device, while the children's PCs use wired network adapters. What option must the gateway include so that you can connect all the PCs to the Internet?

   a. Ethernet switch

   b. Print server

   c. VPN

   d. Firewall

4. Which methods can you use to manage and configure a wireless residential gateway? (Choose three.)

   a. Jumpers

   b. Browser

   c. Telnet

   d. USB console

Extended Activity

Use the Internet or visit your local computer store and compare wireless residential gateways to traditional APs. What features do gateways include that APs do not? What compromises do residential gateway manufacturers make to add usability features and keep costs low? Are these good solutions for providing enterprise wireless network access? Why or why not?

_____

_____

_____

_____

Lesson 6—Enterprise Wireless Gateways

An enterprise wireless gateway is a device that can provide specialized authentication and connectivity for wireless clients. As opposed to wireless residential gateways, which provide both wired and wireless network access in small office/home office (SOHO) environments, enterprise wireless gateways are appropriate for medium-scale and large-scale wireless local area network (LAN) environments. They provide a multitude of manageable wireless LAN services such as rate limiting, VPN Services, RADIUS support, Quality of Service (QoS), and profile management. This lesson discusses enterprise wireless gateway capabilities, applications, and configuration and management tools.

Objectives

At the end of this lesson you will be able to:

- Describe key features found in enterprise wireless gateways

- Explain network Quality of Service (QoS) services provided by enterprise wireless gateways

- Explain network security services supported by enterprise wireless gateways

- Describe enterprise wireless gateway configuration and management tools

 **Key Point**

Enterprise wireless gateways do not directly connect clients to the wireless network; instead, they support advanced network mobility, QoS, and security services for wireless clients.

Enterprise Wireless Gateway Features

Because an Enterprise Wireless Gateway provides advanced network services to wireless clients, such as assigning service levels to network traffic and securing wireless connections, it is important that it include a powerful central processing unit (CPU) and fast Ethernet interfaces. The gateway may support many access points, all of which send traffic to and through the enterprise wireless gateway. Enterprise wireless gateway units usually support a variety of wireless LAN and wireless personal area networks (WPAN) technologies, such as 802.11 standard devices, Bluetooth, HomeRF, and more.

Enterprise wireless gateways support Simple Network Management Protocol (SNMP) and allow enterprise-wide simultaneous upgrades of user profiles. They may be configured for hot fail-over (when installed in pairs), and support authentication services such as RADIUS, LDAP, Windows NT, or Windows 2000 authentication databases, and data encryption using industry-standard VPN tunnel types. The Sample Enterprise Wireless Gateway Diagram shows an example of an enterprise wireless gateway, and the Enterprise Wireless Gateway Installed on a Network Diagram illustrates where it is used on a wireless LAN.

Sample Enterprise Wireless Gateway

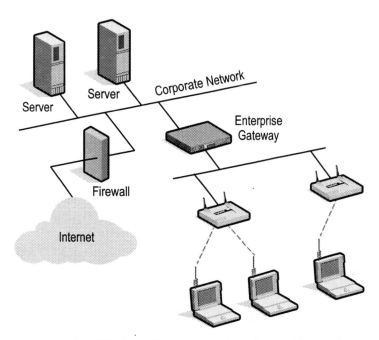

Enterprise Wireless Gateway Installed on a Network

Authentication technologies incorporated into enterprise wireless gateways are often built into the more advanced levels of access points. For example, virtual private network (VPN) and 802.1x/EAP connectivity are supported in many brands of enterprise level access points.

Enterprise wireless gateways do have features, such as Role-Based Access Control (RBAC), that are not found in any access points. RBAC allows an administrator to assign a certain level of wireless network access to a particular job position in the company. If the person doing that job is replaced, the new person automatically gains the same network rights as the replaced person. Having the ability to limit a wireless user's access to corporate resources, as part of the "role," can be a useful security feature.

Class of service (CoS) is typically supported, and an administrator can assign levels of service to a particular user or role. For example, a guest account might be able to use only 500 kbps on a wireless network, whereas an administrator might be allowed 2 Mbps connectivity.

In some cases, the enterprise wireless gateway supports Mobile IP, allowing a user to roam across a layer 3 boundary. User roaming may even be defined as part of an enterprise wireless gateway policy, allowing users to roam only where the administrator allows. Some enterprise wireless gateways support packet queuing and prioritization (Quality of Service [QoS], user tracking, and even time/date controls to specify when users may access the wireless network).

MAC spoofing prevention and complete session logging are also supported and aid greatly in securing wireless LANs. Many more features vary significantly between manufacturers. Enterprise wireless gateways are so comprehensive that we highly recommend that an administrator take the manufacturer's training class before making a purchase so the deployment of the enterprise wireless gateway will go more smoothly.

Consultants finding themselves in a situation of having to provide a security solution for a wireless LAN deployment with many access points that do not support advanced security features might find enterprise wireless gateways to be a good solution. Enterprise wireless gateways are expensive, but considering the number of management and security solutions they provide, they are usually worth the expense.

Configuration and Management

Enterprise wireless gateways are installed in the main data path on the wired LAN segment just past the access point(s) as seen in the Enterprise Wireless Gateway Installed on a Network Diagram. Enterprise wireless gateways are configured through console ports (using CLI), telnet, internal HTTP or HTTPS servers, SNMP software, and so forth. Centralized management of only a few devices is one big advantage of using enterprise wireless gateways. An administrator, from a single console, can easily manage a large wireless deployment using only a few central devices instead of a very large number of access points.

Enterprise wireless gateways are normally upgraded through use of Trivial File Transfer Protocol (TFTP) in the same fashion as many switches and routers on the market today. Configuration backups can often be automated to prevent administrators from having to spend additional management time backing up or recovering from lost configuration files. Enterprise wireless gateways are mostly manufactured as rack-mountable 1U or 2U devices that can fit into your existing data center design.

Activities

1. Which of the following are methods you can use to configure an enterprise wireless gateway? (Choose three.)

    a. CLI on the console port

    b. Client USB port

    c. HTTPS server

    d. SNMP management software

2. You are designing a wireless network to which several functional workgroups are connected. You want to configure your enterprise wireless gateway to allow you to quickly assign identical network access rights to persons within the same workgroup. Which enterprise wireless gateway feature provides this capability?

    a. LDAP

    b. RBAC

    c. EAP

    d. HTTP

3. Which of the following are authentication services that enterprise wireless gateways support? (Choose two.)

    a. RADIUS

    b. MAC filters

    c. Windows NT authentication

    d. VLAN tunnels

4. You are designing a wireless network segment to support real-time voice over IP traffic. You want to ensure that the network gives the voice traffic twice the bandwidth it gives to other network traffic. Which enterprise wireless gateway feature provides this elevated treatment to the voice traffic?

    a. 802.1x/EAP

    b. RBAC

    c. Mobile IP

    d. Class of service

5. Which enterprise wireless gateway feature allows mobile users to roam between routed network segments?

   a. Class of service roaming

   b. Mobile IP

   c. VPN tunneling

   d. RADIUS

Extended Activities

1. Draw a wireless campus network design that meets the following requirements:

   - Four buildings, each with point-to-point wireless network connections to the other three buildings

   - Three floors per building: the first floor is the Main Distribution Frame (MDF), and the other two floors house Intermediate Distribution Frames (IDFs)

   - An Ethernet wired backbone connects the floors

   - Each floor houses 100 wired, Ethernet clients

   - Each floor supports 20 mobile wireless clients

   - The mobile clients use laptop PCs

   - Each floor is not wired for network connectivity, and will not be wired in the near future

   Label each wireless device with its type and operating mode. For example, if you install an access point, label it as such, and list whether it operates in root mode, repeater mode, or bridge mode. For building-to-building bridge links, label the antenna type used. Label the wireless client devices by type (USB, PC Card, ISA, and so forth). Use gateways as appropriate.

2. Explain why you chose to place a particular type of device in each network location, and why you chose its specific operating mode. What other type of wireless devices could you have used in its place?

   _____

   _____

   _____

   _____

Summary

This unit covered the different categories of wireless network infrastructure equipment and some of the variations within each category. The hardware items within each category are the physical building blocks of every wireless LAN. By teaching you to configure and install each type of hardware, this unit enabled you to become more versed in the implementation of wireless LANs.

The wireless LAN hardware devices discussed in this unit include access points, wireless bridges, wireless workgroup bridges, clients, wireless gateways, and enterprise wireless gateways.

Unit 4 Quiz

1. Why would it NOT be a good idea to have a number of access points in repeater mode in series? (Choose two.)

    a. Throughput would be reduced to unacceptable levels.

    b. The access points would be required to be physically connected to the network.

    c. Data corruption can occur over the series of hops back to the root access point.

    d. Legacy serial devices would not be able to communicate with the root access point.

2. You are installing a wireless LAN in a factory, and the laptop client computers have no USB support. Which one of the following client devices could be used as a stand-alone client connection to the wireless LAN?

    a. ISA adapter

    b. PCI adapter

    c. PCMCIA card

    d. Ethernet converter

3. You need to connect two wired networks together that currently share no network connectivity. Using only access points to connect the networks, in what mode do the access points need to be placed?

    a. Root mode

    b. Repeater mode

    c. Bridging mode

    d. Access mode

4. Access point A connects wirelessly to access point B. Access point B extends the wireless network segment to clients out of access point A's range. Access point A connects to the wired network segment, while access point B has no wired network connectivity. In this configuration, in which mode is access point B operating?

    a. Root

    b. Repeater

    c. Bridge

    d. Access

5. Wireless bridges are most often used for which of the following functions? (Choose two.)

   a. Connecting mobile users to the wired LAN

   b. Point-to-multipoint configurations

   c. Building-to-building connectivity

   d. Wireless security

6. Your friend owns a small business and asks you what he could buy to provide low-cost wireless Internet access for the five salespeople in his office. Which one of the following devices would be an appropriate solution?

   a. Access point

   b. Wireless workgroup bridge

   c. Enterprise wireless gateway

   d. Wireless residential gateway

7. A company has hired you to recommend wireless LAN equipment that will allow it to place limits on the bandwidth used by each of their wireless users. Which one of the following devices would you recommend?

   a. Access point

   b. Wireless workgroup bridge

   c. Enterprise wireless gateway

   d. Wireless residential gateway

8. In a situation in which you need to allow outdoor users to connect to your network by means of a wireless LAN, which one of the following features would allow you to use an indoor access point with an outdoor antenna?

   a. Antenna diversity

   b. Detachable antennas

   c. Plug and play support

   d. Modular radio cards

9. Which of the following wireless client devices is not a plug and play (PnP) device?

   a. USB Client

   b. PCMCIA Card

   c. ISA Card

   d. Compact Flash Card

10. Your client has a number of sales people who are located in a remote office building. Each sales person has both a PC and a laptop. The client wants to purchase a hardware solution that will permit each sales person to have wireless network connectivity for his or her PC and laptop. Only the PC or the laptop needs network access at any given time, and both have USB support. Which of the following solutions would work? (Choose two.)

    a. 1 PCMCIA card

    b. 1 PCMCIA card, 1 PCI adapter

    c. 1 PCMCIA card, 1 USB adapter

    d. 1 PCMCIA card, 1 CF card

11. You have configured an access point in a small office and are concerned about hackers intruding on your wireless network. What settings will you adjust (from the manufacturer's default settings) on the unit to address this potential problem? (Choose three.)

    a. Detachable antennas

    b. MAC Filtering

    c. Radio card position

    d. Output power

    e. WEP configuration

12. Which of the following are common security options that most wireless residential gateways include? (Choose three.)

    a. PPPoE

    b. Virtual Servers

    c. Routing

    d. PAT

    e. VPN Client or VPN Client Passthrough

13. Which of the following are wired connectivity options that a wireless bridge can include? (Choose three.)

    a. 10baseTX

    b. 10baseFL

    c. 10/100baseTX

    d. 1000baseSX

    e. 100baseFX

14. A workgroup bridge is which type of device?

    a. Client

    b. Infrastructure

    c. Gateway

    d. Antenna

15. Which one of the following is not a hardware or software option on a wireless bridge?

    a. Fixed or detachable antennas

    b. Advanced filtering capabilities

    c. Removable (modular) radio cards

    d. Full duplex radio links

    e. Varied Types of Wired Connectivity

16. Ethernet and serial converters are used with devices having which of the following physical connectivity? (Choose two.)

    a. 9-pin serial ports

    b. Ethernet ports

    c. USB Ports

    d. Parallel Ports

17. Why is an access point considered a portal?

    a. An access point allows client connectivity from an 802.11 network to either 802.3 or 802.5 networks.

    b. An access point always connects users to the Internet.

    c. An access point connects clients to one another.

    d. An access point is a gateway to another collision domain.

18. A USB adapter is used with which type of wireless LAN device?

    a. Gateway

    b. Access point

    c. Bridge

    d. Client

    e. Converter

19. The statement that an access point is a half-duplex wireless device is which of the following?

    a. Always true

    b. Always false

    c. Dependent on the maker of the access point

Unit 5
Antennas and Accessories

In earlier reading, we discussed the many different pieces of wireless LAN equipment that are currently available on the market for creating simple and complex wireless LANs. In this unit, we discuss a basic element of the devices that make access points, bridges, PC cards, and other wireless devices communicate: antennas.

Antennas are most often used to increase the range of wireless LAN systems, but proper antenna selection can also enhance the security of a wireless LAN. A properly chosen and positioned antenna can reduce the signal leaking out of your workspace, and make signal interception extremely difficult. In this unit, we explain the radiation patterns of different antenna designs and how antenna positioning makes a difference in signal reception.

All wireless LAN antennas fall into three general categories: omnidirectional, semidirectional, and highly directional. We discuss the attributes of each of these groups in-depth, as well as the proper methods for installing each kind of antenna. We also explain polarization, coverage patterns, and appropriate uses of antennas. Additionally, we describe the many different items that are used to connect antennas to other wireless LAN hardware.

Previously, we have discussed RF theory and some of the major categories of wireless LAN devices that an administrator uses on a daily basis. Although this knowledge provides a good foundation, it is of little value without a solid working knowledge of antennas.

This unit also addresses the following wireless LAN accessories:

- RF Amplifiers
- RF Attenuators
- Lightning Arrestors

- RF Connectors
- RF Cables
- RF Splitters
- Pigtails

Knowing these devices' uses, specifications, and effects on RF signal strength is essential for building a functional wireless LAN.

We also discuss Power over Ethernet (PoE), an important technology in today's wireless networks that has spawned new product lines and new standards. We explain PoE technology along with the different types of PoE equipment that can be used to deliver power to a PoE-enabled device.

Lessons

1. RF Antennas
2. PoE Devices
3. Wireless LAN Accessories

Terms

802.3af—IEEE 802.3af is a standard proposed by the Institute of Electrical and Electronic Engineers (IEEE) for powering Ethernet devices over twisted pair cabling. IEEE 802.3af is a legacy Ethernet-compatible, internationally standard power distribution technique.

amplifier—An amplifier is used to increase signal strength between the transmitter/receiver and the antenna along the antenna cable.

bandwidth control unit (BCU)—A BCU is a network device installed between a wired network device, such as a switch or router, and an access point; it controls the amount of network bandwidth used by wireless users.

bidirectional amplifier—A bidirectional amplifier is an RF amplifier that boosts (adds gain) to both the transmitted and received signal.

BNC—Short for British Naval Connector (or Bayonet Nut Connector), BNC connectors are small devices used to connect computers to a thin coaxial cable bus (10Base2) or terminate the ends of a bus. There are several different types of BNC connectors. A BNC barrel connector joins two Thinnet cables. A BNC terminator is used to terminate the end of a cable. It acts as a resistive load that absorbs the signal that reaches one end of the bus. (Two terminators are needed on each bus.) BNC adapters connect different types of cable, such as Thinnet to Thicknet. BNC connectors can also be used to connect some monitors, which increases the accuracy of the signals sent from the video adapter.

Canadian Department of Communications (DOC)—The DOC is the Canadian equivalent to the U.S. Federal Communications Commission (FCC) and is now called "Industry Canada."

coverage area—An RF signal's coverage area is the area around the access point where the radio signal is of sufficient strength and quality to provide acceptable throughput to wireless clients.

Drip loop—A drip loop is installed in a cable run to provide a path for moisture to run away from the connectors and entry facilities. Hence, the drip loop is installed below the cable entrance.

Earth ground—Earth ground is a rod or grid driven into or buried in the Earth for the purpose of providing electrical signals a path to ground. Earth ground provides lightning and over-current protection and is often used as a zero-reference voltage point.

F connector—A coaxial cable F connector is a screw-on connector of the type used for cable television connections and typically has a 75-ohm impedance.

Federal Communications Commission (FCC)—The Federal Communications Commission (FCC) is an independent United States government agency, directly responsible to Congress. The FCC was established by the Communications Act of 1934 and is charged with regulating interstate and international communications by radio, television, wire, satellite and cable. The FCC's jurisdiction covers the 50 states, the District of Columbia, and United States possessions.

frequency converter—A frequency converter is an RF device used to convert one frequency range to another. A frequency converter converts a wireless link from a congested Industrial Scientific Medical (ISM) band to one that is less congested.

horizontal beamwidth—Horizontal beamwidth is the measure of an RF signal's focus as it travels parallel to the Earth's surface.

horizontal polarization—In reference to antennas, horizontal polarization references the alignment of the electrical field parallel to the surface of the Earth.

insertion loss—Insertion loss is the reduction in signal strength caused by connecting any RF-rated device into a transmission path between the transmitter and the antenna.

lobes—Lobes are the electrical fields emitted by an antenna; also called beams.

N-type connector—An N-type connector is a large, threaded connector used on many commercial antennas. The connector was named for Paul Neill of Bell Labs, its inventor. N-type connectors are rated at either 50 ohms or 75 ohms and come in an assortment of types, such as reverse polarity, reverse thread, and standard. NIST certifies these connectors to 18 GHz, but they are sometimes used in transmission circuits up to 26 GHz.

pigtail—Pigtails are used for adapting proprietary connectors on bridges and access points to standard connectors.

radiation pattern—A radiation pattern is the pattern in which radio signals propagate from an antenna.

reverse polarity N-type—A reverse polarity N-type is an N-type connector with the positive and negative contacts reversed.

reverse threaded N-type—A reverse threaded N-type is an N-type connector with the threads reversed.

subminiature type A (SMA) connector—An SMA connector is a small, threaded connector used on coaxial cables. The male component includes six flat lands to facilitate tightening the connector with a wrench. These connectors almost always have a 50-ohm impedance and are typically used up to 26 GHz.

TNC connector—A TNC connector is a small, threaded connector, knurled around its circumference to facilitate finger tightening.

transient current—A transient current is a momentary, additional, unintentional current introduced into a circuit by some external phenomena, such as a nearby lightning strike, high current device, or high voltage line.

unidirectional amplifier—A unidirectional RF amplifier boosts the signal's power level in only one direction, typically on the radio's transmit side.

unused pair—Unused pairs become available in Ethernet UTP networks. Typical Ethernet unshielded twisted pair (UTP) networks only use two pairs of a 4-pair Category 5 cable for data transmission. The remaining unused pairs can be used for other purposes, such as supplying Power over Ethernet.

vertical beamwidth—Vertical beamwidth is the measure of an RF signal's focus as it travels perpendicular to the Earth's surface.

vertical polarization—In reference to antennas, vertical polarization is the orientation or alignment of the electrical field perpendicular to the surface of the Earth.

war driving—War driving is a slang term that describes the practice of listening in on and capturing information from wireless LANs by intercepting RF signals emanating outside of a network coverage area. For example, an individual who parks in a company's parking lot, points a directional antenna at the building, and captures packets from RF signals "leaking" beyond the building's walls, is war driving.

Lesson 1—RF Antennas

An RF antenna is a device that converts high frequency radio frequency (RF) signals on a transmission line (a cable or waveguide, for example) into propagated waves in the air. The electrical fields emitted from antennas are called beams or lobes. Antennas are the devices that actually radiate and receive the RF signals. In this lesson, we discuss RF antenna types, their radiation patterns, antenna concepts, and antenna installation considerations.

Objectives

At the end of this lesson you will be able to:

- Describe the basic attributes, purpose, and functions of the general RF antenna types used in wireless networks

- Recognize each RF antenna type's radiation pattern

- Explain RF antenna concepts that apply to implementing antenna solutions

- Describe proper locations and methods for installing antennas

 **Key Point**

Antenna choice determines the RF signal coverage area and range.

RF Antenna Categories

The three generic categories of RF antennas are:

- Omnidirectional
- Semidirectional
- Highly directional

By possessing different RF characteristics and appropriate uses, each category encompasses multiple antenna types. As the gain of an antenna goes up, the coverage area narrows. Therefore, high-gain antennas offer longer coverage areas than low-gain antennas at the same input power level. There are many types of antenna mounts, each suited to fit a particular need. After studying this section, you will understand which antenna and mount best meets your needs.

Omnidirectional (Dipole) Antennas

The most common wireless LAN antenna is a dipole antenna. Simple to design, the dipole antenna is standard equipment on most access points. The dipole is an omnidirectional antenna, because it radiates its energy equally in all directions around its axis. Directional antennas concentrate their energy into a cone, called a "beam." The dipole has a short radiating element (just inches long) that performs an equivalent function to the "rabbit ears" antennas on television sets. Dipole antennas used with wireless LANs are much smaller because wireless LAN frequencies are in the 2.4 GHz microwave spectrum, instead of the 100 MHz TV spectrum. As frequency gets higher, wavelength and the antennas become smaller.

The Dipole Doughnut Diagram shows that a dipole's radiant energy is concentrated into a region that looks like a doughnut, with the dipole vertically through the "hole" of the "doughnut." The signal from an omnidirectional antenna radiates in a 360-degree horizontal beam. If an antenna radiates in all directions equally (forming a sphere), it is called an isotropic radiator. The sun is a good example of an isotropic radiator. We cannot make an isotropic radiator, which is the theoretical reference for antennas. However, practical antennas all have some type of gain over that of an isotropic radiator. The higher the gain, the more we horizontally squeeze our doughnut until it starts looking like a pancake, as is the case with very high gain antennas.

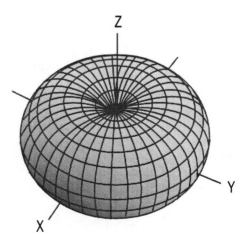

Dipole Doughnut

The dipole radiates equally in all directions around its axis, but does not radiate along the length of the wire itself - this creates the doughnut pattern. Notice the side view of a dipole radiator as it radiates waves in the Dipole Side-View Diagram. This figure also illustrates that dipole antennas form a "figure 8" in their radiation pattern if viewed standing beside a perpendicular antenna.

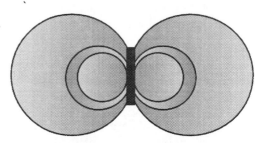

Dipole Side-View

If a dipole antenna is placed in the center of a single floor of a multi-story building, most of its energy will be radiated along the length of that floor, with some significant fraction sent to the floors above and below the antenna. The Sample Omnidirectional Antennas Diagram shows examples of some different types of omnidirectional antennas. The Coverage Area of an Omnidirectional Antenna Diagram shows a two-dimensional example of the top view and side view of a dipole antenna.

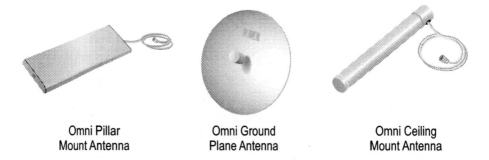

Omni Pillar
Mount Antenna

Omni Ground
Plane Antenna

Omni Ceiling
Mount Antenna

Sample Omnidirectional Antennas

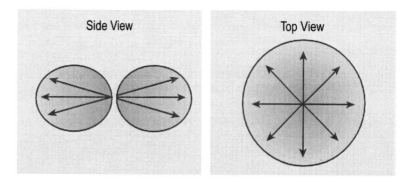

Coverage Area of an Omnidirectional Antenna

High-gain omnidirectional antennas offer more horizontal coverage area, but the vertical coverage area is reduced, as can be seen on the Coverage Area of a High-Gain Omnidirectional Antenna Diagram. This characteristic can be an important consideration when mounting a high-gain omni antenna indoors on the ceiling. If the ceiling is too high, the coverage area may not reach the floor where the users are located.

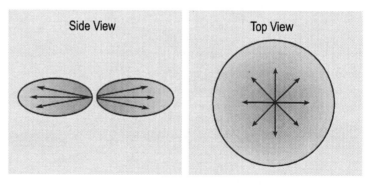

Coverage Area of a High-Gain Omnidirectional Antenna

Usage

Omnidirectional antennas are used when coverage in all directions around the horizontal axis of the antenna is required. Omnidirectional antennas are most effective where large coverage areas are needed around a central point. For example, placing an omnidirectional antenna in the middle of a large, open room would provide good coverage. Omnidirectional antennas are commonly used for point-to-multipoint designs with a star topology, as shown on the Point-to-Multipoint Link Diagram. Used outdoors, an omnidirectional antenna should be placed on top of a structure, such as a building, in the middle of the coverage area. For example, on a college campus the antenna might be placed in the center of the campus for the greatest coverage area. When used indoors, for optimum coverage, the antenna should be placed near the ceiling, in the middle of the building or desired coverage area. Omnidirectional antennas transmit over a large coverage area in a circular pattern and are suitable for warehouses or tradeshows, where coverage is usually from one corner of a building to the other.

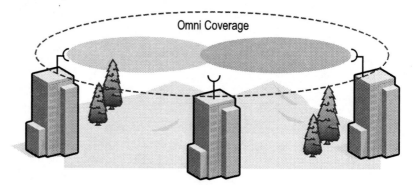

Point-to-Multipoint Link

Semidirectional Antennas

Semidirectional antennas come in many different styles and shapes. Some semidirectional antenna types frequently used with wireless LANs are Patch, Panel, and Yagi (pronounced "YAH-gee"). Patch and panel antennas are generally flat and designed for wall mounting. Yagis are generally elongated, ribbed, and usually housed in an enclosure for moisture protection. Each type has different coverage characteristics. The Sample Semidirectional Antennas Diagram shows some examples of semidirectional antennas.

Yagi Antenna   Patch Antenna   Panel Antenna

Sample Semidirectional Antennas

Semidirectional antennas direct the energy from the transmitter significantly more in one particular direction, rather than the uniform, circular pattern that is common with the omnidirectional antenna. Semidirectional antennas often radiate in a hemispherical or cylindrical coverage pattern, as can be seen on the Coverage Area of a Semidirectional Antenna Diagram.

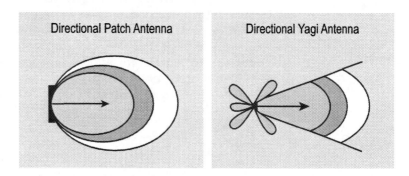

Coverage Area of a Semidirectional Antenna

Usage
Semidirectional antennas are ideally suited for short- and medium-range bridging. For example, an appropriate scenario for implementing semidirectional antennas is when two office buildings that are across the street from one another need to share a network connection. In a large indoor space, if the access point must be located in the corner or at the end of a building, corridor, or large room, a semidirectional antenna would provide the proper coverage. The Point-to-Point Link Using Semidirectional Antennas Diagram illustrates a link between two buildings using semidirectional antennas.

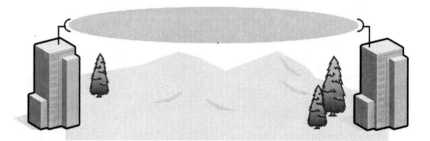

Point-to-Point Link Using Semidirectional Antennas

Many times, during an indoor site survey, engineers focus on how to best locate omnidirectional antennas. In some cases, semidirectional antennas provide such long-range coverage that they eliminate the need for multiple access points in a building. For example, in a long hallway, as an alternative to several access points with omni antennas, it may be possible to use only one or two access points with properly placed semidirectional antennas with sufficiently wide beams. This alternative saves customers a significant amount of money, and in some cases, semidirectional antennas have back and side lobes that, if used effectively, may further reduce the need for additional access points. Specifically, Yagi antennas are appropriate for signal coverage down pathways or aisles in warehouses, rail yards, retail stores, and manufacturing facilities.

Highly Directional Antennas

As their name suggests, highly directional, or high-gain antennas emit the most narrow signal beam of any antenna type and have the greatest gain of these three groups of antennas. Highly directional antennas are typically concave, dish-shaped devices, as can be seen on the Sample of a Highly Directional Parabolic Dish Antenna and Sample of a Highly Directional Grid Antenna Diagrams. These antennas are ideal for long distance, point-to-point wireless links. Some models are referred to as parabolic dishes because they resemble small satellite dishes. Others are called grid antennas because of their perforated design for resistance to wind loading.

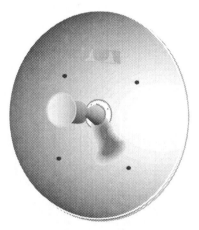

Sample of a Highly Directional Parabolic Dish Antenna

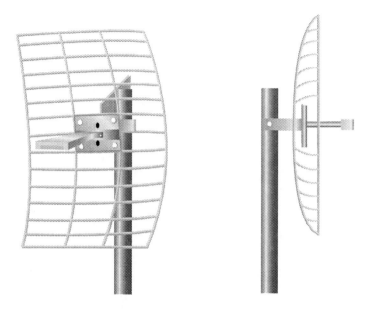

Sample of a Highly Directional Grid Antenna

The Radiation Pattern of a Highly Directional Antenna Diagram illustrates the radiation pattern of a high-gain antenna.

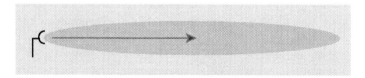

Radiation Pattern of a Highly Directional Antenna

Usage

High-gain antennas do not have a coverage area that client devices can use. These antennas are used for point-to-point communication links and can transmit at distances up to 25 miles (42 km). Highly directional antennas can connect two buildings that are miles away from each other, but have no obstructions in their path. Additionally, these antennas can be aimed directly at each other within a building in order to "blast" through an RF signal absorbing obstruction. This setup would be used to get network connectivity to places that cannot be wired and where normal wireless networks will not work.

Note: Highly directional antennas have a very narrow beamwidth and must be accurately aimed at each other.

RF Antenna Concepts

Several concepts are essential to know when implementing solutions that require RF antennas. Among those that will be described are:

- Polarization
- Gain
- Beamwidth
- Free Space Path Loss

The above list is not a comprehensive list of all RF antenna concepts, but rather a set of fundamentals that allows an administrator to understand how wireless LAN equipment functions over the wireless medium. A solid understanding of basic antenna functionality is the key to moving forward in learning more advanced RF concepts.

Knowing where to place antennas, how to position them, how much power they are radiating, the distance that radiated power is likely to travel, and how much of that power can be picked up by receivers is, many times, the most complex part of an administrator's job.

Polarization

A radio wave is actually made of two fields, one electric and one magnetic. These two fields are on planes perpendicular to each other, as shown on the E-Planes and H-Planes Diagram.

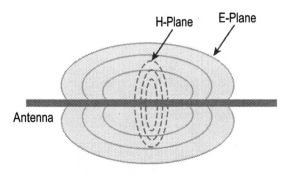

E-Planes and H-Planes

The sum of the two fields is called the electromagnetic field. Energy is transferred back and forth from one field to the other, in a process called "oscillation." The plane that is parallel with the antenna element is referred to as the "E-plane;" the plane that is perpendicular to the antenna element is referred to as the "H-plane." We are interested primarily in the E-plane (electric field) because its position and direction with reference to the Earth's surface (the ground) determines wave polarization.

Polarization is the orientation of the electric field in an electromagnetic wave. The electric field may be either perpendicular or parallel to the radiating elements (the antenna element is the metal part of the antenna that is doing the radiating). An antenna's orientation determines the emitted electric field's relationship to the Earth's surface or plane. The two types of relationships are as follows:

- **Horizontal polarization**—the electric field is parallel to the radiating element.

- **Vertical polarization**—the electric field is perpendicular to the radiating element.

A vertically polarized antenna, which is typically used in wireless LANs, emits a field perpendicular to the radiating element. You have probably noticed the dual antennas protruding from almost any access point; these antennas are typically vertically polarized in their position. A horizontally polarized antenna emits a field parallel to the radiating element. The Polarization Diagram illustrates the effects polarization can have when antennas are not aligned correctly. Antennas that are not polarized in the same way cannot communicate effectively with each other. Additionally, changing an antenna's position changes the emitted signal's orientation referenced to ground, and therefore changes the antenna's ability to communicate effectively with an antenna that is polarized the same, but orientated differently.

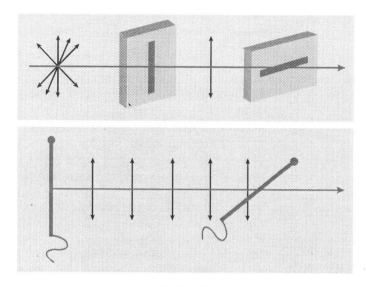

Polarization

Practical Use

The designers of the antennas for Personal Computer Memory Card International Association (PCMCIA) cards face a real problem. It is not easy to form antennas onto the small circuit board inside the plastic cover that protrudes from the end of a PCMCIA card. Rarely do antennas built into PCMCIA cards provide adequate coverage, especially when a client is roaming. The polarization of PCMCIA cards and access points is sometimes not the same, which is why turning your laptop in different directions generally improves reception. Personal digital assistants (PDAs), which usually have a vertically oriented PCMCIA card, normally exhibit good reception. External, detachable antennas vertically mounted with Velcro to the laptop computer almost always show great improvement over the snap-on antennas included with most PCMCIA cards. In areas with a high number of PCMCIA card users, it is often recommended that access point antennas be oriented horizontally for better reception.

Some PCMCIA card antennas only provide adequate coverage in the shape of half of a doughnut, instead of the whole doughnut. This is due to a ground plane in the middle of the circuit board to which the antenna attaches. For this reason, rotating a PCMCIA card or computer in a 360-degree radius can help improve reception.

Gain

Antenna gain is specified in decibels referenced to an isotropic radiator (dBi). An isotropic radiator is a sphere that radiates power equally in all directions simultaneously. We do not have the ability to make an isotropic radiator, but instead we can make omni-directional antennas, such as dipoles, that radiate power in a 360-degree horizontal fashion (but not 360 degrees vertically). RF signal radiation in this fashion creates a doughnut pattern. The more we horizontally squeeze this doughnut, the flatter it becomes, forming more of a pancake shape when the gain is very high. Antennas have passive gain, which means they do not increase the power that is input into them, but rather shape the radiation field to lengthen or shorten the distance the propagated wave will travel. The higher the antenna gain, the farther the wave will travel, concentrating its output wave more tightly so that more of the power is delivered to the destination (the receiving antenna) at long distances. As was shown earlier on the Coverage Area of a Semidirectional Antenna Diagram, the coverage has been squeezed vertically so the coverage pattern is elongated and reaches further.

Beamwidth

As we have discussed previously, narrowing, or focusing antenna beams increases an antenna's gain (measured in dBi). An antenna's beamwidth means just what it sounds like; it is the "width" of the RF signal beam that the antenna transmits. The Beamwidth of an Antenna Diagram illustrates this concept.

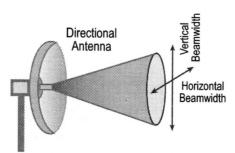

Beamwidth of an Antenna

There are two vectors to consider when discussing an antenna's beamwidths: the vertical and the horizontal. The vertical beamwidth is measured in degrees and is perpendicular to the Earth's surface. The horizontal beamwidth is measured in degrees and is parallel to the Earth's surface. Beamwidth is important to know because each type of antenna has different beamwidth specifications. The Beamwidth Table can be used as a quick reference guide for beamwidths.

Beamwidth

Antenna Type	Horizontal Beamwidth (in degrees)	Vertical Beamwidth (in degrees)
Omnidirectional	360	Ranges from 7-80
Patch/Panel	Ranges from 30-180	Ranges from 6-90
Yagi	Ranges from 30-78	Ranges from 14-64
Parabolic Dish	Ranges from 4-25	Ranges from 4-21

Selecting an antenna with appropriately wide or narrow beamwidths is essential for achieving the desired RF coverage pattern. For example, imagine a long hallway in a hospital. Rooms are located on both sides of the hallway, and instead of using several access points with omni antennas, you have decided to use a single access point with a semidirectional antenna, such as a patch antenna.

The access point and patch antenna are placed at one end of the hallway, facing down the hallway. For complete coverage on the floors directly above and below this floor, a patch antenna could be chosen with a significantly large vertical beamwidth, such as 60-90 degrees. After some testing, you may find that your selection of a patch antenna with 80 degrees vertical beamwidth does the job well.

Now we must decide the horizontal beamwidth needed. Due to the length of the hallway, testing may reveal a high-gain patch antenna must be used in order to have adequate signal coverage at the opposite end. Because of its high gain, the patch antenna's horizontal beamwidths are significantly narrowed such that the rooms on each side of the hallway do not have adequate coverage. Additionally, the high-gain antenna does not have a large enough vertical beamwidth to cover the floors immediately above and below. In this case, you might decide to use two patch antennas facing each other, one at each end of the hallway. They would both be low gain with wide horizontal and vertical beamwidths such that the rooms on each side of the hallway are covered along with the floors above and below. Due to the low gain, the antennas may each only cover a portion (approximately half) of the length of the hallway.

Free Space Path Loss

Free space path loss (or Path Loss) refers to the loss incurred by an RF signal due largely to signal dispersion, which is a natural broadening of the wave front. The wider the wave front, the less power can be induced into the receiving antenna. As the transmitted signal traverses the atmosphere, its power level decreases at a rate inversely proportional to the distance traveled and proportional to the wavelength of the signal. The power level becomes a very important factor when considering link viability.

To envision free space path loss, think of a person blowing a balloon. If you were standing directly in front of the person at a distance of 2 feet, and you pinched a piece of the balloon as it expanded, you would have a given amount of the balloon's mass between your fingers. If you backed up 300 feet and again pinched that same balloon (provided that the balloon-blowing individual had very strong lungs), the amount of the balloon's mass between your fingers would be dramatically less than that which you had at the 2-foot range. This is how a receiving antenna perceives the RF wave front.

The Path Loss equation is one of the foundations of link budget calculations. Path Loss represents the single greatest source of loss in a wireless system. Below is the formula for Path Loss.

$$PathLoss = 20LOG_{10}\left[\frac{4\Pi d}{\lambda}\right]\{dB\}$$

Note: You will not be tested on the Path Loss formula in the CWNA exam, but it is provided for administrative reference.

The 6dB Rule

Close inspection of the Path Loss equation reveals a relationship that is useful in dealing with link budget issues. Each 6 dB increase in EIRP equates to a doubling of range. Conversely, a 6 dB reduction in EIRP translates into cutting the range in half. The Path Loss Table gives you a rough estimate of the Path Loss for given distances between transmitter and receiver at 2.4 GHz.

Path Loss

Distance	Loss (in dB)
100 meters	80.23
200 meters	86.25

Path Loss (Continued)

Distance	Loss (in dB)
500 meters	94.21
1,000 meters	100.23
2,000 meters	106.25
5,000 meters	114.21
10,000 meters	120.23

Note: This Path Loss Table is provided for your reference, and does not appear on the CWNA exam.

Antenna Installation

It is very important to properly install the antennas in a wireless LAN. Improper installation can lead to damage or destruction of equipment and personal injury. Equally as important as personal safety is good performance of the wireless LAN system, which is achieved through proper placement, mounting, orientation, and alignment. In this section we will cover:

- Placement
- Mounting
- Appropriate Use
- Orientation
- Alignment
- Safety
- Maintenance

Placement

Whenever possible, mount omnidirectional antennas attached to access points near the middle of the desired coverage area. Place an antenna as high as possible (within reason) to increase coverage area, being careful that users located somewhat below the antenna still have reception, particularly when using high-gain omni antennas. So no objects encroach on the Fresnel Zone, outdoor antennas should be mounted above obstructions such as trees and buildings.

Mounting

Once you have calculated the necessary output power, gain, and distance required to transmit an RF signal, and have chosen the appropriate antenna for the job, you must mount the antenna. There are numerous options for mounting antennas both indoors and outdoors, as shown on the Mounting Antennas Diagram.

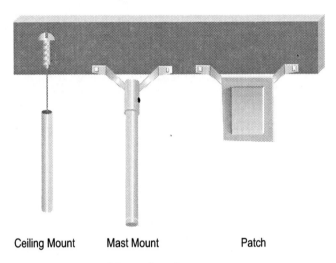

Ceiling Mount   Mast Mount   Patch

Mounting Antennas

Antenna Mounting Options

Some example mounting options are as follows:

- **ceiling mount**—typically hung from crossbars of drop ceilings
- **wall mount**—forces the signal away from a perpendicular surface
- **pillar mount**—mounts flush to a perpendicular surface
- **ground plane**—sits flat on the ground
- **mast mount**—mounts the antenna to a pole
- **articulating mount**—mounts the antenna to a movable mast
- **chimney mount**—mounts to a chimney
- **tripod mast**—mounts the antenna atop a tripod

Determining where to mount your particular antenna can be a complicated decision. The recommended placement and mounting of antennas is part of a proper site survey. There is no substitute for on-the-job training, which is where you are likely to learn how to mount wireless LAN antennas using various types of mounting hardware. Each type of mount comes with installation instructions from the manufacturer. There are many different variations of each mount type because each manufacturer has its own way of designing the mounting kit.

Keep in mind the following when mounting antennas:

- Many times the brackets shipped with the antenna may not work for a desired situation. Modifying brackets or building custom brackets may be necessary.

- Do not hang an antenna by its cable, and make sure the mounting is solid and secure. The cable can break, and cable sway can produce a moving cell.

- Exactly how each antenna is to be mounted should be specified in the site survey.

Mounting Aesthetics

Antennas are usually unsightly and should be hidden. Some manufacturers make ceiling panel antennas. When aesthetics are important, patch or panel antennas may be used rather than omni antennas. If possible, antennas should be hidden to avoid damage by children and also by adults who seek to damage the gear.

Appropriate Use

Use indoor antennas inside of buildings and outdoor antennas outside of buildings unless the indoor area is large enough to warrant use of an outdoor antenna. Outdoor antennas are most often sealed (to prevent water from entering the antenna element area) and their enclosures are made of plastics able to withstand extreme heat and cold. Indoor antennas are not made for outdoor use and generally cannot withstand the elements.

Orientation

Antenna orientation determines polarization, which was discussed previously as having a significant impact on signal reception. If an antenna is oriented with the electrical field parallel to the Earth's surface, then the clients (if the antenna is mounted to an access point) should have this same orientation for maximum reception. Or, both ends of the link should have the electrical field oriented perpendicular to the Earth's surface. The throughput of a bridge link will be drastically reduced if each end of the link does not have the same antenna orientation.

Alignment

Antenna alignment is sometimes critical, and other times is not. Some antennas have very wide horizontal and vertical beamwidths, allowing the administrator to aim two antennas in a building-to-building bridging environment in each other's general direction and achieve near-perfect reception. Alignment is more important when implementing long-distance bridging links using highly directional antennas. Wireless bridges come with alignment software that aids the administrator in optimizing antenna alignment for best reception, which reduces lost packets and high retry counts while maximizing signal strength. When using access points with omnidirectional or semidirectional antennas, proper alignment is usually a matter of covering the appropriate area such that wireless *clients* can connect in places where connectivity is required.

Safety

RF antennas, like other electrical devices, can be dangerous to implement and operate. The following guidelines should be observed whenever you or one of your associates is installing or otherwise working with RF antennas.

Follow the Manual

Carefully follow instructions provided with all antennas. Following all provided instructions will prevent personal injury and damage to the antenna. Most of the safety precautions found in antenna manufacturers' manuals are common sense.

Do Not Touch When Power is Applied

Never touch a high-gain antenna to any part of your body or point it toward your body while it is transmitting. The FCC allows very high amounts of RF power to be transmitted in the license-free bands when configuring a point-to-point link. Putting any part of your body in front of a 2.4 GHz highly directional antenna that is transmitting at high power is equivalent to putting your body in a microwave oven.

Use Professional Installers

For most elevated antenna installations, consider using a professional installer. Professional climbers and installers are trained in proper climbing safety, and they will be able to better install and secure your wireless LAN antenna if it is to be mounted on a pole, tower, or other type of elevated construction.

Keep Antennas Away from Metal Obstructions

Keep antennas away from metal obstructions such as heating and air-conditioning ducts, large ceiling trusses, building superstructures, and major power cabling runs. These types of metal obstructions create a significant amount of multipath. And, because metal obstructions reflect a large portion of the RF signal, if the signal is broadcast at high power, the reflected signal could be dangerous to bystanders.

Keep Antenna Towers Away from Power Lines

Antenna towers should be a safe distance from overhead power lines. The recommended safe distance is twice the antenna height or tower height (depending on which is applicable). It is not safe to have wireless LAN antennas near significant power sources because an electrical short between the power source and the wireless LAN could be dangerous to personnel working on the wireless LAN and would likely destroy the wireless LAN equipment.

Use Grounding Rods

Use quality grounding rods and follow the National Electrical Code and local electrical codes for proper outdoor antenna and tower grounding. Grounding rods should generally have less than 5 ohms to Earth ground after installation. The recommended minimum resistance is 2 ohms or less. Grounding rods can prevent damage to the wireless LAN equipment and might even save the life of anyone climbing on a tower when it is struck by lightning.

Maintenance

To prevent moisture entry into antenna cable, seal all external cable connectors using commercial products such as quality electrical tape or Coax-Seal. Moisture that has entered connectors and cabling is very difficult to remove. It is usually more economical to replace the cable and connectors than to remove the moisture. Connectors and cables with any amount of water will likely make the RF signal erratic and can cause significant signal degradation because the presence of water will change the cable's impedance, and consequently the voltage standing wave ratio (VSWR). You can purchase a test kit for testing cables and connectors for this purpose. The kit will typically consist of a power meter and an RF signal source.

When installing outdoor RF cabling, make sure to mount connectors facing downward and use drip loops in the cabling so that water will be directed away from points where moisture is likely to enter connections. Check seals periodically. Sealant materials can sometimes dry rot when exposed to the sun for long periods of time and may need replacing from time to time.

Activities

1. Which of the following steps should you take to avoid problems with outdoor antenna cabling? (Choose two.)

    a. Install connectors facing upward

    b. Use drip loops

    c. Check antennas periodically

    d. Seal connectors

2. Which of the following are safety considerations to keep in mind when installing wireless LAN antennas? (Choose two.)

    a. Antenna coverage

    b. Tower grounding

    c. Antenna grounding

    d. Antenna alignment

3. You have installed a point-to-point bridge link between buildings 5 miles apart. You installed a parabolic dish antenna on the side of each building, and aimed them appropriately. The link performed flawlessly when installed, but in the afternoons, when wind and rainstorms roll in, the link power drops significantly. What might you do to resolve this problem? (Choose two.)

    a. Replace the parabolic antennas with omnidirectional antennas

    b. Replace the parabolic antennas with grid antennas

    c. Mount the antennas on the building roofs

    d. Tightly secure the dish antennas

4. You are running a ground wire for an outdoor antenna installation. What is the recommended resistance you should measure between the existing ground rod and Earth ground?

    a. 2 ohms

    b. 5 ohms

    c. 7 ohms

    d. 9 ohms

5. Which statements best describe the 6 dB rule? (Choose two.)

    a. For every 6 dB increase in the intentional radiator, the signal range doubles.

    b. For every 6 dB in EIRP loss, the signal range is cut by one-fourth.

    c. For every 6 dB in intentional radiator gain, the signal range is doubled.

    d. For every 6 dB in EIRP gain, the signal range is doubled.

6. You are designing a wireless LAN that needs to cover a long, thin hallway. Off the hallway on each side are offices, each needing wireless network access. You want to limit coverage only to this floor. How might you best install the APs and antennas to properly cover the hallway and offices, while limiting the signal overreach beyond the specified area and using the minimum number of APs?

    a. Install a single access point in the middle of the hall and mount a high-gain dipole antenna at one end of the hallway.

    b. Install three APs and their attached omni antennas, one in the middle and one at each end of the hallway.

    c. Install a single access point in each end of the hallway and use high-gain parabolic dish antennas mounted on the end walls.

    d. Install an access point in each end of the hallway and use low-gain patch antennas mounted on the end walls.

7. As a result of your site survey, you determine that you need to install an antenna with very narrow horizontal and vertical beamwidths. Which one of the following antenna types meets these requirements?

    a. Dipole

    b. Dish

    c. Yagi

    d. Panel

8. What is the electromagnetic field plane parallel to the antenna element called?

   a. E-plane

   b. H-plane

   c. P-plane

   d. A-plane

9. Which of the following are concerns when installing highly directional grid antennas? (Choose two.)

   a. Wind loading

   b. Antenna aim

   c. Low gain

   d. Large coverage area

10. You want to wirelessly share your broadband connection with your neighbors living within a 300-meter radius of your home. What type of antenna would be the best choice for this application?

    a. High-gain parabolic

    b. High-gain Yagi

    c. High-gain patch

    d. High-gain omni

Extended Activities

1. Draw a diagram of one floor or building of your office or school. Based on the antenna coverage areas presented in this lesson, place and label the appropriate antenna type to provide complete wireless coverage. Ensure that your solution limits the RF signals to within the building walls.

2. Using a compatible wireless access point and PC card NIC, configure the access point and NIC to use the same service set ID (SSID), but not to use encryption (turn off Wired Equivalent Privacy [WEP]). Using the client utilities, measure the signal power level as you first change the access point's antenna polarity, then the client's. Did the signals change significantly? Separate the access point and client, and measure again. What did the signals do this time?

_____

_____

_____

_____

Lesson 2—PoE Devices

Power over Ethernet (PoE) is a method of delivering DC voltage to an access point, wireless bridge, or wireless workgroup bridge over the Cat5 Ethernet cable for the purpose of powering the unit. PoE is used when AC power receptacles are not available in the area where wireless LAN infrastructure devices are to be installed. The Ethernet cable is used to carry both the power and the data to the units. This lesson discusses common PoE options, compatibility between PoE devices, and PoE device features.

Objectives

At the end of this lesson you will be able to:

- Describe common PoE device options and features

- Explain components of PoE devices that determine their compatibility with others

- Explain how to install, configure, and manage PoE devices

 **Key Point**

PoE allows you to install wireless networking devices in remote locations far from AC power sources.

When to Use PoE

Consider a warehouse where the access points need to be installed in the ceiling of the building. The labor costs that would be incurred to install electrical outlets throughout the ceiling of the building to power the access points would be considerable. Hiring an electrician to do this type of work would be very expensive and time consuming. However, remember that Ethernet cables can only carry data reliably for 100 meters, so for any distance greater than 100 meters, PoE is not a viable solution. The PoE Installation Diagram illustrates how a PoE device provides power to an access point.

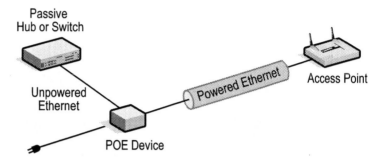

Passive
Hub or Switch

Unpowered
Ethernet

Powered Ethernet

Access Point

POE Device

PoE Installation

As you will learn in Site Surveying Fundamentals, the best locations for installing access points or bridges to ensure optimum RF coverage often have no power source. Therefore, PoE can be a great help in implementing a well-designed wireless network. Some manufacturers allow for only PoE to power up their devices, not standard AC power.

Common PoE Options

PoE devices are available in several types:

- Single-port DC voltage injectors
- Multiport DC voltage injectors
- Ethernet switches designed to inject DC voltage on each port on a given pair of pins

Although configuration and management is generally not necessary for a PoE device, there are some caveats to be aware of if and when you begin to implement PoE. First, there is no industry standard on implementation of PoE. This means that the manufacturers of PoE equipment have not worked together and agreed on how this equipment should interface with other devices. If you are using a wireless device such as an access point and will be powering it using PoE, it is recommended that you purchase the PoE device from the same manufacturer as the access point. This recommendation holds true for any device when considering powering with PoE.

Second, and similar in nature to the first caveat, is that the output voltage required to power a wireless LAN device differs from manufacturer to manufacturer. This caveat is another reason to use the same vendor's equipment when using PoE. When in doubt, ask the manufacturer or the vendor from whom the equipment was purchased.

Third, the unused pins used to carry the current over the Ethernet cable are not standardized. One manufacturer may carry power on pins 4 and 5, while another carries power on pins 7 and 8. If you connect a cable carrying power on pins 4 and 5 to an access point that does not accept power on those pins, the access point will not power up.

Finally, polarity is another issue to be resolved. In deciding on a standard implementation of PoE, most manufacturers choose which pin will be negative (ground) and which pin will be positive.

Single-Port DC Voltage Injectors

Access points and bridges that specify mandatory use of PoE include single-port DC voltage injectors for the purpose of powering a single unit. The Single-Port PoE Injector Diagram shows an example of a single-port DC voltage injector. These single-port injectors are acceptable when used with a small number of wireless infrastructure devices, but quickly become a burden, cluttering wiring closets, when building medium or large wireless networks.

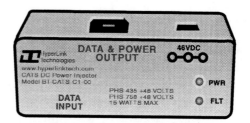

Single-Port PoE Injector

Multiport DC Voltage Injectors

Several manufacturers offer multiport injectors including 4-, 6-, or 12-port models. These models may be more economical or convenient for installations where many devices are to be powered through the Cat5 cable originating in a single wiring closet or from a single switch. Multiport DC voltage injectors typically operate in exactly the same manner as their single-port counterparts. The Multiport PoE Injector Diagram is an example of a multiport PoE injector. A multiport DC voltage injector looks like an Ethernet switch with twice as many ports. A multiport DC voltage injector is a pass-through device to which you connect the Ethernet switch (or hub) to the input port, and then connect the PoE client device to the output device, both by means of Cat5 cable. The PoE injector connects to an AC power source in the wiring closet. These multiport injectors are appropriate for medium-sized wireless network installations where up to 50 access points are required, but in large enterprise rollouts, even the most dense multiport DC voltage injectors combined with Ethernet hubs or switches can create a cluttered environment when installed in a wiring closet.

Multiport PoE Injector

Active Ethernet Switches

The next step up for large enterprise installations of access points is the implementation of active Ethernet switches. These devices incorporate DC voltage injection into the Ethernet switch itself allowing for large numbers of PoE devices without any additional hardware in the network. The Active Ethernet Switch Diagram is an example of an Active Ethernet switch. Wiring closets will not have any additional hardware other than the Ethernet switches that would already be there for a nonPoE network. Several manufacturers make these switches in many different configurations (numbers of ports). In many Active Ethernet switches, the switch can auto-sense PoE client devices on the network. If the switch does not detect a PoE device on the line, the DC voltage is switched off for that port.

Active Ethernet Switch

As you can see from the picture, an Active Ethernet switch looks no different from an ordinary Ethernet switch. The only difference is the added internal functionality of supplying DC voltage to each port. The PoE Using an Injector Diagram illustrates access points (APs) powered by an active switch and a power injector.

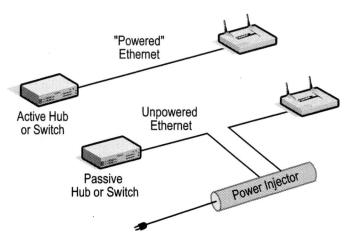

PoE Using an Injector

PoE Compatibility

Devices that are not "PoE Capable" can be converted to Power-over-Ethernet by way of a DC "picker" or "tap". These are sometimes called Active Ethernet "splitters". This device picks-off the DC voltage that has been injected into the CAT5 cable by the injector and makes it available to the equipment through the regular DC power jack.

In order to use Power-over-Ethernet one of the two following device combinations are needed:

(Injector) + (PoE capable device)

or

(Injector) + (nonPoE capable device) + (Picker)

Types of Injectors

There are two basic types of Injectors available: passive and fault protected. Each type is typically available in a variety of voltage levels and number of ports:

- **Passive injectors**—Passive injectors place a DC voltage onto a Cat5 cable. These devices provide no short-circuit or over-current protection.

- **Fault protected injectors**—Fault protected injectors provide continuous fault monitoring and protection to detect short circuits and over-current conditions in the Cat5 cable.

Types of Pickers/ Taps

Two basic types of pickers and taps are available: passive and regulated. A passive tap simply takes the voltage from the Cat5 cable and directs it to the equipment for direct connection. Therefore, if the injector injects 48 VDC (Volts of Direct Current), then 48 VDC will be produced at the output of the passive tap.

A regulated tap takes the voltage on the Cat5 cable and converts it to another voltage. Several standard regulated voltages are available (5 VDC, 6 VDC, and 12 VDC) allowing a wide variety of non-PoE equipment to be powered through the Cat5 cable.

Voltage and Pinout Standards

Although the IEEE and other industry groups are trying to create PoE standards, such as IEEE 802.3af, a definitive standard has yet to be introduced. At present, different equipment vendors use different PoE voltages and Cat5 pin configurations to provide the DC power. Therefore, it is important to select the appropriate PoE devices for each piece of equipment you plan to power through the Cat5 cable. The IEEE has standardized on the use of 48 VDC as the injected PoE voltage. The use of this higher voltage reduces the current flowing through the Cat5 cable.

Fault Protection   The primary purpose of fault protection is to protect the cable, the equipment, and the power supply in the event of a fault or short-circuit. During normal operation, a fault may never occur in the Cat5 cable. However, there are many ways a fault might be introduced into the Cat5 cable, including the following examples:

- The attached device may be totally incompatible with PoE and may have some nonstandard or defective connection that short-circuits the PoE conductors. At present, most nonPoE devices have no connection on the PoE pins.

- Incorrectly wired Cat5 cabling. Cut or crushed Cat5 cable, in which the insulation on one or more of the conductors have come in contact with each other or another conducting material.

During any fault condition, the fault-protection circuit shuts off the DC voltage injected onto the cable. Fault protection circuit operation varies from model to model. Some models continuously monitor the cable and restore power automatically once the fault is removed. Some models must be manually reset by pressing a reset button or cycling power.

Activities

1. When using PoE on a nonPoE compatible device, what other devices are needed? (Choose two.)

    a. Amplifier

    b. Injector

    c. Picker

    d. Regulator

2. What happens when an Active Ethernet switch fails to sense a PoE device on the line?

    a. It disables the port to which the line is attached.

    b. It rejects data traffic destined for that port.

    c. It adjusts the DC output to a lower voltage.

    d. It switches off DC power on that port.

3. You are cabling several wireless APs in the equipment closet. Each access point includes its own single-port injector. You are concerned about clutter in the wiring closet. Which of the following provides a means of powering each access point with PoE, while keeping closet clutter to a minimum? (Choose two.)

    a. Install AC outlets near each access point, and plug the access point directly into the AC outlet

    b. Bundle the injectors together, and strap them to the back of the patch panels

    c. Install a compatible multiport injector, and terminate each access point at the multiport injector

    d. Install a compatible Active Ethernet switch, and terminate each access point at the switch

4. Which one of the following statements concerning PoE equipment is true?

   a. PoE injectors will work with any vendor's access point, bridge, or workgroup bridge

   b. PoE power signals are reliable up to 100 meters on Cat 5 UTP cabling

   c. PoE is used to power wireless client devices, such as PC card or USB radios

   d. PoE devices will damage standard wired network devices, such as hubs or routers

5. Which statement describes a passive injector?

   a. Provides over-current protection

   b. Detects short circuits

   c. Turns off DC power on incorrectly wired Cat 5 cabling

   d. Places DC voltage onto a Cat 5 cable

6. Which voltage has the IEEE suggested for PoE devices?

   a. 12 VDC

   b. 24 VDC

   c. 32 VDC

   d. 48 VDC

Extended Activities

1. You are installing 10 wireless APs in a warehouse. Each is located far from an AC outlet, so you will use PoE to power them. Draw a network diagram showing how you would connect the access point cabling to a 12-port multiport injector.

2. Why do PoE equipment manufacturers pick pins 4, 5, 7, and/ or 8 for carrying power on Cat 5 cabling? Can you install a PoE injector on a full-duplex Ethernet switch port? Why or why not?

_____

_____

_____

_____

Lesson 3—Wireless LAN Accessories

When the time comes to connect all of your wireless LAN devices, you will need to purchase the appropriate cables and accessories that will maximize your throughput, minimize your signal loss, and, most importantly, allow you to make the connections correctly. This lesson discusses these different types of accessories and where they fit into a wireless LAN design.

Objectives

At the end of this lesson you will be able to:

- Describe common wireless LAN accessories

- Choose the appropriate accessory for the application

- Describe how to install, configure, and manage wireless LAN accessories

 **Key Point**

Wireless LAN accessories allow you to maximize your wireless LAN's performance and functionality.

Wireless LAN Accessory Types

Wireless LANs often require accessories in addition to the commonly found devices, antennas, and power sources discussed in previous reading. The following accessory types are discussed in this lesson:

- RF Amplifiers

- RF Attenuators

- Lightning Arrestors

- RF Connectors

- RF Cables

- RF Splitters

- RF Pigtail Adapters

- Frequency Converters

- Bandwidth Control Units

- Test Kits

Each of these devices is important to building a successful wireless LAN. Some items are used more than others because some are mandatory and others are optional. It is likely that an administrator will have to install and use all of these items multiple times while implementing and managing a wireless LAN.

RF Amplifiers

As its name suggests, a radio frequency (RF) amplifier is used to amplify, or increase the amplitude of an RF signal. This positive increase in power is called gain, and is measured in +dB. An amplifier is used to compensate for the loss incurred by the RF signal, either due to the distance between antennas or the length of cable from a wireless infrastructure device to its antenna. Most RF amplifiers used with wireless LANs are powered using DC voltage fed onto an RF cable with a DC injector near the RF signal source, such as an access point or bridge.

Sometimes the DC voltage used to power RF amplifiers is called "phantom voltage" because the RF amplifier seems to magically power up. A DC injector is powered using AC voltage from a wall outlet, so it might be located in a wiring closet. In this scenario, the RF cable carries both the radio frequency (RF) signal and the DC voltage necessary to power the in-line amplifier, which, in turn, boosts the RF signal amplitude. The Sample of a Fixed-Gain RF Amplifier Diagram shows an example of an RF amplifier (top), and a DC power injector (bottom).

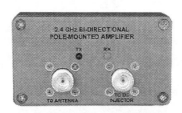

Copyright Young Design, Inc. 2002, YDI.com

Sample of a Fixed-Gain RF Amplifier

Two types of RF amplifiers are available: unidirectional and bidirectional. Unidirectional amplifiers compensate for the signal loss incurred over long RF cables by increasing the signal level before it is injected into the transmitting antenna. Bidirectional amplifiers boost the effective sensitivity of the receiving antenna by amplifying the received signal before it is fed into the access point, bridge, or client device. By locating the amplifier as close to the antenna as possible, a bidirectional amplifier will compensate for cable losses that might be significant at the signal levels typically seen by receiving antennas. Most amplifiers used with wireless LANs are bidirectional.

Common Options

Before you ever get to a point of deciding which amplifier to purchase, you should already know the amplifier specification requirements. Once you know the impedance (ohms), gain (dB), frequency response (range in GHz), voltage standing wave ratio (VSWR), input (mW or dBm), and output (mW or dBm) specifications, you are ready to select an RF amplifier.

Frequency response is likely the first criteria you determine. If a wireless LAN uses the 5-GHz frequency spectrum, an amplifier that operates only in the 2.4 GHz frequency spectrum will not work. Determine how much gain, input, and output power is required by performing the necessary RF math calculations. The amplifier should match impedances with all of the other wireless LAN hardware between the transmitter and the antenna. Generally, wireless LAN components have an impedance of 50 ohms; however, it is always a good idea to check the impedance of every component on a wireless LAN.

The amplifier must be connected into the network; therefore, an amplifier should be chosen with the same kinds of connectors as the cables and/or antennas to which the amplifier will be connected. Typically, RF amplifiers have either subminiature type A (SMA) or N-Type connectors. SMA and N-Type connectors perform well and are widely used.

Note: Make sure that the amplifier you purchase comes with a calibration report and certificate. When the unit is new, check to see if the amplifier meets the manufacturer's stated specifications prior to implementing it in your network. It is further recommended that you store the calibration report and certificate in a proper location in case the report is ever needed.

Also, RF amplifiers should be calibrated once per year to ensure continued accuracy and performance, but this may not be feasible in a network that requires 100 percent up time.

Configuration and Management

RF amplifiers used with wireless LANs are installed in series with the main signal path as illustrated on the RF Amplifier Placement in the Wireless LAN System Diagram. Amplifiers are typically mounted to a solid surface by inserting screws inserted through flange plates. Configuration of an RF amplifier is not required.

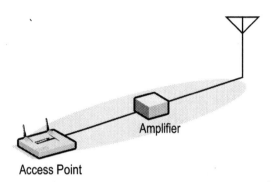

RF Amplifier Placement in the Wireless LAN System

Note: Variable amplifiers are not typically used in wireless LAN configurations because the settings could inadvertently be changed, resulting in damage to the antenna or a violation of FCC rules governing output power in the industrial scientific medical (ISM) or unlicensed national information infrastructure (UNII) bands. Fixed, linear RF amplifiers are recommended, and the RF calculations should be done ahead of time to make sure the RF signal strength meets your application's needs and is within FCC guidelines. The manufacturer usually performs these calculations when it sells the amplifier as part of an FCC-certified system.

Special Stipulations

The FCC's CFR 15.204 states that every system operating in the ISM and UNII bands must be certified as a complete system and given a certification number by the FCC. Accompanying each system should be a certificate that lists the pieces of equipment and the FCC identifiers that are permitted for use with that wireless LAN system. All pieces of the wireless LAN setup that are used must be listed in the certificate. Understanding this requirement becomes especially crucial when dealing with amplifiers. A "system" is defined as the transmitting device, the cabling, connectors, amplifiers, attenuators, splitters, and the antenna. Manufacturers obtain FCC approval or "certification" of their hardware to enable end users to purchase radio devices and antennas and use them as a system without contacting the FCC for testing and certification. When additional devices, such as amplifiers, are added into a system, the manufacturer's certification no longer applies and a user must obtain his own certification, at a cost of as much as $12,000.00 per system. An answer to this solution might be to purchase an FCC-certified system from a reputable vendor that meets the requirements of the wireless network.

CFR 15.204 does not allow an amplifier to be marketed or sold when it is not part of a "certified" system. The FCC maintains a database of certified systems and companies holding these certifications. You can search for the database on the FCC's web site: **http://www.fcc.gov.**

The FCC meticulously maintains this site. Updates usually occur every week, at a minimum. End users are liable for violations of FCC rules while they use the equipment. FCC violations may result in fines of $27,500 - $1,200,000 per violation. The FCC typically allows a violator a brief period (approximately 10 days) to correct a problem and report the corrective action. It is not uncommon for the FCC to audit a wireless Internet service provider (WISP) looking for certified systems infractions.

Many manufacturers do not produce amplifiers to be used with their systems. For this reason, some companies produce amplifiers (but not wireless LAN hardware) that obtain FCC certification of an entire wireless LAN system that combines their amplifiers and another vendor's wireless LAN hardware. Be careful about the type of amplifiers you buy because some amplifiers cause the FCC to certify systems as being able to use DSSS channels 2–10 or 3–9, instead of 1–11, as with an unamplified system. This is due to how the RF signal is amplified and bleeds over into the licensed RF frequency spectrum outside of the ISM or UNII bands.

The FCC's CFR 15.203 says that installers are responsible for ensuring that intentional radiators are used with authorized antennas. Antennas may be made such that they can be repaired, but not attached to noncertified, matching intentional radiators.

One common concern regarding CFR 15.204 is that one manufacturer's antennas may not be used with another manufacturer's intentional radiator (bridge, PC Card, or access point, for example) without FCC system certification. This ruling directly affects individuals who connect a Pringles can antenna to a PC Card radio for the purpose of "war driving," or intercepting wireless radio signals from outside a facility.

When you begin purchasing an RF amplifier to use as part of a wireless LAN, ask for a copy of the FCC certification documenting use of the amplifier before you complete the purchase. There are two classes of changes that can be made to an FCC certification. First is a class I change. This type of change can be made by the manufacturer who may document a change that has no negative affect on RF propagation or signal density (increasing interference with other systems in your immediate environment). The manufacturer notes the change on the FCC certificate, and then writes a brief synopsis on what the change involved and why it had no negative affect. A class II change is a change that negatively affects RF propagation or signal density and requires the system to be recertified by the FCC.

RF Attenuators

An RF attenuator is a device that causes precisely measured loss (in –dB) in an RF signal. An amplifier increases the RF signal, and an attenuator decreases it. Why would you need or want to decrease your RF signal? Consider a case when an access point has a fixed output of 100mW, and the only antenna available is an omnidirectional antenna with +20 dBi gain. Using this equipment together violates FCC rules for power output; thus, an attenuator could be added to decrease the RF signal down to 30mW before it entered the antenna. This configuration would put the power output within FCC parameters. However, as mentioned in the previous section on RF amplifiers, you cannot simply install any RF attenuator in a circuit. The attenuator must be a component of an FCC-certified system. Therefore, if you must alter the antenna output of an FCC-certified system, you must replace it with another certified system. The Sample of a Fixed-Loss RF Attenuator Diagram shows examples of fixed-loss RF attenuators with BNC connectors (left) and Subminiature Type A (SMA) connectors (right). The Sample of an RF Step Attenuator (Variable-Loss) Diagram shows an example of an RF step attenuator.

Sample of a Fixed-Loss RF Attenuator

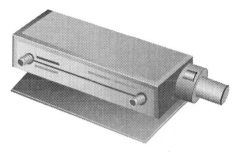

Sample of an RF Step Attenuator (Variable-Loss)

Common Options   RF attenuators are available as either fixed-loss or variable-loss. Like variable amplifiers, variable attenuators allow administrators to precisely configure the amount of loss caused in the RF signal. Variable RF attenuators are not used in wireless LAN systems due to the FCC's regulations on certified systems. They are typically used in site surveys to determine antenna gain, necessity of amplifiers, and so forth.

Note: Variable attenuators are not recommended for final configurations because the settings can inadvertently be changed, resulting in damage to the antenna or receiving equipment. Fixed RF attenuators are recommended where the RF calculations are done ahead of time to ensure the signals are within FCC guidelines. Once the necessary attenuation is calculated, the appropriate fixed-loss attenuator can be purchased. Variable attenuators are mostly used during site surveying to aid in coverage pattern discovery.

When determining what kind of attenuator is required, consider the similar items as when choosing an RF amplifier, as shown on the RF Attenuator Placement in a Wireless LAN Diagram. The type of attenuator (fixed-loss or variable-loss), impedance, ratings (input power, loss, and frequency response), and connector types should all be part of the decision-making process.

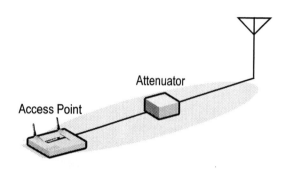

RF Attenuator Placement in a Wireless LAN

Note: All attenuators should come with a calibration report and certificate, and should be calibrated once per year thereafter to ensure proper operation and continued performance. In some production environments, taking the network down to perform these types of tests may not be feasible. Thus, it is best to ensure that the attenuator meets the manufacturer's specifications prior to installation.

Configuration and Management

The RF Attenuator Placement in a Wireless LAN Diagram shows the proper placement in a wireless LAN for an RF attenuator, which is directly in series with the main signal path. Fixed, coaxial attenuators are connected directly between any two connection points between the transmitter and the antenna. For example, a fixed, coaxial antenna might be connected directly on the output of an access point, at the input to the antenna, or anywhere between these two points if multiple RF cables are used.

Configuration of RF attenuators is not required unless a variable attenuator is used; in which case, the amount of attenuation required is configured according to tests you are performing. Configuration instructions for attenuators are included in the manufacturers' user manuals, but usually the configuration method consists only of turning a dial. Again, the FCC will not likely certify a system that includes a variable attenuator.

Lightning Arrestors

Lightning arrestors shunt (turn aside or move to an alternate course) lightning-induced transient currents into the Earth ground. Transient currents are electrical currents created when lightning strikes a nearby object or area. Lightning arrestors protect wireless LAN hardware, such as access points, bridges, and workgroup bridges, attached to coaxial transmission lines. Coaxial transmission lines are susceptible to surges from nearby lightning strikes.

Note: One common misconception about lightning arrestors is that they are installed to protect against a direct lightning strike. If a bolt of lightning strikes a wireless LAN antenna with the best lightning arrestor on the market, the antenna will be destroyed and the wireless LAN will probably be damaged. A lightning arrestor is not meant to withstand a direct lightning strike or protect your network from such a strike.

A lightning arrestor can generally shunt (redirect) surges of up to 5000 Amperes at up to 50 Volts. Lightning arrestors function as follows:

1. Lightning strikes a nearby object.

2. Transient currents induce into an antenna or RF transmission line.

3. The lightning arrestor senses these currents and immediately ionizes the gases held internally to cause a short (a path of almost no resistance) directly to Earth ground.

The Sample Lightning Arrestors Diagram shows some types of lightning arrestors. The one on the right shunts transient currents to ground by way of the physical characteristics of the lightning arrestor itself, while allowing the appropriate RF signals to pass.

Copyright Young Design, Inc. 2002, YDI.com

Sample Lightning Arrestors

The Lightning Arrestor Installed on a Network Diagram shows how a lightning arrestor is installed on a wireless LAN. When an object is struck by lightning, an electric field is built around that object for just an instant. When the lightning ceases to induce electricity into the object, the field collapses. When the field collapses, it induces high amounts of current into nearby objects, which are, in this case, the wireless LAN antenna or coaxial transmission line. Lightning is discharged as a direct current (DC) pulse, but then causes an alternating current (AC) component to be formed, resonating as high as 1 GHz. However, most of the power is dissipated from DC to 10 Mhz.

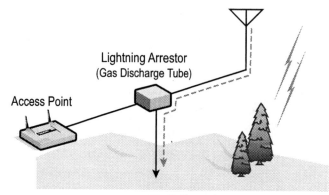

Lightning Arrestor Installed On a Network

Common Options

There are few options on a lightning arrestor, and the cost is between $50 and $150 for any brand. However, the following attributes should be considered for any lightning arrestor that is purchased:

- **IEEE Standards**—Most lightning arrestors are able to trigger a short to Earth ground in under 2 microseconds (μS), but the IEEE specifies that this process should happen in no more than 8 μS. It is very important that the lightning arrestor you choose at least meet the IEEE standard.

- **Reusability**—Some lightning arrestors are reusable after a lightning strike, and some are not. It is more cost effective to own an arrestor that can be used a number of times. Some reusable models have replaceable gas discharge tube elements that are cheaper to replace than the entire lightning arrestor. Other models may have physical characteristics that allow the lightning arrestor to do its job properly multiple times with no replaceable parts.

- **Voltage Breakdown**—Some lightning arrestors support passing DC voltage for powering RF amplifiers, and others do not. If you plan to place an RF amplifier closer to the antenna than the lightning arrestor, the lightning arrestor should be able to pass the DC voltage. The gas tube breakdown voltage (the voltage at which the arrestor begins shorting current to ground) should be higher than the voltage required to operate inline RF amplifiers. It is suggested that you place lightning arrestors as the last component on the RF transmission line, before the antenna, so they can protect amplifiers, attenuators, and the bridge or access point.

- **Connector Types**—Make sure the connector types of the lightning arrestor you choose match those on the cable you plan to use on your wireless LAN. If they do not match, adapter connectors will have to be used, inserting more loss into the RF circuit than is necessary.

- **Frequency**—The frequency response specification of the lightning arrestor should be at least as high as the highest frequency used in a wireless LAN. For example, if you are using only a 2.4 GHz wireless LAN, a lightning arrestor that is specified for use at up to 3 GHz is best.

- **Impedance**—The impedance of an arrestor should match all the other devices in the circuit between the transmitter and the antenna. Impedance is 50 ohms in most wireless LANs.

- **Insertion Loss**—The insertion loss should be significantly low (perhaps around 0.1 dB) to prevent high RF signal amplitude loss as the signal passes through the arrestor.

- **VSWR Rating**—The VSWR rating of a good quality lightning arrestor will be around 1.1:1, but some may be as high as 1.5:1. Because reflected voltage degrades the main RF signal, the lower the ratio of the device, the better.

- **Warranty**—Regardless of the quality of a lightning arrestor, the unit can malfunction. Seek a manufacturer that offers a good warranty on their lightning arrestors. Some manufacturers offer a highly desirable "no matter what" type of warranty.

Configuration and Maintenance

No configuration is necessary for a lightning arrestor. Lightning arrestors are installed in series with the main RF signal path, and the grounding connection should be attached to an Earth ground with a measurable resistance of 5 ohms or less. It is recommended that you test an Earth ground connection with an appropriate Earth ground resistance tester before deciding that the installation of the lightning arrestor is satisfactory. Make it a point, along with other periodic maintenance tasks, to check the Earth ground resistance and the gas discharge tube regularly.

RF Splitters

An RF Splitter is a device that has a single input connector and multiple output connectors. An RF Splitter splits a single signal into multiple independent RF signals. Use of splitters in everyday implementations of wireless LANs is not recommended. Sometimes two 120-degree panel antennas or two 90-degree panel antennas may be combined with a splitter and equal-length cables when the antennas are pointing in opposite directions. This configuration will produce a bidirectional coverage area, which may be ideal for covering the area along a river or major highway. Back-to-back 90 degree panels may be separated by as little as 10 inches or as much as 40 inches on either side of the mast or tower. Each panel in this configuration may have a mechanical down tilt; the resultant gain in each of the main radiation lobes is reduced by 3 to 4 dB.

When installing an RF splitter, the input connector should always face the source of the RF signal. The output connectors (sometimes called "taps") are connected facing the destination of the RF signal (the antenna). The Sample RF Splitters Diagram shows two examples of RF splitters. The RF Splitter Installed on a Network Diagram illustrates how an RF splitter is used in a wireless LAN installation.

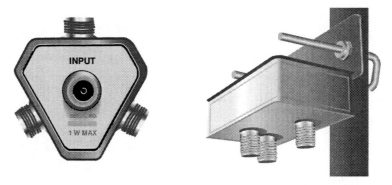

Sample RF Splitters

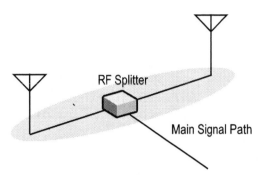

RF Splitter Installed on a Network

Splitters may be used to keep track of power output on a wireless LAN link. By hooking a power meter to one output of the splitter and the RF antenna to the other, an administrator can actively monitor the output at any given time. In this scenario, the power meter, the antenna, and the splitter must all have equal impedance. Although it is an uncommon practice, removing the power meter from one output of the splitter and replacing it with a 50-ohm dummy load allows an administrator to move the power meter from one connection point to another throughout the wireless LAN while making output power measurements.

Power splitters are yet another device that can be used as part of a wireless LAN. Keep in mind that the splitter must be included as part of a certified system if used in your wireless LAN.

Choosing an RF Splitter

Below is a list of things to consider when choosing an RF splitter:

- **Insertion Loss**—Low insertion loss (loss incurred by simply introducing a splitter into a circuit) is necessary because simply putting the splitter in the RF circuit can cause a significant RF signal amplitude decrease. Insertion loss of 0.5 dB or less is considered good for an RF splitter.

Note: Do not confuse insertion loss with the loss of amplitude incurred between the input connector and any output connector (called "through loss"). The number of connectors on an RF splitter determines the number of ways (speaking in terms of power division) that the RF amplitude will split. A two-way splitter should have a 3 to 4 dB loss between the input connector and either output connector. Loss higher than this can be attributed either to insertion loss (which is added to through loss when measured) or to inaccuracies in the splitter's ability to divide the power between output connectors.

- **Frequency Response**—The frequency response specification of a splitter should be at least as high as the highest frequency used in the wireless LAN. For example, if you were using only a 2.4 GHz wireless LAN, a splitter that is specified for use at up to 3 GHz would be best.

- **Impedance**—The impedance of the splitter, usually 50 ohms in wireless LANs, should match all of the other devices in the circuit between the transmitter and the antenna.

- **VSWR Rating**—As with many other RF devices, VSWR ratings should be as close to 1:1 as possible. Typical VSWR ratings on RF splitters are less than 1.5:1. Low VSWR ratings on splitters are much more critical than on many other devices in an RF system, because reflected RF power in a splitter may be reflected in multiple directions inside the splitter, affecting both the splitter input signal and all splitter output signals.

- **High Isolation Impedance**—High isolation impedance between ports on an RF splitter is important for several reasons. First, a load on one output port should not affect the output power on another output port of the splitter. Second, a signal arriving into the output port of a splitter (such as the received RF signal) should be directed to the input port rather than to another output port. These requirements are accomplished through high impedance between output connectors. Typical isolation (resistance causing separation) is 20 dB or more between ports.

- **Power Ratings**—Splitters are rated for power input maximums, which means that the amount of power you can feed into your splitter is limited. Exceeding the manufacturer's power rating will result in damage to the RF splitter.

- **Connector Types**—RF splitters generally have N-type or SMA connectors. It is very important to purchase a splitter with the same connector types as the cable being used. Doing so cuts down on adapter connectors, which reduce RF signal amplitude. This knowledge is especially important when using splitters, because splitters already cut the signal amplitude in an RF system.

- **Calibration Report**—All RF splitters should come with a calibration report that shows insertion loss, frequency response, through loss at each connector, and so forth. Having splitters calibrated once per year is recommended so that the administrator will know before initial installation whether or not the splitter meets the manufacturer's specifications. Continued calibration requires taking the wireless LAN off line for an extended period of time, and may not be practical in some network environments.

- **Mounting**—Mounting an RF splitter is usually a matter of putting screws through the flange plates into whatever surface the splitter will be mounted. Some models come with pole-mounting hardware using "U" bolts, mounting plates, and standard-sized nuts. Depending on the manufacturer, the splitter might be weatherproof, which means it can be mounted outside on a pole without fear of water causing problems. When this is the case, be sure to seal cable connections and use drip loops.

- **DC Voltage Passing**—Some RF splitters have the option of passing the required DC voltage to all output ports in parallel. This feature is helpful when there are RF amplifiers, which power internal circuitry with DC voltage originating from a DC voltage injector in a wiring closet, located on the output of each splitter port.

RF Connectors

RF connectors are specific types of connection devices used to connect cables to devices or devices to devices. Traditionally, N, F, SMA, BNC, and TNC connectors (or derivatives) have been used for RF connectors on wireless LANs.

In 1994, the FCC and Canadian DOC (Department of Communications now called "Industry Canada") ruled that connectors for use with wireless LAN devices should be proprietary between manufacturers. For this reason, many variations on each connector type exist, such as:

- N-type
- Reverse polarity N-type
- Reverse threaded N-type

The Sample N-type and SMA Connectors Diagram illustrates the N and SMA type connectors.

Sample N-Type and SMA Connectors

Choosing an RF Connector

Five things should be considered when purchasing and installing any RF connector, and they are similar in nature to the criteria for choosing RF amplifiers and attenuators. The five considerations are as follows:

1. The RF connector should match the impedance of all other wireless LAN components (generally 50 ohms). Because center-pin sizing will prevent components from properly fitting together, this is normally not a problem even when you purchase like connectors with different impedances.

2. Know how much insertion loss each connector inserted into the signal path causes. The amount of loss caused will factor into your calculations for signal strength required and distance allowed.

3. Know the upper frequency limit (frequency response) speci-fied for the particular connectors. This point will be very important as 5-GHz wireless LANs become more and more common. Some connectors are rated only as high as 3 GHz, which is fine for use with 2.4 GHz wireless LANs, but will not work for 5 GHz wireless LANs. Some connectors are rated only up to 1 GHz and will not work with wireless LANs, except for legacy 900 MHz wireless LANs.

4. Beware of bad quality connectors. First, always consider pur-chasing from a reputable company. Second, purchase only high-quality connectors made by name-brand manufacturers. Being particular about your purchase will help eliminate many prob-lems with sporadic RF signals, VSWR, and bad connections.

5. Make sure you know both the type of connector (N, F, SMA, etc.) that you need and the sex of the connector. Connectors come in male and female. Male connectors have a center pin, and female connectors have a center receptacle.

RF Cables

In the same manner that you must choose the proper cables for your 10 Gbps wired infrastructure backbone, you must choose the proper cables for connecting an antenna to an access point or wireless bridge. Below are some criteria to consider when choos-ing the proper cables for your wireless network:

•   Cables introduce loss into a wireless LAN, so make sure the shortest cable length possible is used.

•   Plan to purchase pre-cut lengths of cable with pre-installed connectors. Doing so minimizes the possibility of bad con-nections between the connector and the cable. Professional manufacturing practices are almost always superior to cables manufactured by untrained individuals.

•   Look for the lowest loss cable available at your particular price range (the lower the loss, the more expensive the cable). Cables are typically rated for loss in dB/100-feet. The Coaxial Cable Attenuation Ratings (in dB/foot at x MHz) Table lists the loss that is introduced by adding a given manufacturer's cables to a wireless LAN.

Coaxial Cable Attenuation Ratings (in dB/foot at x MHz)

LMR CABLE	30	50	150	220	450	900	1500	1800	2000	2500
100A	3.9	5.1	8.9	10.9	15.8	22.8	30.1	33.2	35.2	39.8
195	2.0	2.6	4.4	5.4	7.8	11.1	14.5	16.0	16.9	19.0
200	1.8	2.3	4.0	4.8	7.0	9.9	12.9	14.2	15.0	16.9
240	1.3	1.7	3.0	3.7	5.3	7.6	9.9	10.9	11.5	12.9
300	1.1	1.4	2.4	2.9	4.2	6.1	7.9	8.7	9.2	10.4
400	0.7	0.9	1.5	1.9	2.7	3.9	5.1	5.7	6.0	6.8
400UF	0.8	1.1	1.7	2.2	3.1	4.5	5.9	6.6	6.9	7.8
500	0.54	.70	1.2	1.5	2.2	3.1	4.1	4.6	4.8	5.5
600	0.42	.55	1.0	1.2	1.7	2.5	3.3	3.7	3.9	4.4
600UF	0.48	.63	1.15	1.4	2.0	2.9	3.8	4.3	4.5	5.1
900	0.29	0.37	0.66	0.80	1.17	1.70	2.24	2.48	2.63	2.98
1200	0.21	0.27	0.48	0.59	0.89	1.3	1.7	1.9	2.0	2.3
1700	0.15	0.19	0.35	0.43	0.63	0.94	1.3	1.4	1.5	1.7

- Purchase cable that has the same impedance as all of your other wireless LAN components (usually 50 ohms).

- Consider the frequency response of the cable as a primary decision factor in your purchase. With 2.4 GHz wireless LANs, a cable with a rating of at least 2.5 GHz should be used. With 5 GHz wireless LANs, a cable with a rating of at least 6 GHz should be used.

- You may have to use an extension cable when an access point and its remote antenna are far apart (such as in an outdoor installation). In this case, be aware that connectors drop ~0.25dB and cable loss can be very significant (depending on the cable type used). Use of longer Cat5 cable can sometimes remedy the situation by allowing the access point to be moved closer to the antenna. RG-58 cable should never be used for extension cables because of its poor frequency response. LMR, Heliax, and other appropriate high-frequency cable should be used for extensions.

If the FCC performs an inspection on your wireless LAN (which it is authorized to do at any time), it will note the manufacturer, model number, length, and type of connectors on your RF cable. This information should be documented in your system's FCC certificate.

Note: Three major manufacturers build RF cables used with wireless LANs. These are Andrew, Times Microwave, and Belden. Andrew's Heliax cable, Times Microwave's LMR, and Belden's RF-series are all popular in the wireless LAN industry. LMR cable has become somewhat of an industry standard in the same way Xerox became known for copiers. Sometimes the term "LMR" is used in place of "RF cable" in the same way "Xerox" is used in place of "copy."

RF "Pigtail" Adapter Cable

Pigtail adapter cables are used to connect cables that have industry-standard connectors to manufacturer's wireless LAN equipment. Pigtails adapt proprietary connectors to industry standard connectors such as N-type and SMA connectors. One end of the pigtail cable is the proprietary connector, and the other end is the industry-standard connector. The Sample RF "Pigtail" Adapter Diagram shows an example of a pigtail cable.

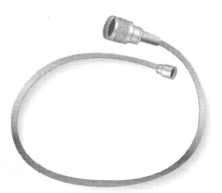

Sample RF "Pigtail" Adapter

The DOC and FCC ruling of June 23, 1994, stated that connectors manufactured after June 23, 1994 must be manufactured with proprietary antenna connectors. The 1994 rule was intended to discourage use of amplifiers, high-gain antennas, or other means of significantly increasing RF radiation. The rules are further intended to discourage "home brew" systems which are installed by inexperienced users and which (either accidentally or intentionally) do not comply with FCC regulations for use in the ISM band.

Since this rule was enacted, consumers have had to obtain proprietary connectors from manufacturers to connect to an industry standard connector. Third party manufacturers have begun custom making these adapter cables (called "pigtails") and selling them inexpensively on the open market. Keep in mind that the FCC's CFR 15.204 does not allow "home brew" systems of any kind. All systems must be certified, and a system is defined as an intentional radiator, an antenna, and everything in between. Thus, individuals using security utilities, such as NetStumbler, with a Pringles can antenna, are violating this FCC regulation. Any pigtails or antennas used with a wireless LAN in the ISM or UNII bands must be part of a certified system and documented by the FCC.

Frequency Converters

Frequency converters are used for converting one frequency range to another for the purpose of decongesting a frequency band. Suppose that many companies located in the same multitenant office building have wireless LANs, a common occurrence. Each of these companies wants building-to-building wireless connectivity with an adjacent building, because each has offices in the other building. It is easy to see that only three companies will be able to communicate wirelessly between buildings, due to the limited number of nonoverlapping 802.11b wireless LAN channels available. In this example, a frequency converter may be deployed to convert the existing 2.4GHz wireless equipment to a less congested band, such as the 5.8GHz upper UNII band, for this wireless bridge segment. The Sample Frequency Converter Diagram illustrates an example of a frequency converter.

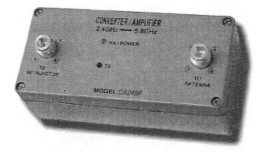

Copyright Young Design, Inc. 2002, YDI.com

Sample Frequency Converter

Proper antennas and cables must be used when employing a frequency converter, due to both antennas and cables having limited frequency response. This measure can be a very economical solution in a congested area. The alternative would be to replace all wireless LAN hardware with new 5GHz hardware. The Using a Frequency Converter Diagram shows how a frequency converter is installed in a wireless LAN configuration.

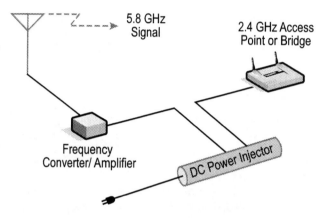

Using a Frequency Converter

Bandwidth Control Units

Wireless LANs are a shared medium with very low throughput compared with today's wired LAN technologies. For this reason, bandwidth on wireless LANs must be conserved and protected, especially in outdoor environments such as would be found with WISPs. It is recommended that bandwidth be controlled to ensure that users have a reliable and consistent connectivity experience and receive what they have purchased. With indoor wireless LAN installations, it is not as common to use a Bandwidth Control Unit (BCU) because many users expect to have the same experience they had on a wired LAN. This simply is not feasible considering the extreme bandwidth differences. However, administrators strive to give indoor LAN users as much bandwidth as possible by not overloading access points. In a wireless LAN, the BCU is placed between the access point or bridge and the network, as shown on the Using a Bandwidth Control Unit Diagram.

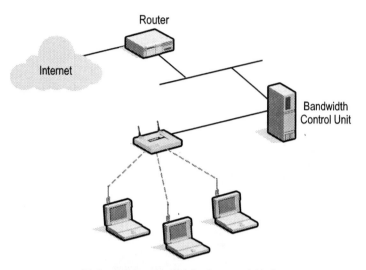

Using a Bandwidth Control Unit

BCUs typically work by filtering on MAC addresses in order to drop each user into a preassigned queue. Each queue has particular properties, such as upstream and downstream bandwidth. Multiple users might be put into the same queue. This allows for precise bandwidth control and accounting per user. BCUs are managed through various software packages, such as the one shown on the Manager Application for a BCU Diagram.

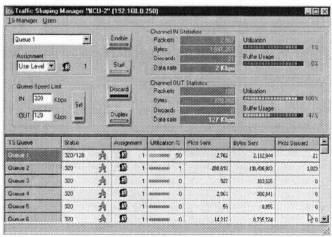

Copyright Young Design, Inc. 2002, YDI.com

Manager Application for a BCU

Test Kits

Many types of test kits are on the market. One of the most valuable types of test kits in the wireless LAN industry is one used for testing cables and connectors. The kit might also consist of an RF signal generator and a through-line power meter. The signal generator can be hooked directly to the power meter to get a baseline measurement. A baseline measurement can be determined when putting cables and connectors between the signal generator and the power meter, if the generator and meter meet the manufacturer's specifications, and if they are intermittent. The connections on cables can become worn and loose, making a bad or intermittent bad connection. They can also take on water, which is highly detrimental to their RF characteristics. It is important to test cables and connectors before deployment and as regularly as possible thereafter. The Sample Test Kit Diagram illustrates one type of RF test kit.

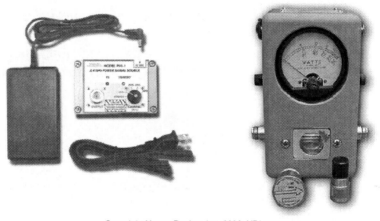

Sample Test Kit

Activities

1. How is coaxial antenna cable typically rated for loss?

   a. dB/100 feet

   b. dBm/100 feet

   c. dB/100 meters

   d. dB/1000 feet

2. Which of the following are important criteria to consider when choosing RF cabling? (Choose three.)

   a. The cables should come in kit form so you can build your own.

   b. Know the connector type you need on each end of the cable.

   c. Purchase cable with the appropriate frequency response.

   d. Cables should match the impedance of the other components.

3. How frequently should you calibrate an RF splitter if the network does not require 100 percent up time?

   a. Once a year

   b. Every six months

   c. Monthly

   d. Every 5 years

4. How much through loss is normally between a two-way splitter's input and output ports?

   a. .5dB

   b. 1dB

   c. 3dB

   d. 5dB

5. Which term describes the loss incurred by introducing an item into an RF circuit?

   a. VSWR

   b. RF loss

   c. Impedance loss

   d. Insertion loss

6. Which statements are true concerning lightning arrestors installed in wireless LANs? (Choose two.)

   a. The breakdown voltage should be less than the voltage used to operate inline RF amplifiers.

   b. They will not pass DC voltages.

   c. The IEEE states that they must short to ground in less than 2us.

   d. They must have a frequency response as high as the highest RF frequency used.

7. Which types of RF amplifiers and attenuators are recommended for use with wireless LANs?

   a. Fixed attenuators

   b. Fixed amplifiers

   c. Variable attenuators

   d. Variable amplifiers

8. You recently installed a wireless network on top of your school's administration building. The access point radio transmits at a fixed 80mW, and you installed a high-gain, +20dB omnidirectional antenna to ensure that the RF signal covers the entire campus. You compute the EIRP and determine that you have exceeded the FCC output power rules. You want to install an RF attenuator to reduce the output power to the FCC allowed maximum for point-to-multipoint links. To meet FCC rules, what size fixed RF attenuator should be included with the new, certified system?

   e. -3dB

   f. –6dB

   g. –10dB

   h. –16dB

9. What effect will using poor quality connectors have on RF signals? (Choose two.)

   a. Sporadic quality

   b. VSWR

   c. Free space path loss

   d. Incorrect polarity

10. You operate a wireless LAN and notice that some of your wireless users tend to use more of the network's resources than others. Further investigation shows that these users spend a good deal of time downloading large audio and video files over the Internet, which causes congestion on the wireless network segment. Which one of the following devices can you install in the network to control how much of the network resources each user may use?

    a.   Bandwidth control unit

    b.   Frequency converter

    c.   RF splitter

    d.   Active Ethernet switch

Extended Activities

1. FCC rules state that a vendor cannot sell RF amplifiers unless they are sold as part of an FCC-certified system. Research wireless vendors for complete, FCC-certified systems. What components do they include? What FCC rule states this?

_____

_____

_____

_____

2. Using a wireless access point and compatible NIC, attach external antennas to each. Be aware of such issues as VSWR, insertion loss, and so forth. Use your client utilities to measure and compare gain (or loss) the signals experience in each configuration.

Summary

This unit discussed a basic element of the devices that enable access points, bridges, PC cards, and other wireless devices to communicate: antennas. Several different items used to connect antennas to other wireless LAN hardware were reviewed. Antennas are most often used to increase the range of wireless LAN systems; proper antenna selection can also enhance the security of a wireless LAN. All wireless LAN antennas fall into three general categories: omnidirectional, semidirectional, and highly directional. This unit described the attributes of each category and the proper methods for installing each kind of antenna.

This unit also described the following wireless LAN accessories: RF amplifiers, RF attenuators, and lightening arrestors. Knowing these devices' uses, specifications, and effects on RF signal strength is essential for building a functional wireless LAN. PoE, an important technology in today's wireless networks that has spawned new product lines and standards, was also discussed.

Unit 5 Quiz

1. Properly aligning two wireless bridges will optimize their throughput. This statement is:

   a. Always true

   b. Always false

   c. Depends on the manufacturer

2. In a small warehouse installation, you must provide the greatest coverage area possible for the users inside the warehouse. The warehouse is free from tall obstructions, such as shelving, but has a high ceiling. You have decided to use a low-gain omnidirectional antenna to achieve your goal. For the best coverage area, where should the antenna be installed?

   a. In the center of the building on the roof

   b. In the center of the building on the ceiling

   c. In one of the corners of the building

   d. On one of the walls of the building

3. When purchasing RF connectors, which of the following should be considered when making your decision? (Choose three.)

   a. Impedance

   b. Insertion loss

   c. Gain

   d. Maximum frequency allowed

4. You have been hired as a consultant to install a wireless LAN that will connect only two buildings that are 1.5 miles (2.5 km) apart at 11 Mbps. Which of the following antennas could you use? (Choose two.)

   a. Omnidirectional

   b. High-gain Dipole

   c. High-gain Yagi

   d. Parabolic dish

5. You have been hired as a consultant to install a wireless LAN that will connect two buildings that are 10 miles (16.7 km) apart. In this particular area, wind gusts are a problem. Which one of the following antennas would you use?

    a. High-gain Grid

    b. High-gain Dipole

    c. High-gain Yagi

    d. Parabolic dish

6. You have been hired as a consultant to install a wireless LAN that will connect four buildings that are 100 meters apart. Which of the following antennas could you use? (Choose two.)

    a. Four dipole antennas

    b. Four patch antennas

    c. One dipole and three patch antennas

    d. Two parabolic dish antennas and two Yagi antennas

    e. Four panel antennas

7. A wireless LAN installation has a 50-meter cable running between the access point and a highly directional antenna. The output signal being sent and received is very weak at each end of the link. What device should you add to the configuration that would fix the problem?

    a. Unidirectional amplifier

    b. Bidirectional amplifier

    c. Unidirectional attenuator

    d. Bidirectional attenuator

8. The RF signal amplitude loss that occurs because of the natural broadening of the RF wave front is referred to as which one of the following?

    a. Fresnel zone loss

    b. Coverage area loss

    c. Radiation pattern loss

    d. Free space path loss

9. PoE could be used in which one of the following scenarios?

   a. To power an antenna that is less than 100 meters away from an access point

   b. To power an antenna that is more than 100 meters away from an access point

   c. To power an access point that is less than 100 meters away from a wiring closet

   d. To power an access point that is more than 100 meters away from a wiring closet

10. You are performing an outdoor installation of an omnidirectional antenna. Which of the following will you need to do to ensure proper installation? (Choose three.)

   a. Check that RF LOS exists with the other antennas in the installation.

   b. Check that visual LOS exists with the other antennas in the installation.

   c. Install a lightning arrestor to protect against transient currents.

   d. Seal all the cable connections in the series to prevent water damage.

11. Which one of the following statements is true about PoE devices from different manufacturers?

   a. They always use the same unused pairs for sending current.

   b. They are guaranteed to interoperate with devices from other vendors.

   c. They use the same output voltage.

   d. They may cause damage to devices from other vendors.

12. You have purchased a semidirectional antenna from Vendor A, and an access point from Vendor B that the FCC has certified as a system through a third party. What type of cables or connectors must be used as part of this system in order to connect the access point to the antenna?

    a. An RF cable with industry standard connectors and a pigtail cable with appropriate connectors

    b. An RF cable with connectors matching the access point and a pigtail cable with appropriate connectors for the antenna and RF cable connection

    c. An RF cable with N connectors and a pigtail with N connectors on both sides

    d. An RF cable with SMA connectors and a pigtail with N connectors on both sides

13. An antenna's beamwidth refers to which one of the following?

    a. The width of the RF signal beam that the antenna transmits

    b. The width of the antenna main element

    c. The width of the mounting beam on which the antenna is mounted

    d. The width of the beam of the RF signal relative to the Earth's surface

14. When should an omnidirectional antenna be used?

    a. When coverage in all horizontal directions from the antenna is required

    b. When coverage in a specific direction is required

    c. When coverage is required over more than 7 miles (11.7 km) in a specific direction

    d. Indoors only, for short-range coverage of nonroaming wireless LAN clients

15. Which of the following are names of semidirectional antenna types? (Choose three.)

    a. Yagi

    b. Omni

    c. Patch

    d. Panel

    e. Point-to-point

16. The coverage area of a Yagi antenna is only in the direction that the antenna is pointing. This statement is:

    a. Always true

    b. Always false

    c. Sometimes true, depending on the antenna manufacturer

    d. Depends on how the antenna itself is installed

17. Polarization is defined as which one of the following?

    a. The direction of the RF antenna in relation to the north and south poles

    b. The magnetic force behind the antenna element

    c. The power sources of an antenna that cause the antenna to transmit signal in more than one direction

    d. The orientation of the electric field emitted from an antenna in relation to the Earth's plane

18. Which one of the following is an accurate description of an access point with vertically polarized antennas?

    a. Both antennas emit signals perpendicular to the Earth's surface

    b. Both antennas emit signals parallel to the Earth's surface

    c. One antenna emits signals parallel to the Earth's surface and the other emits signals perpendicular to the Earth's surface

    d. The client will receive the best signal when its antenna is oriented to receive signals parallel to the Earth's surface

19. What is the unit of measurement for gain as related to an RF antenna?

    a. Decibels

    b. Watts

    c. dBi

    d. dBm

    e. dB

20. Which one of the following defines free space path loss?

    a. The loss incurred by an RF signal whose path has crossed a large free space

    b. What occurs as an RF signal is deflected off of its intended path into free space

    c. The loss incurred by an RF signal due largely to "signal dispersion," which is a natural broadening of the wave front

    d. The weakening of the RF signal propagation due to an infinite amount of free space

21. Which of the following are variations of the "N-type" connector? (Choose three.)

    a. Standard N-type

    b. Reverse threaded N-type

    c. Reverse polarity N-type

    d. Dual head N-type

Unit 6
Wireless LAN Organizations and Standards

Most computer-related hardware and technologies are based on some standard, and wireless LANs are no exception. Some organizations that define and support the standards allow hardware from different manufacturers to function together seamlessly. In this unit we discuss the role of the Federal Communications Commission (FCC) role in defining and enforcing the regulations governing wireless communication and the role of the Institute of Electrical and Electronics Engineers (IEEE) in creating standards that allow wireless devices to work together. We also cover the different frequency bands on which wireless LANs operate, and examine the IEEE 802.11 family of standards. We discuss some of the major organizations in the wireless LAN marketplace and the roles they fill in the industry. We cover some of the emerging technologies and standards and discuss their impact on the wireless LAN industry.

By understanding the regulations and the standards that govern and guide wireless LAN technology, you will be able to ensure that any wireless system you implement will be interoperable and comply with the regulations. Furthermore, familiarity with these statutes and standards, as well as the organizations that create them, will greatly enhance your ability to research and find the latest information about wireless LANs.

Lessons

1. FCC
2. IEEE
3. Major Organizations
4. Competing Technologies

Terms

5-Unified Protocol (5-UP™)—5-UP is a standard proposed by Atheros Communications to enhance the features of 802.11a and HiperLAN/2 into one interoperable standard.

802.1p—802.1p is the IEEE extension to the 802.1D media access control (MAC) bridges standard. IEEE 802.1p allows MAC layer frames on the network to be prioritized. IEEE 802.1p uses a portion of the 802.1Q VLAN tag to represent one of eight possible priority values, each mapped to one of eight traffic classes.

802.1Q—IEEE 802.1Q is a vendor-neutral standard for modifying a frame header to represent the frame's virtual local area network (VLAN) membership. This modified header is transferred between 802.1Q-capable switches and bridges, but is not passed to clients.

Barker code—Barker code is one of the spreading codes (a.k.a. chipping codes) used in 802.11- based wireless LANs.

Binary Phase Shift Keying (BPSK)—BPSK is a signal modulation technique that shifts the carrier frequency between two states to represent the transmitted data.

complementary code keying (CCK)—CCK is one of the spreading codes used in 802.11b wireless LANs operating at 5.5 and 11 Mbps. The spreading code determines how large a frequency range the signal covers.

chip—A chip is a component of a spread spectrum radio frequency (RF) signal that determines the frequency shift rate. The number of chips in the chipping code determines the amount of spreading that occurs; the number of chips per bit and the speed of the code determine the data rate.

Carrier Sense Multiple Access with Collision Detection (CSMA/CD)—CSMA/CD is the technique Ethernet uses for controlling access to the shared transmission medium (the bus). In CSMA/CD, a node may not transmit unless the medium is idle (carrier sense). If the transmitting node detects (collision detection) that another station (multiple access) has begun to transmit at the same time, both nodes stop, then wait a random time interval before attempting to retransmit.

data encryption standard (DES)—DES is a cryptographic algorithm that protects unclassified computer data. DES is a National Institute of Standards and Technology (NIST) standard and is available for both public and government use. DES is a popular single-key encryption system that uses a 56-bit key. 3DES uses the DES algorithm to encrypt a message three times, using two 56-bit keys. It is considered a hardware solution to encryption because of the time necessary to encrypt and decrypt a message.

Differentiated Services (DiffServ)—DiffServ is an IETF recommended protocol used to provide IP traffic preferential treatment across a network. DiffServ uses the IP packet header priority bits to represent traffic forwarding classes (FCs). These forwarding classes tell network routers and switches how each is to handle the DiffServ marked packets. Packets needing QoS can be routed over high-bandwidth, low-delay paths, while routine data packets may be routed over busier, lower throughput links.

equivalent isotropically radiated power (EIRP)—EIRP is the power actually radiated by the antenna element. This concept is important because the FCC regulates EIRP, and EIRP is used in calculating whether or not a wireless link is viable. EIRP takes into account the gain of the antenna.

Extended SSID (ESSID)—See Service Set Identifier (SSID).

HiperLAN—HiperLAN is a wireless LAN protocol developed by ETSI (European Telecommunications Standards Institute) that provides a 23.5 Mbps data rate in the 5-GHz band.

HiperLAN/2—HiperLAN/2 is an extension to the HiperLAN protocol developed by ETSI that provides a 54 Mbps data rate in the 5-GHz band.

IEEE 1363 (Public Key Encryption)—Public-key encryption is a cryptographic system that uses two mathematically related keys: one key is used to encrypt a message, and the other to decrypt it. People who need to receive encrypted messages distribute their public keys but keep their private keys secret.

IEEE 1394 (Firewire)—IEEE 1394, named Firewire by Apple Computer, is a high speed serial bus technology designed to support fast PC peripherals. IEEE 1394 supports such real-time, high-bandwidth applications as full-motion video and CD–quality audio. Current versions 1394a and 1394b are rated at 800Kbps and 1600Mbps, respectively.

infrared light—Infrared light is composed of light waves that have wavelengths ranging from about 0.75 to 1,000 microns, which is longer (lower in frequency) than the spectral colors, but much shorter (higher in frequency) than radio waves. Therefore, under most lighting conditions, infrared light is invisible to the naked eye.

Industrial, Scientific, and Medical (ISM) bands—ISM bands are radio frequency bands that the Federal Communications Commission (FCC) authorized for wireless LANs. The ISM bands are located at 915+/- 13 MHz, 2450+/- 50 MHz, and 5800+/- 75 MHz.

Initialization vector (IV)—The IV is a 24-bit number used to start and track wireless frames moving between nodes. The IV is concatenated with (appended to) the secret key to yield the WEP key.

Orthogonal Frequency Division Multiplexing (OFDM)—OFDM is a communications technique that divides a communications channel into a number of equally spaced frequency bands. A subcarrier carrying a portion of the user information is transmitted in each band. Each subcarrier is orthogonal with (independent of) every other subcarrier.

Power Save Polling (PSP) mode—A wireless client operating in PSP mode can sleep for short time periods. This sleep mode conserves power on client nodes that operate on batteries, such as laptops and handhelds.

probe request frame—Probe request frames are sent by a wireless client when actively scanning for access points to locate a network to join. The probe frame contains the desired network SSID, or a broadcast SSID, and indicates the need for the access point to respond with connectivity information.

Quadrature Phase Shift Keying (QPSK)—QPSK is a modulation technique that represents digital data with a four-phase shift in the radio frequency (RF) carrier frequency.

Resource Reservation Setup Protocol (RSVP)—RSVP is a network protocol that allows a network node to reserve the transmission medium for a specified period of time for Quality of Service (QoS)-oriented applications, such as video.

Service Set Identifier (SSID)—The SSID is a unique, case-sensitive, alphanumeric network name used to identify a wireless LAN. The SSID can be used to segment wireless networks, but is only a rudimentary security measure. Access points broadcast SSIDs in their beacon frames; therefore, SSIDs can be easily intercepted.

Shared Wireless Access Protocol (SWAP)—SWAP is a wireless protocol used in HomeRF networks that combines CSMA and TDMA technologies for wireless voice and data networking.

Third Generation (3G)—3G is the latest Global System for Mobile Communications (GSM) cellular communications technology, which combines code division multiple access (CDMA) technologies with Internet Protocol (IP) services.

Time Division Multiple Access (TDMA)—TDMA is a technology for delivering digital wireless service using time division multiplexing (TDM). TDMA works by dividing a radio frequency into time slots, and then allocating slots to multiple calls. In this way, a single frequency can support multiple, simultaneous data channels. TDMA is used by HomeRF, HiperLAN/1 and /2, and cellular systems (GSM).

Wired Equivalent Privacy (WEP)—WEP is an optional IEEE 802.11 function that offers frame transmission privacy similar to a wired network. WEP generates secret shared encryption keys that both source and destination stations can use to alter frame bits to avoid data disclosure to eavesdroppers.

Wireless LAN Association (WLANA)—Founded in March 1996, WLANA's charter is the promotion of wireless LAN education, technology, and awareness.

Lesson 1—FCC

The Federal Communications Commission (FCC) is an independent United States government agency, directly responsible to Congress. The FCC was established by the Communications Act of 1934 and is charged with regulating interstate and international communications by radio, television, wire, satellite, and cable. The FCC's jurisdiction covers not only the 50 states and the District of Columbia, but also all U.S. possessions, such as Puerto Rico, Guam, and the Virgin Islands.

The FCC makes the regulations within which wireless LAN devices must operate. The FCC mandates where on the radio frequency spectrum wireless LANs may operate and at what power, using which transmission technologies, and how and where various pieces of wireless LAN hardware may be used. You can visit the FCC Web site at **http://www.fcc.gov.**

Objectives

At the end of this lesson you will be able to:

* Describe the role the FCC plays in governing wireless LAN operations

* Identify the license-free bands over which wireless LANs operate

* Explain the FCC's power output rules for wireless LANs

 **Key Point**

The FCC makes regulations that control the frequencies over which wireless LANs operate, and how those frequencies are used.

ISM and UNII Bands

The FCC establishes rules limiting which frequencies wireless LANs can use and the output power on each of those frequency bands. The FCC has specified that wireless LANs can use the Industrial, Scientific, and Medical (ISM) bands, which are license free. The ISM bands are located starting at 902 MHz, 2.4 GHz, and 5.8 GHz and vary in width from about 26 MHz to 150 MHz.

In addition to the ISM bands, the FCC specifies three Unlicensed National Information Infrastructure (UNII) bands. Each one of these UNII bands is in the 5-GHz to 6-GHz range and is 100 MHz wide. The ISM and UNII Spectra Diagram illustrates the ISM and UNII bands available.

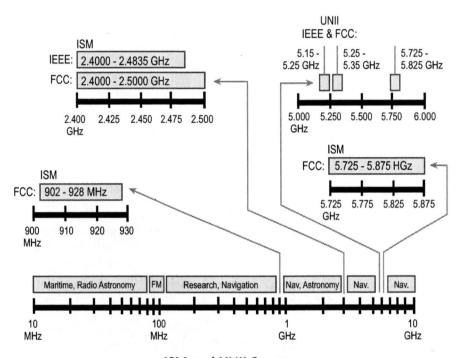

ISM and UNII Spectra

Advantages and Disadvantages of License-Free Bands

When implementing any wireless system on a license-free band, there is no requirement to petition the FCC for bandwidth and power needs. Limits on the power of transmission exist, but there is no procedure for receiving permission to transmit on these frequencies. Furthermore, there are no licensing requirements and, thus, no cost associated with licensing. The license-free nature of the ISM and UNII bands is very important because it allows entities such as small businesses and households to implement wireless systems, and fosters the growth of the wireless LAN market.

This freedom from licensing carries with it a major disadvantage to license-free band users. The same license-free band you use (or intend to use) is also license-free to others. Suppose you install a wireless LAN segment on your home network. If your neighbor also installs a wireless LAN segment in his or her home, the system may interfere with yours, and vise versa. Furthermore, if he or she uses a higher-power system, the wireless LAN may disable yours by "whiting out" your wireless traffic. The two competing systems do not necessarily have to be on the same channel, or even be the same spread spectrum technology to interfere with each other.

ISM Bands

The FCC has specified three license-free ISM bands that wireless LANs may use. They are the 900-MHz, 2.4-GHz, and 5.8-GHz bands.

900-MHz ISM Band

The 900-MHz ISM band is defined as the range of frequencies from 902 MHz to 928 MHz. This band may be additionally (and correctly) defined as 915 MHz ± 13 MHz. Although the 900-MHz ISM band was once used by wireless LANs, it has been largely abandoned in favor of the higher frequency bands, which have wider bandwidths and allow more throughput. Wireless home phones and wireless camera systems are some of the wireless devices that still use the 900- MHz band. Organizations that use 900-MHz wireless LANs find out the hard way that obsolete equipment is expensive to replace should any piece of their hardware malfunction. A single 900-MHz radio card may cost as much as $800.00 and might only be able to transmit at speeds up to 1 Mbps. In comparison, an 802.11b compliant wireless card will support speeds up to 11 Mbps and sell for roughly $70.00. Finding support or replacements for these older 900-MHz units is almost impossible.

2.4-GHz ISM Band

The 2.4-GHz ISM band is used by all 802.11, 802.11b, and 802.11g compliant devices and is by far the most populated space of the three bands presented in this chapter. The FCC defines the 2.4-GHz ISM band as bound by 2.4000 GHz and 2.5000 GHz (2.4500 GHz ± 50 MHz). Of the 100 MHz between 2.4000 and 2.5000 GHz, only the frequencies 2.4000 to 2.4835 GHz are actually used by wireless LAN devices. The principal reason for this limitation is that the FCC has specified power output only for this range of frequencies within the 2.4-GHz ISM band.

5.8-GHz ISM Band

This band is also frequently called the 5-GHz ISM Band. The 5.8-GHz ISM, which yields a 150-MHz bandwidth, is bound by 5.725 GHz and 5.875 GHz. This band of frequencies is not specified for use by wireless LAN devices, so it tends to present some confusion. The 5.8-GHz ISM band overlaps part of another license-free band, the Upper UNII band, causing the 5.8-GHz ISM band to be confused with the 5-GHz Upper UNII band, which *is* used with wireless LANs.

UNII Bands

Three separate 100-MHz-wide bands make up the 5-GHz UNII bands, which are used by 802.11a compliant devices. The three bands are known as the lower, middle, and upper bands. Within each of these three bands, are four, 20 MHz-wide, nonoverlapping orthogonal frequency division multiplexing (OFDM) channels, each separated by 5 MHz. The FCC mandates that the lower band be used indoors, the middle band be used indoors or outdoors, and the upper band be allocated for outdoor use. Because access points are mostly mounted indoors, the 5-GHz UNII bands allow for eight nonoverlapping access points indoors using both the lower and middle UNII bands.

Lower Band

The lower band is bound by 5.15 GHz and 5.25 GHz and is specified by the FCC to have a maximum output power of 50 mW at the intentional radiator. When implementing 802.11a compliant devices, the IEEE has specified 40 mW (80 percent) as the maximum output power for 802.11a-compliant radios, reserving the lower band for indoor operation only.

Note: It is important to realize that it is possible for a radio to transmit at 50 mW and operate within the limits of the regulation, and not be compliant with the 802.11a standard. It is also important to distinguish between what the regulation allows for and what the standard specifies. In some rare installation scenarios, you may be required to work outside the specifications of the standards in order to accomplish a business goal.

Middle Band

The middle UNII band is bound by 5.25 GHz and 5.35 GHz and is specified at 250 mW of output power at the intentional radiator by the FCC. The power output specified by IEEE for the middle UNII band is 200 mW. This power limit allows operation of devices either indoors or outdoors and is commonly used for short outdoor hops between closely spaced buildings. In the case of a home installation, such a configuration might include an RF link between the house and the garage, or the house and a neighbor's house. Due to reasonable power output and flexible indoor/outdoor use restrictions, products manufactured to work in the middle UNII band could enjoy wide acceptance in the future.

Upper Band	The upper UNII band is reserved for outdoor links and is limited by the FCC to 1 Watt (1000 mW) of output power at the intentional radiator. This band occupies the range of frequencies between 5.725 GHz and 5.825 GHz, and is often confused with the 5.8-GHz ISM band. The IEEE specifies the maximum output power for this band as 800 mW, which is plenty of power for almost any outdoor implementation.

Power Output Rules

The FCC enforces certain rules regarding the power radiated by the antenna element, depending on whether the implementation is a point-to-multipoint or a point-to-point implementation. The term used for the power radiated by the antenna is Equivalent Isotropically Radiated Power (EIRP).

PtMP	PtMP links have a central point of connection and two or more noncentral connection points. PtMP links are typically configured in a star topology. The central connection point may or may not have an omnidirectional antenna (an omnidirectional antenna produces a 360 degree horizontal beam). It is important to note that when an omnidirectional antenna is used, the FCC automatically considers the link a PtMP link. Regarding the setup of a PtMP link, the FCC limits the EIRP to 4 Watts in both the 2.4-GHz ISM band and upper 5-GHz UNII band. Furthermore, the power limit set for the intentional radiator (the device transmitting the RF signal) in each of these bands is 1 Watt. If the transmitting wireless LAN devices are adjustable with respect to their output power, the system can be customized to the needs of the user. The 4-Watt EIRP limit for a PtMP link is based on a 1-Watt maximum at the intentional radiator and a 6-dBi gain at the antenna.

Suppose a radio transmitting at 1 Watt (+30 dBm) is connected directly to a 12-dBi omnidirectional antenna. The total output power at the antenna is about 16 Watts, which is well above the 4-Watt limit. The FCC stipulates that for each 3 dBi above the antenna's initial 6 dBi of gain, the power at the intentional radiator must be reduced by 3 dB below the initial +30 dBm. For our example, because the antenna gain is 12 dBi, the power at the intentional radiator must be reduced by 6 dB. This reduction will result in an intentional radiator power of +24 dBm (30 dBm minus 6 dB) or 250 mW, and an EIRP of 36 dBm (24 dBm plus 12 dBi), or 4 Watts. Clearly, this rule can become confusing, but the end result must be that the power at the intentional radiator never be more than 1 Watt, as shown on the PtMP Power Output

Limits Table, and the EIRP must never be above 4 Watts for a PtMP connection.

PtMP Power Output Limits

Power at Antenna (dBm)	Antenna Gain (dBi)	EIRP (dBm)	EIRP (watts)
30	6	36	4
27	9	36	4
24	12	36	4
21	15	36	4
18	18	36	4
15	21	36	4
12	24	36	4

Note: The specific information contained in the PtMP Power Output Limits Table is not covered on the CWNA exam. The information is provided as a resource for your administrative tasks.

When using an omnidirectional antenna, the rules for point-to-multipoint links must be followed, regardless of whether the actual implementation is point-to-point or point-to-multipoint.

PtP

PtP links include a single directional transmitting antenna and a single directional receiving antenna. These connections will typically include building-to-building or similar links and must abide by special rules. When installing a PtP link, the 4-Watt power limit all but disappears in favor of a sliding power limit. Regarding a PtP link, the FCC mandates that for every 3 dBi above the initial 6 dBi of antenna gain, the power at the intentional radiator must be reduced by 1 dB, starting at the initial +30 dBm.

Consider our previous example, using the same values: 1 Watt (+30 dBm) at the intentional radiator and a 12 dBi antenna (in this case the antenna will be a directional antenna). The total output power is still 16 Watts. In this example, because the antenna gain is 12 dBi, the power at the intentional radiator must be reduced by 2 dB, as opposed to a 6 dB reduction in the previous example. This reduction will result in an intentional radiator power of 28 dBm (30 dBm minus 2 dB), or about 630 mW and an

EIRP of 40 dBm (28 dBm plus 12 dBi), or 10 Watts. In the case of PtP links, the power at the intentional radiator is still limited to 1 Watt, but the limit of the EIRP increases with the antenna gain, as shown on the Point-to-Point Power Output Limits Table. It is very important to clearly distinguish between the rules that govern PtP and PtMP wireless links.

Point-to-Point Power Output Limits

Power at Antenna (dBm)	Max Antenna Gain (dBi)	EIRP (dBm)	EIRP (watts)
30	6	36	4
29	9	38	6.3
28	12	40	10
27	15	42	16
26	18	44	25
25	21	46	39.8
24	24	48	63
23	27	50	100
22	30	52	158

Note: The specific information contained in the Point-to-Point Power Output Limits Table is not covered on the CWNA exam. The information is provided as an administrative resource.

The FCC has a different set of rules for PtP links in the upper UNII band. Fixed point-to-point UNII devices operating in the 5.725 to 5.825 GHz band may employ transmitting antennas with directional gain up to 23 dBi, without any corresponding reduction in the transmitter peak output power. For fixed, point-to-point UNII transmitters that employ a directional antenna gain greater than 23 dBi, a 1 dB reduction in peak transmitter power for each 1 dBi of antenna gain in excess of 23 dBi is required. Notice that an output power maximum of +30 dBm at the intentional radiator, and a maximum of 23 dBi of antenna gain before any reduction in transmitter output power is required, allows these 5-GHz UNII systems to have an output of 200 Watts EIRP.

Activities

1. Which is a reason why 900 Mhz wireless LANs have lost favor to higher frequency systems?

   a. 900 Mhz systems require licensing from the IEEE.

   b. 900 MHz systems support only point-to-point wireless links.

   c. 900 MHz devices are more expensive and slower.

   d. 9000 MHz devices cannot interoperate with each other.

2. Why do 2.4 GHz wireless networks leave the top 16.5 Mhz of the 2.4 GHz ISM frequency band unused?

   a. This portion of the frequency band does not have defined power levels.

   b. This portion of the frequency band interferes with FAA communications.

   c. This portion of the frequency band overlaps the 2.5 Ghz ISM band.

   d. This portion of the frequency band is reserved for medical devices.

3. What does the IEEE specify as the maximum allowable power output for 802.11a devices operating on the lower UNII band?

   a. 40 mW

   b. 50 mW

   c. 200 mW

   d. 250 mW

4. What is the maximum number of nonoverlapping access points you can have indoors if operating both 802.11a and 802.11b wireless LANs?

   a. 3

   b. 8

   c. 11

   d. 12

5. Which frequency range defines the upper license-free UNII band?

   a. 5.15-5.25 GHz

   b. 5.25-5.35 GHz

   c. 5.725-5.875 GHz

   d. 5.725-5.825 Ghz

6. You want to operate a short-distance 802.11a link between buildings. Which frequency range is commonly used for this sort of configuration?

   a. 5.15-5.25 GHz

   b. 5.25-5.35 GHz

   c. 5.725-5.875 GHz

   d. 5.725-5.825 Ghz

Extended Activities

1. You are designing a point-to-multipoint wireless link. Your hub access point's intentional radiator is 1 Watt. You are considering several antennas. For each of the antennas listed below, determine the amount of attenuation you will need to add to the IR to meet FCC regulations for EIRP output power.

Antenna Gain	Attenuation
6dBi	
12dBi	
15dBi	
21dBi	
24dBi	

2. You are designing a point-to-point wireless link. Your access point's IR is 1 Watt. You are considering several antennas. For each of the antennas listed below, determine the amount of attenuation you will need to add to the IR to meet FCC regulations for EIRP output power.

Antenna Gain	Attenuation
6dBi	
12dBi	
15dBi	
21dBi	
24dBi	

Lesson 2—IEEE

The Institute of Electrical and Electronics Engineers (IEEE) is the key standards maker for most things related to information technology in the United States. The IEEE creates its wireless LAN standards within the regulations created by the Federal Communications Commission (FCC). The IEEE specifies many technology standards, such as Public Key Cryptography (IEEE 1363), FireWire (IEEE 1394), Ethernet (IEEE 802.3), and Wireless LANs (IEEE 802.11). You can visit the IEEE Web site at **http://www.ieee.org**.

Objectives

At the end of this lesson you will be able to:

- Describe the role the IEEE plays in setting wireless LAN standards

- Identify the IEEE standards that describe wireless LAN operations

 **Key Point**

The IEEE develops technology standards to ensure interoperability across vendor product lines.

IEEE Wireless LAN Standards

It is part of the mission of the IEEE to develop standards for wireless LAN operation within the framework of the FCC rules and regulations. Following are the four main IEEE standards for wireless LAN connectivity that are either in use or in draft form:

- 802.11

- 802.11b

- 802.11a

- 802.11g

IEEE 802.11

The 802.11 standard was the first standard to describe the operation of wireless LANs. This standard contained all of the available transmission technologies, including Direct Sequence Spread Spectrum (DSSS), Frequency Hopping Spread Spectrum (FHSS), and infrared.

Note: Infrared's wireless LAN market share is quite small and the technology is very limited by its functionality. Due to the lack of popularity of infrared technology in the wireless LAN marketplace, infrared will be mentioned, but not covered in detail in this book.

One type of technology included in the IEEE 802.11 standard is Direct Sequence Spread Spectrum (DSSS). It describes DSSS systems that operate at 1 Mbps and 2 Mbps. If a DSSS system operates at other data rates as well, such as 1 Mbps, 2 Mbps, and 11 Mbps, it may still be an 802.11-compliant system. If, however, the system is operating at any rate other than 1 or 2 Mbps, then, even though the system is 802.11-compliant because of its ability to work at 1 and 2 Mbps, it is not operating in an 802.11-compliant mode and cannot be expected to communicate with other 802.11-compliant devices. If a system cannot operate at these two speeds, it is not 802.11 compliant.

IEEE 802.11 is one of several standards that describe the operation of frequency hopping spread spectrum (FHSS) wireless LAN systems. If a wireless LAN administrator encounters an FHSS system, it is likely to be either an 802.11-compliant or OpenAir-compliant system (discussed in the next section). The 802.11 standard describes use of FHSS systems at 1 and 2 Mbps. Many FHSS systems on the market extend this functionality by offering proprietary modes that operate at 3-10 Mbps, but just as with DSSS, if the system operates at speeds other than 1 and 2 Mbps, it cannot be expected to automatically communicate with other 802.11-compliant devices.

802.11-compliant spread spectrum products operate strictly in the 2.4-GHz ISM band between 2.4000 and 2.4835 GHz. Infrared, also covered by 802.11, is light-based technology, does not fall into the 2.4 GHz ISM band, and is not considered spread spectrum RF.

IEEE 802.11b

Although the 802.11 standard was successful in allowing DSSS as well as FHSS systems to interoperate, the technology has outgrown the standard. Soon after the approval and implementation of 802.11, DSSS wireless LANs began exchanging data at up to 11 Mbps. Without a standard to guide the operation of such devices, problems with interoperability and implementation developed. The manufacturers ironed out most of the implementation problems. Thus, the job of IEEE was relatively easy: create a standard that complied with the general operation of wireless LANs on the market. It is not uncommon for the standards to follow the technology in this way, particularly when the technology evolves quickly.

IEEE 802.11b, referred to as "high-rate" and Wi-Fi™, specifies direct-sequence spread spectrum (DSSS) systems that operate at 1, 2, 5.5 and 11 Mbps. The 802.11b standard does not describe any FHSS or infrared systems, and 802.11b-compliant devices are also 802.11-compliant by default, meaning they are backward compatible and support both 1 and 2 Mbps data rates for DSSS only. Backward compatibility is very important because it allows a wireless LAN to be upgraded without the cost of replacing the core hardware. This low-cost feature, together with the high data rate, has made the 802.11b-compliant hardware very popular.

The high data rate of 802.11b-compliant devices is the result of using a different coding technique. Although the system is still a direct sequencing system, the way the chips are coded (Complimentary Code Keying [CCK] rather than Barker Code) and the way the information is modulated (Quadrature Phase Shift Keying [QPSK] at 2, 5.5, and 11 Mbps and Binary Phase Shift Keying [BPSK] at 1 Mbps) allows for a greater amount of data to be transferred in the same time frame. Products that are 802.11b-compliant operate only in the 2.4-GHz ISM band between 2.4000 and 2.4835 GHz. Modulation and coding are discussed in further reading.

IEEE 802.11a

The IEEE 802.11a standard describes wireless LAN device operation in the 5-GHz UNII bands. Operation in the UNII bands automatically makes 802.11a devices incompatible with all other devices complying with the other 802.11 series of standards. The reason for this incompatibility is simple: systems using 5-GHz frequencies do not communicate with systems using 2.4 -GHz frequencies.

Using the UNII bands, most devices are able to achieve data rates of 6, 9, 12, 18, 24, 36, 48, and 54 Mbps. Some of the devices employing the UNII bands have achieved data rates of 108 Mbps by using proprietary technology, such as rate doubling. The highest rates of some of these devices are the result of newer technologies not specified by the 802.11a standard. IEEE 802.11a specifies data rates of only 6, 12, and 24 Mbps. A wireless LAN device must support at least these data rates in the UNII bands in order to be 802.11a-compliant. The maximum data rate specified by the 802.11a standard is 54 Mbps.

IEEE 802.11g

802.11g provides the same maximum speed as 802.11a, coupled with backwards compatibility for 802.11b devices. This backwards compatibility will make upgrading wireless LANs simple and inexpensive. Because 802.11g technology is new, 802.11g devices are not yet available as of this writing.

IEEE 802.11g specifies operation in the 2.4-GHz ISM band. To achieve the higher data rates found in 802.11a, 802.11g-compliant devices utilize Orthogonal Frequency Division Multiplexing (OFDM) modulation technology. These devices can automatically switch to QPSK modulation in order to communicate with the slower 802.11b- and 802.11-compatable devices. With all of the apparent advantages, 802.11g's use of the crowded 2.4-GHz band could prove to be a disadvantage.

Note: As of this writing, 802.11g is in draft form. Final specifications for the 802.11g standard are expected in late 2002. To read about the status of this standard, visit **http://www.ieee802.org/11/**.

Activities

1. Infrared is defined in which IEEE standard?

    a. 802.11

    b. 802.11a

    c. 802.11b

    d. 802.11g

2. Why are 802.11a devices incompatible with other 802.11 series devices?

    a. Because they operate outside of FCC-regulated power limits

    b. Because they operate only over short distances

    c. Because they operate in the 5-MHz frequency range

    d. Because they operate at their own unique data rates

3. Which of the following data rates must a device support in order to be IEEE 802.11a compliant? (Choose two.)

    a. 6 Mbps

    b. 11 Mbps

    c. 18 Mbps

    d. 24 Mbps

4. How do IEEE 802.11g devices achieve 802.11a data rates?

    a. They can switch from QPSK to OFDM.

    b. They use rate-doubling technologies.

    c. They can switch from the 2.4-GHz range to the 5-GHz range.

    d. They can switch from barker code to CCK.

5. Which is a potential disadvantage of the 802.11g standard?

    a. It is not backward compatible with DSSS systems.

    b. It uses the crowded 2.4-GHz ISM band.

    c. It uses the low power lower UNII band.

    d. It can only operate in the 5-GHz ISM band.

Extended Activities

1. Major wireless vendors are positioning themselves to be first in the marketplace with 802.11g-standard devices. Using the Web, research vendors that have products ready for release as soon as the standards are approved.

2. Some wireless vendors have chosen to develop their own techniques for providing higher bandwidths to wireless networks. How are these vendors supplying faster 802.11a data rates while still supporting legacy 802.11 and 802.11b DSSS systems?

_____

_____

_____

_____

Lesson 3—Major Organizations

Whereas the Federal Communications Commission (FCC) and the IEEE are responsible for defining the regulations and standards as they apply to wireless LANs in the United States, several other organizations, both in the United States and in other countries, contribute to growth and education in the wireless LAN marketplace. In this lesson, we will look at three of these organizations:

- Wireless Ethernet Compatibility Alliance (WECA)

- European Telecommunications Standards Institute (ETSI)

- Wireless LAN Association (WLANA)

Objectives

At the end of this lesson you will be able to:

- Describe the major organizations who support the continued growth of the wireless LAN marketplace

 **Key Point**

Other major organizations, both in the U.S. and abroad, ensure wireless LAN product compatibility and marketability.

WECA

The Wireless Ethernet Compatibility Alliance (WECA) promotes and tests for wireless LAN interoperability of 802.11b devices and 802.11a devices. WECA's mission is to certify interoperability of IEEE 802.11b and 802.11a products and to promote Wi-Fi™as the global wireless LAN interoperability standard across all market segments. As an administrator, you must resolve conflicts among wireless LAN devices that result from interference, incompatibility, or other problems.

When a product meets the interoperability requirements as described in WECA's test matrix, WECA grants the product a certification of interoperability, which allows the vendor to use the Wi-Fi logo on advertising and packaging for the certified product. The Wi-Fi seal of approval ensures end users of interoperability with other wireless LAN devices that also bear the Wi-Fi logo.

Among WECA's list of interoperability checks is the use of 40-bit WEP keys. Note that 40- and 64-bit keys are the same thing. A 40-bit "secret" key is concatenated with a 24-bit initialization vector (IV) to reach the 64 bits. In the same manner, 104- and 128-bit keys are the same. WECA does not specify interoperability of 128-bit keys; therefore, no compatibility is to be expected between vendors displaying the Wi-Fi seal when using 128-bit WEP keys. Nevertheless, many 128-bit systems from different vendors are interoperable.

Many other factors besides use of 40-bit WEP keys are required to meet WECA's Wi-Fi criteria. These factors include support of fragmentation, PSP mode, Probe Request Frames, and so forth. Some of these topics will be discussed in later reading. The WECA Web site is found at **http://www.wirelessethernet.org**.

ETSI

The European Telecommunications Standards Institute (ETSI) is chartered with producing communications standards for Europe in the same way that the IEEE is responsible for standards for the United States. The standards ETSI has established, HiPerLAN/2 for example, directly compete against standards created by the IEEE, such as 802.11a. There has been much discussion about IEEE and ETSI unifying on certain wireless technologies, but nothing has materialized as of this writing. This effort is referred to as the "5UP" initiative for "5 GHz Unified Protocol initiative," or simply "5UP."

ETSI's original HiPerLAN standard for wireless, dubbed "Hiper-LAN/1," supported rates of up to 24 Mbps using direct sequence spread spectrum (DSSS) technology with a range of approximately 150 feet. HiperLAN/1 used the lower and middle UNII bands, as do HiperLAN/2, 802.11a, and the new 802.11h draft. The new HiperLAN/2 standard supports rates of up to 54 Mbps and uses all three of the UNII bands, as does 802.11a and 802.11h.

ETSI's HiperLAN/2 standard has interchangeable convergence layers, support for Quality of Service (QoS), and supports DES and 3DES encryption. The supported convergence layers are ATM, Ethernet, Point-to-Point Protocol (PPP), FireWire, and 3G. Supported QoS awareness includes 802.1p, RSVP, and DiffServ-FC. The ETSI Web site is located at **http://www.etsi.org**.

WLANA

WLANA's mission is to educate and raise consumer awareness regarding the use and availability of wireless LANs and to promote the wireless LAN industry in general. The WLANA is an educational resource for those seeking to learn more about wireless LANs. WLANA can also help if you are looking for a specific wireless LAN product or service.

WLANA has many partners within the industry that contribute content to the WLANA directory of information. It is this directory, along with the many white papers and case studies that WLANA provides, that offer you valuable information for making your own decisions about wireless LAN implementation. You can visit WLANA's Web site at **http://www.wlana.org**.

Activities

1. In which instance can Wi-Fi-compliant systems be incompatible?

   a. In their use of 40-bit WEP keys

   b. In their use of 128-bit WEP keys

   c. In their support of fragmentation

   d. In their use of SSIDs

2. Which IEEE draft specifies wireless networks operating in all three UNII bands?

   a. 802.11b

   b. 802.11c

   c. 802.11g

   d. 802.11h

3. You are building a wireless network segment that will carry Voice over IP traffic. You want to supply QoS to the voice traffic. Which one of the following standards supports QoS awareness?

   a. IEEE 802.11a

   b. IEEE 802.11b

   c. ETSI HiperLAN/2

   d. WLIF OpenAir

4. You are looking for information concerning a particular wireless product or service. Which organization will you contact?

   a. WLANA

   b. WECA

   c. ETSI

   d. IEEE

Extended Activities

1. Visit the ETSI portal Web site at **http://portal.etsi.org/ Portal_Common/home.asp** and research some of the wireless standards in work. How do they compare to the IEEE standards?

_____

_____

_____

_____

2. Research information on the 802.11h draft. How does it differ from the 802.11a standard? HiperLAN/2? What do EU laws state concerning 802.11a use? What do they say about 802.11h use?

_____

_____

_____

_____

Lesson 4—Competing Technologies

Several technologies compete with the 802.11 family of standards. As business needs change, and technologies improve, new standards will be created that support the marketplace as well as new inventions that drive enterprise spending. Other wireless LAN technologies and standards that are used today include:

- HomeRF
- Bluetooth
- Infrared
- OpenAir

Objectives

At the end of this lesson you will be able to:

- Describe technologies competing against the IEEE standards for a share of the wireless LAN marketplace
- Describe key features of each of the competing technologies

 **Key Point**

Competing wireless standards aim to better focus wireless network technologies on specific applications, such as home networks and WPANs.

HomeRF

HomeRF operates in the 2.4-GHz band and uses frequency-hopping technology. HomeRF devices hop at about 50 hops per seconds, about 5 to 20 times faster than most 802.11-compliant frequency-hopping spread spectrum (FHSS) devices. The new version of HomeRF, HomeRF 2.0, uses the new "wideband" frequency hopping rules approved by the Federal Communications Commission (FCC), and is the first to do so. Recall that these rules, implemented after August 31, 2000, include:

- Maximum of 5-MHz-wide carrier frequencies
- Minimum of 15 hops in a sequence
- Maximum of 125 mW of output power

Because HomeRF allows an increase over the former 1-MHz-wide carrier frequencies, and flexibility in implementing less than the previously required 75 hops, one might think that wideband frequency hopping would be quite popular among corporations and vendors alike. This, however, is not the case. As advantageous as the resulting 10 Mbps data rate is, it does not overshadow the disadvantage of 125 mW of output power, which limits use of wideband frequency-hopping devices to an approximate range of 150 to 300 feet (46 to 92 meters). This outcome limits the use of wideband frequency-hopping devices primarily to small office/home office (SOHO) environments.

HomeRF units use the Shared Wireless Access Protocol (SWAP), which is a combination of Carrier Sense Multiple Access (CSMA), used in LANs, and Time Division Multiple Access (TDMA), used in cellular phones. SWAP is a hybrid of the 802.11 and Digital Enhanced Cordless Telecommunications (DECT) standards and was developed by the HomeRF working group. HomeRF devices are the only devices currently on the market that follow the wideband frequency-hopping rules. HomeRF devices are considered more secure than 802.11 products using WEP because of the 32-bit initialization vector (IV) HomeRF uses--in contrast to 802.11's 24-bit IV. Additionally, HomeRF has specified how the IV is to be chosen during encryption, whereas 802.11 does not, leaving 802.11 open for attack due to weak implementations.

Some particularly interesting features of HomeRF 2.0 are:

- ~50 hops per second

- Use of 2.4-GHz ISM band

- Compliance with FCC regulations for spread spectrum technologies

- 10 Mbps data rate with fallback to 5 Mbps, 1.6 Mbps, and 0.8 Mbps

- Backward compatibility with the OpenAir standard

- Simultaneous host/client and peer/peer topology

- Built in security measures against eavesdropping and denial-of-service

- Support for prioritized streaming media sessions and toll-quality two-way voice connections

- Enhanced roaming capabilities

The Web site for HomeRF is located at **http://www.homerf.org**.

Bluetooth

Bluetooth is another frequency-hopping technology that operates in the 2.4-GHz ISM band. The hop rate of Bluetooth devices is about 1600 hops per second (about 625 microseconds dwell time). Thus, this technology has considerably more overhead than 802.11-compliant frequency hopping systems. The high hop rate also gives Bluetooth greater resistance to spurious narrowband noise. Bluetooth systems are not designed for high throughput, but rather for simple use, low power, and short range WPANs. The new IEEE 802.15 draft for WPANs includes specifications for Bluetooth.

A major disadvantage of using Bluetooth technology is that it tends to completely disrupt other 2.4-GHz networks. The high hop rate of Bluetooth over the entire usable 2.4-GHz band makes the Bluetooth signal appear to all other systems as all-band noise, or all-band interference. Bluetooth also affects other FHSS systems. All-band interference, as the name implies, disrupts the signal over its entire range of useable frequencies, rendering the main signal useless. Curiously, the counter-interference (interference provided by the wireless LAN interfering with Bluetooth) does not impact Bluetooth devices as severely as Bluetooth impacts the 802.11-compliant wireless LAN. It is now common for placards to be mounted in wireless LAN areas that read "No Bluetooth" in eye-catching print.

Bluetooth devices operate in three power classes: 1 mW, 2.5 mW, and 100 mW. Currently there are few implementations of Class 3 (100 mW) Bluetooth devices; thus, range data is not readily available; however, Class 2 (2.5 mW) Bluetooth devices have a maximum range of 10 meters (33 feet). Naturally, if extended ranged is desired, the use of directional antennas is a possible solution; although, most Bluetooth devices are mobile devices. Information on Bluetooth technology can be found at the Bluetooth Special Interest Group (SIG) Web site located at **http://www.bluetooth.com**.

IrDA

The Infrared Data Association (IrDA) is not a standard such as HomeRF and the 802.11 series of standards; rather, IrDA is an organization. Founded in June of 1993, IrDA is a member-funded organization whose charter is "to create an interoperable, low-cost, low-power, half-duplex, serial data interconnection standard that supports a walk-up point-to-point user model that is adaptable to a wide range of computer devices." Infrared data transmission is known by most for its use in calculators, printers, some building-to-building and in-room computer networks, and now in handheld computers.

Infrared

Infrared is a light-based transmission technology and is not spread spectrum; spread spectrum technologies all use radio frequency (RF) radiation. Infrared devices can achieve a maximum data rate of 4 Mbps at close range, but as a light-based technology, other sources of infrared light can interfere with infrared transmissions. The typical data rate of an infrared device is about 115 kbps, which is effective for exchanging data between handheld devices. An important advantage of infrared networks is that they do not interfere with spread spectrum RF networks. For this reason, the two are complementary and can easily be used together.

Security

The security of infrared devices is inherently excellent for two main reasons. First, infrared cannot travel though walls at such a low power (2 mW maximum), and second, a hacker or eavesdropper must directly intercept the beam in order to gain access to the information being transferred. Single room networks that need wireless connectivity can be ensured of the security benefit from IR networks. With personal digital assistants (PDAs) and laptop computers, infrared is used for point-to-point connectivity at very short ranges; thus, security concerns would be almost irrelevant in these instances.

Stability

Although infrared will not pass through walls, it will bounce off walls and ceilings, which aids in single room networking. Infrared is not disrupted by electromagnetic signals, which promotes the stability of an infrared system. Broadcast infrared devices are available and can be mounted on ceilings. An infrared broadcast device (which is analogous to an RF antenna) transmits the infrared carrier and information in all directions so that these signals can be picked up by nearby infrared clients. For power consumption reasons, broadcast infrared is normally implemented indoors. Point-to-point infrared transmitters can be used outdoors, and have a maximum range of about 3280 feet (1 km), but this range may be shortened by the presence of sunlight. Sunlight is approximately 60 percent infrared light, which severely dilutes broadcast infrared signals. On sunny days, when transferring data between laptop computers or PDAs, the two devices may have to be held closer together for good infrared data transfer.

WLIF

The OpenAir standard was created by the Wireless LAN Interoperability Forum (WLIF) (now defunct), for which many wireless LAN systems were created to comply as an alternative to 802.11. OpenAir specified FHSS technology at 800 kbps and 1.6 Mbps. OpenAir and 802.11 FHSS systems are not compatible and will not interoperate. Because several product lines are available that still comply with the OpenAir standard, it is important that wireless LAN administrators know that OpenAir exists; however, OpenAir is quickly losing support among vendors and no new products are being made that comply with this standard. OpenAir was the first attempt at interoperability and standardization among wireless LANs.

Activities

1. You are designing a wireless network that will support users working in a single room. The network must protect data from interception, and not be susceptible to interference from existing DSSS networks. Which technology meets these requirements?

   a. Infrared

   b. Bluetooth

   c. OpenAir

   d. HomeRF

2. Which of the following statements is true concerning HomeRF 2.0 networks? (Choose two.)

   a. They are more secure than 802.11 networks running WEP

   b. They support data rates up to 11 Mbps

   c. They adhere to the pre-08/31/00 narrowband frequency hopping rules

   d. They can transmit at up to 125 mW output power

3. Which one of the following products adheres to the FCC's wideband frequency hopping rules?

   a. Infrared

   b. Bluetooth (class 3)

   c. OpenAir

   d. HomeRF 2.0

4. Which of the following statements is true concerning Bluetooth technology?

   a. Devices can operate in any ISM frequency band.

   b. The short dwell time creates less overhead than on 802.11 networks.

   c. To 802.11 networks, it appears as all-band noise.

   d. The FCC-specified maximum output power is 1W.

5. Which is the hop rate for Bluetooth devices?

    a. 5 hops per second

    b. 50 hops per second

    c. 800 hops per second

    d. 1600 hops per second

Extended Activities

1. Bluetooth and 802.11b devices do not normally operate together in the same area. Some vendors have found ways to work around this. Research wireless and computer system vendors marketing combined Bluetooth/802.11b solutions. How do they make the technologies work together?

    _____

    _____

    _____

    _____

2. When would Bluetooth technology be a better wireless LAN solution than 802.11 series technologies?

    _____

    _____

    _____

    _____

Summary

This unit discussed the FCC's role in defining and enforcing the regulations governing wireless communication, and the role of IEEE in creating standards that allow wireless devices to work together. This unit covered the different frequency bands on which wireless LANs operate, and examined the IEEE 802.11 family of standards. Three major organizations contribute to growth and education in the wireless LAN marketplace: WECA, ETSI, and WLANA. This unit also detailed some of the emerging technologies and standards that compete with the IEEE 802.11 family of standards and drive enterprise spending, including HomeRF, Bluetooth, Infrared, and OpenAir.

By understanding the regulations and standards that govern and guide wireless LAN technology, you will be able to ensure that any wireless system you implement will be interoperable and comply with the regulations.

Unit 6 Quiz

1. What data rates does the 802.11 standard specify when using DSSS?

   a. 1 Mbps only

   b. 2 Mbps only

   c. 4 Mbps only

   d. 1 and 2 Mbps

   e. 1, 2, and 4 Mbps

2. How wide is each of the three wireless LAN UNII bands?

   a. 100 MHz

   b. 102 MHz

   c. 110 MHz

   d. 120 MHz

3. The FCC specifies rules for wireless LANs regarding which of the following? (Choose two.)

   a. Power output

   b. Frequencies

   c. Modulation

   d. Data rates

4. Which one of the following is an ISM band used with wireless LANs?

   a. 900 MHz

   b. 2.4 MHz

   c. 4.5 GHz

   d. 5.8 GHz

5. The 802.11b standard specifies which one of the following sets of data rates using DSSS technology?

   a. 1 and 2 Mbps

   b. 5.5 and 11 Mbps

   c. 1, 2, and 11 Mbps

   d. 1, 2, 5.5, and 11 Mbps

6. The 802.11b standard specifies which one of the following spread spectrum technologies?

  a. FHSS

  b. DSSS

  c. Infrared

  d. Key hopping

7. Which of the following standards specifies use of FHSS technology? (Choose two.)

  a. 802.11

  b. 802.11b

  c. 802.11a

  d. 802.11g

  e. OpenAir

8. What is the FCC limit on EIRP for a point-to-multipoint link?

  a. 1 Watt

  b. 2 Watts

  c. 3 Watts

  d. 4 Watts

9. Why are 802.11a devices incompatible with all other 802.11 family devices?

  a. 802.11a devices operate at a maximum of 54 Mbps

  b. 802.11a devices operate in the 5-GHz ISM band

  c. 802.11a devices operate in the 5-GHz UNII bands

  d. 802.11a devices use Barker Code modulation

10. Which one of the following statements is true?

  a. The IEEE is government regulated.

  b. The FCC is a government agency.

  c. The IEEE sets the allowable RF power outputs in the United States.

  d. The FCC specifies connectivity speeds for the 802.11 standard.

11. What does the Wi-Fi™ seal of approval indicate?

    a. A vendor's hardware has a WECA chipset in it.

    b. A vendor's hardware has been proven interoperable with other vendor's hardware.

    c. A wireless LAN meets the IEEE 802.11 standard.

    d. A wireless LAN meets FCC regulations.

12. Which organization creates the regulations that wireless LANs must follow?

    a. IEEE

    b. FCC

    c. WECA

    d. WLANA

13. You have been hired to take over the administration of a wireless LAN on a small college campus. The campus uses one omnidirectional antenna to connect six buildings. One day an inspector with the FCC tells you that the power output at the element of your antenna is too high and violates FCC regulations. What is the maximum power output at which you can set the EIRP to comply with the regulation?

    a. 125 mW

    b. 1 W

    c. 2 W

    d. 4W

14. The FCC's jurisdiction covers which of the following areas?

    a. The 50 United States only

    b. The 50 United States and the District of Columbia

    c. The 50 United States, the District of Columbia, and all U.S. territories such as Puerto Rico, Guam, and the Virgin Islands

    d. All of Europe

15. Which one of the following is a disadvantage of a license-free radio frequency band?

    a. No licensing fees or paperwork

    b. Regulation by the FCC in the US

    c. Possible random interference with other networks

    d. Lower cost of equipment

16. "ISM" stands for which one of the following?

    a. International Scientific Measurement

    b. International Standards Makers

    c. Industrial Standard Machine

    d. Industrial, Scientific, and Medical

17. Which one of the following does NOT specify equipment that uses the 2.4-GHz ISM band?

    a. 802.11

    b. 802.11a

    c. 802.11b

    d. 802.11g

18. Which one of the following defines the acronym "UNII"?

    a. Unlicensed National Information Invention

    b. Unlicensed National Information Infrastructure

    c. Unlicensed Nominal Information Infrastructure

    d. Unlicensed National Innovation Infrastructure

19. Which one of the following is the key standards maker for most information technology arenas in the United States?

    a. WECA

    b. FCC

    c. IEEE

    d. WLANA

    e. IrDA

20. Which one of the following was the first IEEE standard describing the operation of wireless LANs?

    a. 802.11

    b. 802.11a

    c. 802.11b

    d. 802.11g

Unit 7
The 802.11 Network Architecture

This unit covers some of the key concepts found in the 802.11 network architecture. Most of the topics in this unit are defined directly in the 802.11 standard, and are required for implementation of 802.11-compliant hardware. This unit examines the process by which clients connect to an access point, the terms used for organizing wireless LANs, and how power management is accomplished in wireless LAN client devices.

Without a solid understanding of the principals covered in this unit, it would be quite difficult to design, administer, or troubleshoot a wireless LAN. This unit presents some of the most elementary steps of both wireless LAN design and administration. As you administer wireless LANs, your understanding of these concepts will allow you to more intelligently manage day-to-day operations.

Lessons

1. Locating a Wireless LAN
2. Authentication and Association
3. Service Sets
4. Power Management Features

Terms

802.11f—IEEE 802.11f is an IEEE draft specification that proposes a set of functions and protocols that will enable multivendor access points to support roaming on a wireless network. An Interaccess Point Protocol (IAPP) will map media access control (MAC) addresses to distributed system (access point) addresses, in order to support client reassociation as they move between APs.

802.1x authentication server—An 802.1x authentication server is a network device that determines if a client is authorized to access the network. The authenticator contacts the authentication server to verify client credentials.

802.1x authenticator—An 802.1x authenticator is a network device that desires to authenticate a network client. The authenticator is the port with which the client, or supplicant, wishes to authenticate.

802.1x supplicant—An 802.1x supplicant is a client device that uses the services of the authenticator.

Announcement Traffic Information Message (ATIM)—ATIM is used in ad hoc mode to indicate to stations the presence of transmissions bound for a particular station. ATIM tells stations not to enter sleep mode before receiving their transmitted frames.

association service—An association service is an IEEE 802.11 service that enables the mapping of a wireless station to the distribution system by means of an access point.

authentication—Authentication is the process a station uses to announce its identity to another station. The IEEE 802.11 standard specifies two forms of authentication: open system and shared key.

authentication, authorization, and accounting (AAA)—AAA is the method by which users are authenticated, authorized, and tracked to gain access and move about inside a network.

basic service set (BSS)—BSS is a set of 802.11-compliant stations and an access point that operate as a fully connected wireless network.

basic service set identifier (BSSID)—A BSSID is a 6-byte address that distinguishes a particular access point from others.

beacon—See beacon management frame.

beacon management frame—Beacon management frames are short frames sent from the access point to the stations in infrastructure mode or from station-to-station in ad-hoc mode. They are used to organize and synchronize wireless LAN communications.

bit error rate (BER)—BER is the number of erroneous bits divided by the total number of bits transmitted, received, or processed over some stipulated period.

Challenge Handshake Authentication Protocol (CHAP)—CHAP is a protocol used to authenticate remote network access over Point-to-Point Protocol. CHAP initiates a three-way handshake between the remote access service client and the server. The server responds to the client authentication request with a randomly generated challenge value. The client requestor generates and sends to the server a one-way hashed response, which the server uses to verify the user's identity and access permissions.

channel reuse—During channel reuse, a technique used in large wireless LANs, nonoverlapping channels alternatively provide multicell seamless roaming while avoiding co-channel and adjacent channel interference. Cells are arranged side-by-side to form a mesh of nonoverlapping channels.

EAPCisco Wireless (Cisco LEAP)—LEAP, developed by Cisco Systems, Inc., is an authentication algorithm that enhances WEP by supporting 802.1x port-level access control. LEAP requires mutual authentication between the user and the access point, ensuring that rogue APs cannot masquerade as authentic network APs. As with other EAP versions, LEAP uses authentication servers to perform the client authentication process.

EAP-Secure Remote Password (SRP)—EAP-SRP uses the authentication mechanism defined in RFC 2945 to eliminate the vulnerability of password-based authentication to interception and subsequent cracking. EAP-SRP uses hashing algorithms and secure-key exchanges between the client and the authenticator. The authenticator stores a verifier for each client, and uses this to ensure the client's password is not compromised.

EAP-Subscriber Identity Module (EAP-SIM [GSM])—EAP-SIM is an EAP authentication mechanism for use on GSM networks. EAP-SIM uses a challenge-response mechanism based on a 128-bit long random number (RAND) challenge generated by the SIM installed inside a wireless device. The calling client contacts the carrier network, which refers the caller to the EAP authenticator. The EAP authenticator requests the caller's identity, and the client responds with its unique identity. The authenticator then asks for the client's SIM packet, and the client responds with a 32-bit response and 64-bit key. The authenticator verifies the response and sends back a challenge. The client runs the authentication algorithm on the SIM, and responds to the challenge. Assuming all progressed as desired, and the client is authenticated, communications can commence.

EAP-Transport Layer Security (TLS)—EAP-TLS uses the TLS protocol to ensure private communications between two users over a public network. TLS protects client/server applications from eavesdropping, interception, and forgery by using two protocol layers: the Record Protocol and the Handshake Protocol. The Record Protocol ensures privacy through the use of data encryption and reliability with a message integrity check. The Handshake Protocol verifies peer entity identities, negotiates a secure shared secret, and verifies the integrity of the negotiation process.

EAP Tunneled Transport Layer Security (TTLS)—EAP-TTLS extends EAP-TLS by tunneling legacy, password-based authentication over the secure connection created during the TLS handshake. Therefore, less secure password-passing algorithms can still authenticate over an EAP-TLS secured communications channel.

extended service set (ESS)—An ESS is a collection of basic service sets, tied together by means of a distribution system, that share a common network name (Service Set Identifier).

Extensible Authentication Protocol (EAP)—EAP is a general protocol for Point-to-Point Protocol (PPP) authentication that supports multiple authentication mechanisms. EAP does not select a specific authentication mechanism at link control phase, but rather postpones this step until the authentication phase. This allows the authenticator to request more information before determining the specific authentication mechanism. This also permits the use of a "back-end" server, which actually implements the various mechanisms while the PPP authenticator merely passes through the authentication exchange. EAP serves as a flexible replacement for CHAP and/or PAP.

Global System for Mobile Communications (GSM)—GSM is a family of global cellular network services providing voice, data, and messaging in over 170 countries. GSM is nonproprietary, uses time division multiple access (TDMA) technologies, and performs digital voice encoding.

GSM Subscriber Identity Module (SIM)—A GSM SIM is a smartcard installed in a cell phone that stores cryptographic codes used to authenticate callers and bill them for services. The SIM stores a customer unique key used to authenticate the caller. The SIM runs an algorithm that generates random numbers used to respond to authenticator challenges.

independent basic service set (IBSS)—IBSS is an IEEE 802.11-based wireless network that has no backbone infrastructure and consists of at least two wireless stations. This type of network is often referred to as an ad hoc network because it can be constructed quickly, without much planning, and it has no access point with which to connect. Client stations connect directly to each other.

Inter Access Point Protocol (IAPP)—Developed by several wireless product vendors, IAPP is a protocol designed to support roaming across multivendor APs. The protocol supports roaming both on single subnets and across subnet boundaries.

LEAP—See EAPCisco Wireless.

load balancing—Load balancing is the practice of spreading processing work or communications requests evenly across multiple devices, communication links, or agents. For example, large Web sites load balance among two or more identical Web servers. Contact centers use load balancing software to distribute work fairly among its agents.

Message Digest 5 (MD5)—MD5 is a one-way hash algorithm that converts a message into a fixed string of digits called a "message digest." It is used to create digital signatures.

Novell Directory Services (NDS)—NDS is Novell's global database that stores all information about network objects (resources) and user permissions, and provides secure access to those objects.

Password Authentication Protocol (PAP)—PAP is a method to identify and authenticate Point-to-Point (PPP) peers.

reassociation service—Reassociation service enables an IEEE 802.11 station to change its association with different access points as the station moves throughout the facility.

Remote Authentication Dial-In User Service (RADIUS)—
RADIUS is an authentication service specified by the IETF that utilizes a computer-based database (RADIUS server) to compare usernames and passwords to allow access to a network.

Service Set Identifier (SSID)—The SSID is a unique, case-sensitive, alphanumeric network name used to identify a wireless LAN. The SSID can be used to segment wireless networks, but is only a rudimentary security measure. Access points broadcast SSIDs in their beacon frames; therefore, SSIDs can be easily intercepted.

signal-to-noise ratio (SNR)—The signal-to-noise ratio is a measure of the useful information being communicated relative to anything else, including external noise or interference.

Lesson 1—Locating a Wireless LAN

When you install, configure, and finally start up a wireless LAN client device, such as a universal serial bus (USB) client or Personal Computer Memory Card International Association (PCMCIA) card, the client will automatically "listen" to see if there is a wireless LAN within range. The client is also discovering if it can associate with that wireless LAN. This process of listening is called "scanning." Scanning occurs before any other process, because scanning is how a client finds the network.

There are two kinds of scanning: passive scanning and active scanning. In finding an access point, client stations follow a trail of breadcrumbs left by the access point. These breadcrumbs are called service set identifiers (SSID) and beacons. These tools serve as a means for a client station to find any and all access points.

Objectives

At the end of this lesson you will be able to:

- Describe the tools and scanning methods clients use to locate wireless LANs

- Explain terminology used to describe the processes wireless clients use to locate wireless LANs

 **Key Point**

Wireless clients automatically scan for wireless LANs operating nearby.

Service Set Identifier

The service set identifier (SSID) is a unique, case sensitive, alphanumeric value from 2-32 characters long, used by wireless LANs as a network name. This naming handle is used for segmenting networks, as a rudimentary security measure, and in the process of joining a network. The SSID value is sent in beacons, probe requests, probe responses, and other types of frames. A client station must be configured for the correct SSID in order to join a network, unless the network access points are configured to allow a station to join using any SSID value. The administrator configures the SSID (sometimes called the ESSID [Extended Service Set Identifier]) in each access point. Some stations have the ability to use the access point-broadcasted SSID value, rather than just the SSID manually specified by the administrator. If clients are to roam seamlessly among a group of access points, the clients and all access points must be configured with matching SSIDs. The most important point about an SSID is that it must match exactly between access points and clients.

Do not confuse the SSID (or ESSID) with the Basic Service Set Identifier (BSSID). The BSSID is a 6-byte hex number that identifies the access point where the frame originated or was relayed. In contrast, the SSID and ESSID are interchangeable terms denoting the network name or identifier.

Beacons

Beacons (short for beacon management frames) are short frames sent from the access point to stations (infrastructure mode) or from station-to-station (ad hoc mode) in order to organize and synchronize wireless communication on the wireless LAN. Beacons serve several functions, including those discussed in the following sections. Although more information is passed within beacons, this list covers everything that could be considered important from an administrator's point of view.

Time Synchronization

Beacons synchronize clients by way of a time stamp at the exact moment of transmission. When the client receives the beacon, it changes its own clock to reflect the clock of the access point. Once this change is made, the two clocks are synchronized. Synchronizing the clocks of communicating units will ensure that all time-sensitive functions, such as hopping in frequency hopping spread spectrum (FHSS) systems, are performed without error. The beacon also contains the beacon interval, which informs stations how often to expect the beacon.

FH or DS Parameter Sets

Beacons contain information specifically geared to the spread spectrum technology the system is using. For example, in an FHSS system, hop and dwell time parameters and hop sequence are included in the beacon. In a direct sequence spread spectrum (DSSS) system, the beacon contains channel information.

SSID Information   Stations look in beacons for the SSID of the network they wish to join. When this information is found, the station looks at the media access control (MAC) address of the beacon's origination and sends an authentication request in hopes of associating with that access point. If a station is set to accept any SSID, the station will attempt to join the network through the first access point that sends a beacon or the one with the strongest signal strength if there are multiple access points.

TIM   The traffic indication map (TIM) indicates which sleeping stations have packets queued at the access point. When operating in power management mode, a wireless client "sleeps" to save power.   The lesson entitled "Power Management Features" discusses sleeping stations. This information is passed in each beacon to all associated stations. While sleeping, synchronized stations power up their receivers, listen for the beacon, and check the TIM to see if they are listed. If they are not listed, they power down their receivers and continue sleeping.

Supported Rates   With wireless networks, many supported speeds depend on the standard of the hardware in use. For example, an 802.11b-compliant device supports 11, 5.5, 2, and 1 Mbps speeds. This capability information is passed in the beacons to inform the stations what speeds are supported on the access point.

Passive Scanning

Passive scanning is the process of listening for beacons on each channel for a specific period of time after the station is initialized. These beacons are sent by access points (infrastructure mode) or client stations (ad hoc mode), and the scanning station catalogs characteristics about the access points or stations based on these beacons. The station searching for a network listens for beacons until it hears a beacon listing the SSID of the network it wishes to join. The station then attempts to join the network through the access point that sent the beacon. The Passive Scanning Diagram illustrates clients passively scanning for APs.

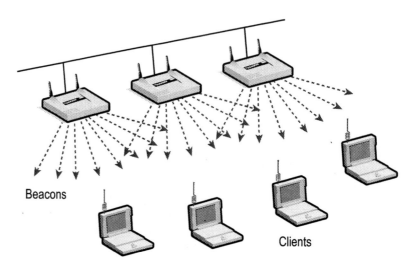

Passive Scanning

In configurations with multiple access points, the SSID of the network the station wishes to join may be broadcast by more than
one of these access points. In this situation, the station will
attempt to join the network through the access point with the
strongest signal strength and the lowest bit error rate.

Stations continue passive scanning even after associating to an
access point. Passive scanning saves time reconnecting to the network if the client is disconnected (disassociated) from the access
point to which the client is currently connected. By maintaining
a list of available access points and their characteristics (channel,
signal strength, SSID, and so forth), the station can quickly locate
the best access point should its current connection be broken for
any reason.

Stations will roam from one access point to another after the
radio signal from the access point where the station is connected
gets to a certain low level of signal strength. Roaming is implemented so that the station can stay connected to the network.
Stations use the information obtained through passive scanning
for locating the next best access point (or ad hoc network) to use
for connectivity back into the network. For this reason, overlap
between access point cells is usually specified at approximately
20-30 percent. This overlap allows stations to seamlessly roam
between access points while disconnecting and reconnecting

without a user's knowledge. Roaming is not specified as part of the 802.11 series of standards, but is being directly addressed as part of the new IEEE 802.11f draft.

Note: Because the sensitivity threshold on some radios does not work properly, sometimes an administrator sees a radio stay attached to an access point until the signal is broken due to extremely low signal strength instead of roaming to another access point that has a better signal. This situation is a known problem with some hardware and should be reported to the manufacturer.

Active Scanning

Active scanning involves sending a probe request frame from a wireless station. Stations send this probe frame when they are actively seeking a network to join. The probe frame will contain either the SSID of the network they wish to join or a broadcast SSID. If a probe request is sent specifying an SSID, only access points servicing that SSID will respond with a probe response frame. If a probe request frame is sent with a broadcast SSID, all access points within reach will respond with a probe response frame, as can be seen on the Active Scanning Diagram.

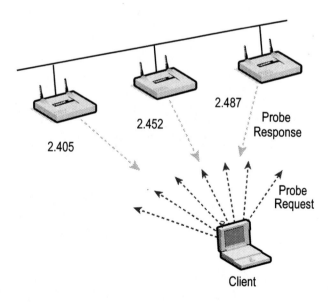

Active Scanning

The point of probing in this manner is to locate access points through which the station can attach to the network. After an access point with the proper SSID is found, the station initiates the authentication and association steps of joining the network through that access point.

The information passed from the access point to the station in probe response frames is almost identical to that of beacons. Probe response frames differ from beacons only in that they are not time stamped and do not include a TIM. Active and passive scanning can occur simultaneously on the network.

The signal strength of the probe response frames that the PC card receives helps determine the access point with which the PC card will attempt to associate. The station generally chooses the access point with the strongest signal strength and lowest bit error rate (BER). The BER is a ratio of corrupted packets to good packets and is typically determined by the signal-to-noise ratio (SNR) of the signal. If the peak of an RF signal is somewhere near the noise floor, the receiver may confuse the data signal with noise.

Beacons and probe response frames include the SSID of the network to which the access point belongs. Some access point manufacturers include a feature called "closed system" that allows the administrator to remove the SSID from the beacons through a simple check box in the access point's configuration screen. This serves to hide the available networks from some client-scanning utilities. However, because probe response frames include the SSID, a hacker can use a wireless protocol analyzer, commonly called a "sniffer," to obtain the clear text SSID from these response frames. ("SNIFFER" is a registered trademark of Network Associates, Inc.) Additionally, although closed networks do not send the SSID in beacon frames, some utilities are designed specifically for the task of locating closed networks.

Activities

1. When a wireless station is set to accept any SSID and receives beacon frames from several access points (APs) at once, how will it choose the access point it will use to join the network?

    a. It chooses the nearest access point.

    b. It chooses the first beacon it receives.

    c. It chooses the access point with the strongest signal.

    d. It chooses the access point with an SSID that matches its own.

2. Which two are functions served by beacon frames on wireless LANs? (Choose two.)

    a. Setting the WEP encryption key size

    b. Performing client and access point time synchronization

    c. Set the physical distance between the access point and the client

    d. Passing network FHSS hop and dwell time parameters

3. Why is time synchronization between wireless FHSS clients and APs important?

    a. The client must know what times it is allowed to sleep when in power save mode.

    b. The client must know when to change DSSS channels.

    c. The client must know when to hop on FHSS systems.

    d. The client must know when to change WEP keys.

4. Which statement is true concerning wireless LAN SSIDs?

    a. The client and access point SSIDs must match.

    b. The SSID is case-insensitive.

    c. The SSID must be at least 2 bits long.

    d. The SSID can only be an alpha character string.

5. You are building a multiple access point network to enable wireless roaming. Which one of the following tasks must you perform to provide this capability?

   a. Set each access point to a unique SSID.

   b. Set the access point radios to different power levels.

   c. Set each access point to a different data rate.

   d. Place the access points so that the cells overlap.

6. How do active scanning probe response frames differ from beacon frames? (Choose two.)

   a. They do not pass the SSID.

   b. They contain no TIM.

   c. They contain no time stamp.

   d. They do not set the data rate.

Extended Activity

NetStumbler is a wireless, network-monitoring utility written by Marius Milner and available for download from **http://www.netstumbler.com**. Note that the utility will only run on certain operating systems and wireless client devices. Download the utility to a compatible system, and capture information about your access point. What type of information do you see displayed?

Lesson 2—Authentication and Association

The process of connecting to a wireless LAN consists of two separate subprocesses. These subprocesses always occur in the same order, and are called authentication and association. For example, when we speak of a wireless PC card connecting to a wireless LAN, we say that the PC card has been authenticated by and has associated with a certain access point. Keep in mind that when we speak of association, we are speaking of Layer 2 connectivity, and authentication pertains directly to the radio PC card, not to the user. Understanding the steps involved in connecting a client to an access point is crucial to security, troubleshooting, and management of the wireless LAN.

Objectives

At the end of this lesson you will be able to:

- Describe the steps client devices take to connect to a wireless LAN

- Explain each of the three wireless LAN authentication and association states

- Describe the authentication methods used on 802.11 wireless LANs

- Identify emerging authentication protocols used on wireless LANs

 **Key Point**

Wireless clients connect to wireless LANs in three distinct stages.

Authentication

The first step in connecting to a wireless LAN is authentication. Authentication is the process through which a wireless node (PC Card, universal serial bus [USB] client, and so forth) has its identity verified by the network (usually the access point) to which the node is attempting to connect. This verification occurs when the access point to which the client is connecting verifies the client's identity. To put it another way, the access point responds to a client requesting to connect by verifying the client is who it says

305

it is before any connection happens. Sometimes the authentication process is null, meaning that, although both the client and access point have to proceed through this step in order to associate, there is really no special identity required for association. This is the case when most brand new access points and PC cards are installed in their default configuration. We will discuss two types of authentication processes in further reading.

The client begins the authentication process by sending an authentication request frame to the access point (in infrastructure mode). The access point will either accept or deny this request, thereafter notifying the station of its decision with an authentication response frame. The authentication process can be accomplished at the access point, or the access point might pass along this responsibility to an upstream authentication server, such as RADIUS. The RADIUS server would perform the authentication based on a list of criteria, and then return its results to the access point so that the access point could return the results to the client station. A wireless client may authenticate (or preauthenticate) to many access points simultaneously, but may only be associated (connected) to one access point at a time.

Association

After a wireless client has been authenticated, the client associates with the access point. Association is the state at which a client is allowed to pass data through an access point. If your PC card is associated to an access point, you are connected to that access point, and therefore to the network.

The process of becoming associated is as follows:

1. When a client wishes to connect, the client sends an authentication request to the access point and then receives an authentication response.

2. After authentication is completed, the station sends an association request frame to the access point. The access point replies to the client with an association response frame, either allowing or disallowing association.

States of Authentication and Association

The complete process of authentication and association occurs in the following three distinct states:

- Unauthenticated and unassociated
- Authenticated and unassociated
- Authenticated and associated

Unauthenticated and Unassociated

In this initial state, the wireless node is completely disconnected from the network and unable to pass frames through the access point. Access points keep a table of client connection statuses known as the association table. It is important to note that different vendors refer differently to the unauthenticated and unassociated state in their access points' association table. This table will typically show "unauthenticated" for any client that has not completed the authentication process or has attempted authentication and failed.

Authenticated and Unassociated

In this second state, the wireless client has passed the authentication process, but is not yet associated with the access point. The client is not yet allowed to send or receive data through the access point. The access point's association table will typically show "authenticated." Because clients pass the authentication stage and immediately (within milliseconds) proceed into the association stage, very quickly, you rarely see the "authenticated" step on the access point. It is far more likely that you will see "unauthenticated" or "associated," which brings us to the last stage.

Authenticated and Associated

In this final state, the wireless node is completely connected to the network and able to send and receive data through the access point to which the node is connected (associated). The Association Diagram illustrates a client associating with an access point. You will likely see "associated" in the access point's association table denoting that this client is fully connected and authorized to pass traffic through the access point. As you can deduce from the description of each of these three states, advanced wireless network security measures would be implemented at the point at which the client is attempting to authenticate.

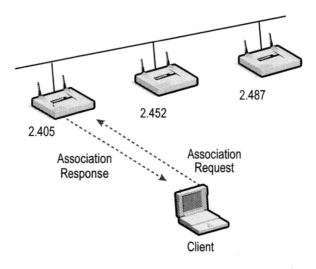

Association

Authentication Methods

The IEEE 802.11 standard specifies two methods of authentication: Open System authentication and Shared Key authentication. The simpler and also the more secure of the two methods is Open System authentication. For a client to become authenticated, the client must walk through a series of steps with the access point. This series of steps varies, depending on the authentication process used. In the following sections, we will discuss each authentication process specified by the 802.11 standard, how they work, and why they are used.

Open System Authentication

Open System authentication is a method of null authentication and is specified by the IEEE 802.11 as the default setting in wireless LAN equipment. Using this method of authentication, a station can associate with any access point that uses Open System authentication based only on having the right service set identifier (SSID). The SSIDs must match on both the access point and client before a client is allowed to complete the authentication process. Uses of the SSID relating to security will be discussed in further reading on Security. The Open System authentication process is used effectively in both secure and nonsecure environments.

Open System Authentication Process

The Open System authentication process occurs as follows:

1. The wireless client makes a request to authenticate to the access point.

2. The access point authenticates the client and sends a positive response that completes authentication; and then the client becomes associated (connected).

These steps are shown on the Open System Authentication Process Diagram.

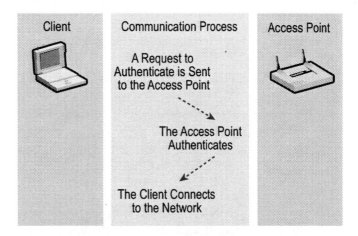

Open System Authentication Process

Open System authentication is a very simple process. As a wireless LAN administrator, you have the option of using wired equivalent privacy (WEP) encryption with Open System authentication. If WEP is used with the Open System authentication process, there is still no verification of the WEP key on each side of the connection during authentication. Rather, the WEP key is used only for encrypting data after the client is authenticated and associated.

Open System authentication is used in several scenarios, but there are two main reasons to use it. First, Open System authentication is considered the more secure of the two available authentication methods for reasons explained below. Second, Open System authentication is simple to configure because it requires no configuration at all. All 802.11-compliant wireless LAN hardware is configured to use Open System authentication by default, making it easy to get started building and connecting your wireless LAN right out of the box.

Shared Key Authentication

Shared Key authentication is a method of authentication that requires use of WEP. WEP encryption uses keys that are entered (usually by the administrator) into both the client and the access point. These keys must match on both sides for WEP to work properly. Shared Key authentication uses WEP keys in two ways, as we will describe here.

Shared Key Authentication Process

The authentication process using Shared Key authentication occurs as follows:

1. **A client requests authentication to an access point—** This step is the same as that of Open System authentication.

2. **The access point issues a challenge to the client—**This challenge is randomly generated plain text, which is sent from the access point to the client in the clear.

3. **The client responds to the challenge—**The client responds by encrypting the challenge text using the client's WEP key and sending it back to the access point.

4. **The access point responds to the client's response—** The access point decrypts the client's encrypted response to verify that the challenge text is encrypted using a matching WEP key. Through this process, the access point determines whether or not the client has the correct WEP key. If the client's WEP key is correct, the access point will respond positively and authenticate the client. If the client's WEP key is not correct, the access point will respond negatively, and will not authenticate the client, leaving the client unauthenticated and unassociated.

This process is shown on the Shared Key Authentication Process Diagram.

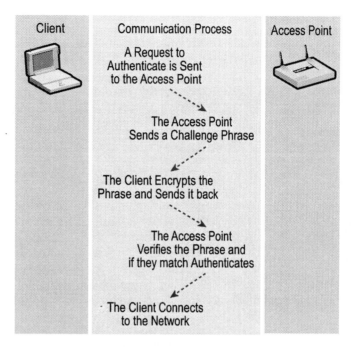

Shared Key Authentication Process

It would seem that the shared key authentication process is more secure than that of Open System authentication, but as you will soon see, it is not. Rather, Shared Key authentication opens the door for would-be hackers. It is important to understand both ways that WEP is used. The WEP key is used during the shared key authentication process to verify a client's identity, and it is also used for encryption of the data payload sent by the client through the access point. This type of WEP is discussed in further reading on Security.

Authentication Security

Shared Key authentication is not considered secure because the access point transmits the challenge text in the clear and receives the same challenge text encrypted with the WEP key. This scenario allows a hacker using a sniffer to see both the plaintext challenge and the encrypted challenge. Having both of these values, a hacker can use a simple cracking program to derive the

WEP key. After obtaining the WEP key, the hacker could decrypt encrypted data traffic in real time by simply entering the WEP key into his or her own computer. It is for this reason that Open System authentication is considered more secure than Shared Key authentication.

Note: It is important for the wireless network administrator to understand that neither Open System nor Shared Key authentication types are secure. For this reason, a wireless LAN security solution that is above and beyond what the 802.11 standard specifies is important and necessary.

Shared Secrets and Certificates

Shared secrets are strings of numbers or text that are commonly referred to as the WEP key. Certificates are another method of user identification used with wireless networks. Just as with WEP keys, certificates (which are authentication documents) are placed on the client machine ahead of time. This placement is done so that when the user wishes to authenticate to the wireless network, the authentication mechanism is already in place on the client station. Both of these methods have historically been implemented in a manual fashion, but applications are available today that allow automation of this process.

Emerging Wireless Security Solutions

Many new authentication security solutions and protocols are on the market today, including Virtual Private Network (VPN) and IEEE 802.1x port-based access control, using Extensible Authentication Protocol (EAP). Use of 802.1x and EAP involves passing authentication from the access point through to the authentication server located upstream from the access point, while keeping the client waiting during the authentication phase. Windows XP has native support for 802.11, 802.1x, and EAP. Cisco and other wireless LAN manufacturers also support these standards. For this reason, it is easy to see that the 802.1x and EAP authentication solution could be a common solution in the wireless LAN security market.

802.1x and EAP
The IEEE 802.1x standard is relatively new, and devices that support it have the ability to allow a connection into the network at layer 2 only if user authentication is successful. This protocol works well for access points that need the ability to keep users disconnected if they are not supposed to be on the network. EAP is a layer 2 protocol that is a flexible replacement for Password Authentica-

tion Protocol (PAP) or Challenge Handshake Authentication Protocol (CHAP) under Point-to-Point Protocol (PPP) that works over local area networks. Extensible Authentication Protocol (EAP) allows plug-ins at either end of a link through which many methods of authentication can be used. In the past, PAP and/or CHAP have been used for user authentication, and both support using passwords. The need for a stronger, more flexible alternative is clear with wireless networks because more varied implementations are available with wireless than with wired networks.

Typically, user authentication is accomplished using a remote authentication dial-in user service (RADIUS) server and some type of user database (Native RADIUS, NDS, Active Directory, LDAP, and so forth). The process of authenticating using EAP is shown on the 802.1x and EAP Diagram. The forthcoming 802.11i standard includes support for 802.1x, EAP, Authentication, Authorization, and Accounting (AAA), mutual authentication, and key generation, none of which were included in the original 802.11 standard. AAA is an acronym for authentication (identifying who you are), authorization (attributes to allow you to perform certain tasks on the network), and accounting (shows what you have done and where you have been on the network).

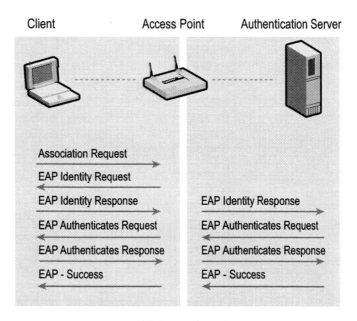

802.1x and EAP

In the 802.1x standard model, network authentication consists of three pieces: the supplicant, the authenticator, and the authentication server. The supplicant is the client who is requesting authentication. The authenticator is typically the access point that supports the 802.1x protocol and relays authentication information between the supplicant and the authentication server. The authentication server is the software application that supports EAP and authenticates supplicants based on information contained in a database.

Because wireless LAN security is essential, and EAP authentication types provide the means of securing the wireless LAN connection, vendors are rapidly developing and adding EAP authentication types to their authentication software. Many RADIUS implementations now support various flavors of EAP, and many custom RADIUS-like software applications that various EAP authentication types support are being developed specifically for wireless networks. Knowing the type of EAP being used is important in understanding the characteristics of the authentication method, such as passwords, key generation, mutual authentication, and protocol. Some of the commonly deployed EAP authentication types include:

- **EAP-MD-5 Challenge**—The earliest EAP authentication type, this essentially duplicates CHAP password protection on a wireless LAN. EAP-MD5 represents a kind of base-level EAP support among 802.1x devices.

- **EAP-Cisco Wireless**—Also called LEAP (Lightweight Extensible Authentication Protocol), this EAP authentication type is used primarily in Cisco wireless LAN access points. LEAP provides security during credential exchange, encrypts data transmission using dynamically generated WEP keys, and supports mutual authentication.

- **EAP-TLS**—EAP-Transport Layer Security (TLS) provides for certificate-based mutual authentication of the client and the network. Using dynamically generated user-based and session-based WEP keys distributed to secure the connection, EAP-TLS relies on client-side and server-side certificates to perform authentication. Windows XP includes an EAP-TLS client, and EAP-TLS is also supported by Windows 2000.

- **EAP-TTLS**—Funk Software and Certicom have jointly developed EAP-Tunneled Transport Layer Security (TTLS). EAP-TTLS is an extension of EAP-TLS, which provides for certificate-based mutual authentication of the client and network. Unlike EAP-TLS, however, EAP-TTLS requires only server-side certificates, eliminating the need to configure certificates for each wireless LAN client.

  In addition, EAP-TTLS supports legacy password protocols; thus, you can deploy it against your existing authentication system (such as Active Directory or NDS). EAP-TTLS securely tunnels client authentication within TLS records, ensuring that the user remains anonymous to eavesdroppers on the wireless link. Dynamically generated user-based and session-based WEP keys are distributed to secure the connection.

- **EAP-SRP**—EAP-Secure Remote Password (SRP) is a secure, password-based authentication and key-exchange protocol. It solves the problem of authenticating clients to servers securely in cases where the user of the client software must memorize a small secret (like a password) and carries no other secret information. The server carries a verifier for each user, which allows the server to authenticate the client. However, if the verifier were compromised, the attacker would not be allowed to impersonate the client. In addition, SRP exchanges a cryptographically strong secret as a byproduct of successful authentication, which enables the two parties to communicate securely.

- **EAP-SIM (GSM)**—EAP-Subscriber Identity Module (SIM) is a mechanism for Mobile IP network access authentication and registration key generation using the GSM Subscriber Identity Module (SIM). The rationale for using the GSM SIM with Mobile IP is to leverage the existing GSM authorization infrastructure with the existing user base and the existing SIM card distribution channels. By using the SIM key exchange, no preconfigured security association other than the SIM card is required on the mobile node. The idea is not to use the GSM radio access technology, but to use GSM SIM authorization with Mobile IP over any link layer, for example on Wireless LAN access networks.

It is likely that this list of EAP authentication types will grow as more vendors enter the wireless LAN security market, and until the market chooses a standard.

Note: The different types of EAP authentication are not covered on the CWNA exam, but understanding what EAP is and how it is used in general is a key element in being effective as a wireless network administrator.

VPN Solutions

Virtual private network (VPN) technology provides the means to securely transmit data between two network devices over an insecure data transport medium. It is commonly used to link remote computers or networks to a corporate server by means of the Internet. However, VPNs are also a solution for protecting data on a wireless network. VPNs work by creating a tunnel on top of a protocol such as IP. Traffic inside the tunnel is encrypted and totally isolated, as can be seen on the Access Point with an Integrated VPN Server and the Access Point with an External VPN Server Diagrams.

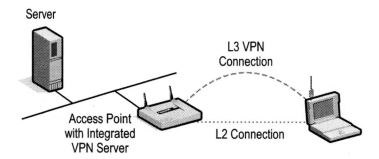

Access Point with an Integrated VPN Server

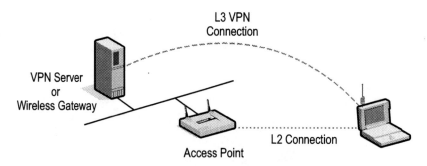

Access Point with an External VPN Server

VPN technology provides the following three levels of security:

- User authentication ensures that only authorized users (over a specific device) are able to connect, send, and receive data over the wireless network.

- Encryption offers additional protection as it ensures that even if transmissions are intercepted, they cannot be decoded without significant time and effort.

- Data authentication ensures the integrity of data on the wireless network, guaranteeing that all traffic is from authenticated devices only.

For the following reasons, applying VPN technology to secure a wireless network requires a different approach than when it is used on wired networks:

- The inherent repeater function of wireless access points automatically forwards traffic between wireless LAN stations that communicate together and that appear on the same wireless network.

- The range of the wireless network will likely extend beyond the physical boundaries of an office or home, giving intruders the means to compromise the network.

The ease and scalability with which wireless LAN solutions can be deployed makes them ideal solutions for many different environments. As a result, implementation of VPN security varies based on the needs of each type of environment. For example, if a hacker with a wireless sniffer obtained the WEP key, he or she could decode packets in real time. With a VPN solution, the packets would not only be encrypted, but also tunneled. This extra layer of security provides many benefits at the access level.

It is notable that not all VPNs let wireless users roam between subnets or networks without breaking the secure tunnel, and not all VPNs permit Transport and Application Layer connections to remain established while roaming occurs. Another problem is the operating system the mobile clients run because it determines whether or not the client can use VPN services.

Activities

1. How would a VPN solution protect a wireless LAN from unauthorized access?

   a. By tunneling the WEP key to protect it from interception

   b. By encapsulating wireless frames within tunnel packets

   c. By securing the wireless medium

   d. By encrypting data packets carried within wireless frames

2. During Shared Key authentication, a wireless client responds incorrectly to an access point's WEP challenge. At which authentication and association states does the access point leave the client?

   a. Authenticated and associated

   b. Unauthenticated and associated

   c. Authenticated and unassociated

   d. Unauthenticated and unassociated

3. Which of the following are reasons to use Open System instead of Shared Key authentication on a wireless LAN? (Choose two.)

   a. Open System authentication encrypts the access point challenge text sent to the client.

   b. Open System authentication works on any client operating system.

   c. Open System authentication is more secure.

   d. Open System authentication takes less effort to configure.

4. Which statement describes the use of WEP with Open System authentication?

   a. The WEP key and the data are sent in clear text.

   b. The access point and client use the WEP key to encrypt the data only.

   c. The WEP key is broadcast to all clients on the wireless segment.

   d. The client can communicate with the access point using any key size from 40- to 128-bit.

5. A wireless client has attempted authentication and failed. A typical access point's association table will show the client in which state?

   a. Authenticated

   b. Associated

   c. Unauthenticated

   d. Unassociated

6. Which one of the following is considered among 802.1x devices as the base-level EAP authentication type?

   a. EAP-MD-5 Challenge

   b. EAP-Cisco Wireless

   c. EAP-TTLS

   d. EAP-TTL

Extended Activity

Design a wireless VPN. Show how you would configure the network segments to protect wired network traffic, such as shared resources, from the wireless network users. Draw a state diagram showing the 802.11 client authentication and association process (Open System, no WEP) and the process of building and connecting the VPN tunnel. You may use any tunnel protocol you wish. Start by researching wireless VPNs at **http://www.nwfusion.com** and **http://www.dell.com**.

Lesson 3—Service Sets

A service set is a term that describes the basic components of a fully operational wireless LAN. There are three ways to configure a wireless LAN, and each way requires a different set of hardware. The three ways to configure a wireless LAN are:

- Basic service set
- Extended service set
- Independent basic service set

This lesson discusses the three wireless LAN service sets, and how clients roam across service set cell boundaries.

Objectives

At the end of this lesson you will be able to:

- Describe concepts associated with wireless LAN service sets
- Explain how wireless devices communicate in each service set
- Explain how roaming occurs across service sets
- Describe how roaming clients maintain Layer 2 and 3 connectivity when moving between service sets

 **Key Point**

Service sets describe the basic hardware configuration of a wireless LAN.

BSS

When one access point is connected to a wired network and a set of wireless stations, the network configuration is referred to as a basic service set (BSS). A basic service set consists of only one access point and one or more wireless clients, as shown on the Basic Service Set Diagram. A basic service set uses infrastructure mode, a mode that requires use of an access point and in which all of the wireless traffic traverses the access point. No direct client-to-client transmissions are allowed.

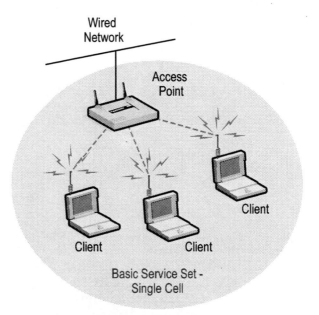

Basic Service Set

Each wireless client must use an access point to communicate with any other wireless client or any wired host on the network. The BSS covers a single cell, or radio frequency (RF) area, around the access point with varying data rate zones (concentric circles) of differing data speeds, measured in Mbps. The data speeds in these concentric circles will depend on the technology utilized. If the BSS were made up of 802.11b equipment, the concentric circles would have data speeds of 11, 5.5, 2, and 1 Mbps, respectively, moving away from the access point. In other words, the data rates decrease as the zones get farther away from the access point. A BSS has one unique service set identifier (SSID).

ESS

An extended service set (ESS) is defined as two or more basic service sets connected by a common distribution system, as shown on the Extended Service Set Diagram. The distribution system can be wired, wireless, LAN, WAN, or any other method of network connectivity. An ESS must have at least two APs operating in infrastructure mode. Similar to a BSS, all packets in an ESS must go through one of the APs.

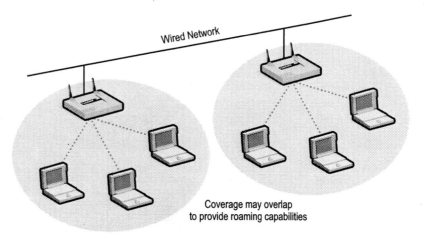

Extended Service Set

Other characteristics of extended service sets, according to the 802.11 standard, are that an ESS covers multiple cells, allows (but does not require) roaming capabilities, and does not require the same SSID in both basic service sets.

IBSS

An independent basic service set (IBSS) is also known as an ad hoc network. An IBSS has no access point or any other access to a distribution system, but it covers one single cell and has one SSID, as shown on the Independent Basic Service Set Diagram. The clients in an IBSS alternate the responsibility of sending beacons because there is no access point to perform this task.

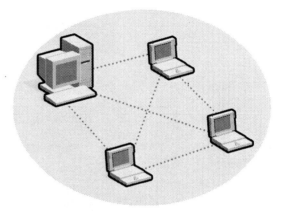

Independent Basic Service Set

In order to transmit data outside an IBSS, one of the clients in the IBSS must be act as a gateway or router, using a software solution for this purpose. In an IBSS, clients make direct connections to each other when transmitting data. For this reason, an IBSS is often referred to as a peer-to-peer network.

Roaming

Roaming is the process or ability of a wireless client to move seamlessly from one cell (or BSS) to another without losing network connectivity. APs hand off a client to one another in a way that is invisible to the client and ensures unbroken network connectivity. The Roaming in an ESS Diagram illustrates a client roaming from one BSS to another BSS.

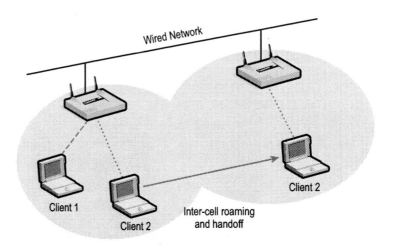

Roaming in an ESS

When any area in the building is within reception range of more than one access point, the cells' coverage overlaps. Overlapping coverage areas are an important attribute of the wireless LAN setup, because it enables seamless roaming between overlapping cells. Roaming allows mobile users with portable stations to move freely between overlapping cells, constantly maintaining their network connection.

When roaming is seamless, a work session can be maintained while moving from one cell to another. Multiple APs can provide wireless roaming coverage for an entire building or campus.

When the coverage area of two or more APs overlap, stations in the overlapping area can establish the best possible connection with one of the APs while continuously searching for the best access point. In order to minimize packet loss during switchover, the "old" and "new" APs communicate to coordinate the roaming process. This function is similar to a cellular phones' handoff, with two main differences:

- On a packet-based LAN system, the transition from cell to cell may be performed between packet transmissions, as opposed to telephony where the transition may occur during a phone conversation.

- On a voice system, a temporary disconnection may not affect the conversation. In contrast, in a packet-based environment, it significantly reduces performance because the upper layer protocols then retransmit the data.

Standards

The 802.11 standard does not define how roaming should be performed, but it does define the basic building blocks. These building blocks include active and passive scanning and a reassociation process. The reassociation process occurs when a wireless station roams from one access point to another, becoming associated with the new access point.

The 802.11 standard allows a client to roam among multiple APs operating on the same or separate channels. For example, every 100 ms, an access point might transmit a beacon signal that includes a time stamp for client synchronization, a traffic indication map (TIM), an SSID, channel information, spread spectrum type used, an indication of supported data rates, and other parameters. Roaming clients use the beacon to gauge the strength of their existing connection to the access point. If the connection is weak, the roaming station can attempt to associate itself with a new access point.

To meet the needs of mobile radio communications, the 802.11b standard must tolerate connections being dropped and reestablished. The standard attempts to ensure minimum disruption to data delivery, and provides some features for caching and forwarding messages between BSSs.

Particular implementations of some higher layer protocols, such as Transmission Control Protocol/Internet Protocol (TCP/IP), may be less tolerant. For example, in a network where Dynamic Host Configuration Protocol (DHCP) is used to assign IP addresses, a roaming node may lose its connection when it moves across cell boundaries. The node will then have to reestablish the connection when it enters the next BSS or cell. Software solutions are available to address this particular problem.

One such solution is Mobile IP. Mobile IP is an Internet Engineering Task Force (IETF) Request for Comment (RFC), RFC 2002, that was created to explain how to best enable mobile users to stay connected to the Internet while moving between connection points. This is accomplished by use of home agents and foreign agents. These two agents work together to ensure that traffic destined to a mobile node reaches the node wherever it is connected. A home agent or foreign agent can be a computer, a router, or other similar device that is capable of running the Mobile IP protocol. There are some caveats in many Mobile IP solutions that are briefly addressed in this text so that you understand what to look for in a Mobile IP solution.

First, Mobile IP does not allow mobile devices and mobility agents on the network to share state information about each session that a mobile device has established. This means that applications cannot persist between periods when the mobile device cannot be reached. When the mobile device reattaches to the network, the operating system, applications, and protocols may need to clean up broken application sessions and reauthenticate the client, while a user might need to log back in to the network, restart applications, and reenter lost data.

Second, "session persistence" involves more than forwarding packets to a user's new location. If you do not have transport and application session persistence, the solution breaks down. The reason is that when a transport protocol cannot communicate to its peer, underlying protocols, such as TCP, assume that network congestion has caused the disruption of service. When this occurs, these protocols back off, which reduces performance and eventually terminates the connection. The only way to solve this problem is to deploy mobile nodes with a software solution that acts on behalf of the mobile device when it is unreachable.

The 802.11b standard leaves much of the detailed functioning of what it calls the distribution system to manufacturers. This was a deliberate decision on the part of the standard designers, because they were most concerned with making the standard entirely independent of any other existing network standards. As a practical matter, an overwhelming majority of 802.11b wireless LANs using ESS topologies are connected to Ethernet LANs and make heavy use of TCP/IP. Wireless LAN vendors have stepped into the gap to offer proprietary methods of facilitating roaming between nodes in an ESS.

Note: When a station roams from an old access point to a new access point, the new access point is responsible for ensuring that any bridges between the two APs are properly notified of the station's new location. The manner in which this is accomplished is not specified. The only requirement is that some method is implemented that ensures that packets will flow properly to the station's new access point. The new IEEE 802.11f draft addresses the issue of standardizing roaming with the introduction of the Inter Access Point Protocol (IAPP).

Connectivity

The 802.11 media access control (MAC) layer is responsible for how a client associates with an access point. When an 802.11 client enters the range of one or more APs, the client chooses an access point to associate with (also called joining a BSS), based on signal strength and observed frame error rates.

After it is associated with the access point, the station periodically surveys all 802.11 channels in order to assess whether a different access point would provide better performance characteristics. If the client determines that there is a stronger signal from a different access point, the client reassociates with the new access point, tuning to the radio channel to which that access point is set. The station will not attempt to roam from its existing association until it drops below a manufacturer-defined signal strength threshold.

Reassociation

Reassociation usually occurs because the wireless station has physically moved away from the original access point, causing the signal to weaken. In other cases, reassociation occurs due to a change in radio characteristics in the building, or due simply to high network traffic on the original access point. In the latter case, this function is known as load balancing, because its primary function is to distribute the total wireless LAN load most efficiently across the available wireless infrastructure in a given area.

Association and reassociation differ only slightly in their use. Association request frames are used when joining a network for the first time. Reassociation request frames are used when roaming between APs so that the new access point knows to negotiate transfer of buffered frames from the old access point and to inform the distribution system that the client has moved. Reassociation is illustrated on the Roaming with Reassociation Diagram.

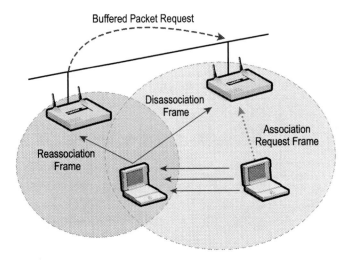

Roaming with Reassociation

By creating a series of overlapping 802.11 cells throughout a building or across a campus, this process of dynamically associating and reassociating with APs allows network managers to set up wireless LANs with very broad coverage. To be successful, an IT manager ideally will employ channel reuse, taking care to configure each access point on an 802.11 DSSS channel that does not overlap with a channel used by a neighboring access point. While 14 partially overlapping channels are specified in 802.11 DSSS (11 channels can be used within the U.S.), only three channels do not overlap at all, and these are the best to use for multicell coverage. If two APs are in range of one another and are set to the same or partially overlapping channels, they may cause some interference for one another, therefore lowering the total available bandwidth in the area of overlap.

VPN Use

Wireless virtual private network (VPN) solutions are typically implemented in two fashions. First, a centralized VPN server is implemented upstream from the APs. This VPN server could be a proprietary hardware solution or a server running a VPN application. Both serve the same purpose and provide the same type of security and connectivity. Placing this VPN server (also acting as a gateway and firewall) between the wireless user and the core network provides a level of security similar to wired VPNs.

The second approach is a distributed set of VPN servers. Some manufacturers implement a VPN server into their APs. This type of solution provides security for small-office and medium-size organizations without use of an external authentication mechanism, such as RADIUS. For scalability, these same access point/ VPN servers typically support RADIUS.

Tunnels are built from the client station to the VPN server, as illustrated on Roaming within VPN Tunnels Diagram. When a user roams, the client is roaming between APs across layer 2 boundaries. This process is seamless to the layer 3 connectivity. However, if a tunnel is built to the access point or centralized VPN server and a layer 3 boundary is crossed, a mechanism of some kind must be provided for keeping the tunnel alive when the boundary is crossed.

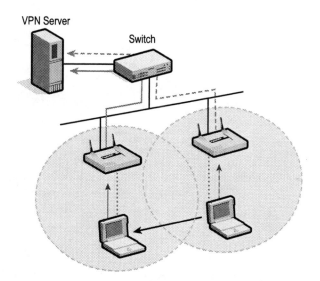

Roaming within VPN Tunnels

Layer 2 and Layer 3 Boundaries

A constraint of existing technology is that wired networks are often segmented for manageability.   Enterprises with multiple buildings, such as hospitals or large businesses, often implement a LAN in each building and then connect these LANs with routers or switch-routers. This layer 3 segmentation has two major advantages. First, it contains broadcasts effectively, and second, it allows access control between segments on the network. This type of segmentation can also be done at layer 2 using VLANs on switches. VLANs are often implemented floor-by-floor in multifloor office buildings or for each remote building in a campus for the same reasons. Segmenting at layer 2 in this fashion completely segments the networks, as if multiple networks were being implemented. When using routers such as those seen on the Roaming Across Layer 3 Boundaries Diagram, users must have a method of roaming across router boundaries without losing their layer 3 connection. The APs still maintain the layer 2 connection; however, because the IP subnet has changed while roaming, the connection to servers, for example, will be broken. Without subnet-roaming capability (such as that used with a Mobile IP solution or using DHCP), wireless LAN APs must all be connected to a single subnet (also called a "a flat network"). This work-around can be done at a loss of network management flexibility, but customers may be willing to incur this cost if they perceive that the value of the end system is high enough.

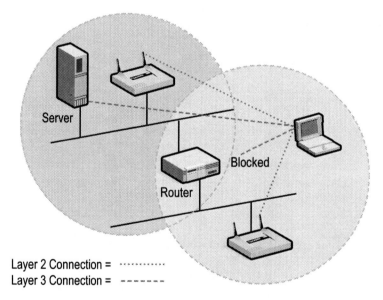

Layer 2 Connection = ·············
Layer 3 Connection = ~ ~ ~ ~ ~ ~ ~

Roaming Across Layer 3 Boundaries

Many network environments (multibuilding campuses, multifloor high rises, or older or historical buildings) cannot embrace a single subnet solution as a practical option. This wired architecture is at odds with current wireless LAN technology. APs cannot hand off a session when a remote device moves across router boundaries, because crossing routers changes the client device's IP address. The wired system no longer knows where to send the message. When a mobile device reattaches to the network, all application end points are lost, and users are forced to log in again, reauthenticate, relocate themselves in their applications, and recreate lost data. The same type of problem is incurred when using VLANs. Switches see users as roaming across VLAN boundaries. The Roaming Across VLANs Diagram illustrates this problem.

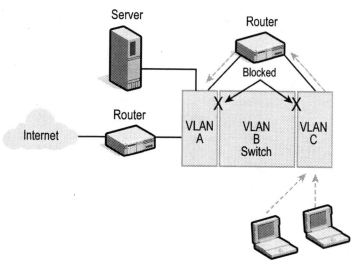

Roaming across VLANs

A hardware solution to this problem is to deploy all APs on a single VLAN using a flat IP subnet for all APs so that no change of IP address for roaming users occurs, and a Mobile IP solution is not required. Using a firewall, a router, a gateway device, and so forth, users are then routed as a group back into the corporate network. This solution can be difficult to implement in many instances, but it is generally accepted as the "standard" methodology. In many more instances, an enterprise must forego using a wireless LAN altogether because such a solution simply is not practical.

Even with all APs on a single subnet, mobile users can still encounter coverage problems. If a user moves out of range, into a coverage hole, or simply suspends the device to prolong battery life, all application end points are lost. Users in these situations must log back in to the network and resume their application sessions where they left off.

Note: Several layer 3 solutions are on the market as of this writing. One such solution is an access point that has a built in VPN server and performs full routing, including routing protocols, such as RIP. Another solution is implemented on a series of servers using the Mobile IP standard (RFC 2002). Many of the software solutions are implemented in somewhat the same manner.

Load Balancing

Congested areas with many users and heavy traffic load per access point may require a multicell structure. In a multicell structure, multiple co-located APs "illuminate" the same area, creating a common coverage area, which increases aggregate throughput. Stations inside the common coverage area automatically associate with the access point that is less loaded and provides the best signal quality. This feature is only available on enterprise-class APs.

As illustrated on the Load Balancing Diagram, the stations are equally divided between the APs in order to equally share the load between all APs. Efficiency is maximized because all APs are working at the same low-level load. Load balancing is also known as load sharing and is usually configured on both the stations and the access point.

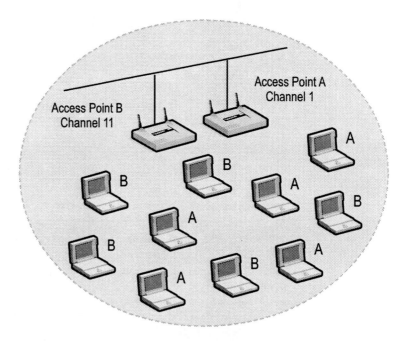

Load Balancing

Activities

1. A wireless client roamed across service set boundaries. Although the client maintained its network association, the user's open network application stopped responding, forcing the user to log off and back onto the network and restart the application. The network is designed to isolate wireless clients on routed VLAN segments separated from the wired network, and each access point is located on a separate VLAN. How can you best resolve the client's VLAN connectivity issue?

   a. Place a VPN server on each VLAN, have the client log out before moving between APs, and then log in to the new VLAN VPN server.

   b. Leave each access point on a different VLAN segment, and implement load balancing across the APs.

   c. Place all APs on single, flat IP network segments so that when roaming, no change of IP address is necessary.

   d. Use DHCP to dynamically assign the wireless client an IP address whenever she moves to a new segment.

2. Which statement best describes load balancing across wireless network APs?

   a. It creates a common coverage area to increase aggregate wireless network throughput.

   b. It builds a network environment that only allows the highest priority clients network access.

   c. Clients automatically associate with the access point operating at the highest data rate.

   d. Clients automatically log off and on VPN servers, based on network load and error rates.

3. When entering the range of one or more APs, how does a roaming client choose an access point with which to associate? (Choose two.)

   a. Data rate

   b. Signal strength

   c. Channel number

   d. Error rates

4. Which term describes the operation mode of a BSS?

   a. Peer-to-peer mode

   b. Infrastructure mode

   c. Ad hoc mode

   d. Client-to-client mode

5. Which statement is true concerning a wireless IBSS?

   a. No client-to-client communications are allowed.

   b. Clients may seamlessly roam between service sets.

   c. The service set must include at least two APs.

   d. It consists of a single cell and one SSID.

Extended Activities

Log in to the WestNet Learning Technologies, Inc. Online Student Resources Center found at **http://www.westnetinc.com**. Download and perform the following wireless networking labs:

- Lab 1: Infrastructure Mode Connectivity

- Lab 2: Infrastructure Mode Throughput Test

- Lab 5: Rudimentary Security Features with Seamless Roaming in an Extended Service Set

Note that you must first register to gain access to the Student Resources Center.

To complete the labs, you will require access to a wireless network and several PCs. The labs list the hardware and software required.

Lesson 4—Power Management Features

While operating, wireless client devices use a significant amount of power. Because many wireless nodes are battery-powered devices, such as laptops and PDAs, conserving power using a power-saving mode is especially important to mobile wireless network users. Extending battery life allows the user to stay up and running longer without a recharge. This lesson discusses the two power management modes used in 802.11 networks, and how they affect wireless client device operations.

Objectives

At the end of this lesson you will be able to:

- Describe the two power management modes used by 802.11 wireless LAN clients

- Explain how power management affects communications in wireless networks.

 **Key Point**

Wireless client device power management can significantly increase mobile node battery life, but can negatively impact network throughput.

Power Management Modes

802.11 wireless clients operate in one of two power management modes specified by the IEEE 802.11 standard: continuous aware mode (CAM) and power save polling (PSP) mode. CAM is the always-on mode; PSP mode allows a wireless client to conserve battery power by "sleeping" for a short time period.

CAM

Continuous aware mode is the setting during which a wireless client uses full power, does not "sleep," and is constantly in regular communication with the access point. Any computers that are continuously plugged into an AC power outlet, such as a desktop or server, should always be set for CAM. Under these circumstances, there is no reason to have the PC card conserve power.

PSP Mode

Using power save polling (PSP) mode allows a wireless client to "sleep." By sleep, we mean that the wireless client device actually powers down for a very short amount of time, perhaps a small fraction of a second, while it is not communicating. This sleep is enough time to save a significant amount of power on the wireless client over a period of time. In turn, the power saved by the wireless client enables a laptop computer user, for example, to work for a longer period of time on batteries, making that user more productive. Sleep time is generally measured in milliseconds, and is sometimes configurable in the wireless-client utility software.

When using PSP, the wireless client behaves differently within basic service sets and independent basic service sets. The one similarity in behavior from a Basic Service Set (BSS) to an Independent Basic Service Set (IBSS) is the sending and receiving of beacons.

The processes that operate during PSP mode, in both BSS and IBSS, are described below. Keep in mind that these processes occur many times per second. That fact allows a wireless LAN to maintain its connectivity, but also causes a certain amount of additional overhead. An administrator should consider this overhead when planning for the needs of the users on the wireless LAN. Some vendors have proprietary sleep modes, which are supposedly more effective. The more the wireless client device sleeps, the greater the impact will be on its throughput.

PSP Mode in a BSS

When using PSP mode in a BSS, stations first send a frame to the access point to inform the access point that they are going to sleep (temporarily powering down). The access point then records the sleeping stations as asleep. The access point buffers any frames that are intended for the sleeping stations. Traffic for those clients who are asleep continues arriving at the access point, but the access point cannot send traffic to a sleeping client. Therefore, frames get queued in a buffer marked for the sleeping client.

The access point is constantly sending beacons at a regular interval. Because clients are time synchronized with the access point, they know exactly when to receive the beacon. Clients that are sleeping power up their receivers to listen for beacons, which contain the traffic indication map (TIM). The length of the sleeping period for which a client is configured is based on how many beacons it will 'skip'. If a station sees itself listed in the TIM, it powers up, and sends a frame to the access point. The frame notifies the access point that the station is now awake. The client then has to request its buffered frames by sending another frame to the access point. After the client has received its frames from the access point, the client sends a message to the access point stating that it is going back to "sleep." The process repeats itself over and over again. This process creates some overhead that would not be present if PSP mode were not being utilized. The steps of this process are shown on the PSP Mode in a BSS Diagram.

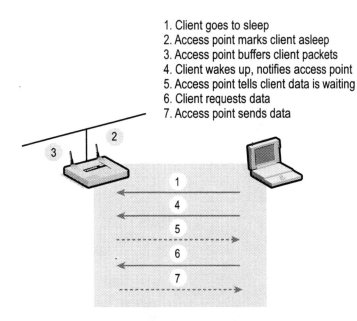

1. Client goes to sleep
2. Access point marks client asleep
3. Access point buffers client packets
4. Client wakes up, notifies access point
5. Access point tells client data is waiting
6. Client requests data
7. Access point sends data

PSP Mode in a BSS

PSP in an IBSS

The power saving communication process in an IBSS is very different than when power saving mode is used in a BSS. An IBSS does not contain an access point, so there is no device to buffer frames. Therefore, every station must buffer frames destined from itself to every other station in the ad hoc network. Stations alternate sending beacons on an IBSS network using varied methods, which each depend on the manufacturer.

When stations are using power saving mode, during a period of time called an announcement traffic indication messages (ATIM) window, each station is fully awake and ready to receive data frames. ATIMs are unicast frames that stations use to notify other stations that data is destined to them and that they should stay awake long enough to receive it. ATIMs are sent during the ATIM window. The process followed by stations in order to pass traffic between peers is:

1. Stations are synchronized through the beacons so they wake up before the ATIM window begins, in order to receive the beacon.

2. The ATIM window begins, and stations send ATIM frames notifying other stations of buffered traffic destined to them.

3. Stations receiving ATIM frames during the ATIM window stay awake to receive data frames. If no ATIM frames are received, stations may go back to sleep.

4. The ATIM window closes, and stations begin transmitting data frames. After receiving data frames, stations may go back to sleep awaiting the next ATIM window.

This PSP process for an IBSS is illustrated on the PSP Mode in an IBSS Diagram.

PSP Mode in an IBSS

Again, stations may be configured to awaken for beacons at a given interval in lieu of every beacon. For example, a station may awake for every third or fifth beacon. This methodology applies to PSP mode in both IBSS and BSS networks. As a wireless LAN administrator, you need to know what effect power management features will have on performance, battery life, broadcast traffic on your LAN, and so forth. In the example described above, the effects could be significant.

Activities

1. How do PSP clients operating within a BSS know when to expect the next access point beacon that contains the TIM?

   a. They listen for power save beacons that tell them when the next TIM will arrive.

   b. They are time synchronized with the access point and thus know when the next beacon will arrive.

   c. They use probability algorithms to calculate when the next beacon will arrive.

   d. They scan frames in low power mode, and then switch to high power when the TIM arrives.

2. What does the access point do with frames destined for a sleeping station?

   a. It buffers them until the station awakens.

   b. It returns them to the sending station.

   c. It forwards them in the TIM.

   d. It sends beacons to the target station only.

3. Which of the following describes a similarity between how a BSS and an IBSS operate in PSP mode?

   a. Both service sets send TIMs in beacon frames.

   b. Stations locally buffer frames destined for other sleeping stations.

   c. Stations notify each other that they are awake and ready to accept frames.

   d. Both service set types notify receiving stations of buffered frames

4. IBSS stations operating in PSP mode receive data frames during which time period?

   a. ATIM window

   b. Ad hoc window

   c. Data window

   d. IBSS window

5. Which is a disadvantage to using PSP mode on a wireless network?

   a. Power save mode reduces network bandwidth.

   b. Power save mode increases network overhead.

   c. Clients cannot hear beacon frames sent by other devices.

   d. Users must periodically reconnect to the network.

Extended Activities

Log in to the WestNet Learning Technologies, Inc. Online Student Resources Center found at **http://www.westnetinc.com**. Download and perform the following wireless networking lab:

• Lab 3: Ad Hoc Connectivity and Throughput Tests

Note that you must first register to gain access to the Student Resources Center.

To complete the lab you will require access to a wireless network and several PCs. The lab lists the hardware and software required.

Summary

This unit described the process by which clients connect to an access point, the terms used for organizing wireless LANs, and how power management is accomplished in wireless LAN client devices. Some of the key concepts encountered in the 802.11 network architecture were covered. Most of the topics discussed in this unit are defined directly in the 802.11 standard, and are required for implementation of 802.11-compliant hardware.

This unit began by describing scanning, the process by which a client locates a wireless LAN. The client automatically "listens" to see whether a wireless LAN is within range. During scanning, the client is also discovering whether it can associate with that wireless LAN. The two types of scanning for an access point are active scanning and passive scanning. Scanning must occur before any other process, because it is how a client finds a network.

This unit then explained that the process of connecting to a wireless LAN consists of two separate subprocesses. These subprocesses, authentication and association, always occur in the same order. The role of service sets in configuring wireless LANs was also discussed. A service set includes the basic components of a fully operational wireless LAN. The three types of service sets, which represent the three ways of configuring a wireless LAN are basic service set, extended service set, and independent service set. Clients can roam across each type of service set cell boundaries.

By understanding the steps involved in connecting a client to an access point, you now possess the knowledge crucial to securing, troubleshooting, and managing a wireless LAN.

Unit 7 Quiz

1. Which of the following is a client that can transmit data over a wireless network considered to be? (Choose two.)

   a. Unauthenticated

   b. Unassociated

   c. Authenticated

   d. Associated

2. Which one of the following supports Authentication, Authorization, and Accounting (AAA)?

   a. Open System authentication

   b. Shared Key authentication

   c. 802.11 standard

   d. 802.11i draft

3. A basic service set has how many APs?

   a. None

   b. 1

   c. 2

   d. Unlimited

4. Shared key authentication is more secure than open system authentication.

   a. This statement is always true.

   b. This statement is always false.

   c. It depends on whether or not WEP is utilized.

5. Which one of the following power management features populates a traffic indication map (TIM) in a basic or extended service set?

   a. Continuous aware mode

   b. Continuous power mode

   c. Power save polling mode

   d. Power aware polling mode

6. An announcement traffic indication message (ATIM) is sent when using which one of the following power management features in an independent basic service set (IBSS)?

   a. Continuous aware mode

   b. Continuous power mode

   c. Power save polling mode

   d. Power aware polling mode

7. An IBSS is also commonly referred to as which one of the following?

   a. Ad hoc mode

   b. Infrastructure mode

   c. Network mode

   d. Power save polling mode

8. The 802.11 standard specifies which of the following authentication processes? (Choose two.)

   a. Open system authentication

   b. 802.1x/EAP

   c. Shared key authentication

   d. RADIUS

9. Using power save polling (PSP) mode in a wireless LAN will result in which of the following? (Choose two.)

   a. Increased throughput on the network due to less overhead traffic

   b. Decreased throughput on the network due to more overhead traffic

   c. Network traffic is not affected by using PSP

   d. Longer battery life on the clients that use PSP

10. In an ad hoc network using PSP mode, every client station buffers packets.

    a. This statement is always true.

    b. This statement is always false.

    c. It depends on whether one station is acting as a gateway.

11. Which of the following are functions of the beacon management frame? (Choose two.)

    a. Load balancing all clients across multiple APs

    b. Broadcasting the SSID so clients can locate and identify the access point and its network

    c. Synchronizing the time between the access point and clients

    d. Allowing client authentication with the access point when using Shared Key authentication

12. What is passive scanning used for in a wireless LAN?

    a. Allowing clients to authenticate with an access point

    b. Allowing clients to actively search for any APs within range

    c. Reducing the time it takes clients to locate and associate to APs when roaming

    d. Helping determine to which bridge the client will connect

13. What does the acronym "SSID" stand for?

    a. Security Set Identifier

    b. Service Set Information Directory

    c. Service Set Identifier

    d. Security Service Information Dependency

14. How many distinct states does the process of authentication and association have?

    a. 1

    b. 2

    c. 3

    d. 4

    e. 5

15. Why is Shared Key authentication considered a security risk?

    a. The access point transmits the challenge text in the clear and receives the same challenge text encrypted with the WEP key.

    b. The keys are shared through broadcast with all network nodes.

    c. A hacker can see the keys with a sniffer.

    d. The WEP keys used on all computers are the same.

16. What is a basic service set?

    a. The basic components of a wireless LAN

    b. All clients in a wireless LAN that are being serviced by one access point

    c. The area around an access point that can be serviced by the access point

    d. One or more APs transmitting an RF signal

17. In a BSS, in which mode must the access point operate?

    a. Repeater

    b. Router

    c. Bridge

    d. Infrastructure

    e. Gateway

18. Which of the following can an IBSS also be called? (Choose two.)

    a. Peer-to-peer

    b. Incremental Basic Service Set

    c. Ad hoc network

    d. Internet Bindery Set Solution

19. In which of the following situations should Continuous Aware Mode (CAM) be configured on wireless LAN clients? (Choose two.)

    a. Portable laptop stations whose users need the ability to roam away from power sources

    b. Desktop stations that are rarely moved from their permanent location

    c. PDAs with limited battery life

    d. Laptop computers that can remain connected to a power source

20. Which of the following statements about power save polling (PSP) is true? (Choose two.)

    a. Using PSP mode allows a wireless client to sleep.

    b. Using PSP mode forces a wireless client to accept an access point's polling.

    c. Using PSP mode allows a wireless client to accept packets while asleep.

    d. Using PSP mode causes overhead in an ad hoc network.

Unit 8
Physical Layers

We mentioned earlier that most of the technology used in any wireless LAN is the same, but that wireless LAN product manufacturers approach and utilize that technology differently. In this unit we discuss some of the media access control (MAC) and Physical Layer characteristics of wireless LANs that are common to all wireless LAN products, regardless of the manufacturer. We explain the difference between Ethernet and wireless LAN frames and how wireless LANs avoid collisions. We also describe how wireless LAN stations communicate with one another under normal circumstances, and how collision handling occurs in a wireless LAN.

As a wireless LAN administrator, you must understand information at this level in order to properly configure and administer an access point, as well as to diagnose and solve problems that commonly occur in wireless LANs.

Lessons

1. How Wireless LANs Communicate
2. Interframe Spacing
3. RTS/CTS
4. Modulation

Terms

Acknowledgment (ACK)—In networking, an acknowledgement is an indication from the receiving device that information has been successfully received. In wireless LANs, an ACK frame indicates that the target device received the data frame.

AppleTalk—AppleTalk is Apple's proprietary, seven-layer, peer-to-peer network communications protocol for MacIntosh networks. AppleTalk runs on Apple network topologies and over Ethernet and Token Ring networks.

automatic rate selection (ARS)—See Dynamic Rate Shifting.

broadcast—The term broadcast is used in several different ways in communications and networking. With respect to LANs, the term refers to information (frames) sent to all devices on the physical segment. For example, a bus topology, in which a common cable is used to connect devices, is considered a broadcast technology.

Carrier Sense Multiple Access/Collision Avoidance (CSMA/CA)—CSMA/CA is a type of contention protocol. It is a set of rules determining use of the wireless medium, and it is used to prevent collisions in a wireless network. Use of this protocol means that all stations that want to transmit will listen for other transmissions in the air, and if there are transmissions, they will back off for a random period of time, and then try again. As soon as no transmissions are detected, the station will begin transmitting.

Carrier Sense Multiple Access/Collision Detection (CSMA/CD)—CSMA/CD is a type of contention protocol. It is a set of rules determining how network devices respond when two devices attempt to use a data channel simultaneously (called a collision). Standard Ethernet networks use CSMA/CD. This standard enables devices to detect a collision. After detecting a collision, a device waits a random delay time and then attempts to retransmit the message. If the device detects a collision again, it waits a longer period of time to attempt retransmission of the message. This is known as exponential back off.

contention—Contention in data communications networks occurs when two stations attempt to send data over a shared communications medium at the same time. The most common occurrence of this is found with the Ethernet protocol (CSMA/CD). When this occurs, the data on the bus is corrupted and each station must retransmit its data.

contention period—The contention period is the portion of the superframe that allows DCF mode stations to contend for access to the medium. No polling of PCF stations occurs during the contention period.

contention-free period—The contention-free period is the portion of the superframe that the access point uses to poll those stations operating in PCF mode for data. During the contention-free period, DCF modes sense the medium as busy through Network Allocation Vector (NAV) timers and clear channel assessments and wait to transmit.

distributed coordination function (DCF)—DCF mode is a mode during which all stations, including the access point, contend for access using the CSMA/CA protocol.

distributed coordinated function interframe space (DIFS)—DIFS is the longest 802.11 fixed interframe space used to control when DCF nodes can contend for the network medium.

Domain Name System (DNS)—DNS is the online distributed database system used to map human-readable computer names into IP addresses. DNS servers throughout the connected Internet implement a hierarchical namespace that allows sites freedom in assigning computer names and addresses. In addition, DNS supports separate mappings between mail destinations and IP addresses.

dynamic rate shifting—Dynamic rate shifting is a method by which wireless LAN clients will fall back to lower data rates when bit error rates exceed a predefined level due to interference or radio signal attenuation. Clients will shift to higher rates when signal attenuation or interference is no longer present.

Extended Interframe Space (EIFS)—EIFS is a variable-length space used as a waiting period after a device receives a frame with a bad frame check sequence. EIFS is used in DCF mode to allow enough time for a node on the network to acknowledge the receipt of a frame that was received in error by another node. The EIFS allows the node that received the erred frame to resynchronize to the current state of the medium.

File Transfer Protocol (FTP)—FTP is a TCP/IP protocol for file transfer.

fragmentation threshold—In a wireless LAN, the fragmentation threshold is the point at which the network divides large frames into smaller ones for transmission. Each smaller frame is sent on its own and requires its own acknowledgement.

hidden node—Hidden node occurs when two wireless clients cannot hear each other's transmissions, but the access point can hear both; it causes excessive collisions on a wireless LAN. RTS/CTS can reduce collisions that are due to hidden node.

Internet Packet Exchange (IPX)—IPX is Novell's Network Layer protocol that is a derivative of the Xerox Network Systems Internet Datagram Protocol (XNS IDP) developed by Xerox. It is used in Novell NetWare networks.

Internet Protocol (IP)—IP is a Layer 3 protocol that assigns IP addresses to devices in a network for routing purposes.

multicast—A multicast is a frame addressed to a specific group of nodes. A unicast is a frame addressed to a single node. A broadcast is a frame destined for all nodes on a network.

NetBIOS Extended User Interface (NetBEUI)—NetBEUI is a Network and Transport Layer protocol designed to work within a single physical LAN. (It does not provide packet routing between networks.) NetBEUI is typically integrated with NetBIOS.

Network Allocation Vector (NAV)—The NAV is a virtual carrier sense mechanism used to predict future network traffic based on the time set in the RTS and CTS frames' NAV field. When the NAV equals a value of zero, the medium is assumed idle, while any other state indicates the medium is busy. This carrier-sensing mechanism is considered virtual because nodes do not listen to the physical medium, but instead reference the timer state to determine when to access the medium.

Network Basic Input/Output System (NetBIOS)—NetBIOS is a software system developed by Sytek and IBM that has become the de facto standard for application interface to LANs. It operates at the Session Layer of the OSI protocol stack. Applications can call NetBIOS routines to carry out functions, such as data transfer, across a LAN.

packet binary convolutional code (PBCC)—PBCC is a Texas Instruments-developed coding technology for wireless LANs designed to support data rates of 22 Mbps on 802.11b networks. Its current version is called PBCC-22.

Physical Layer Convergence Protocol (PLCP)—PLCP is the Physical Layer convergence function through which the Physical Layer communicates with the Data Link Layer in 802.11 wireless networks. PLCP maps the MAC layer frames into a format suitable for the transmission of data (user and management) between wireless devices.

Point Coordination Function (PCF)—PCF is an IEEE 802.11 mode that enables contention-free frame transfer based on a priority mechanism; stations are polled for the need for frame transmission. It enables time-bounded services that support the transmission of voice and video.

Point Coordination Function Interframe Space (PIFS)—PIFS is used as interframe spacing on PCF mode networks to allow an access point to gain control of the medium before any DCF node.

polling—Polling is sequential interrogation of devices for various purposes, such as avoiding contention, determining operational status, or determining readiness to send or receive data.

probe frame—When a wireless station is actively scanning for access points, it sends a probe frame containing the SSID of the target network. The answering access points respond to the probe frame with a probe response frame that contains basically the same information as a beacon management frame.

Received Signal Strength Indicator (RSSI)—The RSSI is the indicator of the received RF signal energy at the network device. This is an optional parameter ranging from 0 to the maximum RSSI intended to be used as a relative measure of the received signal.

Request to Send/Clear to Send (RTS/CTS)—RTS/CTS is a virtual carrier sense protocol used on WLANs. When RTS/CTS is enabled on a wireless LAN, a station wishing to communicate effectively reserves the medium for a period of time. All other stations then must wait for the communications to complete before they can use the medium.

Routing Information Protocol (RIP)—RIP is a common routing protocol. RIP bases its routing path on the distance (number of hops) to the destination. RIP maintains optimum routing paths by sending out routing update messages if the network topology changes. For example, if a router finds that a particular link is faulty, it will update its routing table and then send a copy of the modified table to each of its neighbors.

Short Interframe Space (SIFS)—SIFS are the short interframe spaces between RTS, CTS, and ACK frames that are designed to give these frames priority over all others on the network. To enable a receiving station to formulate a response to the received frame, SIFSs are used as a time for processing or turn-around.

superframe—A superframe is a special timeframe during which a network in Point Coordination Function (PCF) mode is allowed to alternatively have both a contention-free period and a contention period. This allows DCF and PCF mode clients to coexist on the same network at the same time. The superframe consists of a beacon, a contention-free period (CFP), and a contention period (CP).

unicast—A unicast is a transmission sent to a single network address. A unicast functions differently than a broadcast, which is sent to all network addresses simultaneously, and a multicast, which is sent to several addresses at once.

Lesson 1—How Wireless LANs Communicate

To understand how to configure and manage a wireless LAN, the administrator must understand communication parameters that are configurable on the equipment and how to implement those parameters. In order to estimate throughput across wireless LANs, one must understand the effects of these parameters and collision handling on system throughput. This lesson conveys a basic understanding of many configurable parameters and their effects on network performance.

Objectives

At the end of this lesson you will be able to:

- Explain how wireless LAN frames differ from wired Ethernet frames

- Describe how wireless LANs handle medium contention

- Describe the effect frame fragmentation has on wireless LAN throughput

- Explain how wireless devices adjust connection speeds

 **Key Point**

Wireless LAN devices contend for access to the shared RF communications medium.

Wireless LAN Frames vs. Ethernet Frames

After a wireless client has joined a network, the client and the rest of the network will communicate by passing frames across the network in almost the same manner as any other Institute of Electrical and Electronics Engineers (IEEE) 802 network. To clear up a common misconception, wireless LANs do not use 802.3 Ethernet frames. The term wireless Ethernet is somewhat of a misnomer. Wireless LAN data frames contain more information than common Ethernet frames do. The actual structure of a wireless LAN data frame versus that of an Ethernet frame is beyond the scope of both the CWNA exam, as well as a wireless LAN administrator's job, but is useful knowledge, nonetheless.

Consider that although there are many types of IEEE 802 frames, there are three types of wireless frames: control, management, and data. Each frame type is put together in a different fashion, and for comparison purposes, only the data frame type compares to the 802.3 Ethernet frame type. After a network administrator chooses 802.3 Ethernet frames, the same frame type is used to send all data across the wire, just as with wireless data frames. One similarity between wireless data frames and 802.3 Ethernet frames is that the payload of both types of data frames is a maximum of 1500 bytes. Ethernet's maximum frame size is 1518 bytes, whereas 802.11 wireless LANs have a maximum frame size of 2346 bytes. It is typical to see 1518-byte frames used on the wireless segment because the 1500-byte wired segment frame payload is dropped into the 802.11 wireless frame that has 18 bytes of overhead. The only time this is not be the case is when the wired segment uses jumbo frames (frames larger than the maximum of 1518 bytes allowed by the 802.3 standard).

A subject seldom discussed is the preamble and header of a wireless frame. A few pieces of information on this topic are important to know, especially if you are going to do any wireless protocol analysis. The preamble (a series of 1s and 0s used for bit synchronization at the beginning of each frame) is always sent at 1 Mbps to provide a common data rate that any receiver can interpret. There are two lengths of preamble (also called "Physical layer convergence procedure [PLCP] preamble"): long (128 bits) and short (56 bits). It is important that nodes at each end of a wireless link use the same preamble type. The 802.11b standard requires support of long preambles and provides an option for short preambles for the purpose of improving network efficiency when transmitting special types of traffic, such as Voice over IP (VoIP). After the preamble is sent, the header (also called PLCP header) is sent. For long preambles, the preamble and the header are both sent at 1 Mbps. For short preambles, the preamble is sent at 1 Mbps, and the header is sent at 2 Mbps. The Data Rate (DR) field in the header specifies the rate at which the data will be transmitted. After sending the header, the transmitter can then change the data rate to whatever the header specifies. This same premise applies to beacons, which are also sent at 1 Mbps for the same reasons.

These three different categories of frames are as follows:

- Management Frames
    - Association request frame
    - Association response frame
    - Reassociation request frame
    - Reassociation response frame
    - Probe request frame
    - Probe response frame
    - Beacon frame
    - ATIM frame
    - Disassociation frame
    - Authentication frame
    - Deauthentication frame

- Control Frames
    - Request to send (RTS)
    - Clear to send (CTS)
    - Acknowledgement (ACK)
    - Power-Save Poll (PS Poll)
    - Contention-Free End (CF End)
    - CF End + CF Ack

- Data Frames

Each type of frame (listed above) uses certain fields within its particular frame type. What a wireless LAN administrator needs to know is that wireless LANs support practically all Layer 3-7 protocols – Internet Protocol (IP), Internetwork Packet Exchange (IPX), NetBEUI, AppleTalk, Router Information Protocol (RIP), Domain Name System (DNS), File Transfer Protocol (FTP), and so forth. The main differences from 802.3 Ethernet frames are implemented at the media access control (MAC) sublayer of the Data Link Layer and the entire Physical Layer. Upper layer protocols are simply considered payload by the Layer 2 wireless data frames.

Collision Handling

Because radio frequency is a shared medium, wireless LANs have to deal with the possibility of collisions, just as traditional wired LANs do. The difference on a wireless LAN is that there is no means through which the sending station can determine that a collision has actually occurred. It is impossible to detect a collision on a wireless LAN, and for this reason, wireless LANs use the Carrier Sense Multiple Access/Collision Avoidance protocol (CSMA/CA). CSMA/CA is somewhat similar to the CSMA/Collision Detection (CD) protocol (commonly used on Ethernet networks) in the way nodes check the status of the medium before proceeding.

The most significant difference between CSMA/CA and CSMA/CD is that CSMA/CA avoids collisions and uses positive acknowledgements (ACKs), instead of arbitrating use of the medium when collisions occur. The use of acknowledgements, or ACKs, works in a very simple manner. When a wireless station sends a packet, the receiving station sends back an ACK after that station actually receives the packet. If the sending station does not receive an ACK, the sending station assumes a collision occurred and resends the data.

CSMA/CA, added to the large amount of control data used in wireless LANs, causes overhead that uses approximately 50 percent of the available bandwidth on a wireless LAN. This overhead, plus the additional overhead of protocols that enhance collision avoidance (Request to Send/Clear to Send [RTS/CTS], for example), is responsible for the actual throughput of approximately 5.0 - 5.5 Mbps on a typical 802.11b wireless LAN rated at 11 Mbps. CSMA/CD also generates overhead, but only about 30 percent on an average use network. When an Ethernet network becomes congested, CSMA/CD can cause overhead of up to 70 percent, while a congested wireless network remains somewhat constant at around 50 - 55 percent throughput.

The CSMA/CA protocol avoids the probability of collisions among stations sharing the medium by using a random back off time when a station's physical or logical sensing mechanism indicates a busy medium. The period of time immediately following a busy medium is when the highest probability of collisions occurs, especially under high utilization. At this point in time, many stations may be waiting for the medium to become idle and will attempt to transmit at the same time. Once the medium is idle, a random back off time defers a station from transmitting a frame, minimizing the chance that stations will collide.

Fragmentation

Fragmentation of packets into shorter fragments adds protocol overhead and reduces protocol efficiency (decreases network throughput) when no errors are observed, but reduces the time spent on retransmissions if errors occur. Larger packets have a higher probability of collisions on the network; therefore, a method of varying packet size is needed. The IEEE 802.11 standard provides support for fragmentation of packets.

By decreasing the length of each frame payload, the probability of interference during transmission can be reduced, as illustrated on the Fragmentation Diagram. A tradeoff must be made between the lower packet error rate, which can be achieved by using shorter packets, and the increased overhead of more frames on the network due to fragmentation. Each fragment requires its own headers and ACK, so the adjustment of the fragmentation level is also an adjustment of the amount of overhead associated with each packet transmitted. To prevent unnecessary overhead being introduced into the network, stations only fragment unicast frames, and never multicast and broadcast frames. Finding the optimal fragmentation setting to maximize the network throughput on an 802.11 network is an important part of administering a wireless LAN. Keep in mind that a 2346-byte frame is the largest frame that can traverse a wireless LAN segment without fragmentation.

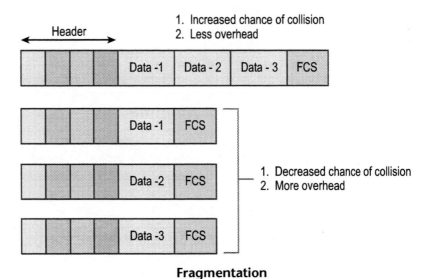

Fragmentation

One way to use fragmentation to improve network throughput in times of heavy packet errors (faulty packets) is to monitor the packet error rate on the network and manually adjust the fragmentation threshold level. It is recommended that you monitor the network at multiple times throughout a typical day to see what impact fragmentation adjustment will have at various times.

If your network is experiencing a high packet error rate (faulty packets), increase the fragmentation threshold on the client stations and/or the access point (depending on which units allow these settings on your particular equipment). Start with the maximum value and gradually decrease the fragmentation threshold size until you observe an improvement in throughput. If fragmentation is used, the network will experience a performance hit due to the overhead incurred with fragmentation. Sometimes this hit is acceptable in order to gain more throughput due to a decrease in packet errors and subsequent retransmissions.

DRS

Adaptive Rate Selection (ARS) also called Automatic Rate Selection, and Dynamic Rate Shifting (DRS) are both terms that describe the method of dynamic speed adjustment on wireless LAN clients. This speed adjustment occurs as distance increases between the client and the access point, or as interference increases. It is imperative that a network administrator understand how this function works in order to plan for network throughput, cell sizes, power outputs of access points and stations, and security.

Modern spread spectrum systems are designed to make discrete jumps only to specified data rates, such as 1, 2, 5.5, and 11 Mbps. As distance increases between the access point and a station, the signal strength will decrease to a point where the current data rate cannot be maintained. When this signal strength decrease occurs, the transmitting unit drops its data rate to the next lower supported data rate (from 11 Mbps to 5.5 Mbps, for example, or from 2 Mbps to 1 Mbps). The Dynamic Rate Shifting Diagram illustrates that as the distance from the access point increases the data rate decreases.

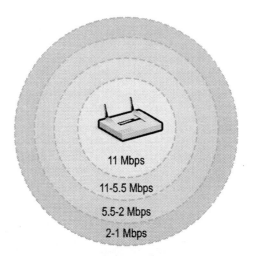

Dynamic Rate Shifting

A wireless LAN system never drops from 11 Mbps to 10 Mbps, for example, because 10 Mbps is not a supported data rate. The method of making such discrete jumps is typically called either ARS or DRS, depending on the manufacturer. Both frequency hopping spread spectrum (FHSS) and direct sequence spread spectrum (DSSS) implement DRS, and the IEEE 802.11, IEEE 802.11b, IEEE 802.11a, HomeRF, and OpenAir standards require it.

DCF

Distributed Coordination Function (DCF) is an access method specified in the 802.11 standard that allows all stations on a wireless LAN to contend for access on the shared transmission medium (radio frequency [RF]) using the CSMA/CA protocol. In this case, the transmission medium is a portion of the radio frequency band that the wireless LAN uses to send data. Basic service sets (BSS), extended service sets (ESS), and independent basic service sets (IBSS) can (and must) all use DCF mode. The access points in these service sets act in the same manner as IEEE 802.3-based wired hubs to transmit their data, and DCF is the mode in which the access points send the data.

PCF

Point Coordination Function (PCF) is a transmission mode that allows for contention-free frame transfers on a wireless LAN by making use of a polling mechanism. PCF has the advantage of guaranteeing a known amount of latency so that applications requiring quality of service (QoS) (voice or video for, example) can be used. When using PCF, the access point on a wireless LAN performs the polling. For this reason, an ad hoc network cannot utilize PCF, because an ad hoc network has no access point to do the polling. PCF is never implemented in a standalone fashion; rather, it is implemented in such a way that both clients configured for DCF mode and PCF mode are supported simultaneously.

The PCF Process

First, a wireless station must tell the access point that the station is capable of answering a poll. Then the access point asks, or polls, each wireless station to see if each station needs to send a data frame across the network. PCF, through polling, generates a significant amount of overhead on a wireless LAN.

Note: When multiple access points located in the same coverage area operate in PCF mode and share the same channel, they can significantly interfere with DCF systems as well as each other. DCF mode systems may coexist with other DCF systems, even on the same channel, and although they do discernibly interfere with each other, they can still function. However, a PCF mode system operating alongside a DCF mode system or another PCF mode system set to the same (or an adjacent) channel, would likely cause one of the adjacent units to fail entirely.

DCF can be used without PCF, but PCF cannot be used without DCF. We will explain how these two modes coexist as we discuss interframe spacing. DCF is scalable due to its contention-based design, whereas PCF, by design, limits the scalability of the wireless network by adding the additional overhead of polling frames.

Activities

1. Which is the largest 802.11 data frame that can traverse a wireless LAN without fragmentation?

    a. 1500 bytes

    b. 1514 bytes

    c. 2346 bytes

    d. 2034 bytes

2. Which of the following are the three frame types defined by the IEEE 802.11 standard? (Choose three.)

    a. Collision frames

    b. Control frames

    c. Data frames

    d. Management frames

3. What does a wireless station do if it fails to receive acknowledgements to its data frames?

    a. It goes to sleep for a random period of time.

    b. It sends the frames to the next node in line.

    c. It waits for the next token and resends the data.

    d. It contends for the medium again and resends the data.

4. Why would a wireless LAN use fragmentation?

    a. To reduce overhead caused by large packets monopolizing network bandwidth

    b. To reduce the time spent retransmitting packets due to packet errors

    c. To allow receiving nodes to acknowledge multiple frames at once

    d. To provide increased Quality of Service for real-time applications

5. Which type of frame will a wireless LAN device fragment?

    a. broadcast

    b. multicast

    c. unicast

    d. omnicast

6. Which statement best describes the use of a fragment threshold on a wireless network?

   a. It manually adjusts the frame fragmentation rate based on observed fragmentation over a period of time.

   b. It sets the number of frame fragments that can be acknowledged at once by the receiver.

   c. It defines the number of 802.3 Ethernet frame fragments carried within each 802.11 frame.

   d. It is a method of adjusting frame sizes to maximize an 802.11 network's throughput.

Extended Activity

Log in to the WestNet Learning Technologies, Inc. Online Student Resources Center found at **http://www.westnetinc.com**. Download and perform the following wireless networking lab:

- Lab 4: Cell sizing and Automatic Rate Selection (ARS) in Infrastructure Mode

Note that you must first register to gain access to the Student Resources Center.

To complete the lab, you will require access to a wireless network and several PCs. The lab lists the hardware and software required.

Lesson 2—Interframe Spacing

Interframe spacing does not sound like something an administrator would need to know; however, if you do not understand the types of interframe spacing, you cannot effectively grasp Request to Send/Clear to Send (RTS/CTS), which helps you solve problems, or Distributed Coordination Function (DCF), and Point Coordination Function (PCF), which are manually configured in the access point. Both of these functions are integral in the ongoing communications process of a wireless LAN. In this lesson, we define each type of interframe space (IFS) and explain how each type works on the wireless LAN.

As we learned when we discussed beacons, all stations on a wireless LAN are time synchronized. All the stations on a wireless LAN are effectively 'ticking' time in sync with one another. Interframe spacing is the term we use to refer to standardized time spaces that are used on all 802.11 wireless LANs.

Objectives

At the end of this lesson you will be able to:

- Explain how wireless LANs use interframe spacing to manage communications

- Explain the three types of interframe spacing used on wireless LANs

- Describe the use of slot times on wireless LANs

- Describe a superframe and its use on a wireless network

 **Key Point**

Wireless networks use interframe spacing to control how and when devices are allowed to access the medium.

Three Types of Spacing

Three main spacing intervals (interframe spaces) are used on wireless LANs: Short Interframe Spacing (SIFS), Distributed Coordination Function Interframe Spacing (DIFS), and Point Coordination Function Interframe Spacing (PIFS). Each type of interframe space is used either to send certain types of messages across the network or to manage the intervals during which the stations contend for the transmission medium. The Interframe Spacing Table illustrates the actual times that each interframe space takes for each type of 802.11 technology.

Interframe Spacing

IFS	DSSS	FHSS	Diffused Infrared
SIFS	10 uS	28 uS	7 uS
PIFS	30 uS	78 uS	15 uS
DIFS	50 uS	128 uS	23 uS

Note: The Extended Interframe Space (EIFS), which is not covered on the CWNA exam, is a fourth interframe space. EIFS is a variable length space used as a waiting period when a frame transmission results in a bad reception of the frame due to an incorrect frame check sequence (FCS) value. EIFS is not a main focus of this section and an in-depth understanding of its functionality is not essential knowledge for a wireless network administrator.

Interframe spaces are measured in microseconds and are used to defer a station's access to the medium and provide various levels of priority. On a wireless network, everything is synchronized and all stations and access points use standard amounts of time (spaces) to perform various tasks. Each node knows these spaces and uses them appropriately. A set of standard spaces is specified for direct sequence spread spectrum (DSSS), frequency hopping spread spectrum (FHSS), and Infrared as you can see in the Interframe Spacing Table. By using these spaces, each node knows when and if it is supposed to perform a certain action on the network.

SIFS

Short interframe spaces (SIFS) are time spaces the network provides to allow a communicating node to formulate an appropriate response to a received message, similar to the way you would stop to think about an answer to a question before replying. SIFS are used directly before and after messages between wireless nodes. Below is a partial list of frame types that call for use of SIFS:

- **RTS**—Request-to-Send frame, used for reserving the medium by stations

- **CTS**—Clear-to-Send frame, used as a response by access points and wireless clients to the RTS frame generated by a station in order to ensure all stations have stopped transmitting

- **ACK**—Acknowledgement frame used for notifying sending stations that data arrived in readable format at the receiving station

SIFSs provide the highest level of priority on a wireless LAN. The reason for this is that stations constantly listen to the medium (carrier sense) awaiting a clear medium. Once the medium is clear, each station must wait a given amount of time (spacing) before proceeding with a transmission. The function the station needs to perform determines the length of time a station must wait. Each function on a wireless network falls into a spacing category. Tasks that are high priority fall into the SIFS category. If a station only has to wait a short period of time after the medium is clear to begin its transmissions, it would have priority over stations having to wait longer periods of time. SIFS is used for functions that require a very short period of time, yet need high priority in order to accomplish the goal.

PIFS

An point coordination function interface space (PIFS) interframe space is neither the shortest nor longest fixed interframe space; thus, it gets more priority than DIFS and less than SIFS. Access points use a PIFS interframe space only when the network is in point coordination function mode, which is manually configured by the administrator. PIFSs are shorter in duration than DIFSs, so the access point will always win control of the medium before other contending stations in distributed coordination function (DCF) mode. PCF only works with DCF, not as a stand-alone operational mode so that, once the access point is finished polling, other stations can continue to contend for the transmission medium using DCF mode.

DIFS

A distributed coordinated function interframe space (DIFS) is the longest fixed interframe space and is used by default on all 802.11-compliant stations that are using the distributed coordination function. Each station on the network using DCF mode is required to wait until DIFS has expired before any station can contend for the network. All stations operating according to DCF use DIFS for transmitting data frames and management frames. This spacing makes the transmission of these frames lower priority than PCF-based transmissions. Instead of all stations assuming the medium is clear and arbitrarily and simultaneously beginning transmissions after DIFS (which would cause collisions), each station uses a random back off algorithm to determine how long to wait before sending its data.

The period of time directly following DIFS is referred to as the contention period (CP). All stations in DCF mode use the random back off algorithm during the contention period. During the random back off process, a station chooses a random number and multiplies it by the slot time to determine the length of time to wait. To see if the medium is busy, the stations count down these slot times one by one, performing a clear channel assessment (CCA) after each slot time. Whichever station's random back off time expires first, that station does a CCA, and provided the medium is clear, it then begins transmission.

After the first station has begun transmissions, all other stations sense that the medium is busy, and remember the remaining amount of their random back off time from the previous CP. This remaining amount of time is used in lieu of picking another random number during the next CP. This process ensures fair access to the medium among all stations.

Once the random back off period is over, the transmitting station sends its data and receives back the ACK from the receiving station. This entire process then repeats. It stands to reason that most stations will choose different random numbers, eliminating most collisions. However, it is important to remember that collisions do happen on wireless LANs, but they cannot be directly detected. Collisions are assumed by the fact that the ACK is not received back from the destination station.

Slot Times

A slot time, which is preprogrammed into the radio in the same fashion as the SIFS, PIFS, and DIFS timeframes, is a standard period of time on a wireless network. Slot times are used in the same method as a clock's second hand is used. A wireless node ticks slot times just like a clock ticks seconds. These slot times are determined by the wireless LAN technology being utilized. Slot times for FHSS, DSSS, and Infrared are as follows:

- FHSS Slot Time = 50uS
- DSSS Slot Time = 20uS
- Infrared Slot Time = 8uS

Notice the following:

- PIFS = SIFS + 1 Slot Time
- DIFS = PIFS + 1 Slot Time

Also notice that FHSS has noticeably longer slot times, DIFS times, and PIFS times than DSSS. These longer times contribute to FHSS overhead, which decreases throughput.

The Communications Process

When you consider the PIFS process described above, it may seem that the access point would always have control over the medium, because the access point does not have to wait for DIFS, but the stations do. This would be true, except for the existence of what is called a superframe. A superframe is a period of time, and it consists of three parts:

1. Beacon
2. Contention-Free Period (CFP)
3. Contention Period (CP)

A superframe is shown on the Superframe Diagram. The purpose of the superframe is to allow peaceful, fair coexistence between PCF and DCF mode clients on the network, allowing QoS for some, but not for others.

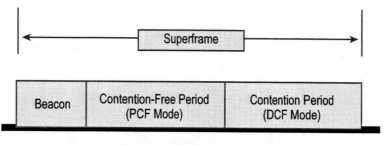

Superframe

Again, remember that PIFS, and therefore the superframe, only occur when the following conditions are met:

- The network is in point coordination function mode

- The access point has been configured to do polling

- The wireless clients have been configured to announce to the access point that they are pollable

Therefore, if we start from a hypothetical beginning point on a network that has the access point configured for PCF mode, and some of the clients are configured for polling, the process is as follows:

1. The access point broadcasts a beacon as the first part of the CFP.

2. During the contention-free period, the access point polls stations to see if any station needs to send data.

3. If a station needs to send data, it sends one frame to the access point in response to the access point's poll.

4. If a station does not need to send data, it returns a null frame to the access point in response to the access point's poll.

5. Polling continues throughout the contention-free period.

6. Once the contention-free period ends and the contention period begins, the access point can no longer poll stations. During the contention period, stations using DCF mode contend for the medium and the access point uses DCF mode.

7. The superframe ends with the end of the CP, and a new cycle begins with the following beacon.

Think of the CFP as using a "controlled access policy" and the CP as using a "random access policy." During the CFP, the access point is in complete control of all functions on the wireless network, whereas during the CP, stations arbitrate and randomly gain control over the medium. In PCF mode, the access point does not have to wait for the DIFS to expire, but rather uses the PIFS, which is shorter than the DIFS, to capture the medium before any client using DCF mode does. Because the access point captures the medium and begins polling transmissions during the CFP, the DCF clients sense the medium as being busy and wait to transmit. Additionally, the access point sets the NAV field in all other nodes to a nonzero value while transmitting the beacon during the CFP. The use of PIFS for priority is a backup mechanism. After the CFP, the CP begins, during which all stations using DCF mode may contend for the medium and the access point switches to DCF mode.

The DCF/PCF Mode Timeline Diagram illustrates a short timeline for a wireless LAN using DCF and PCF modes. Note that SIFS and other details are not shown for the sake of brevity.

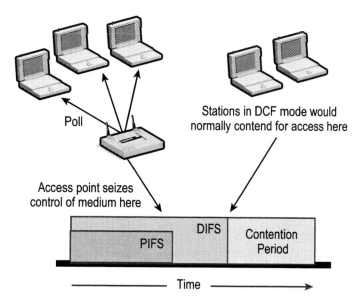

Poll

Stations in DCF mode would
normally contend for access here

Access point seizes
control of medium here

| PIFS | DIFS | Contention Period |

Time ⟶

DCF/PCF Mode Timeline

The process is somewhat simpler when a wireless LAN is only in DCF mode, because there is no polling and, therefore, no super-frame. This process is as follows:

1. Stations wait for DIFS to expire.

2. During the CP, which immediately follows DIFS, stations calculate their random back off time based on a random number multiplied by a slot time.

3. Stations tick down their random time with each passing slot time, checking the medium (CCA) at the end of each slot time. The station with the shortest time gains control of the medium first.

4. A station sends its data.

5. The receiving station receives the data and waits a SIFS period before returning an ACK back to the station that transmitted the data.

6. The transmitting station receives the ACK, and the process starts over from the beginning with a new DIFS.

The DCF Timeline Diagram illustrates a timeline for a DCF mode wireless LAN. Keep in mind that this timeline is a few milliseconds long. The whole process happens many times every second. Note that SIFS and other details are not shown for the sake of brevity.

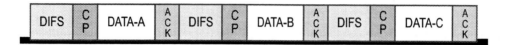

DCF Timeline

Activities

1. A superframe only occurs on a wireless LAN under which three conditions? (Choose three.)

   a. The access point has been configured to do polling.

   b. The contention-free period has expired.

   c. The wireless clients have been configured to announce to the access point that they are pollable.

   d. The network is in point coordination function mode.

2. Which wireless technology has the longest slot time?

   a. DSSS

   b. FHSS

   c. Infrared

   d. Bluetooth

3. What does a wireless station do immediately after its backoff time expires?

   a. Immediately sends its data.

   b. Transmits a DIFS to test the medium.

   c. Performs a clear channel assessment.

   d. Waits for all other stations to transmit.

4. Which type of interframe space allows high priority network functions control over the medium for a short time period?

   a. DIFS

   b. EIFS

   c. PIFS

   d. SIFS

5. Which statement is true concerning a wireless network's use of interframe spacing?

   a. PCF stations must wait until the contention-free period expires before they can contend for the medium.

   b. DIFS occur before and after high priority messages.

   c. Interframe spacing controls station medium access timing.

   d. Station polling only occurs during the contention period.

Extended Activities

1. On a wireless network, what types of applications do you think would benefit from the use of the Point Coordination Function mode? Research wireless products that provide this capability.

_____

_____

_____

_____

2. Draw a state diagram illustrating a wireless network operating in PCF mode.

Lesson 3—RTS/CTS

Two carrier sense mechanisms are used on wireless networks. The first is physical carrier sense. Physical carrier sense functions by checking the signal strength, called the Received Signal Strength Indicator (RSSI), on the RF carrier signal to see if there is a station currently transmitting. The second is virtual carrier sense. Virtual carrier sense works by using a field called the "Network Allocation Vector (NAV)," which acts as a timer on the station. If a station wishes to broadcast its intention to use the network, the station sends a frame to the destination station, which will set the NAV field on all stations hearing the frame to the time necessary for the station to complete its transmission, plus the returning ACK frame. In this way, any station can reserve use of the network for specified periods of time. Virtual carrier sense is implemented with the Request to Send/Clear to Send (RTS/CTS) protocol.

Objectives

At the end of this lesson you will be able to:

- Explain how wireless devices use RTS/CTS to reserve the network for short time periods

- Describe the effects RTS/CTS has on network performance

- Explain how to configure RTS/CTS on a wireless network

 **Key Point**

RTS/CTS, if used properly, can increase throughput on a wireless network segment experiencing high collision rates.

Use of RTS/CTS on a Wireless Network

The RTS/CTS protocol is an extension of the CSMA/CA protocol. As the wireless LAN administrator, you can use this protocol to solve problems, such as Hidden Node, discussed in further reading on troubleshooting. Using RTS/CTS allows stations to broadcast their intent to send data across the network.

As you can imagine by the brief description above, RTS/CTS will cause significant network overhead. For this reason, RTS/CTS is turned OFF by default on a wireless LAN. If you are experiencing an unusual amount of collisions on your wireless LAN (evidenced by high latency and low throughput), using RTS/CTS can actually increase the traffic flow on the network by decreasing the number of collisions. Use of RTS/CTS should not be done haphazardly. RTS/CTS should be configured after careful study of the network's collisions, throughput, latency, and so forth.

Note: Some manufacturers do not allow administrators to change a station's RTS/CTS settings (and many other settings) unless they obtain the special password from the manufacturer. By default, an administrator is locked out of those features of the station's driver software. Normally, getting this password is not easy. These manufacturers require an administrator to take their one to two day product seminar before they allow the administrator to fill out a series of paperwork to obtain the necessary password(s).

The RTS/CTS Handshaking Diagram illustrates the four-way handshake process used for RTS/CTS. In short, the transmitting station broadcasts the RTS, followed by the CTS reply from the receiving station, both of which go through the access point. Next, the transmitting station sends its data payload through the access point to the receiving station, which immediately replies with an acknowledgement (ACK) frame. This process is used for every frame that is sent across the wireless network.

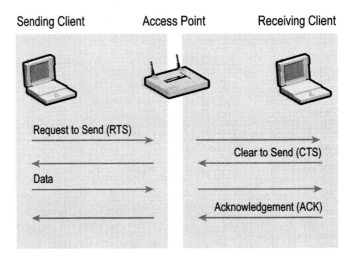

RTS/CTS Handshaking

Configuring RTS/CTS

The following three settings are on most access points and nodes for RTS/CTS:

- Off

- On

- On with Threshold

When RTS/CTS is turned on, every packet that goes through the wireless network is announced and cleared between the transmitting and receiving nodes prior to transmission, creating a significant amount of overhead and significantly less throughput. Generally, RTS/CTS should only be used in diagnosing network problems and when large frames are flowing across a congested wireless network.

However, the "on with threshold" setting allows an administrator to control which frames over a certain size (called the "threshold") are announced and cleared to send by the stations. Because collisions affect larger frames more than smaller ones, you can set the RTS/CTS threshold to work only when a node wishes to send frames over a certain size. This setting allows you to customize the RTS/CTS setting to your network data traffic and optimize the throughput of your wireless LAN while assisting with problems such as Hidden Node.

The RTS/CTS Data Transmission in DCF Mode Diagram depicts a DCF network using the RTS/CTS protocol to transmit data. Notice that the RTS and CTS transmissions are spaced by SIFS. The NAV is set with RTS on all nodes, and then reset on all nodes by the immediately following CTS.

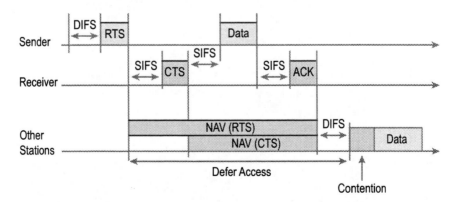

RTS/CTS Data Transmission in DCF Mode

Activities

1. Physical carrier sense mechanisms refer to which one of the following in order to check the wireless network's RF signal strength?

    a. NAV

    b. RTS/CTS

    c. RSSI

    d. CSMA/CD

2. When should you consider enabling RTS/CTS on a wireless LAN?

    a. When small frames experience high collision rates

    b. To improve throughput when collision rates are low

    c. To enable wireless nodes to transmit multiple frames without acknowledgement

    d. When large frames experience high collision rates

3. Which statement best describes how RTS/CTS operates?

    a. The CTS frame indicates that the transmitting station can send its data.

    b. The transmitting station sends its data in the RTS frame.

    c. The receiving station sends an ACK for each RTS frame.

    d. The receiving station sends a CTS immediately after the ACK frame.

4. Which interframe space separates RTS/CTS frames?

    a. DIFS

    b. EIFS

    c. PIFS

    d. SIFS

Extended Activities

1. The RTS/CTS Data Transmission in DCF Mode Diagram shows two NAV field lengths.

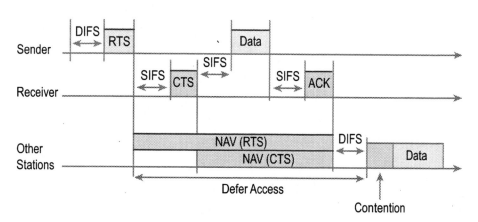

The RTS/CTS Data Transmission in DCF Mode

Why do you think the NAV (CTS) time period is shorter than the NAV (RTS) time period? Why is a second NAV field used?

_____

_____

_____

_____

2. Research wireless products that allow you to configure the RTS/CTS settings. Do they require you to attend a vendor training course before allowing you access to these settings?

_____

_____

_____

_____

Lesson 4—Modulation

Modulation, which is a Physical Layer function, is a process in which the radio transceiver prepares the digital signal within the network interface card (NIC) for transmission over the airwaves. Modulation is the process of adding data to a carrier by altering the amplitude, frequency, or phase of the carrier in a controlled manner. Knowing the many different kinds of modulations used with wireless LANs is helpful when trying to build a compatible network piece-by-piece.

Objectives

At the end of this lesson you will be able to:

- Describe the modulation technologies used by wireless LANs

- Identify the spreading code used by each wireless technology and data rate

 **Key Point**

Wireless LAN technologies use a variety of spreading codes and modulation techniques.

Modulation and Spreading Code Types

FHSS and DSSS wireless LANs use differing spreading codes and modulation technologies, depending on the data rate and the type of spread spectrum technology used. The Modulation and Spreading Code Types for 802.11 and 802.11b Table shows the details of the modulation and spreading code types used with frequency hopping and direct sequence wireless LANs in the 2.4-GHz ISM band.

Modulation and Spreading Code Types for 802.11 and 802.11b

	Spreading Code	Modulation Technology	Data Rate
2.4 GHz DSSS	Barker Code	DBPSK	1 Mbps
	Barker Code	DQPSK	2 Mbps
	CCK	DQPSK	5.5 Mbps
	CCK	DQPSK	11 Mbps
2.4 GHz FHSS	Barker Code	2GFSK	1 Mbps
	Barker Code	4GFSK	2 Mbps

Differential Binary Phase Shift Keying (DBPSK), Differential Quadrature Phase Shift Keying (DQPSK), and Gaussian Frequency Shift Keying (GFSK) are the types of modulation used by 802.11 and 802.11b products on the market today. Barker Code and Complementary Code Keying (CCK) are the types of spreading codes used in 802.11 and 802.11b wireless LANs.

As higher transmission speeds are specified, such as when a system is using DRS, modulation techniques change to provide more data throughput. For example, 802.11g- and 802.11a- compliant wireless LAN equipment specify use of orthogonal frequency division multiplexing (OFDM), allowing speeds of up to 54 Mbps, which is a significant improvement over the 11 Mbps specified by 802.11b. The Modulation Types and Data Rates for 802.11a Table shows the modulation types used for 802.11a networks. The 802.11g standard provides backwards compatibility by supporting CCK coding; it even supports packet binary convolution coding (PBCC) as an option. Bluetooth and HomeRF are both FHSS technologies that use GFSK modulation technology in the 2.4 GHz ISM band.

Modulation Types and Data Rates for 802.11a

Coding Technique	Modulation Technology	Data Rate
OFDM	BPSK	6 Mbps
OFDM	BPSK	9 Mbps
OFDM	QPSK	12 Mbps
OFDM	QPSK	18 Mbps
OFDM	16QAM	24 Mbps
OFDM	16QAM	36 Mbps
OFDM	64QAM	48 Mbps
OFDM	64QAM	54 Mbps

OFDM is a communications technique that divides a communications channel into a number of equally spaced frequency bands. A subcarrier that carries a portion of the user information is transmitted in each band. Each subcarrier is orthogonal (independent of each other) with every other subcarrier, differentiating OFDM from the commonly used frequency division multiplexing (FDM).

Activities

1. At 1 Mbps, which spreading code do 802.11 FHSS wireless networks use?

   a. CCK

   b. Barker Code

   c. 2GFSK

   d. DQPSK

2. Which of the following are modulation technologies used by 802.11 and 802.11b networks? (Choose two.)

   a. CCK

   b. DBPSK

   c. 6GFSK

   d. QPSK

3. How do 802.11g wireless networks provide backward compatibility for 802.11b networks?

   a. They can switch to OFMD coding.

   b. They support CCK coding.

   c. They use 16QAM modulation technology.

   d. They support GFSK modulation technology.

4. Which two wireless technologies use GFSK modulation? (Choose two.)

   a. HomeRF

   b. Bluetooth

   c. 802.11b

   d. HiperLAN/2

5. Which modulation technology does an 802.11a network use at 54Mbps?

   a. 16QAM

   b. 64QAM

   c. BPSK

   d. QPSK

Extended Activities

Research the following modulation techniques, and describe how each represents digital data as analog radio waves.

1. BPSK

   _____

   _____

   _____

2. GFSK

   _____

   _____

   _____

3. QPSK

   _____

   _____

   _____

4. 16QAM

   _____

   _____

   _____

5. 64QAM

   _____

   _____

   _____

Summary

This unit discussed some of the MAC and Physical Layer characteristics of wireless LANs common to all wireless LAN products, regardless of the manufacturer. This unit presented basic instruction on many configurable parameters and their effects on network performance, as well as the difference between Ethernet and wireless LAN frames and how wireless LANs avoid collisions. This unit also described how wireless LAN stations communicate with one another under normal circumstances, and how collision handling occurs in a wireless LAN.

To estimate throughput across wireless LANs, you must understand the effects of communication parameters and collision handling on system throughput. This unit described the types of IFS so that you can effectively grasp how RTS/CTS, DCF, and PCF work on wireless LANs. These functions are essential in the ongoing communications process of a wireless LAN.

Two carrier sense mechanisms are used on wireless networks, physical carrier sense and virtual carrier sense. Physical carrier sense functions by checking the signal strength (the RSSI) on the RF carrier signal to see whether a station is currently transmitting. Virtual carrier sense works by using the NAV field, which acts as a timer on the station.

Unit 8 then described the process of modulation, a Physical Layer function, in which a radio transceiver prepares the digital signal within the NIC for transmission over the airwaves. Modulation is the process of adding data to a carrier by altering the amplitude, frequency, or phase of the carrier in a controlled manner.

Unit 8 Quiz

1. Which of the following service sets can use distributed coordination function (DCF) mode? (Choose three.)

   a. BSS

   b. IBSS

   c. ESS

   d. IESS

2. Which of the following service sets can use point coordination function (PCF) mode? (Choose two.)

   a. BSS

   b. IBSS

   c. ESS

   d. IESS

3. You have a large number of users on one access point, and collisions are becoming a problem, causing reduced throughput. Some of the users are developers that do a significant amount of large file transfers during the day. Which RTS/CTS setting would best fix this problem?

   a. On

   b. Off

   c. On with threshold

   d. Off with threshold

4. Which one of the following is an advantage to using point coordination function (PCF) mode over distributed coordination function (DCF) mode?

   a. PCF has a lower overhead than using DCF.

   b. PCF can be used in and IBSS while DCF cannot.

   c. PCF uses CSMA/CA while DCF does not.

   d. PCF provides a level of QoS.

5. After a client station sends a data packet to another client station, the receiving station replies with an acknowledgement after which interframe space?

   a. IFS

   b. SIFS

   c. PIFS

   d. DIFS

6. Why is the CSMA/CA protocol used in order to avoid collisions in a wireless LAN?

   a. PCF mode requires use of a polling mechanism.

   b. The overhead of sending acknowledgements is high.

   c. All clients must acknowledge packets received while they are asleep.

   d. It is impossible to detect collisions on a wireless LAN.

7. What will wireless end stations broadcast when actively scanning for access points on the network?

   a. Beacon management frames

   b. Superframes

   c. Probe request frames

   d. Request to send frames

8. PIFS are only used during the communications of a wireless LAN when which of the following have occurred?

   a. The network is in point coordination function mode.

   b. The access point has been configured to use RTS/CTS.

   c. The access point has been configured to use CSMA/CD.

   d. The network is configured for fragmentation.

9. You have just finished installing your first wireless LAN with 802.11b equipment rated at 11 Mbps. After testing the throughput of the clients, you find your actual throughput is only 5.5 Mbps. What is the likely cause of this throughput?

   a. Wireless LANs use RTS/CTS by default.

   b. Wireless LANs use the CSMA/CA protocol.

   c. Use of PCF is reducing network throughput.

   d. DRS has caused all of the clients to decrease their data rates.

10. You have just finished installing your first wireless LAN with 802.11b equipment rated at 11 Mbps. After testing the throughput of the clients, you find your actual throughput is only 5.5 Mbps. What can you change to get 11 Mbps of total system throughput?

    a. Turn off RTS/CTS.

    b. Move all of the clients closer to the access point.

    c. Turn up the power on the access point.

    d. Purchase another access point and co-locate both together using nonoverlapping channels.

11. What type of modulation do 802.11b devices use at 11 Mbps?

    a. BPSK

    b. DPSK

    c. QPSK

    d. CCK

12. At 24 Mbps, what type of modulation do 802.11a devices use?

    a. BPSK

    b. 16QAM

    c. OFDM

    d. CCK

13. If the sending station on a wireless LAN does not receive an ACK, the sending station assumes which one of the following?

    a. The receiving station is sleeping.

    b. The receiving station is a hidden node.

    c. A collision occurred.

    d. That RTS/CTS is turned on.

14. Modulation is which of one of the following?

    a. The process by which digital data is modified to become RF data

    b. The process of adding data to a carrier by altering the amplitude, frequency, or phase of the carrier in a controlled manner

    c. The process of propagating an RF signal through the airwaves

    d. The means by which RF signals are received and processed by RF antennas

15. Which of the following are parts of a superframe? (Choose three.)

    a. Beacon

    b. Beacon Free Period

    c. Contention-Free Period

    d. Contention Period

16. A superframe is used when which of the following is true? (Choose two.)

    a. The access point has been configured for point coordination function mode

    b. When beacons are disabled in the access point

    c. The wireless clients have been configured to announce to the access point that they are pollable

    d. The access point has been configured for distributed coordination function mode

17. What is the purpose of the superframe?

    a. To increase the throughput of all wireless LANs

    b. To ensure QoS for all voice and video applications running on wireless LANs

    c. To ensure that PCF-mode and DCF-mode clients do not communicate within the same wireless LAN

    d. To allow fair coexistence between PCF-mode and DCF-mode clients on the network

18. The acronym CCA stands for which one of the following?

    a. Close Client Association

    b. Clear Current Authentication

    c. Clear Channel Assessment

    d. Clean Channel Association

    e. Calculate Clear Assessment

19. Which statement describes the Network Allocation Vector (NAV)?

    a. It is a timer on the station.

    b. It is a navigational feature for RF signal propagation.

    c. It is a location discovery tool for wireless LANs.

    d. It is a tool for allocating the bandwidth of a wireless LAN.

20. Using RTS/CTS allows wireless stations to do which of the following?

    a. Broadcast their intent to send data across the network to the receiving station

    b. Send their packets across the network at the maximum rated speed of the network

    c. Eliminate hidden nodes on the network

    d. Diagnose and reduce high overhead between stations

Unit 9
Troubleshooting Wireless LAN Installations

Just as traditional wired networks have challenges during implementation, wireless LANs have their own set of challenges, mainly dealing with the behavior of RF signals. In this unit, we discuss the more common obstacles to successful implementation of a wireless LAN, and how to troubleshoot them. There are different methods of discovering when these challenges exist, and each of the challenges discussed has its remedies and workarounds.

Many consider the challenges to implementing any wireless LAN to be "textbook" problems that can commonly occur and, therefore, can be avoided by careful planning and simply being aware that these problems can and will occur.

Lessons

1. Multipath
2. Hidden Node
3. Near/Far
4. System Throughput
5. Types of Interference
6. Range Considerations

Terms

adjacent channel interference—Adjacent channel interference is interference caused when a channel exceeds its assigned frequency band, and "spills over" into the band assigned to another channel.

all-band interference—All-band interference is radio frequency (RF) interference that covers the entire usable RF spectrum of a certain wireless technology. For example, 802.15 Bluetooth creates interference across the entire 2.4-GHz ISM band.

antenna diversity—Antenna diversity is the use of multiple antennas in order to overcome multipath.

co-channel interference—Co-channel interference is RF interference caused by wireless access points operating on the same channel in close proximity to each other.

downfade—Downfade is the reduction of the received RF signal amplitude as a result of multipath.

free-space path loss—Free-space path loss refers to the loss incurred by an RF signal due largely to "signal dispersion," which is a natural broadening of the wave front. The wider a wave front is, the less power that can be induced into the receiving antenna. This loss of signal strength is a function of distance alone and becomes a very important factor when considering link viability.

narrowband interference—Narrowband interference is RF interference that occurs over a small portion of the RF spectrum.

nulling—Nulling is the multipath condition that occurs when one or more reflected RF signals arrive at the receiver 180 degrees out-of-phase with the main wave, at such an amplitude that they cancel, or null, the main wave.

spectrum analyzer—A spectrum analyzer is an instrument that identifies the amplitude of signals at various frequencies.

stratification—Stratification occurs when air layers of different temperatures or densities are stacked one on top of the other. Stratification causes RF waves to bend as they pass through the layers.

upfade—Upfade describes the condition when multipath causes an RF signal to gain strength.

Lesson 1—Multipath

As discussed in our reading on radio frequency (RF) fundamentals, there are two types of line of sight (LOS). First, there is visual LOS, which is what the human eye sees. Visual LOS is the first and most basic LOS test. If you can see the RF receiver from the installation point of the RF transmitter, you have visual line of sight. Second, and different from visual LOS, is RF line of sight. RF LOS is what an RF device can "see." RF signals meet with many obstacles as they travel from the source to the destination, and these obstacles can cause all or part of the signal to change its course or shape. This lesson discusses these signal changes, their effects on the network, and the steps we can take to compensate for them.

Objectives

At the end of this lesson you will be able to:

- Describe the causes of multipath on a wireless LAN

- Troubleshoot multipath

- Resolve multipath on a wireless network segment

 **Key Point**

Multipath is the creation of multiple waveforms from a single signal caused by obstacles in the original signal's path.

Causes of Multipath

The general behavior of an RF signal is to grow wider as it is transmitted farther. Because of this type of behavior, the RF signal will encounter objects in its path that will reflect, diffract, or otherwise interfere with the signal. When an RF wave is reflected off an object (water, tin roof, other metal object, and so forth) while moving toward its receiver, multiple wave fronts are created, one for each reflection point. These waves move in many directions, and many of these reflected waves still head toward the receiver. The term multipath is derived from this behavior, as shown on the Multipath Diagram. Multipath is defined as the composition of a primary signal plus duplicate or echoed wave fronts caused by reflections of waves off objects between the transmitter and receiver. The delay between the instant that the main signal arrives and the instant that the last reflected signal arrives is known as delay spread.

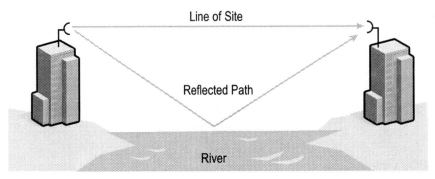

Multipath

Effects of Multipath

Multipath can cause several different conditions, all of which can affect the transmission of the RF signal differently. These conditions include:

- Decreased Signal Amplitude (downfade)
- Corruption
- Nulling
- Increased Signal Amplitude (upfade)

Decreased Signal Amplitude

When an RF wave arrives at the receiver, many reflected waves may arrive at the same time from different directions. The combination of these waves' amplitudes is additive to the main RF wave. Reflected waves, if out-of-phase with the main wave, can cause decreased signal amplitude at the receiver, as illustrated on the Downfade Diagram. This occurrence is commonly referred to as downfade and should be taken into consideration when conducting a sight survey and selecting appropriate antennas.

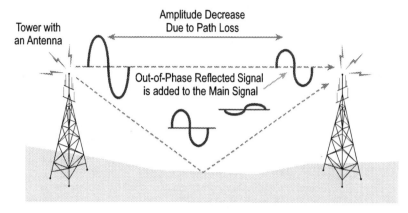

Downfade

Corruption

Corrupted signals (waves) due to multipath can occur as a result of the same phenomena that cause decreased amplitude, but to a greater degree. When reflected waves arrive at the receiver out-of-phase with the main wave, as illustrated on the RF Signal Corruption Diagram, they can cause the wave to be greatly reduced in amplitude instead of only slightly reduced. The amplitude reduction is such that the receiver is sensitive enough to detect most of the information carried on the wave, but not all the information.

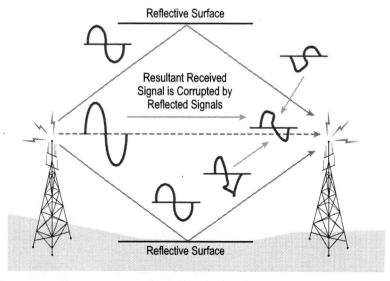

RF Signal Corruption

In such cases, the signal-to-noise ratio (SNR) is generally very low, where the signal itself is very close to the noise floor. The receiver is unable to clearly decipher between the information signal and noise, causing the data that is received to be only part (if any) of the transmitted data. This corruption of data will require the transmitter to resend the data, increasing overhead and decreasing throughput in the wireless LAN.

Nulling

The condition known as nulling occurs when one or more reflected waves arrive at the receiver out-of-phase with the main wave with such amplitude that the main wave's amplitude is cancelled. As illustrated on the RF Signal Nulling Diagram, when reflected waves arrive out-of-phase with the main wave at the receiver, the condition can cancel or "null" the entire set of RF waves, including the main wave.

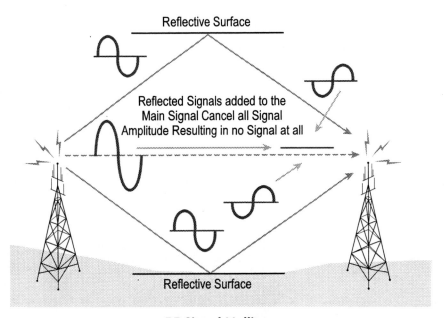

RF Signal Nulling

When nulling occurs, retransmission of the data will not solve the problem. The transmitter, receiver, or reflective objects must be moved. Sometimes more than one of these must be relocated to compensate for the nulling effects on the RF wave.

Increased Signal Amplitude

Multipath conditions can also cause a signal's amplitude to be increased from what it would have been without reflected waves present. Upfade is the term used to describe when multipath causes an RF signal to gain strength. Upfade, as illustrated on the Upfade Diagram, occurs due to reflected signals arriving at the receiver in phase with the main signal. Similar to a decreased signal, all of these waves are additive to the main signal. Under no circumstance can multipath cause the signal that reaches the receiver to be stronger than the transmitted signal when the signal left the transmitting device. If multipath occurs in such a way as to be additive to the main signal, the total signal that reaches the receiver will be stronger than the signal would have otherwise been without multipath present.

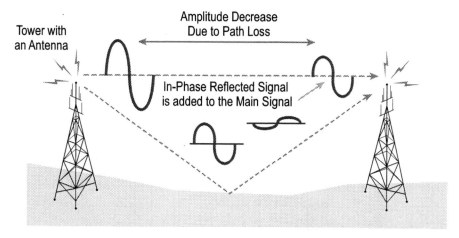

Upfade

It is important to understand that a received RF signal can never be as large as the signal that was transmitted due to the significance of free space path loss (usually called path loss). Path loss is the effect of a signal losing amplitude, due to expansion, as the signal travels through open space.

Another way to think of path loss is to consider what happens when someone is blowing a bubble with bubble gum. As the gum expands, the gum at any point in the bubble becomes thinner. If someone reached out and grabbed a 1-inch square piece of this bubble, the amount of gum he or she would actually get would decrease as the bubble expanded. If a person grabbed a piece of the bubble while it was still small (close to the person's mouth, which is the transmitter) the person would get a significant amount of gum. If the person waited until the bubble was large (further from the transmitter) to get a piece the same size, the piece would be only a very small amount of gum. This illustration shows that path loss is affected by two factors: the distance between transmitter and receiver and the size of the receiving aperture (the size of the piece of gum that was grabbed).

Troubleshooting Multipath

An in-phase or out-of-phase RF wave cannot be seen; thus, we must look for the effects of multipath in order to detect its occurrence. When doing a link budget calculation, to find out just how much power output you will need to have a successful link between sites, you might calculate an output power level that should work, but doesn't. Such an occurrence is one way to determine that multipath is occurring.

Another common method of finding multipath is to look for RF coverage holes in a site survey discussed in further reading on site surveys. These holes are created both by lack of coverage and by multipath reflections that cancel the main signal. Understanding the sources of multipath is crucial to eliminating its effects.

Reflected RF waves cause multipath; thus, obstacles that more easily reflect RF waves, such as metal blinds, bodies of water, and metal roofs, should be removed from or avoided in the signal path if possible. This procedure may include moving the transmitting and receiving antennas. Multipath is likely the most common "textbook" wireless LAN problem. Administrators and installers deal with multipath daily. Because they are mobile, even wireless LAN users experience problems with multipath. Users may roam into an area with high multipath, not knowing why their RF signal has been so significantly degraded.

Solutions for Multipath

Antenna diversity was devised to compensate for multipath. Antenna diversity means using multiple antennas, inputs, and receivers to compensate for the conditions that cause multipath. There are four types of receiving antenna diversity, one of which is predominantly used in wireless LANs. The types of transmission diversity used by wireless LANs are as follows:

- **Antenna Diversity**—Not active. Multiple antennas are on single input. This diversity is rarely used.

- **Switching Diversity**—Multiple antennas are on multiple receivers. The radios switch receivers based on signal strength.

- **Antenna Switching Diversity**—Active (the radio takes an action based on a condition) and used by most wireless LAN manufacturers. Multiple antennas are on multiple inputs. Signal is received through only one antenna at a time.

- **Phase Diversity**—Patented proprietary technology. This diversity adjusts the phase of the antenna to the phase of the signal in order to maintain signal quality.

- **Diversity Transmission**—Used by most wireless LAN manufacturers. Transmits out of the antenna last used for reception and can alternate antennas for transmission retries. A unit can either transmit or receive, but cannot do both simultaneously.

The Antenna Diversity Diagram illustrates an access point with multiple antennas to compensate for multipath.

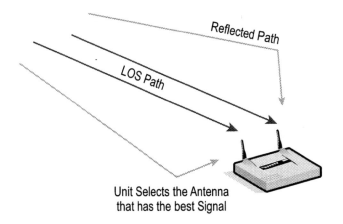

Antenna Diversity

Antenna diversity is made up of the following characteristics that work together to compensate for the effects of multipath:

1. Antenna diversity uses multiple antennas on multiple inputs to bring a signal to a single receiver.

2. The incoming RF signal is received through one antenna at a time. The receiving radio is constantly sampling the incoming signals from both antennas to determine which signal is of a higher quality. The receiving radio then chooses to accept the higher quality signal.

3. The radio transmits its next signal out of the antenna that was last used to receive an incoming signal because the received signal was a higher quality signal than from the other antenna. If the radio must retransmit a signal, it will alternate antennas until a successful transmission is made.

4. Finally, each antenna can be used to transmit or receive, but not both at the same time. Only one antenna may be used at a time, and that antenna may only transmit or receive; it may not do both.

Most access points in today's wireless LANs are built with dual antennas for exactly this purpose: to compensate for the degrading effects of multipath on signal quality and throughput.

Activities

1. Which of the following are common methods used to locate multipath on a wireless network? (Choose two.)

    a. Measure throughput at the access point and compare to the bandwidth at the wireless nodes.

    b. Look for holes in the RF coverage during the site surveys.

    c. Set the transmit power to one that should work and measure network performance.

    d. Turn off the multipath option on the access point and the wireless clients.

2. Which of the following could cause multipath? (Choose three.)

    a. A lake next to the antenna

    b. A tree in the signal's path

    c. A metal roof in the Fresnel zone

    d. Metal blinds in the office area

3. Which statement describes the nulling of an RF signal?

    a. Multiple signals combine to increase the signal amplitude at the receiver.

    b. Out-of-phase signals at the receiver cancel the transmitted waveform.

    c. Signals received out-of-phase reduce the signal-to-noise ratio.

    d. The transmitted signal wavefront widens as it travels toward the receiver.

4. You are working a trouble ticket on a wireless bridge link between two buildings. The buildings are 1.5 miles (2.4 km) apart. The data received by either building is virtually unrecognizable and the received signal power level is close to the noise floor. Which of the following examples of multipath caused this situation?

    a. Nulling

    b. Diversity

    c. Increase amplitude

    d. Corruption

5. You are completing a site survey for a building-to-building point-to-point wireless bridge link. The buildings are located about 200m apart. You are verifying your signal level measurements, and notice today that the received signal amplitude has increased significantly over what was previously measured. The site received a great deal of rain overnight and a significant amount of standing water in the area between the buildings. Which of the following multipath effects is present in this example?

   a. Upfade

   b. Nulling

   c. Downfade

   d. Corruption

6. Which two factors affect path loss on a wireless LAN? (Choose two.)

   a. Distance between transmitter and receiver

   b. Transmitter power

   c. Size of the transmitter aperture

   d. Size of the receiver aperture

Extended Activity

Configure a wireless LAN with two bridged APs. Turn off WEP, set the SSIDs, and verify communications. Separate the APs and experiment with the multipath sources mentioned in this lesson. Can you duplicate the behaviors discussed in the lesson?

_____

_____

_____

_____

Lesson 2—Hidden Node

Multiple access protocols that enable networked computing devices to share a medium, such as Ethernet, are well developed and understood. However the nature of the wireless medium makes traditional methods of sharing a common connection more difficult. As we have learned, collisions do occur on wireless networks. However, wireless nodes have no way to detect collisions, and rely instead on collision avoidance techniques and frame acknowledgements to reduce collisions and their effect on wireless performance. Although wireless nodes perform a CCA before transmission, also designed to reduce the likelihood that a collision will occur, there is a situation where the transmitting node may not sense the presence of another node transmitting simultaneously. This lesson discusses this situation, called hidden node.

Objectives

At the end of this lesson you will be able to:

- Describe the causes of hidden node
- Troubleshoot hidden nodes
- Resolve hidden node on a wireless network segment

 **Key Point**

Obstacles in the RF signal path cause hidden node.

Causes of Hidden Node

Collisions can cause many problems in wired networking, and even more so for wireless networks. Collisions occur when two or more nodes sharing a communication medium simultaneously transmit data. The two signals corrupt each other and the result is a group of unreadable packet fragments. Collisions have always been a problem for computer networks, and the simplest protocols often do not overcome this problem. More complex protocols, such as Carrier Sense Multiple Access/Collision Detection (CSMA/CD) and Carrier Sense Multiple Access/ Collision Avoidance (CSMA/CA) check the channel before transmitting data. CSMA/CD is the protocol used with Ethernet and involves checking the voltage on the wire before transmitting. However, the process is considerably more difficult for wireless systems because collisions are undetectable. A condition known as the hidden node problem has been identified in wireless systems and is caused by problems in transmission detection.

Hidden node is a situation encountered with wireless LANs in which at least one node is unable to hear (detect) one or more of the other nodes connected to the wireless LAN. In this situation, a node can see the access point, but cannot see that other clients are also connected to the same access point due to some obstacle or a large amount of distance between the nodes. This situation causes a problem in medium access sharing, causing collisions between node transmissions. These collisions can result in significantly degraded throughput in the wireless LAN, as illustrated on the Hidden Node Diagram.

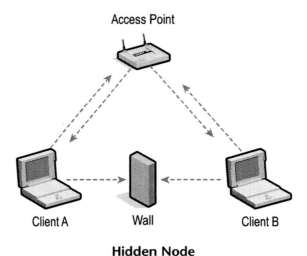

Hidden Node

The Hidden Node Diagram illustrates a brick wall with an access point sitting on top. On each side of the wall is a wireless station. These wireless stations cannot hear each other's transmissions, but both can hear the transmissions of the access point. If station A is transmitting a frame to the access point, and station B cannot hear this transmission, station B assumes that the medium is clear and can begin a transmission of its own to the access point. At this stage, the access point will be receiving transmissions that have originated at two points, and a collision will occur. The collision will cause retransmissions by both stations A and B, and again, because they cannot hear each other, they will transmit at will, thinking the medium is clear. Another collision is likely to occur. This problem is exacerbated with many active nodes on the wireless LAN that cannot hear one another.

Troubleshooting Hidden Node

The primary symptom of a hidden node is degraded throughput over the wireless LAN. Many times you will discover that you have a hidden node by hearing the complaints of users connected to the wireless LAN who detect that the network is unusually sluggish. Throughput may be decreased by up to 40 percent because of a hidden node problem. Because wireless LANs use the CSMA/CA protocol, they already have an approximate overhead of 50 percent. However, during a hidden node problem, it is possible to lose almost half of the remaining throughput on the system.

Because the nature of a wireless LAN increases mobility, you may encounter a hidden node at any time, despite a flawless design of your wireless LAN. If a user moves his computer to a conference room, another office, or into a data room, the new location of that node can potentially be hidden from the rest of the nodes connected to your wireless LAN.

Note: To proactively troubleshoot a hidden node, you must test for degraded throughput and also find as many potential locations for a hidden node as possible during the initial and any subsequent site surveys.

Solutions for Hidden Node

After you have performed the troubleshooting and discovered a hidden node problem, you must locate the problem node. Finding the node(s) will include a manual search for nodes that might be out of reach of the main cluster of nodes. This process is usually trial and error at best. Once these nodes are located, there are several remedies and workarounds for the problem:

- Use RTS/CTS
- Increase power to the nodes
- Remove obstacles
- Move the node

Use RTS/CTS

The RTS/CTS protocol is not necessarily a solution to the hidden node problem. Instead, it is a method of reducing the negative impact that hidden nodes have on the network. Hidden nodes cause excessive collisions, which have a severely detrimental impact on network throughput. The Request to Send/Clear to Send (RTS/CTS) protocol involves sending a small packet (RTS) to the intended recipient to prompt it to send back a packet (CTS), clearing the medium for data transmission before sending the data payload. This process informs any nearby stations that data is about to be sent, and tells them to delay transmissions (and thereby avoids collisions). Both the RTS and the CTS contain the length of the impending data transmission so that stations overhearing either the RTS or CTS frames know how long the transmission will take and when they can start to transmit again.

Three settings for RTS/CTS are on most access points and clients: On, Off, and On with Threshold. A network administrator must manually configure RTS/CTS settings. The Off setting is the default in order to reduce unnecessary network overhead caused by the RTS/CTS protocol. The threshold refers directly to the packet size that will trigger use of the RTS/CTS protocol. Because hidden nodes cause collisions, and collisions mainly affect larger packets, you may be able to overcome the hidden node problem by using the packet size threshold setting for RTS/CTS. What this setting essentially does is tell the access point to transmit all packets that are greater in size than "x" (your setting) using RTS/CTS, and to transmit all other packets without RTS/CTS. If the hidden node only has a minor impact on network throughput, activating RTS/CTS might have a detrimental effect on throughput.

Try using RTS/CTS in the "On" mode as a test to see if your throughput is positively affected. If RTS/CTS increases throughput, you have most likely confirmed the hidden node problem. You will encounter some additional overhead when using RTS/CTS, but your overall throughput should increase over what it was when the hidden node problem occurred.

Increase Power to the Nodes

Increasing the power (measured in milliwatts) of the nodes can solve the hidden node problem by allowing the cell around each node to increase in size, encompassing all of the other nodes. This configuration enables the nonhidden nodes to detect, or hear, the hidden node. If the nonhidden nodes can hear the hidden node, the hidden node is no longer hidden. Because wireless LANs use the CSMA/CA protocol, nodes will wait their turn before communicating with the access point.

Remove Obstacles

Increasing the power on your mobile nodes may not work if, for example, the reason one node is hidden is that a cement or steel wall prevents communication with other nodes. It is doubtful that you would be able to remove such an obstacle, but removal of the obstacle is another method of remedy for the hidden node problem. Keep these types of obstacles in mind when performing a site survey.

Move the Node

Another method of solving the hidden node problem is moving the nodes so that they can all hear each other. If you have found that the hidden node problem is the result of a user moving his or her computer to an area that is hidden from the other wireless nodes, you may have to force that user to move again. The alternative to forcing users to move is extending your wireless LAN to add proper coverage to the hidden area, perhaps using additional access points.

Activities

1. You are working a trouble ticket concerning reduced through-put on the second floor wireless LAN segment. Construction has been ongoing on that floor, and a new firewall was installed in the middle of the building. A hallway passes through the wall, and includes a fire door that, according to the local fire code, must remain closed. You notice that the throughput improves dramatically when the door is opened, then drops again when it is closed. When you installed the access point you installed two antennas, each connected to a splitter, one on each side of the wall.

   How can you best resolve this throughput problem while adhering to the fire code?

   a. Move all clients to one side of the wall

   b. Leave the door open during business hours

   c. Replace the access point with a higher-powered unit

   d. Install APs on each side of the wall

2. Which of the following are used to resolve the hidden node problem? (Choose three.)

   a. Use directional antennas

   b. Remove obstacles

   c. Add APs

   d. Increase node power

3. How might you confirm the presence of a hidden node on the network?

   a. Turn off the access point and observe wireless client throughput.

   b. Use the Search for Hidden Node capability built into the access point.

   c. Add reflective surfaces around the facility walls to increase signal coverage.

   d. Turn on RTS/CTS and watch for increased network throughput.

4. You are planning a wireless network installation. In order to proactively search for hidden nodes, at which point would you test for degraded throughput resulting from hidden nodes on the network?

   a. Requirements analysis

   b. Site survey

   c. Network installation

   d. System configuration

5. Which of the following would you look for when trouble-shooting hidden node?

   a. Sources of all-band interference

   b. APs running RTS/CTS

   c. Reflective surfaces

   d. Nodes transmitting at low power

Extended Activity

Configure a wireless LAN with a single access point and two clients. Turn off WEP, set the SSIDs, and verify communications. Separate the clients by a wall of some sort, and observe throughput. Experiment with the different solutions to hidden node discussions in this lesson. Can you duplicate the behaviors discussed in the lesson?

_____

_____

_____

_____

Lesson 3—Near/Far

The near/far problem occurs when multiple client nodes are located very near to the access point and transmitting at high power settings. At least one client is located much farther away from the access point than the other client nodes. The access point receives its setting at a much lower setting than the other nodes. The result is that the client(s) located farther away from the access point simply cannot be heard over the traffic from the nearer clients. This lesson discusses the near/far problem.

Objectives

At the end of this lesson you will be able to:

- Describe the causes of near/far
- Troubleshoot the near/far problem
- Resolve near/far on a wireless network segment

 Key Point

Wireless nodes located near the access point can overpower those located farther away.

Causes of Near/Far

The Near/Far Diagram illustrates the near/far problem on a wireless network segment.

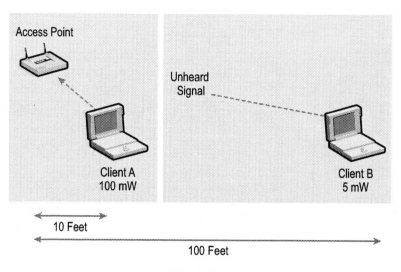

Near/Far

Near/far is similar in nature to a crowd of people all screaming at one time into a microphone, and one person whispering from 50 feet (15.2 meters) away from that same microphone. The voice of the person 50 feet (15.2 meters) away is not going to reach the microphone over the noise of the crowd shouting near the microphone. Even if the microphone is sensitive enough to pick up the distant whisper under silent conditions, the high-powered, close-range conversations have effectively raised the noise floor to a point where low-amplitude inputs are not heard.

Getting back to wireless LANs, the node that is being drowned out is well within the normal range of the access point, but it simply cannot be heard over the signals of the other clients. What this means to you as an administrator is that you must be aware of the possibility of the near/far problem during site surveys and understand how to overcome the problem through proper wireless LAN design and troubleshooting techniques.

Troubleshooting Near/Far

Troubleshooting the near/far problem is usually as simple as taking a good look at a network layout, locations of stations on the wireless network, and transmission output power of each node. These steps will give the administrator clues to what is likely going on with the stations having connectivity problems. Because near/far prevents a node from communicating, the administrator should check to see if the station has drivers loaded properly for the wireless radio card and has associated with the access point (shown in the association table of the access point).

The next step in troubleshooting near/far is to use a wireless sniffer. A wireless sniffer picks up transmissions from all stations it hears. One simple method of finding nodes whose signals are not heard by the access point is to move around the network looking for stations with a faint signal in relation to the access point and nodes near the access point. Depending on the size of the network and the complexity of the building structure, it should not be too time-consuming to locate such a node using this method. Locating this node and comparing its signal strength to that of nodes near the access point can solve the near/far problem fairly quickly.

Solutions for Near/Far

Although the near/far problem can be debilitating for those clients whose RF signals get drowned out, near/far is a relatively easy problem to overcome in most situations. It is imperative to understand that the CSMA/CA protocol solves much of the near/far problem with no intervention of the administrator. If a node can hear another node transmitting, it will stop its own transmissions, and comply with shared medium access rules of CSMA/CA. However, if for any reason the near/far problem still exists in the network, below is a list of remedies that are easily implemented and can overcome the near/far problem:

- Increase power to remote node (the one that is being drowned out)
- Decrease power of local nodes (the close, loud ones)
- Move the remote node closer to the access point

One other solution is moving the access point to which the remote node is associated. However, this solution should be viewed as a last resort, because moving an access point will likely disrupt more clients than it would help.

Activities

1. You are troubleshooting a near/far problem on your wireless network. You find that the access point is located much closer to some clients than others. What likely flaw does this reveal in the network?

   a. All the clients should have been placed in a central location.

   b. The access point cannot handle the client count.

   c. The site survey was not performed properly.

   d. The clients use different layer 3 protocols.

2. Why is near/far relatively easy to resolve?

   a. Clients can be easily moved nearer to the access point.

   b. CSMA/CA controls medium access.

   c. access point power levels can be easily adjusted.

   d. Obstacles are easily moved.

3. What steps can a network administrator take to check for causes of near/far on the network? (Choose two.)

   a. Look for reflective surfaces in the signal path.

   b. Look for clients running protocols that support network QoS.

   c. Check for the correct drivers installed on the wireless clients.

   d. Use a wireless sniffer to check for faint signals.

4. Which one of the following tasks is the best choice for troubleshooting the near/far problem?

   a. Review the locations of the stations on the network

   b. Check the access point receiver gain

   c. Check that antenna diversity is used on the wireless clients

   d. Review the access point's transmit power settings

Extended Activity

Configure a wireless LAN with a single access point and two clients. Turn off WEP, set the SSIDs, and verify communications. Move one of the clients down the hall, into another room, or somewhere else remote from the access point. Can you duplicate the near/far problem? How can you resolve it?

_____

_____

_____

_____

Lesson 4—System Throughput

Throughput on a wireless LAN is based on many factors. For example, the amount and type of interference may impact the amount of data that can be successfully transmitted. If additional security solutions, such as WEP, are implemented, the additional overhead of encrypting and decrypting data will also cause a decrease in throughput. Using VPN tunnels will add additional overhead to a wireless LAN system in the same manner as will turning on WEP. This lesson discusses some of the many sources of overhead on a wireless LAN, the effect co-located APs have on network throughput, and how we can resolve throughput problems co-located APs may cause.

Objectives

At the end of this lesson you will be able to:

- Describe key sources of overhead on wireless LANs

- Explain the effect co-located APs and channel selection have on network throughput

- Increase network throughput through the proper configuration and placement of wireless APs

 **Key Point**

Co-located APs can improve network performance if properly installed and configured.

Sources of Overhead

As mentioned earlier, there are many sources of overhead on a wireless network. As more of the network bandwidth is used to move data, less bandwidth is available for the data itself. We have learned that the best throughput we can hope for on a wireless network is 50 percent of the bandwidth. Network performance will degrade appreciably when other factors decrease throughput even further. The following sections provide some additional examples of network overhead sources.

Distance
Greater distances between the transmitter and receiver cause the throughput to decrease because an increase in the number of errors (bit error rate) creates a need for retransmissions. Modern spread spectrum systems are configured to make discrete jumps to specified data rates (1, 2, 5.5, and 11 Mbps). If 11 Mbps cannot be maintained, for example, the device will drop to 5.5 Mbps. Because the throughput is about 50 percent of the data rate on a wireless LAN system, changing the data rate will have a significant impact on the throughput.

Hardware
Hardware limitations will also dictate the data rate. If an IEEE 802.11 device is communicating with an IEEE 802.11b device, the data rate can be no more than 2 Mbps, despite the 802.11b device's ability to communicate at 11 Mbps. Correspondingly, the actual throughput will be less still—about 50 percent, or 1 Mbps. With wireless LAN hardware, another consideration must be taken into account: the amount of CPU power given to the access point. A slow central processing unit (CPU) that cannot handle the full 11 Mbps data rate with 128-bit WEP enabled will affect throughput.

Spread Spectrum Technology
The type of spread spectrum technology used, frequency hopping spread spectrum (FHSS) or direct sequence spread spectrum (DSSS), will make a difference in throughput for two specific reasons. First, the data rates for FHSS and DSSS systems are quite different. FHSS systems typically comply with either the OpenAir standard, which allows them to transmit at 800 kbps or 1.6 Mbps, or the IEEE 802.11 standard, which allows them to transmit at 1 Mbps or 2 Mbps. Currently, DSSS systems comply with either the IEEE 802.11 standard or the 802.11b standard, supporting data rates of 1, 2, 5.5, and 11 Mbps. The second reason that the type of spread spectrum technology affects throughput is that FHSS incurs the additional overhead of hop time.

Request to Send/Clear to Send (RTS/CTS), a protocol used on some wireless LAN implementations, which communicates similarly to the way that some serial links communicate, creates significant overhead because of the amount of handshaking that takes place during the transfer.

User Count
The number of users attempting to simultaneously access the medium will have an impact. An increase in simultaneous users decreases the throughput each station receives from the access point.

PCF Mode Using Point Coordination Function (PCF) mode on an access point, thereby invoking polling on the wireless network decreases throughput. Polling causes lower throughput by introducing the extra overhead of a polling mechanism and mandatory responses from wireless stations even when no data needs to be sent by those stations.

Other Factors Other factors limiting the throughput of a wireless LAN include proprietary Data Link Layer protocols, the use of fragmentation (which requires the reassembly of packets), and packet size. Larger packets result in greater throughput (assuming the radio frequency [RF] link is good) because the ratio of data to overhead is better.

Co-location Throughput (Theory vs. Reality)

Co-location is a common wireless LAN implementation technique used to provide more bandwidth and throughput to wireless users in a given area. RF theory, combined with FCC regulations, allows wireless LAN users in the United States three nonoverlapping RF channels (1, 6, and 11). These three channels can be used to co-locate multiple (three) access points within the same physical area using 802.11b equipment, as can be seen on the Co-location Throughput Diagram.

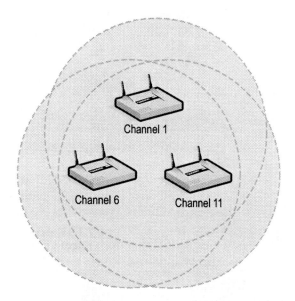

Co-location Throughput

When co-locating multiple access points, it is highly recommended that you:

1. Use the same spread spectrum technology (either direct sequence or frequency hopping, but not both) for all access points.

2. Use the same vendor for all access points.

Note: Several vendors' access point configurations allow you to load balance, either automatically or manually. If this feature is available, it's use is recommended.

The portion of the 2.4-GHz Industrial, Scientific, Medical (ISM) band that is useable for wireless LANs consists of 83.5 MHz. DSSS channels are 22 MHz wide, and 11 channels are specified for use in the United States. These channels are specifically designated ranges of frequencies within the ISM band. According to the center frequency and the width given to each of these channels by the FCC, only three nonoverlapping channels can exist in this band. Co-location of access points using nonoverlapping channels in the same physical space has advantages in implementing wireless LANs, so we will first explain what should happen when you properly co-locate these access points, and then we will explain what will happen.

Theory: What Should Happen

For purposes of simplicity in this explanation, we will assume that all access points being used in this scenario are 802.11b-compliant, 11-Mbps access points. When using only one access point in a simple wireless LAN, you should experience actual throughput of somewhere between 4.5 Mbps and 5.5 Mbps. You will never see the full 11 Mbps of rated bandwidth due to the half-duplex nature of the RF radios and overhead requirements for wireless LAN protocols, such as CSMA/CA.

The RF theory of three nonoverlapping channels should allow you to set up one access point on channel 1, one access point on channel 6, and one access point on channel 11 without any overlap in these access points' RF band usages. Therefore, you should see normal throughput of approximately 5 Mbps on all co-located access points, with no adjacent-channel interference. Adjacent-channel interference causes degradation of throughput on one or both of the other access points.

Reality: What Does Happen

What actually happens is that channel 1 and channel 6 have a small amount of overlap, as do channel 6 and channel 11. The DSSS Channel Overlap Diagram illustrates this overlap. The reason for this overlap is typically that both access points are transmitting at approximately the same high output power and are located relatively close to each other. Thus, instead of getting normal half-duplex throughput on all access points, a detrimental effect is seen on all three. Throughput can decrease to 4 Mbps or less on all three access points, or may be unevenly distributed where the access points might have 3, 4, and 5 Mbps, respectively.

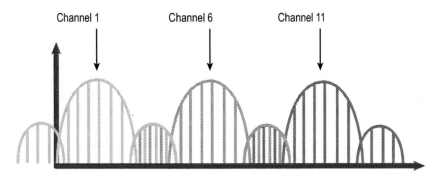

Channel 1   Channel 6   Channel 11

DSSS Channel Overlap

The portion of the theory that holds true is that adjacent channels (1, 2, 3, 4, and 5, for example) have significant overlap, to the point that using an access point on channel 1 and another on channel 3, for example, results in even lower throughput (2 Mbps or less) on the two access points. In this case, in particular, a partial overlapping of channels occurs. It is typically seen that a full overlap results in better throughput for the two systems than does a partial overlap between systems.

All this discussion is not to say that you simply cannot co-locate three access points using channels 1, 6, and 11. Rather, it is to point out that when you do so, you should not expect the theory to hold completely true. You will experience degraded throughput that is significantly less than the normally expected rate of approximately 5 Mbps per access point unless care is taken to turn down the output power and spread the access points across a broader amount of physical space.

Note: If you do co-locate three access points in this manner, it is recommended that you implement the co-location using the same manufacturer's hardware for all three access points. It has been noted in many lab scenarios that using differing vendors' equipment for co-location has a negative effect on throughput of one or more of the access points. This negative effect could be simply due to differing output power and proximity between access points, but could also be related to many other factors.

Solutions for Co-location Throughput Problems

As a wireless LAN installer or administrator, you really have two choices when considering access point co-location. You can accept the degraded throughput, or you can attempt a workaround. Accepting the fact that your users will not have 5 Mbps of actual throughput to the network backbone on each access point may be an acceptable scenario. First, however, you must make sure that the users connecting to the network in this situation can still be productive and that they do not actually require the full 5 Mbps of throughput. The last thing you want to be responsible for as a wireless LAN administrator is a network that does not allow the users to do their jobs or achieve the connections that they require. An administrator's second option in this case is to attempt a workaround. Below, we describe some of the alternatives to co-location problems.

Use Two Access Points

One option, which is the easiest, is to use channels 1 and 11 with only 2 access points, as illustrated on the Using Two Access Points Instead of Three Diagram. Using only these two channels will ensure that you have no overlap between channels regardless of proximity between systems, and therefore, no detrimental effect on the throughput of each access point. By way of comparison, two access points operating at the maximum capacity of 5.5 Mbps (about the best that you can expect by any access point), give you a total capacity of 11 Mbps of aggregate throughput, whereas three access points operating at approximately 4 Mbps each (degraded from the maximum due to actual channel overlap) on average yield only 12 Mbps of aggregate throughput. For an additional 1 Mbps of throughput, an administrator would have to spend the extra money to buy another access point, the time and labor to install it, and the continued burden of managing it.

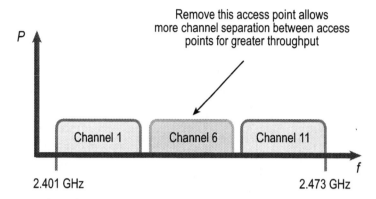

Using Two Access Points Instead of Three

In certain instances, the extra 1 Mbps of bandwidth might still be advantageous, but in a small environment, it might not be practical. Remember that this scenario applies only to access points located in the same physical space serving the same client base, but using different, nonoverlapping channels. This configuration does not apply to channel reuse, where cells on different nonoverlapping channels are alternately spread throughout an area to avoid co-channel interference.

Use 802.11a Equipment

As a second option, you could use 802.11a-compliant equipment operating in the 5-GHz UNII bands. The 5-GHz UNII bands, which are each wider than the 2.4-GHz ISM band, have three usable bands, and each band allows for four nonoverlapping channels. By using a mixture of 802.11b and 802.11a equipment, more systems can be co-located in the same space without fear of interference between systems. With two (or three) co-located 802.11b systems and up to eight co-located 802.11a systems, there is the potential for an incredible amount of throughput in the same physical space. The reason that we specify 8 instead of 12 co-located access points with 802.11a is that only the lower and middle bands (with four nonoverlapping channels each) are specified for indoor use. Therefore, indoors, where most access points are placed, there is normally only the potential for up to eight access points using 802.11a-compliant devices.

Issues with 802.11a Equipment

802.11a equipment is now available from several vendors, but is still more expensive than equipment that uses the 2.4-GHz frequency band. However, the 5-GHz band has the advantage of many more nonoverlapping channels than the 2.4-GHz band (eight vs. three) for any given area, allowing you to implement many more co-located access points.

You must keep in mind that while the 2.4-GHz band allows for less expensive gear, the 2.4-GHz band is much more crowded, which means you are more likely to encounter interference from other nearby wireless LANs. Remember that 802.11a devices and 802.11b devices are incompatible. These devices do not see, hear, or communicate with one another because they utilize different frequency bands and different modulation techniques.

Summary

Why do nonoverlapping channels overlap? There could be many answers to this question; however, it seems that the greatest cause is access points that are located too close together. By separating the access points by a greater distance, the overlap between theoretically nonoverlapping channels is reduced. Watching this configuration on a spectrum analyzer, you can see that for close-quarters co-location, channel separation needs to be larger than 3 MHz; however, because that is what we, as administrators, have to work with, we have to find a workaround.

We can either physically separate the radios by a farther distance or we can use channels farther apart than 3 MHz (this is why using channels 1 and 11 is only suggested for close-quarters co-location). It also seems that co-location of different vendors' equipment makes a difference. Using the same vendor's equipment for close-quarters co-location has less severe overlapping than does using multiple vendors' equipment. It is unknown whether this phenomenon is due to inaccuracies in the radios or just due to each vendor's implementation of hardware around the radio is unknown.

Note: Idiosyncrasies such as nonoverlapping channels overlapping will not be tested on the CWNA exam. For the exam it is important to know the theory of how co-channel throughput is supposed to work.

Activities

1. You are building a three-access point, co-located, cross-vendor wireless network. What kind of behavior can you expect from this design?

    a. Lower throughput than if you used the same vendor's equipment

    b. Better network performance under heavy client loads

    c. Lower levels of interference due to variances in radio performance

    d. More nonoverlapping channels as each vendor sets its own channel frequencies

2. You wish to build a wireless network that provides significantly better throughput than does a single 802.11b access point. Which of the following is an acceptable solution?

    a. Co-locate 802.11 FHSS and 802.11b DSSS APs in the same area.

    b. Install two 802.11b radio cards in a single access point, transmitting on channels 1 and 6.

    c. Co-locate two 802.11b and two 802.11a APs in the same area.

    d. Install in the area two load balancing 802.11b APs operating on the same channel.

3. How might a wireless network administrator help alleviate throughput problems caused by two co-located 802.11b APs?

    a. Use only channels 6 and 11.

    b. Choose channels separated by more than 3 MHz.

    c. Turn down the power on one access point.

    d. Configure the clients to use a single channel.

4. You are evaluating an existing wireless network as a part of a system upgrade site survey. You notice on your spectrum analyzer that channels 1, 6, and 11 are all in use in close proximity to each other. Which of the following are network throughput conditions your customer is likely experiencing? (Choose two.)

   a. Throughput somewhat lower than 4 Mbps

   b. Aggregate throughput well above 5.5 Mbps

   c. Throughput unevenly distributed across the APs

   d. Load balanced throughput across the APs

5. Which of the following are steps you should take when considering co-locating access points on your wireless network? (Choose two.)

   a. Mix frequency hopping and direct sequence devices.

   b. Use the same vendor for all equipment.

   c. Implement load balancing if it is an option.

   d. Operate all APs on the same channel.

6. Which of the following are causes of reduced throughput on a wireless network? (Choose three.)

   a. High user counts on the network segment

   b. High access point CPU utilization

   c. High client CPU utilization

   d. Use of frequency hopping technologies

Lesson 5—Types of Interference

Due to the unpredictable behavioral tendencies of radio frequency (RF) technology, you must take into account many kinds of RF interference during implementation and management of a wireless LAN. Narrowband, all-band, RF signal degradation, and adjacent and co-channel interference are the most common sources of RF interference that occur during implementation of a wireless LAN. In this lesson, we will discuss these types of interference, how they affect wireless LANs, how to locate them, and in some cases how to work around them.

Objectives

At the end of this lesson you will be able to:

- Describe sources of wireless LAN RF interference

- Recognize tools used to check for and troubleshoot RF interference

- Explain adjacent channel and co-location interference

 **Key Point**

There are many sources of RF interference, both human made and natural.

RF Interference Sources

The following sections discuss several sources of RF interference on a wireless network. These include narrowband, all-band, weather, and adjacent channel and co-channel interference.

Narrowband

Narrowband RF is basically the opposite of spread spectrum technology. Narrowband signals, depending on output power, frequency width in the spectrum, and consistency, can intermittently interrupt or even disrupt the RF signals emitted from a spread spectrum device, such as an access point. However, as its name suggests, narrowband signals do not disrupt RF signals across the entire RF band. Thus, if the narrowband signal is primarily disrupting the RF signals in channel 3, you could, for example, use Channel 11, where you may not experience any interference. It is also likely that only a small portion of any given channel might be disrupted by narrowband interference. Typically, narrowband interference only disrupts a single carrier frequency (a 1-MHz increment in an 802.11b 22-MHz channel). Given this type of interference, spread spectrum technologies will usually work around this problem without any additional administration or configuration.

To identify narrowband interference, you will need a spectrum analyzer, shown on the Handheld Digital Spectrum Analyzer Showing a Narrowband Signal Diagram. Spectrum analyzers are used to locate and measure narrowband RF signals, among other things. There are even handheld, digital spectrum analyzers available that cost approximately $4,000. That may seem like quite a bit of money to locate a narrowband interference source, but if that source is disabling your network, it might be well worth it.

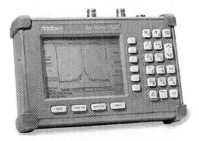

**Handheld Digital Spectrum Analyzer
Showing a Narrowband Signal**

As an alternative, some wireless LAN vendors have implemented a software spectrum analyzer into their client driver software. This software uses a frequency hopping spread spectrum (FHSS) Personal Computer Memory Card International Association (PCM-CIA) card to scan the useable portion of the 2.4-GHz ISM band for RF signals. The software graphically displays all RF signals between 2.4000GHz and 2.4835 GHz, which gives the administrator a way of "seeing" the RF that is present in a given area. An example of the visual aid provided by such a spectrum analyzer is shown on the Screenshot of a Spectrum Analyzer Showing Narrowband Interference Diagram.

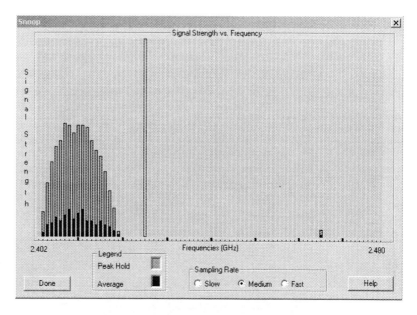

**Screenshot of a Spectrum Analyzer
Showing Narrowband Interference**

To remedy a narrowband RF interference problem, you must first find where the interference originates by using the spectrum analyzer. As you walk closer to the source of the RF signal, the RF signal on the display of your spectrum analyzer grows in amplitude (size). When the RF signal peaks on the screen, you have located its source. At this point, you can remove the source, shield it, or use your knowledge as a wireless network administrator to configure your wireless LAN to efficiently deal with the narrowband interference. Of course, several options are possible within this last category, such as changing channels, changing spread spectrum technologies (DSSS to FHSS or 802.11b to 802.11a), and others that we will discuss in later sections.

All-Band Interference

All-band interference is any signal that interferes with the RF band from one end of the radio spectrum to the other. All-band interference does not refer to interference only across the 2.4-GHz ISM band, but rather is the term used in any case where interference covers the entire range you are trying to use, regardless of frequency. Technologies like Bluetooth, which hops across the entire 2.4-GHz ISM band many times per second, usually interfere significantly with 802.11 RF signals. Bluetooth is considered all-band interference for an 802.11 wireless network. In the Software Spectrum Analyzer Showing All-Band Interference Diagram, a sample screen shot of a spectrum analyzer recording all-band interference is shown.

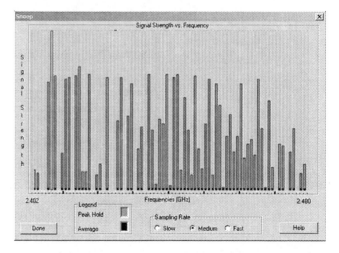

Software Spectrum Analyzer Showing All-Band Interference

A possible source of all-band interference that can be found in homes and offices is a microwave oven. Older, high-power microwave ovens can leak as much as one watt of power into the RF spectrum. One watt is not much leakage for a 1000-watt microwave oven, but considering that one watt is many times as much power as is emitted from a typical access point, you can see what a significant impact it might have. It is not a given that a microwave oven will emit power across the entire 2.4-GHz band, but it is possible, depending on the type and condition of the microwave oven. A spectrum analyzer can detect this kind of problem.

When all-band interference is present, the best solution is to change to a different technology, such as moving from 802.11b, which uses the 2.4-GHz ISM band, to 802.11a, which uses the 5-GHz UNII bands. If changing technologies is not feasible due to cost or implementation problems, the next best solution is to find the source of the all-band interference and remove it from service, if possible. Finding the source of all-band interference is more difficult than finding the source of narrowband interference because you are not watching a single signal on the spectrum analyzer. Instead, you are looking at a range of signals, all with varying amplitudes. You will most likely need a highly directional antenna in order to locate the all-band interference source.

Weather

Severely adverse weather conditions can affect the performance of a wireless LAN. In general, common weather occurrences such as rain, hail, snow, and fog do not have an adverse effect on wireless LANs. However, extreme occurrences of wind, fog, and perhaps smog can cause degradation or even downtime of your wireless LAN. A radome protects an antenna from the elements. If used, radomes must have a drain hole for condensation drainage. Yagi antennas without radomes are vulnerable to rain, because the raindrops will accumulate on the elements and detune the performance. The droplets actually make each element look longer than it really is. Ice accumulation on exposed elements can cause the same detuning effect as rain; however, it stays around longer. Radomes may also protect an antenna from falling objects, such as ice falling from an overhead tree.

A 2.4-GHz signal may be attenuated by up to 0.05 dB/km (0.08 dB/mile) by torrential rain (4 inches/hour). Thick fog produces up to 0.02 dB/km (0.03 dB/mile) attenuation. At 5.8 GHz, torrential rain may produce up to 0.5 dB/km (0.8 dB/mile) attenuation, and thick fog may produce up to 0.07 dB/km (0.11 dB/mile). Even though rain itself does not cause major propagation problems, rain will collect on the leaves of trees and will produce attenuation until it evaporates.

Wind

Wind does not affect radio waves or RF signals, but it can affect the positioning and mounting of outdoor antennas. For example, consider a wireless point-to-point link that connects two buildings that are 12 miles (20 km) apart. Taking into account the curvature of the Earth (Earth bulge), and having only a 5-degree vertical and horizontal beam width on each antenna, the positioning of each antenna has to be exact. A strong wind can easily move one or both antennas enough to completely degrade the signal between the two antennas. This effect is called "antenna wind loading," and is illustrated on the Antenna Wind Loading on Point-to-Point Networks Diagram.

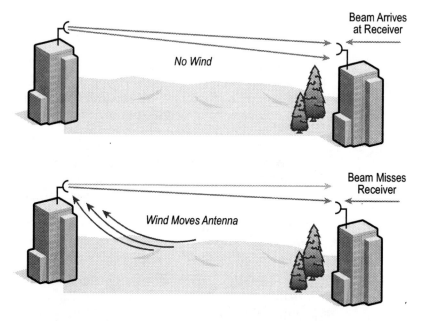

Antenna Wind Loading on Point-to-Point Networks

Other similarly extreme weather occurrences, such as tornadoes and hurricanes, must also be considered. If you are implementing a wireless LAN in a geographic location where hurricanes or tornadoes occur frequently, you should certainly take that into account when setting up any type of outdoor wireless LAN. In such weather conditions, securing antennas, cables, and the like are all very important.

Stratification   When very thick fog or even smog settles (such as in a valley), the air within this fog becomes very still and begins to separate into layers. It is not the fog itself that causes the diffraction of RF signals, but the stratification of the air within the fog. When the RF signal goes through these layers, it is bent in the same fashion as visible light is bent as it moves from air into water.

Lightning   Lightning can affect wireless LANs in two ways. First, lightning can strike either a wireless LAN component, such as an antenna, or it may strike a nearby object. Lightning strikes of nearby objects can damage wireless LAN components if a lightning arrestor does not protect them. A second way that lightning affects wireless LANs is by charging the air through which the RF waves must travel after striking an object lying between the transmitter and receiver. The effect of lightning is similar to the way the Aurora Borealis Northern Lights cause problems for RF television and radio transmissions.

Adjacent Channel and Co-channel Interference

A solid understanding of channel use with wireless LANs is imperative for any good wireless LAN administrator. As a wireless LAN consultant, you will undoubtedly find many wireless networks that have many access points, all of them configured for the same channel. In these types of situations, a discussion with the network administrator who installed the access points will reveal that he or she thought it was necessary for all access points and clients to be on the same channel throughout the network in order for the wireless LAN to work properly. This configuration is very common, and absolutely incorrect. This section will build on your knowledge of how channels are used; explaining how multiple access points using various channels can have a detrimental impact on a network.

Adjacent Channel Interference   Adjacent channels are those channels within the RF band being used that are, in essence, side-by-side. For example, channel 1 is adjacent to channel 2, which is adjacent to channel 3, and so forth. These adjacent channels overlap each other because each channel is 22 MHz wide and their center frequencies are only 5 MHz apart. Adjacent channel interference happens when two or more access points using overlapping channels are located near enough to each other that their coverage cells physically overlap. Adjacent channel interference can severely degrade throughput in a wireless LAN.

It is especially important to pay attention to adjacent channel interference when co-locating access points in an attempt to achieve higher throughput in a given area. Co-located access points on nonoverlapping channels can experience adjacent channel interference if there is not enough separation between the channels used, as illustrated on the Adjacent Channel Interference Diagram.

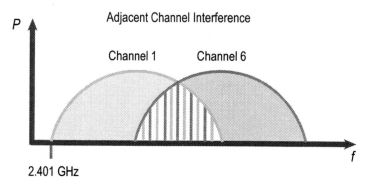

Adjacent Channel Interference

A spectrum analyzer will be needed to find the problem of adjacent channel interference. The spectrum analyzer shows you a picture of how the channels being used overlap each other. Using the spectrum analyzer in the same physical area as the access points show the channels overlapping each other.

There are only two solutions for a problem with adjacent channel interference. The first is to move access points on adjacent channels far enough away from each other that their cells do not overlap, or turn the power down on each access point until the cells do not overlap. The second solution is to use only channels that have no overlap. For example, using channels 1 and 11 in a DSSS system would accomplish this task.

Co-channel Interference

Co-channel interference can have the same effects as adjacent channel interference, but is an altogether different set of circumstances. Co-channel interference as seen by a spectrum analyzer is illustrated on the Co-channel Interference Diagram. How a network configuration produces this problem is shown on the Co-channel Interference in a Network Diagram.

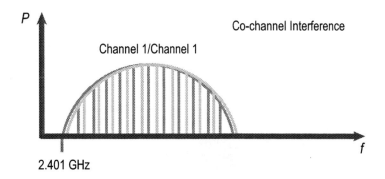

Co-channel Interference

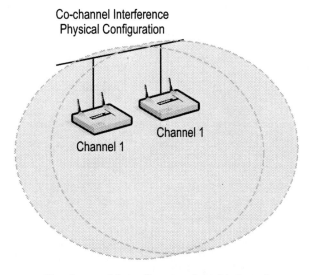

Co-channel Interference in a Network

To understand co-channel interference, consider a three-story building, with a wireless LAN on each floor, with the wireless LANs each using channel 1. The access points' signal ranges, or cells, are likely to overlap in this situation. Because each access point is on the same channel, they will interfere with one another. This type of interference is known as co-channel interference.

To troubleshoot co-channel interference, a wireless network sniffer is needed. The sniffer shows packets coming from each of the wireless LANs using any particular channel. Additionally, it shows the signal strength of each wireless LAN's packets, giving you an idea of just how much one wireless LAN is interfering with the others.

The two solutions for co-channel interference are: first, using a different, nonoverlapping channel for each of the wireless LANs, and second, moving the wireless LANs far enough apart that the access points' cells do not overlap. These solutions are the same remedy as for adjacent channel interference.

In situations where seamless roaming is required, a technique called channel reuse is used to alleviate adjacent and co-channel interference while allowing users to roam through adjacent cells. Channel reuse involves side-by-side locating of nonoverlapping cells to form a mesh of coverage where no cell on a given channel touches another cell on that channel. The Channel Reuse Diagram illustrates channel reuse.

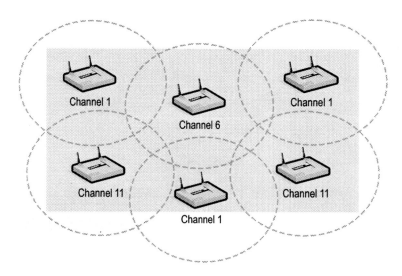

Channel Reuse

Activities

1. Which statement best describes the use of channel reuse to alleviate adjacent and co-channel interference in an area where seamless roaming is required?

    a. Configuring each client device to operate on a different channel

    b. Side-by-side locating of nonoverlapping channels to form a mesh

    c. Combining 802.11 and 802.11a APs in the same area

    d. Configuring the APs to select a new channel for each client device

2. Which condition causes stratification interference on a wireless link?

    a. Earth bulge

    b. Fog or smog

    c. Dust storms

    d. Layered air

3. Of the choices listed, which is the best solution to all-band interference experienced on an 802.11b network?

    a. Convert to a Bluetooth network.

    b. Convert to an 802.11a network.

    c. Increase access point radio power.

    d. Install a highly directional antenna on the access point.

4. Which common home appliance is a possible source of all-band interference in the 2.4-GHz ISM range?

    a. Microwave oven

    b. Cordless phones

    c. Satellite dishes

    d. Infrared remote controls

5. Which one of the following statements describes how narrow-band interference affects an 802.11b network?

   a. Forces the access point to switch to FHSS

   b. Can block an entire channel

   c. Forces the data rate to the next lower increment

   d. Forces the access point to select another channel

Extended Activities

Configure two DSSS access points each on channel 1, each with a different SSID. Configure two clients, each with an SSID matching an access point. Connect each access point directly to a PC running an FTP server daemon or service. Configure each client with an FTP client software application. Transfer data from one server to its client as a baseline, and then do the same for the other pair; using a single, large file (such as a zip file) works well. Record this throughput data using a real time, throughput-measuring utility, such as NetPerSec (freeware available for download from **http://downloads-zdnet.com**) as your baseline. Begin transferring data from both FTP servers to their respective FTP clients and record the data. Monitor the spectrum on a spectrum analyzer to see what happens within the spectrum. This is an example of co-channel interference.

Change one access point to channel 3, then 6, then 11, and repeat the previous process each time. Record the results each time and compare to the previous test. This is an example of adjacent channel interference effects.

Lesson 6—Range Considerations

When considering how to position wireless LAN hardware, the communication range of the units must be taken into account. The maximum communication range of a wireless LAN link is reached when, at some distance, the link begins to become unstable, but is not lost. This lesson discusses three conditions that affect the range of an RF link.

Objectives

At the end of this lesson you will be able to:

* Describe the three general conditions that effect the communication range of wireless LAN devices

* Explain steps to control the transmission range of wireless LANs

 **Key Point**

RF signal range determines how far from the access point and other nodes wireless devices can be located.

Issues that Affect RF Signal Range

Generally, three conditions affect the range of an RF link: transmission power, antenna type and location, and environment.

Transmission Power

The output power of the transmitting radio has an effect on the range of the link. A higher output power causes the signal to be transmitted a greater distance, resulting in a greater range. Conversely, lowering the output power reduces the range.

Antenna Type

The type of antenna used affects the range either by focusing the RF energy into a tighter beam, transmitting it farther (as a parabolic dish antenna does); or by transmitting it in all directions (as an omnidirectional antenna does), reducing the range of communication.

Environment

A noisy or unstable environment can cause the range of a wireless LAN link to be decreased. The packet error rate of an RF link is greater at the fringes of coverage due to a small signal-to-noise ratio. Also, adding interference effectively raises the noise floor, lessening the likelihood of maintaining a solid link.

The frequency of the transmission can also influence the range of an RF link. Although it is not normally a concern within a wireless LAN implementation, frequency might be a consideration when planning a bridge link. For example, a 2.4-GHz system will be able to reach farther at the same output power than a 5-GHz system. The same holds true for an older 900-MHz system: it will go farther than a 2.4-GHz system at the same output power. All of these bands are used in wireless LANs, but 2.4-GHz systems are by far the most prevalent.

Activities

1. Which statement is true concerning how external conditions affect a wireless link's range?

    a. The higher the frequency, the farther the signal travels

    b. An omnidirectional antenna increases a signal's range

    c. Packet error rates increase on the signal's fringe

    d. A dish antenna reduces the signal's range

2. You have installed a wireless access point in a hallway. The RF signal needs to reach users at the end of the hallway, as well as those located in offices on each side of the hallway. You install an omnidirectional antenna, and measure the signal power in several locations. The power level is acceptable in the nearby offices, but deteriorates in the offices near the opposite end of the hall, and is nearly hidden in the noise at the end of the hall. What can you do to extend the signal's range?

    a. Add a second radio and antenna in the access point.

    b. Change the access point to a more powerful channel.

    c. Set the access point to use RTS/CTS.

    d. Change to a semidirectional antenna.

3. You are troubleshooting a throughput problem on an 802.11b wireless network. A user complains that as she moves about the office, her client device looses connections to network resources. The client still shows a signal received from the access point, but cannot access the network. You determine that the client signal cannot reach the access point. How might you best resolve this problem?

    a. Convert the network to 802.11a.

    b. Increase the client radio power.

    c. Move the access point closer to the user.

    d. Increase the access point radio power.

Extended Activities

Configure a wireless LAN with an access point and two clients. Turn off WEP, set the SSIDs, and verify communications. Experiment with each of the three issues mentioned in this lesson, and observe the effects each have on the wireless LAN's range.

Summary

This unit discussed the more common obstacles to successful implementation of a wireless LAN, and how to troubleshoot them. There are different methods of discovering when these challenges exist, and each of the challenges discussed has its remedies and workarounds. Many consider the challenges to implementing any wireless LAN to be "textbook" problems that can commonly occur and be avoided by careful planning.

Unit 9 began by explaining multipath, which is the creation of multiple waveforms from a single signal by obstacles in the original signal's path. RF signals meet with many obstacles as they travel from source to destination, and these obstacles can cause all or part of a signal to change its course or shape. Because wireless nodes have no way to detect collisions, they rely on collision avoidance techniques and frame acknowledgements to reduce collisions and their effect on wireless performance. Although wireless nodes perform a CCA, which is designed to reduce the likelihood a collision will occur, before transmission, hidden node occurs when the transmitting node may not simultaneously sense the presence of another node transmitting.

The near/far problem occurs when multiple client nodes are located very near to the access point and are transmitting at high power settings. At least one client is located much farther away from the access point than the other client nodes. The access point receives a much lower setting than the other nodes. The result is that the client(s) located farther away from the access point simply cannot be heard over the traffic from the nearer clients.

Unit 9 also described the effect co-located access points have on network throughput, and how to resolve associated throughput problems. Other issues discussed include the types of RF interference, how they affect wireless LANs, how to locate them, and in some cases how to work around them.

Unit 9 Quiz

1. Which of the following are solutions to the hidden node problem? (Choose two.)

    a. Using RTS/CTS

    b. Increasing the power to the hidden nodes

    c. Decreasing the power to the hidden node

    d. Increasing the power on the access point

2. Antenna diversity is a solution to which one of the following wireless LAN problems?

    a. Near/Far

    b. Hidden Node

    c. Co-location throughput

    d. Multipath

3. When objects in the Fresnel Zone absorb or block some of the RF wave, which one of the following might result?

    a. Signal fading

    b. A surge in signal amplitude

    c. A change in signal frequency

    d. A change in modulation

4. What is the period of time between the main wave's arrival at the receiver and the reflected wave's arrival at a receiver called?

    a. SIFS

    b. Delay spread

    c. PIFS

    d. Signal spread

5. Which of the following could be used to remedy a near/far problem? (Choose two.)

    a. Decrease the power of the near nodes

    b. Increase the power of the closer nodes

    c. Decrease the power of the distant nodes

    d. Increase the power of the far nodes

6. Which of the following channels on three co-located access points will result in the greatest co-channel interference?

   a. 1, 1, 1

   b. 1, 2, 3

   c. 1, 6, 11

   d. 1, 11

7. Which one of the following can cause all-band interference?

   a. Metal roof

   b. Lake

   c. Bluetooth

   d. HiperLAN

8. Why are most access points built with two antennas?

   a. Access points are half-duplex devices that send on one antenna and receive on the other.

   b. Access points use one antenna as a standby for reliability.

   c. Access points use two antennas to overcome multipath.

   d. Access points use two antennas to transmit on two different channels.

9. Using RTS/CTS can solve the hidden node problem and will not affect network throughput.

   a. This statement is always true.

   b. This statement is always false.

   c. It depends on the manufacturer's equipment.

10. Which of the following can cause RF interference in a wireless LAN? (Choose three.)

    a. Wind

    b. Lightning

    c. Smog

    d. Clouds

11. Multipath is defined as which one of the following?

    a. The negative effects induced on a wireless LAN by reflected RF signals arriving at the receiver along with the main signal

    b. Surges in signal strength due to an RF signal taking multiple paths between the sending and receiving stations

    c. The condition caused by a receiving station having multiple antennas, which causes the signal to take multiple paths to the CPU

    d. The result of using a signal splitter to create multiple signal paths between sending and receiving stations

12. Multipath can cause signals to increase above the power of the signal that was transmitted by the sending station. This statement is:

    a. Always true

    b. Always false

    c. True, when the signal is transmitted in clear weather

    d. False, unless a 12 dBi or higher power antenna is being used

13. Multipath is caused by which one of the following?

    a. Multiple antennas

    b. Wind

    c. Reflected RF waves

    d. Bad weather

14. When can the hidden node problem occur?

    a. Only when a network is at full capacity

    b. When all users of a wireless LAN are simultaneously transmitting data

    c. Anytime, even after a flawless site survey

    d. Every time a wireless LAN client roams from one access point to another

15. Which one of the following is not a solution for correcting the hidden node problem?

    a. Using the RTS/CTS protocol

    b. Increasing power to the node(s)

    c. Removing obstacles between nodes

    d. Moving the hidden node(s)

16. How is the threshold set when using RTS/CTS in "On with Threshold" mode on a wireless LAN?

    a. Automatically by the access points only

    b. Manually by the user of the hidden node

    c. Manually on the clients and access points by the wireless LAN administrator

    d. Automatically by the clients only

17. Which one of the following conditions occurs when an access point receives a distant client's signal at a lower power level than it does a nearer client?

    a. Hidden Node

    b. Near/Far

    c. Degraded throughput

    d. Interference

18. Why should an administrator be able to co-locate three DSSS access points in the same area using the 2.4-GHz ISM band?

    a. Each access point transmits on one band and receives on another.

    b. Each access point will use co-channel interference to stop the others from transmitting data when it is ready to send.

    c. The access points will use channels that do not overlap or cause adjacent channel interference.

    d. There are up to five nonoverlapping DSSS channels in the ISM bands.

19. How many DSSS channels in the 2.4-GHz spectrum are designated for use in the United States?

    a. 3

    b. 14

    c. 10

    d. 11

20. Which one of the following is an advantage of using 5-GHz (802.11a) equipment over 802.11b equipment?

    a. The lower 5-GHz UNII band is wider than the 2.4-GHz ISM band.

    b. The 802.11a equipment is less expensive than 802.11b.

    c. The 5-GHz UNII bands allows for more nonoverlapping channels than the 2.4-GHz ISM band.

    d. 802.11a equipment is backwards compatible with 802.11g equipment.

Unit 10
Wireless LAN Security

Wireless LANs are not inherently secure; however, if you do not take any precautions or configure any defenses with wired LAN or WAN connections, they are not secure either. The key to making a wireless LAN secure, and keeping it secure, is educating those who implement and manage the wireless LAN. Educating the administrator on basic and advanced security procedures for wireless LANs is essential to preventing security breaches into your wireless LAN.

In this unit, we discuss the much-maligned 802.11 specified security solution known as Wired Equivalent Privacy (WEP). As you may already know, WEP alone will not keep a hacker out of a wireless LAN for very long. This unit explains why, and offers some steps for using WEP with some level of effectiveness.

We explain the various methods that can be used to attack a wireless LAN to prepare you (as an administrator) to prevent security problems. We discuss some of the emerging security solutions that are available, but not yet specified by any of the 802.11 standards. Finally, we offer some recommendations for maintaining wireless LAN security and discuss corporate security policy as it pertains specifically to wireless LANs.

This unit does not provide all the information available on wireless LAN security. Rather, it serves as a basic introduction for CWNA candidates to the inherent weaknesses of wireless LANs and the available solutions that compensate for these weaknesses.

Lessons

1. WEP
2. Attacks on Wireless LANs
3. Emerging Security Solutions
4. Corporate Security Policy
5. Security Recommendations

Terms

Advanced Encryption Standard (AES)—AES is an encryption technique that improves upon the RC-4 algorithm used in WEP. AES uses the Rijndael algorithm and is considered uncrackable.

authentication, authorization, and accounting (AAA)—AAA is a method by which users are authenticated, authorized, and tracked to gain access and move about inside a network.

biometrics—Biometric identification techniques identify users by a physical feature, such as fingerprints, the blood vessel pattern in the retina, or voice characteristics.

cipher—Cipher is a generic term used to describe the algorithms an encryption technique uses to scramble data to protect it from interception.

Internet Protocol Security (IPSec)—The IETF has proposed IPSec as a set of protocols and procedures for securing IP packet traffic on publicly accessible IP networks. IPSec supports several cipher algorithms, and enables both payload authentication and encryption.

key server—A key server is a centralized device that dynamically generates WEP keys for each session or packet.

message integrity code (MIC)—A MIC is a cryptographic checksum appended to an encrypted packet used by the recipient to validate that the data was not tampered with in transit.

National Institute of Standards and Technology (NIST)—NIST is a nonregulatory US federal agency whose mission is to "develop and promote measurements, standards, and technology to enhance productivity, facilitate trade, and improve the quality of life." See **http://www.nist.gov** for more information.

Organization Unit Identifier (OUI)—The OUI is the company ID component of a MAC address assigned by the IEEE. The OUI is the first six hex characters (24 bits) of the MAC address.

plaintext—Plaintext is unencrypted information.

Point-to-Point Tunneling Protocol (PPTP)—Microsoft developed PPTP for VPNs using Microsoft Windows 95/98 and Windows NT. PPTP can support tunneling of IP, IPX, NetBios, and NetBEUI protocols inside IP packets. PPTP also works with Windows 2000, XP, Linux, and FreeBSD.

pseudo-random number generator (PRNG)—A PRNG is a hardware device designed to generate a random number string for use in cryptography and other applications. A PRNG emulates a hardware random number generator in software.

RC4—RC4 is an encryption cipher used in WEP to generate the encryption key for wireless node to wireless access point authentication.

Rijndael—The Rijndael algorithm is used to generate the 128-bit, 192-bit, and 256-bit keys used in the AES encryption standard.

Routing Information Protocol (RIP) v2—RIPv2 is a distance vector routing protocol designed to improve on the original RIP by subnet mask information and provide some security to the routing table update messages.

smart card—Smart cards are plastic cards that contain embedded integrated circuit (IC) microprocessors and a standard magnetic strip. A user inserts a smart card into a chip-reading terminal, which reads the information stored on it. Smart cards can eliminate the need for users to remember (and frequently change) passwords and other authentication information.

WEPv2—WEPv2, the latest iteration of the WEP protocol, was designed to add increased security by using technologies such as the AES algorithm to generate encryption keys of 192 bits and 256 bits. See Wired Equivalent Privacy.

Wi-Fi hot spot—A Wi-Fi hot spot location is a location considered likely to host many wireless users.

Wired Equivalent Privacy (WEP)—WEP is an optional IEEE 802.11 function that offers frame transmission privacy similar to a wired network. WEP generates secret shared encryption keys that both source and destination stations can use to alter frame bits to avoid disclosure to eavesdroppers.

Wireless demilitarized zone (WDMZ)—A WDMZ is a security solution typically implemented in medium-scale and large-scale wireless LAN deployments. Using a firewall device, WDMZs separate access points, which are insecure devices, from other network segments.

Lesson 1—WEP

Wired Equivalent Privacy (WEP) is an encryption algorithm used by the shared key authentication process for authenticating users and for encrypting data payloads over the wireless segment of a LAN. The IEEE 802.11 standard specifies the use of WEP. This lesson discusses WEP, its inherent weaknesses, and some tools we can use to augment it.

Objectives

At the end of this unit you will be able to:

- Explain basic WEP concepts and vulnerabilities
- Explain how WEP keys are used to encrypt data on the network
- Describe security solutions designed to augment WEP
- Describe the appropriate use and configuration of SSID, MAC, and protocol filters

 **Key Point**

WEP alone does not provide adequate wireless network security.

What Is WEP?

WEP is a simple algorithm that utilizes a pseudo-random number generator (PRNG) and the RC4 stream cipher. For several years this algorithm was considered a trade secret, and details were not available, but in September of 1994, someone posted the source code in the cypherpunks mailing list. Although the source code is now available, RC4 is still trademarked by RSA Security, Inc. The RC4 stream cipher decrypts and encrypts quickly, which saves on central processing unit (CPU) cycles. RC4 is also simple enough for most software developers to code into software.

When WEP is called "simple," this means that it is weak. The RC4 algorithm was inappropriately implemented in WEP, yielding a less-than-adequate security solution for 802.11 networks. Both 64-bit and 128-bit WEP (the two available types) have the same weak implementation of a 24-bit initialization vector (IV) and use the same flawed process of encryption. The flawed process is that most implementations of WEP initialize hardware using an IV of zero, thereafter incrementing the IV by one for each packet sent. For a busy network, statistical analysis shows that all possible IVs (2^{24} or 16,777,216) would be exhausted in five hours, meaning the IV would be reinitialized starting at zero at least once every five hours. This scenario creates an open door for determined hackers. When WEP is used, the IV is transmitted in the clear with each encrypted packet. The manner in which the IV is incremented and sent in the clear allows the following breaches in security:

- **Active attacks to inject new traffic**—Unauthorized mobile stations can inject packets onto the network, based on known plaintext.

- **Active attacks to decrypt traffic**—Based on tricking the access point.

- **Dictionary-building attacks**—After gathering enough traffic, the WEP key can be cracked using freeware tools. After the WEP key is cracked, real-time decryption of packets can be accomplished by listening to broadcasts packets using the WEP key.

- **Passive attacks to decrypt traffic**—Using statistical analysis, WEP traffic can be decrypted.

Why WEP Was Chosen

If WEP is not secure, why was it chosen and implemented into the 802.11 standard? After the 802.11 standard was approved and completed, the manufacturers of wireless LAN equipment rushed their products to market. The 802.11 standard specifies the following criteria for security:

- Exportable

- Reasonably Strong

- Self-Synchronizing

- Computationally Efficient

- Optional

WEP meets all these requirements. When it was implemented, WEP was intended to support the security goals of confidentiality, access control, and data integrity. What actually happened is that too many early adopters of wireless LANs thought that they could simply implement WEP and have a completely secure wireless LAN. These early adopters found out quickly that WEP was not the complete solution to wireless LAN security. Fortunately for the industry, wireless LAN hardware had gained immense popularity well before this problem was widely known. This series of events led to many vendors and third party organizations scrambling to create wireless LAN security solutions.

The 802.11 standard leaves WEP implementation up to wireless LAN manufacturers; thus, each vendor's implementation of WEP keys may or may not be the same, adding another weakness to WEP. Even WECA's Wi-Fi interoperability standard tests include only 40-bit WEP keys. Some wireless LAN manufacturers have chosen to enhance (fix) WEP, while others have looked to using new standards, such as 802.1x with EAP or virtual private networks (VPNs). Many solutions on the market address the weaknesses found in WEP.

WEP Keys

The core functionality of WEP lies in what are known as keys, which are the basis for the encryption algorithm discussed in the previous section of this chapter. WEP keys are implemented on client and infrastructure devices on a wireless LAN. A WEP key is an alphanumeric character string used in two manners in a wireless LAN. First, a WEP key can be used to verify the identity of an authenticating station. Second, WEP keys can be used for data encryption.

When a WEP-enabled client attempts to authenticate and associate to an access point, the access point determines whether or not the client has the correct WEP key. By "correct," we mean that the client has to have a key that is part of the WEP key distribution system implemented on that particular wireless LAN. The WEP keys must match on both ends of the wireless LAN connection.

As a wireless LAN administrator, it may be your job to manually distribute the WEP keys, or to set up a more advanced method of WEP key distribution. WEP key distribution systems can be as simple as implementing static keys or as advanced as using centralized encryption key servers. Obviously, the more advanced the WEP system is, the harder it will be for a hacker to gain access to the network.

WEP keys are available in two types, 64-bit and 128-bit. Many times you will see them referenced as 40-bit and 104-bit instead. This reference is a bit of a misnomer. The reason for this misnomer is that WEP is implemented in the same way for both encryption lengths. Each uses a 24-bit initialization vector (IV) concatenated (linked end-to-end) with a secret key. The secret key lengths are 40-bit or 104-bit, yielding WEP key lengths of 64 bits and 128 bits.

Entering static WEP keys into clients or infrastructure devices, such as bridges or access points, is quite simple. A typical configuration program is shown on the Entering WEP Keys on Client Devices Diagram. Sometimes there is a checkbox for selecting 40- or 128-bit WEP. Sometimes no checkbox is present; thus, the administrator must know how many characters to enter when asked. Most often, client software allows inputting of WEP keys in alphanumeric (ASCII) or hexadecimal (HEX) format. Some devices may require ASCII or HEX, and some may take either form of input.

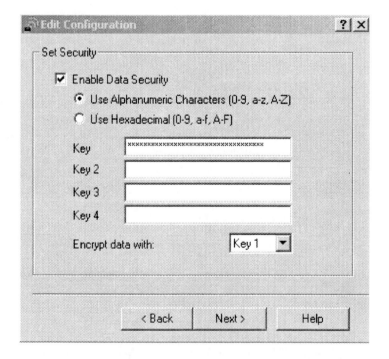

Entering WEP Keys on Client Devices

Note: Many HEX-ASCII conversion charts on the Internet can be found with a simple search engine. You might have to reference such a chart if using mixed vendor hardware across your network. Some vendors include this conversion chart in their client software's HELP section.

The number of characters entered for the secret key depends on whether the configuration software requires ASCII or HEX and whether 64-bit or 128-bit WEP is being used. If your wireless card supports 128-bit WEP, it automatically supports 64-bit WEP as well. When entering your WEP key in ASCII format, five characters are used for 64-bit WEP, and 13 characters are used for 128-bit WEP. When entering your WEP key in HEX format, 10 characters are used for 64-bit WEP, and 26 characters are used for 128-bit WEP.

Static WEP Keys

If you choose to implement static WEP keys, you would manually assign a static WEP key to an access point and its associated clients. These WEP keys never change, making that segment of the network susceptible to hackers who may be aware of the intricacies of WEP keys. For this reason, static WEP keys may be an appropriate basic security method for simple, small wireless LANs, but they are not recommended for enterprise wireless LAN solutions.

When static WEP keys are implemented, it is simple for network security to be compromised. Consider if an employee left a company and "lost" their wireless LAN card. Because the card carries the WEP key in its firmware, that card will always have access to the wireless LAN until the WEP keys on the wireless LAN are changed.

Most access points and clients have the ability to hold up to four WEP keys simultaneously, as can be seen on the Entering WEP Keys on Infrastructure Devices Diagram. One useful reason for having the ability to enter up to four WEP keys is network segmentation. Suppose a network had 100 client stations. Giving out four WEP keys instead of one segments the users into four distinct groups of 25. If a WEP key were compromised, it would entail changing 25 stations and an access point or two instead of the entire network. Access points generally transmit only the first key, but can receive traffic that has been encrypted with any of the four keys it holds.

Use of Data Encryption by Stations is: Not Available
Must set an Encryption Key first

	Open	Shared	Network-EAP
Accept Authentication Type:	☑	☐	☐
Require EAP:	☐	☐	

	Transmit With Key	Encryption Key	Key Size
WEP Key 1:	-		not set ▾
WEP Key 2:	-		not set ▾
WEP Key 3:	-		not set ▾
WEP Key 4:	-		not set ▾

Enter 40-bit WEP keys as 10 hexadecimal digits (0-9, a-f, or A-F).
Enter 128-bit WEP keys as 26 hexadecimal digits (0-9, a-f, or A-F).
This radio supports Encryption for all Data Rates.

| Apply | OK | Cancel | Restore Defaults |

Entering WEP Keys on Infrastructure Devices

Centralized Encryption Key Servers

If possible, centralized encryption key servers should be used for enterprise wireless LANs using WEP as a basic security mechanism, for the following reasons:

- Centralized key generation

- Centralized key distribution

- Ongoing key rotation

- Reduced key management overhead

Any number of different devices can act as a centralized key server. Usually a server, such as a RADIUS server or a specialized application server for the purpose of handing out new WEP keys on a short time interval, is used. Normally, when using WEP, the keys (made up by the administrator) are manually entered into the stations and access points. When using a centralized key server, an automated process between stations, access points, and the key server performs the task of handing out WEP keys. The Centralized Encryption Key Server Diagram illustrates how a typical encryption key server is set up.

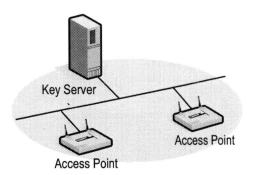

Centralized Encryption Key Server

Centralized encryption key servers allow for key generation on a per-packet, per-session, or other method, depending on each manufacturer's implementation. Per-packet WEP key distribution calls for a new WEP key to be assigned to both ends of the connection for every packet sent, whereas per-session WEP key distribution uses a new WEP key for each new session between nodes.

Note: If you choose to implement per-packet WEP key distribution, be aware that it will add significant overhead to the wireless LAN.

WEP Usage

When WEP is initialized, the data payload of the packet being sent using WEP is encrypted; however, part of the packet header – including the media access control (MAC) address – is not encrypted. All layer 3 information, including source and destination addresses, is encrypted with WEP. When an access point sends out its beacons on a wireless LAN using WEP, the beacons are not encrypted. Remember that the beacons do not include any layer 3 information.

When packets are sent using WEP encryption, those packets must be decrypted. This decryption process consumes CPU cycles and reduces the effective throughput on the wireless LAN, sometimes significantly. Some manufacturers have implemented additional CPUs in their access points for the purpose of performing WEP encryption and decryption. Many manufacturers implement WEP encryption/decryption in software and use the same CPU that is used for access point management, packet forwarding, and so forth. These access points are usually the ones upon which WEP has the most significant effects if enabled. By implementing WEP in hardware, it is very likely that an access point can maintain its 5 Mbps (or more) throughput with WEP enabled. The disadvantage of this implementation is the added cost of a more advanced access point.

WEP can be implemented as a basic security mechanism, but network administrators should first be aware of WEP's weaknesses and how to compensate for them. Administrators should also be aware that each vendor's use of WEP can and may be different, hindering the use of multiple vendor hardware.

AES

The Advanced Encryption Standard (AES) is gaining acceptance as an appropriate replacement for the RC4 algorithm used in WEP. AES uses the Rijndael (pronounced 'RINE-dale') algorithm in the following specified key lengths:

- 128-bit

- 192-bit

- 256-bit

Most cryptographers consider AES uncrackable, and the National Institute of Standards and Technology (NIST) has chosen AES for the Federal Information Processing Standard, or FIPS. As part of the effort to improve the 802.11 standard, the 802.11i working committee is considering the use of AES in WEPv2.

AES, if approved by the 802.11i working group to be used in WEPv2, will be implemented in firmware and software by vendors. Access point firmware and client station firmware (the Personal Computer Memory Card International Association [PCMCIA] radio cards) will have to be upgraded to support AES. Client station software (drivers and client utilities) will support configuring AES with secret key(s).

Filtering

Filtering is a basic security mechanism that can be used in addition to WEP and/or AES. Filtering is the process of keeping out what is not wanted and allowing what is wanted. Filtering works the same way as access lists on a router: by defining parameters to which stations must adhere in order to gain access to the network. With wireless LANs, it is not so much what the stations do, but rather what they are and how they are configured. Three basic types of filtering can be performed on a wireless LAN:

- SSID filtering
- MAC address filtering
- Protocol filtering

This section will explain each of these types of filtering, and how to configure each one.

SSID Filtering

Service Set Identifier (SSID) filtering is a rudimentary method of filtering, and should only be used for the most basic access control. The SSID is just another term for the network name. The SSID of a wireless LAN station must match the SSID on the access point (infrastructure mode) or of the other stations (ad hoc mode) in order for the client to authenticate and associate to the service set. Because the SSID is broadcast in the clear in every beacon that the access point (or set of stations) sends out, it is very simple to find out the SSID of a network using a sniffer. Many access points have the ability to take the SSID out of the beacon frame. When this is the case, the client must have the matching SSID in order to associate to the access point. When a system is configured in this manner, it is said to be a "closed system." SSID filtering is not considered a reliable method of keeping unauthorized users out of a wireless LAN.

Some manufacturer's access points have the ability to remove the SSID from beacons and/or probe responses. In this case, in order to join the service set, a station must have the SSID configured manually in the driver configuration settings. Some common mistakes that wireless LAN users make in administering SSIDs are listed below:

- **Using the default SSID**—This setting is yet another way to give away information about a wireless LAN. It is simple enough to use a sniffer to see the MAC addresses originating from the access point, and then look up the MAC addresses in the Organization Unit Identifier (OUI) table hosted by IEEE. The OUI table lists the different MAC address prefixes that are assigned to each manufacturer. Until Netstumbler, a wireless LAN auditing application came along, this process was manual, but now Netstumbler performs this task automatically.

If you do not know how to use Netstumbler or are unfamiliar with network sniffers, looking for default SSIDs also works well. Each wireless LAN manufacturer uses its own default SSID. Because the number of wireless LAN manufacturers in the industry is still manageable, you can simply obtain each of the user manuals from the support section of the manufacturer's Web site and gather their products' default SSID IP subnet information. Always change the default SSID.

Note: Looking for wireless LANs is also called "netstumbling" (or war-driving)—after the popular wireless LAN auditing application, Netstumbler, written by Marius Milner. More information on this application can be found at **http://www. netstumbler.com**

- **Making the SSID company-related**—This type of setting is a security risk because it simplifies the process of a hacker finding the company's physical location. When looking for wireless LANs in any particular geographic region, finding the physical location of the wireless LAN is half the battle. Even after detecting the wireless LAN using tools such as Netstumbler, finding where the signal originates takes time and considerable effort in many cases. When an administrator uses an SSID that names the company or organization, it makes finding the wireless LAN very easy. Always use noncompany-related SSIDs.

- **Using the SSID as a means of securing wireless networks**—This practice is highly discouraged because a user must only change the SSID in the configuration setting in his or her workstation to join the network. SSIDs should be used as a means of segmenting the network, not securing it. Again, think of the SSID as the network name. Just as with Windows' Network Neighborhood, changing the workgroup your computer is a part of is as simple as changing a configuration setting on the client station.

- **Unnecessarily Broadcasting SSIDs**—If your access points have the ability to remove SSIDs from beacons and probe responses, configure them that way. This configuration aids in deterring casual eavesdroppers from tinkering with or using your wireless LAN.

MAC Address Filtering

Wireless LANs can filter based on the MAC addresses of client stations. Almost all access points (even very inexpensive ones) have MAC filter functionality. The network administrator can compile, distribute, and maintain a list of allowable MAC addresses and program them into each access point. If a PC card or other client with a MAC address that is not in the access point's MAC filter list tries to gain access to the wireless LAN, the MAC address filter functionality will not allow that client to associate with that access point. The MAC Filters Diagram illustrates this point.

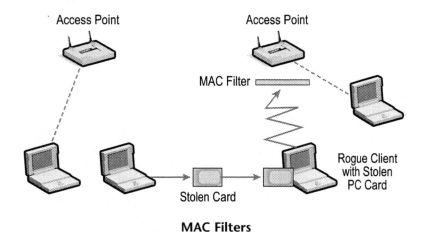

MAC Filters

Of course, programming every wireless client's MAC address into every access point across a large enterprise network would be impractical. MAC filters can be implemented on some RADIUS servers, instead of in each access point. This configuration makes MAC filters a much more scalable security solution. Simply entering each MAC address into RADIUS along with user identity information, which has to be in put anyway, is a good solution. RADIUS servers often point to another authentication source, so that other authentication source would need to support MAC filters.

MAC filters can work in reverse as well. For example, consider an employee who left a company and took their wireless LAN card with them. This wireless LAN card possibly holds the WEP key and an authorized MAC address. The administrator can then create a filter on all access points to deny the MAC address of the client device that was taken by the employee. If MAC filters were already being used on this network when the wireless LAN card was stolen, removing the particular client's MAC address from the allow list would also work.

Although MAC filters may seem to be a good method of securing a wireless LAN in some situations, they are still susceptible to the following intrusions:

- Theft of a PC card that is in the MAC filter of an access point

- Sniffing the wireless LAN and then spoofing with the MAC address after business hours

MAC filters are great for home and small office networks with a small number of client stations. Using WEP and MAC filters provides an adequate security solution in these situations. This solution is adequate because no intelligent hacker is going to spend the hours it takes to break WEP on a low-use network or the energy to circumvent a MAC filter for the purpose of getting to a person's laptop or home desktop PC.

Circumventing MAC Filters

MAC addresses of wireless LAN clients are broadcast in the clear by access points and bridges, even when WEP is implemented. Therefore, a hacker who can listen to traffic on your network can quickly find out most MAC addresses that are allowed on your wireless network. For a sniffer to see a station's MAC address, that station must transmit a frame across the wireless segment.

Some wireless PC cards permit their MAC address to change through software or even operating system configuration changes. Once a hacker has a list of allowed MAC addresses, the hacker can simply change the PC card's MAC address to match one of the PC cards on your network, instantly gaining access to your entire wireless LAN.

Because two stations with the same MAC address cannot peacefully coexist on a LAN, a hacker must find the MAC address of a mobile station that is removed from the premises at particular times of the day. It is during this time when the mobile station (notebook computer) is not present on the wireless LAN that the hacker can gain access into the network. MAC filters should be used when feasible, but not as the sole security mechanism on your wireless LAN.

Protocol Filtering

Wireless LANs can filter packets traversing the network based on layer 2 through 7 protocols. In many cases, manufacturers make protocol filters independently configurable for both the wired segment and wireless segment of the access point.

Imagine a scenario where a wireless workgroup bridge is placed on a remote building in a campus wireless LAN that connects back to the main information technology building's access point. Because all users in the remote building are sharing the 5 Mbps of throughput between these buildings, some amount of control over usage must be implemented. If this link was installed for the express purpose of Internet access for these users, filtering out every protocol except SMTP, POP3, HTTP, HTTPS, FTP, and any instant messaging protocols would prevent users from being able to access, for example, internal company file servers. The ability to set protocol filters such as these is very useful in controlling utilization of the shared medium. The Protocol Filtering Diagram illustrates how protocol filtering works in a wireless LAN.

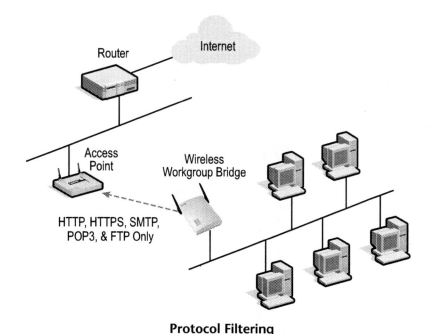

Protocol Filtering

Note: Manufacturers' implementation of protocol filters varies; some manufacturers offer more functionality than others. Ethertype, layer 3 protocols, layer 4 ports, and layer 7 application filters are common.

Activities

1. Which of the following are broadcast in the clear on wireless LANs? (Choose three.)

   a. SSID

   b. WEP key

   c. MAC address

   d. Beacon frames

2. What information stored on a wireless LAN card could compromise network security if the card is lost or stolen? (Choose two.)

   a. IP address

   b. SSID

   c. MAC address

   d. WEP key

3. Where is the most practical place on a large network consisting of many APs to implement MAC filters?

   a. Internet firewall

   b. RADIUS server

   c. EAP

   d. Each client

4. Which term describes a wireless system that does not broadcast the SSID in beacon frames?

   a. Closed system

   b. Beaconless system

   c. Client secured

   d. Unicast system

5. What key lengths does the Rijndale algorithm specify? (Choose three.)

   a. 128

   b. 156

   c. 192

   d. 256

6. You want to use a centralized key generation server to automate WEP key generation and distribution. You also want to reduce the overhead the key generation process creates. Which type of key generation process should you use?

   a. Per bit

   b. Per byte

   c. Per packet

   d. Per session

7. Why would an administrator choose to use a mix of 64-bit and 128-bit WEP keys on the wireless network?

   a. To segment the network by encryption level

   b. The keys are additive, creating a 192-bit key

   c. The 128-bit key ensures compatibility between vendor implementations

   d. To avoid co-channel interference between APs

Extended Activities

1. Visit the IEEE Web site and download the OUI listing. Search for your wireless device's OUI. Does the product brand label match the registered OUI?

   _____

   _____

   _____

   _____

2. What types of filters does your access point support? Configure different filters, and test the results. Did the network behave as you expected?

   _____

   _____

   _____

   _____

Lesson 2—Attacks on Wireless LANs

Hackers are everywhere, each motivated by his or her agenda. Just as an Internet connection is vulnerable to hackers, so is a wireless network. By intercepting your signal with a homemade antenna and freeware packet sniffing software, one of your neighbors could gain free access to your Internet connection. Or, a hacker could be a professional "security consultant" sitting in the parking lot outside corporate headquarters, gathering sensitive data to convince the corporation that it needs his or her services to strengthen network security. For many reasons, wireless networks are vulnerable. This lesson discusses some common attack methods hackers use to gain access to wireless networks.

Objectives

At the end of this unit you will be able to:

• Describe methods hackers use to attack wireless LANs

• Differentiate between passive and active attacks

 **Key Point**

Outsiders wishing to gain access to your networks can easily intercept RF signals.

Attack Methods

A malicious hacker can seek to disable or attempt to gain access to a wireless LAN in several ways. Some of these methods are:

1. Passive attacks (eavesdropping)

2. Active attacks (connecting, probing, and configuring the network)

3. Jamming attacks

4. Man-in-the-middle attacks

The above list is by no means exhaustive, and some of these methods can be orchestrated in several different ways. It is beyond the scope of this text to present every possible method of attacking wireless LANs. Instead, this text is aimed at giving a network administrator insight into some possible methods of attack so that security will be considered a vital part of wireless LAN implementation.

Passive Attacks

Eavesdropping is perhaps the most simple, yet effective type of wireless LAN attack. Passive attacks, such as eavesdropping, leave no trace of a hacker's presence on or near the network because the hacker does not have to actually connect to an access point to listen to packets traversing the wireless segment. Wireless LAN sniffers or custom applications are typically used to gather information about the wireless network from a distance with a directional antenna, as illustrated on the Passive Attack Example Diagram. This method of access allows hackers to keep their distance from a facility, leave no trace of their presence, and listen to and gather valuable information.

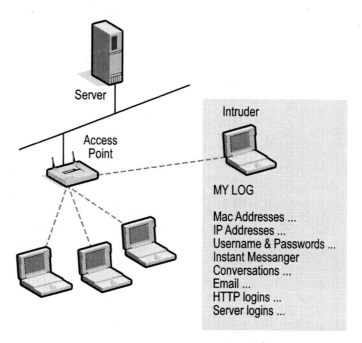

Passive Attack Example

Some applications are capable of gathering clear text passwords from HTTP sites, e-mail, instant messengers, FTP sessions, and telnet sessions. Other applications can snatch password hashes traversing a wireless segment between a client and server for log in purposes. Any information going across the wireless segment in this manner leaves the network and individual users vulnerable to attack. Consider the impact if a hacker gained access to a user's domain login information and caused havoc on the network. Although the hacker caused the damage, network usage logs would point directly to the user. This breach could cost a person his or her job. Consider another situation in which HTTP or email passwords are gathered over the wireless segment and later used by a hacker for personal gain from a remote site.

A hacker who is parked in your facility's parking lot may have a veritable toolkit for breaking into your wireless LAN. All this individual needs is a packet sniffer and some shareware or freeware hacking utilities to acquire your WEP keys and gain access to the wireless network.

Active Attacks

Hackers can stage active attacks in order to perform some type of function on the network. An active attack might be used to gain access to a server to obtain valuable data, use the organization's Internet access for malicious purposes, or even change the network infrastructure configuration. By connecting to a wireless network through an access point, a user can begin to penetrate deeper into the network or perhaps make changes to the wireless network itself. For example, if a hacker progresses past a MAC filter, the hacker can navigate to the access points and remove all MAC filters, making it easier to gain access next time. The administrator might not even notice this change for some time. The Active Attack Example Diagram illustrates an active attack on a wireless LAN.

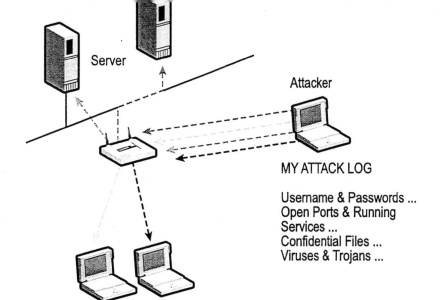

Server

Attacker

MY ATTACK LOG

Username & Passwords ...
Open Ports & Running
Services ...
Confidential Files ...
Viruses & Trojans ...

Active Attack Example

A drive-by spammer or a business competitor who wants access to your files may perpetrate an active attack. A spammer can queue e-mails in his or her laptop, and then connect to your home or business network through the wireless LAN. After obtaining an IP address from your DHCP server, the hacker can send tens of thousands of e-mails using your Internet connection and your Internet service provider (ISP)'s e-mail server without your knowledge. This kind of attack can cause your ISP to cut your connection for e-mail abuse.

A business competitor may try to get your customer list with contact information or perhaps your payroll information to better compete with you or steal your customers. These types of attacks happen regularly without the knowledge of the wireless LAN administrator.

A hacker who has a wireless connection to your network might as well be sitting in his or her own office with a wired connection, because the two scenarios are not much different. Wireless connections offer hackers plenty of speed and access to servers, wide area connections, Internet connections, and users' desktops and laptops. With a few simple tools, it is relatively simple to gather important information, impersonate a user, or even cause damage to the network through reconfiguration. The following harmful actions can be done by following the instructions in off-the-shelf hacker books: probing servers with port scans, creating null sessions to shares, and causing servers to dump passwords to hacking utilities and then logging into servers using existing accounts.

Jamming

Whereas a hacker uses passive and active attacks to gain valuable information from your network or to gain access to your network, jamming is a technique that is used to simply shut down your wireless network. Similar to saboteurs arranging an overwhelming denial of service (DoS) attack aimed at Web servers, an overwhelming RF signal can shut down a wireless LAN. That overwhelming RF signal can be intentional or unintentional, and the signal may be removable or nonremovable. When a hacker stages an intentional jamming attack, the hacker could use wireless LAN equipment, but more likely, the hacker would use a high-power RF signal generator or sweep generator. The Jamming Attack Example Diagram illustrates an example of jamming a wireless LAN.

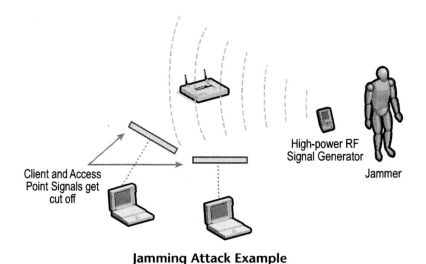

Client and Access
Point Signals get
cut off

High-power RF
Signal Generator

Jammer

Jamming Attack Example

Removing this type of attacker from the premises first requires locating the source of the RF signal. Locating an RF signal source can be done with an RF spectrum analyzer. Many spectrum analyzers are on the market, but having one that is handheld and battery operated is quite useful. Several manufacturers make handheld spectrum analyzers, and a few wireless LAN manufacturers have created spectrum analyzer software utilities for use in wireless client devices.

When a nonmoveable, nonmalicious source (such as a communications tower or other legitimate system) causes jamming, the wireless LAN administrator might have to consider using a wireless LAN system that utilizes a different set of frequencies. For example, if an administrator is responsible for the design and installation of an RF network at a large apartment complex, special considerations might be in order. If an RF interference source was a large number of 2.4-GHz spread spectrum phones, baby monitors, and microwave ovens in this apartment complex, the administrator might choose to implement 802.11a equipment that uses the 5-GHz UNII bands, instead of 802.11b equipment that shares the 2.4-GHz Industrial Scientific Medical (ISM) band with these other devices.

Unintentional jamming occurs regularly due to many different devices across many different industries sharing the 2.4-GHz ISM band with wireless LANs. Malicious jamming is not a common threat. The reason RF jamming is not very popular among hackers is that it is fairly expensive to mount an attack, considering the cost of the required equipment, and the only victory that the hacker gets is temporarily disabling a network.

Man-in-the-Middle Attacks

A man-in-the-middle attack is a situation in which a malicious individual uses an access point to effectively hijack mobile nodes by sending a stronger signal than the legitimate access point is sending to those nodes. The mobile nodes then associate to this rogue access point, sending their data--possibly sensitive data--into the wrong hands. The Man-in-the-Middle Attack Diagram illustrates a man-in-the-middle attack, hijacking wireless LAN clients.

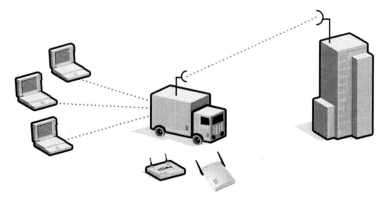

An access point and sometimes a
workgroup bridge are used to hijack users

Man-in-the-Middle Attack

In order to get clients to reassociate with the rogue access point, the rogue access point's power must be much higher than that of the other access points in the area, and something has to actively cause the users to roam to the rogue access point. Losing connectivity with a legitimate access point happens seamlessly as a part of the roaming process, thus some clients connect to the rogue accidentally. Introducing all-band interference into the area around the legitimate access point, as with a Bluetooth device, can cause forced roaming.

The person perpetrating this man-in-the-middle attack must first know the SSID that the wireless clients are using, and, as we have discussed earlier, this piece of information is easily obtained. The perpetrator has to know the network's WEP keys if WEP is being used on the network. Upstream (facing the Network core) connectivity from the rogue access point is handled with a client device, such as a PC card or workgroup bridge. Many times, man-in-the-middle attacks are orchestrated using a single laptop computer with two PCMCIA cards. Access point software is run on the laptop computer where one PC card is used as an access point and a second PC card is used to connect the laptop to nearby legitimate access points. This configuration makes the laptop a "man-in-the-middle," operating between clients and legitimate access points. A man-in-the-middle hacker can obtain valuable information by running a sniffer on the laptop in this scenario.

One particular problem with the man-in-the-middle attack is that the attack is undetectable by users. That being the case, only by the amount of time that the perpetrator can stay in place before getting caught limits the amount of information a perpetrator can gather in this situation. Physical security of the premises is the best remedy for the man-in-the-middle attack.

Activities

1. Your wireless users are unable to connect to the network. You suspect that an external source is jamming an RF signal. What type of device will allow you to locate the jamming source?

    a. Packet sniffer

    b. Oscilloscope

    c. Protocol analyzer

    d. Spectrum analyzer

2. A hacker has gained access to a wireless network. Which of the following are tools she could use to access network resources and impersonate users? (Choose two.)

    a. Port scans for active services

    b. Dump passwords to hacking utilities

    c. Collect SSIDs with a wireless sniffer

    d. Radio frequency spectrum collectors

3. Why are hackers able to intercept wireless users and redirect them to their mobile, illegimate access point?

    a. Wireless devices broadcast the WEP key in the clear

    b. When APs do not send the SSID in beacon frames, the clients choose the SSID at random

    c. Wireless networks allow seamless roaming between APs, even with WEP enabled

    d. Wireless LAN cards can easily overpower the signal transmitted by the legitimate access point

4. Which of the following are methods hackers can use to gain access to a wireless network? (Choose two.)

    a. SSID attacks

    b. Connection probing

    c. Eavesdropping

    d. Frequency repeating

Extended Activity

Configure a wireless LAN with an access point and two clients. Turn off WEP, set the SSIDs, and verify communications. Set up another client with two wireless radio cards and access point software. Using a sniffer, intercept the SSID. Turn on a Bluetooth device to force the clients to roam to the client access point. Were you able to force the clients to the man-in-the-middle access point? What indications did you see on the clients that they roamed?

Lesson 3—Emerging Security Solutions

Because wireless LANs are not inherently secure, and because WEP is not an end-to-end security mechanism for enterprise wireless LANs, there is a significant opportunity for other security solutions to take the forefront in the wireless LAN security market. In this lesson we discuss some of these possible security solutions that, while not yet approved and accepted into the 802.11 family of standards, can play a role in securing your wireless LAN.

Objectives

At the end of this unit you will be able to:

- Identify emerging security solutions for wireless networks

- Describe how emerging security solutions protect a wireless network

 **Key Point**

Vendors have developed their own solutions to wireless network WEP security vulnerabilities.

Vendor Solutions

As of this writing, all of the available security solutions discussed in this book are proprietary in nature. Although the IEEE has accepted 802.1x as a standard, its use as an approved part of an 802.11 series standard is not yet official. Some new standards still in draft form, such as 802.11i, specify use of security mechanisms such as 802.1x and EAP.

WEP Key Management

Instead of using static WEP keys, which can easily be learned or discovered by hackers, wireless LANs can be made more secure by implementing dynamic per-session or per-packet key assignments using a central key distribution system.

Per-session or per-packet WEP key distribution assigns a new WEP key to both the client and the access point for each session or each packet sent between the two. Although dynamic keys add more overhead and reduce throughput, they make hacking the network through the wireless segment much more difficult. The hacker would have to be able to predict the sequence of keys that the key distribution server is using, which is very difficult.

Remember that WEP protects only the layer 3 to 7 information and data payload, but does not encrypt MAC addresses or beacons. A sniffer can capture any information being broadcast in beacons from the access point or any MAC address information in unicast packets from clients.

To put a centralized encryption key server in place, the wireless LAN administrator must find an application that performs this task, buy a server with the appropriate operating system installed, and configure the application according to the organization's needs. This process could be costly and time consuming, depending on the scale of deployment, but will pay for itself in a very short period of time by preventing damage caused by malicious hackers.

Wireless VPNs

Wireless LAN manufacturers are increasingly including virtual private network (VPN) server software in access points and gateways, allowing VPN technology to help secure wireless LAN connections. When the VPN server is built into the access point, clients use off-the-shelf VPN software using protocols such as Point-to-Point Tunneling Protocol (PPTP) or IPSec to form a tunnel directly with the access point.

First, a client associates with the access point, and then the dial-up VPN connection is made in order for the client to pass traffic through the access point. All traffic is passed through the tunnel and can be encrypted and tunneled to add an extra layer of security. The Wireless LAN VPN Solution Diagram shows a VPN configuration.

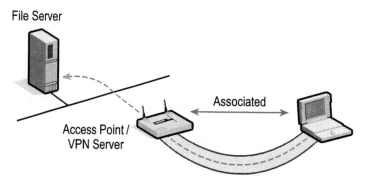

File Server

Associated

Access Point /
VPN Server

Data destined to LAN must pass through tunnel

Wireless LAN VPN Solution

Use of PPTP with shared secrets is very simple to implement and provides a reasonable level of security, especially when added to WEP encryption. In this area, use of IPSec with shared secrets or certificates is generally the solution of choice among security professionals. When the VPN server is implemented in an enterprise gateway, the same process takes place except that, after the client associates to the access point, the VPN tunnel is established with the upstream gateway device, instead of with the access point itself.

Some vendors offer modifications to their existing VPN solutions (hardware and software) to support wireless clients and compete in the wireless LAN market. These devices or applications serve in the same capacity as the enterprise gateway, sitting between the wireless segment and the wired core of the network. Wireless VPN solutions are reasonably economical and fairly simple to implement. If an administrator has no experience with VPN solutions, it might be necessary to get training in that area before implementing such a solution. VPNs that support wireless LANs are usually designed with the novice VPN administrator in mind, which partially explains why these devices have gained such popularity among users.

TKIP

TKIP is essentially an upgrade to WEP that fixes known security problems in WEP's implementation of the RC4 stream cipher. TKIP provides for initialization vector hashing to help defeat passive packet snooping. It also provides a Message Integrity Check to help determine whether an unauthorized user has modified packets by injecting traffic that enables key cracking. TKIP includes use of dynamic keys to defeat capture of passive keys—a widely publicized hole in the existing Wired Equivalent Privacy (WEP) standard.

TKIP can be implemented through firmware upgrades to access points and bridges, as well as software and firmware upgrades to wireless client devices. TKIP specifies rules for the use of initialization vectors, re-keying procedures based on 802.1x, per-packet key mixing, and message integrity code (MIC). A performance loss occurs when using TKIP, but this performance decrease may be a valid trade-off, considering the gain in network security.

AES-Based Solutions

Advanced Encryption Standard (AES)-based solutions may replace WEP using RC4, but in the interim, solutions such as TKIP are being implemented. Although no products that use AES are currently on the market as of this writing, AES has undergone extensive cryptographic review and a few companies have submitted their AES-based products to NIST for review. The current 802.11i draft specifies use of AES, and, considering most wireless LAN industry players are behind this effort, AES will likely remain part of the finalized standard.

Changing data encryption techniques to a solution that is as strong as AES will make a significant impact on wireless LAN security, but scalable solutions, such as centralized encryption key servers to automate the process of handing out keys, must still be implemented on enterprise networks. If a client radio card is stolen with the AES encryption key embedded, it would not matter how strong AES is because the perpetrator would still be able to gain access to the network.

Wireless Gateways

Residential wireless gateways are now available with VPN technology, as well as NAT, DHCP, PPPoE, WEP, MAC filters, and perhaps even a built-in firewall. These devices are sufficient for small office or home office environments with few workstations and a shared connection to the Internet. Costs of these units vary greatly depending on their range of offered services. Some of the high-end units even boast static routing and RIPv2.

Enterprise wireless gateways are a special adaptation of a VPN and authentication server for wireless networks. An enterprise gateway sits on the wired network segment between the access points and the wired upstream network. As its name suggests, a gateway controls access from the wireless LAN onto the wired network, so that, while a hacker could possibly listen to or even gain access to the wireless segment, the gateway protects the wired distribution system from attack.

An example of a good time to deploy an enterprise wireless LAN gateway might be the following hypothetical situation. Suppose a hospital had implemented 40 access points across several floors of their building. Their investment in access points is fairly significant at this point; thus, if the access points do not support scalable security measures, the hospital could be in the predicament of having to replace all of their access points. Instead, the hospital could employ a wireless LAN gateway.

This gateway can be connected between the core switch and the distribution switch (which connects to the access points) and can act as an authentication and VPN server through which all wireless LAN clients can connect. Instead of deploying all new access points, one (or more depending on network load) gateway device can be installed behind all of the access points as a group. Use of this type of gateway provides security on behalf of a nonsecurity-aware access point. Most enterprise wireless gateways support an array of VPN protocols, such as PPTP, IPSec, L2TP, certificates, and even QoS based on profiles.

802.1x and EAP

The 802.1x standard provides specifications for port-based network access control. Port-based access control was originally – and still is – used with Ethernet switches. When a user attempts to connect to the Ethernet port, the port places the user's connection in blocked mode, awaiting verification of the user's identity with a backend authentication system.

The 802.1x protocol has been incorporated into many wireless LAN systems and has become almost a standard practice among many vendors. When combined with extensible authentication protocol (EAP), 802.1x can provide a very secure and flexible environment based on various authentication schemes in use today.

EAP, which was first defined for the point-to-point protocol (PPP), is a protocol for negotiating an authentication method. EAP is defined in RFC 2284 and defines the characteristics of the authentication method, including the required user credentials (password, certificate, and so forth), the protocol to be used (MD5, TLS, GSM, OTP, and so forth), support of key generation, and support of mutual authentication. Perhaps a dozen types of EAP are currently on the market because neither the industry players or IEEE have come together to agree on any single type, or small list of types, from which to create a standard.

The successful 802.1x-EAP client authentication model works as follows:

1. The client requests association with the access point.

2. The access point replies to the association request with an EAP identity request.

3. The client sends an EAP identity response to the access point.

4. The client's EAP identity response is forwarded to the authentication server.

5. The authentication server sends an authorization request to the access point.

6. The access point forwards the authorization request to the client.

7. The client sends the EAP authorization response to the access point.

8. The access point forwards the EAP authorization response to the authentication server.

9. The authentication sends an EAP success message to the access point.

10. The access point forwards the EAP success message to the client and places the client's port in forward mode.

When 802.1x with EAP is used, a situation arises for an administrator in which it is possible to have a double logon procedure when powering up a notebook computer that is attached wirelessly and logging into a domain or directory service. The Two Logon Processes Diagram illustrates this.

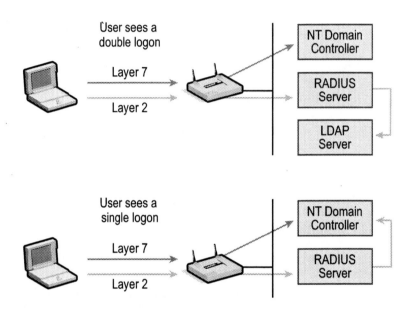

Two Logon Processes

The reason for the possible double logon process is that 802.1x requires authentication in order to provide layer 2 connectivity. In most cases, this authentication is performed by means of a centralized user database. If this database is not the same database used for client authentication into the network (such as with Windows domain controllers, Active Directory, NDS, or LDAP), or at least synchronized with the database used for client authentication, the user will log on each time network connectivity is required. Most administrators choose to use the same database for MAC layer connectivity and client/server connectivity, providing a seamless logon process for the client. A similar configuration can also be used with wireless VPN solutions.

Activities

1. Which statement best describes how the 802.1x standard secures access to the wireless network?

    a. Clients must first create a VPN tunnel with the access point in order to access the network

    b. The 802.1x server and the client must use the same WEP key

    c. The 802.1x standard secures the layer 3 connections between the client and the network

    d. Clients must authenticate at the MAC layer to gain access to the network

2. On which user databases can 802.1x authentication be implemented? (Choose two.)

    a. Active Directory

    b. LDAP

    c. LANMAN

    d. SAM

3. Which security protocols may be used to establish wireless VPN connections? (Choose two.)

    a. IPSec

    b. PPP

    c. LDAP

    d. PPTP

4. Which statements are true concerning wireless client VPN connections? (Choose two.)

    a. The client must authenticate at layer 2 before it can access the wireless network

    b. The client must first associate with the access point

    c. The VPN server must be an external device

    d. The tunnel transports the client data in encrypted packets

5. Which wireless LAN security solution upgrades WEP to fix the protocol's implementation of the RC4 cipher?

    a. VPN

    b. AES

    c. TKIP

    d. 802.1x

Extended Activities

1. Log in to the WestNet Learning Technologies, Inc. Online Student Resources Center found at **http://www.westnetinc.com**. Download and perform the following wireless networking labs:

    Lab 6: Dynamic WEP keys and mutual authentication using 802.1x/EAP and RADIUS

    Lab 7: Wireless VPN using PPTP tunnels and RADIUS

    Note that you must first register to gain access to the Student Resources Center.

    To complete the labs, you will require access to a wireless network and several PCs. The labs list the hardware and software required.

2. Draw a wireless network that includes the following components:

    • Access Point that supports IPSec VPNs

    • Enterprise wireless gateway that acts as the IPSec VPN server

    • Clients that connect to the wireless network using VPN tunnels

    Include a state diagram that shows the client authentication process.

Lesson 4—Corporate Security Policy

A company that uses wireless LANs should have a corporate security policy that addresses the unique risks that wireless LANs introduce to the network. For instance, an inappropriate cell size that allows the drive-by hacker to gain network access from the parking lot is a very good example of one item that should be included in any corporate security policy. Other items that should be covered in the security policy are strong passwords, strong WEP keys, physical security, use of advanced security solutions, and regular wireless LAN hardware inventories (when feasible). This list is far from comprehensive, considering that security solutions will vary between organizations. The depth of the wireless LAN section of the security policy depends on the security requirements of an organization as well as the extent of the wireless LAN segment(s) of the network.

Objectives

At the end of this unit you will be able to:

- Identify key components of corporate wireless network security policy

- Explain in what ways wireless network physical security requirements differ from those of wired networks

 **Key Point**

A corporate security policy puts in place directives that identify and secure sensitive network assets.

Components of a Corporate Security Policy

The benefits of having, implementing, and maintaining a solid security policy are too numerous to count. Preventing data loss and theft, preventing corporate sabotage or espionage, and maintaining company secrets are just a few. Even the suggestion that hackers could have stolen data from an industry-leading corporation may cause confidence in the company to plummet.

The beginning of good corporate policy starts with management. Recognizing the need for security and delegating the tasks of creating the appropriate documentation to include wireless LANs into the existing security policy should be top priority. First, those who are responsible for securing the wireless LAN segments must be educated in the technology. Next, the educated technology professional should interact with upper management and agree on company security needs. This team of educated individuals is then able to construct a list of procedures and requirements that, if followed by personnel at every applicable level, will ensure that the wireless network remains as safely guarded as the wired network.

Keep Sensitive Information Private

Some items that should be known only by network administrators at the appropriate levels are:

- Usernames and passwords of access points and bridges

- SNMP strings

- WEP keys

- MAC address lists

The point of keeping this information only in the hands of trusted, skilled individuals, such as the network administrator, is important because a malicious user or hacker could easily use these pieces of information to gain access into the network and network devices. This information can be stored in one of many secure fashions. Applications using strong encryption on the market for the explicit purpose of password and sensitive data storage are now available.

Physical Security

Although physical security is important when using a traditional wired network, it is even more important for a company that uses wireless LAN technology. For reasons discussed earlier, a person who has a wireless PC card (and perhaps an antenna) does not have to be in the same building as the network to gain access to the network. Even intrusion detection software is not necessarily adequate to prevent wireless hackers from stealing sensitive information. Passive attacks leave no trace on the network because no connection was ever made. Some utilities on the market now can see a network card that is in promiscuous mode, accessing data without making a connection.

When WEP is the only wireless LAN security solution in place, tight controls should be placed on users who have company-owned wireless client devices. For example, not allowing users to take those client devices off of company premises is a tight control. Because the WEP key is stored in the client device's firmware, wherever the card goes, the network's weakest security link also goes. A wireless LAN administrator should know who, where, and when each PC card is taken from the organization's facilities.

Because such knowledge is often unreasonable, an administrator should realize that WEP, by itself, is not an adequate wireless LAN security solution. Even with such tight controls, if a card is lost or stolen, the person responsible for the card (the user) should be required to report the loss or theft immediately to the wireless LAN administrator so that necessary security precautions can be taken. Such precautions should include, at a minimum, resetting MAC filters, changing WEP keys, and so forth.

An effective deterrent to netstumbling is when guards make periodic scans around the company premises looking specifically for suspicious activity. Security guards who are trained to recognize 802.11 hardware and alerting company personnel to always be on the lookout for noncompany personnel lurking around the company building with 802.11-based hardware is also very effective in reducing on-premises attacks.

Wireless LAN Equipment Inventory and Security Audits

As a complement to the physical security policy, all wireless LAN equipment should be regularly inventoried to account for authorized and prevent unauthorized use of wireless equipment to access an organization's network. If the network is too large and contains a significant amount of wireless equipment, periodic equipment inventories might be impractical. In cases such as these, it is very important to implement wireless LAN security solutions that are not based on hardware, but based rather on usernames and passwords or some other type of nonhardware-based security solution. For medium and small wireless networks, performing monthly or quarterly hardware inventories can motivate users to report hardware loss or theft.

Periodic scans of the network with sniffers, in a search for rogue devices, are a very valuable way of keeping the wireless network secure. Consider if a very elaborate (and expensive) wireless network solution were put in place with state-of-the-art security, and, because coverage did not extend to a particular area of the building, a user took it into his or her own hands to install an additional, unauthorized access point in their work area. In this case, this user has just provided a hacker with the necessary route into the network, completely circumventing a very good (and expensive) wireless LAN security solution.

Inventories and security audits should be well documented in the corporate security policy. The types of procedures to be performed, the tools to be used, and the reports to be generated should all be clearly spelled out as part of the corporate policy so that this tedious task does not get overlooked. Managers should expect a report of this type on a regular basis from the network administrator.

Using Advanced Security Solutions

Organizations implementing wireless LANs should take advantage of some of the more advanced security mechanisms available on the market. It should also be required in a security policy that the implementation of any such advanced security mechanism be thoroughly documented. Because these technologies are new, proprietary, and often used in combination with other security protocols or technologies, they must be documented so that if a security breach occurs, network administrators can determine where and how the breach occurred.

Because so few people in the IT industry are educated in wireless technology, the likelihood of employee turnover causing network disruption, or at least vulnerability, is much higher when wireless LANs are part of a network. This turnover of employees is another very important reason that thorough documentation on wireless LAN administration and security functions be created and maintained.

Public Wireless Networks

It is inevitable that corporate users with sensitive information on their laptop computers will connect those laptops to public wireless LANs. It should be a matter of corporate policy that all wireless users--whether wireless is provided by the company or by the user--run both personal firewall software and antivirus software on their laptops. Most public wireless networks have little or no security in order to make connectivity simple for the user and to decrease the amount of required technical support.

Even if upstream servers on the wired segment are protected, the wireless users are still vulnerable. Consider a situation where a hacker is sitting at an airport, considered a "Wi-Fi hot spot." This hacker can sniff the wireless LAN, grab usernames and passwords, log into the system, and then wait for unsuspecting users to log in also. The hacker can then do a ping sweep across the subnet to look for other wireless clients, find the users, and begin hacking into their laptop computer's files. These vulnerable users are considered "low hanging fruit," meaning that they are easy to hack because of their general unfamiliarity with leading edge technology such as wireless LANs.

Limited and Tracked Access

Most enterprise LANs have some method of limiting and tracking a user's access on the LAN. Typically, a system supporting Authentication, Authorization, and Accounting (AAA) services is deployed. This same security measure should be documented and implemented as part of wireless LAN security. AAA services will allow the organization to assign use rights to particular classes of users. Visitors, for example, might only be allowed Internet access, whereas employees would be allowed to access their particular department's servers and the Internet.

Keeping logs of users' rights and the activities they performed while using your network can prove valuable if a question of who did what on the network arises. Consider a user on vacation whose user's account was used almost every day. Keeping logs of activity such as this will give the administrator insight into what is really happening on the LAN. Using the same example, and knowing that the user was on vacation, the administrator could begin looking for where the masquerading user was connecting to the network.

Activities

1. What types of software should you install on your mobile users' laptop computers to protect them from malicious attacks while operating on public wireless networks? (Choose two.)

    a. Packet sniffer

    b. Antivirus software

    c. Firewall

    d. MAC filter

2. How might a network user easily circumvent wireless LAN security?

    a. Use his or her own wireless network card on the company network

    b. Reset the SSID on their wireless client

    c. Install his or her own access point on the network

    d. Connect to the Internet over the wireless network

3. Which statement best describes a rogue device?

    a. An unauthorized access point installed by a network user

    b. A user connecting her home laptop to the wireless network

    c. A malfunctioning wireless LAN card

    d. An access point configured with the wrong WEP key

4. How might a network administrator ensure that security audits and inventories are not overlooked?

    a. Perform daily audits of all network devices

    b. Restrict user network access to work hours only

    c. Make users responsible for performing self audits

    d. Document audit procedures in the security policy

5. Which of the following is an example of a practical physical security step to perform on a wireless network?

    a. Place antennas inside secure enclosures.

    b. Place access points in the wiring closet.

    c. Inventory and track client devices.

    d. Disconnect the access point from the wired network after hours.

Extended Activities

1. Read the white paper "Your Wireless Network has No Clothes," written by William A. Arbaugh, Narendar Shanker, and Y.C. Justin Wan, available at: **http://www.cs.umd.edu/ ~waa/wireless.pdf.**

2. Read several wireless security articles available from the SANS Institute at **http://rr.sans.org/wireless/wireless_list.php.**

Lesson 5—Security Recommendations

This lesson summarizes recommendations for securing your wireless LAN. We revisit WEP, cell sizing, user authentication, security protocols, and rogue hardware, and introduce some new concepts, as well.

Objectives

At the end of this unit you will be able to:

- Explain recommended actions for securing a wireless network
- Choose the appropriate solution to a network vulnerability

 **Key Point**

Some initial thought and effort put towards wireless network security significantly reduces the chances of network compromise.

WEP

Do not rely solely on WEP, no matter how well you have it implemented as an end-to-end wireless LAN security solution. Remember, a wireless environment protected with only WEP should be considered an unsecured environment, and you must take additional steps to secure your system. When using WEP, do not use WEP keys that are related to the service set identifier (SSID) or to the organization. Make WEP keys very difficult to remember and to figure out. In many cases, the WEP key can be easily guessed just by looking at the SSID or the name of the organization.

WEP is an effective solution for reducing the risk of casual eavesdropping. Because an individual who is not maliciously trying to gain access, but just happens to see your network will not have a matching WEP key, that individual is prevented from accessing your network.

Cell Sizing

In order to reduce the chance of eavesdropping, an administrator should make sure that the cell sizes of access points are appropriate. The majority of hackers look for the locations where very little time and energy must be spent gaining access into the network. For this reason, it is important not to have access points emitting strong signals that extend into the organization's parking lot (or similar insecure locations), unless absolutely necessary. Some enterprise-level access points allow for the configuration of power output, which effectively controls the size of the radio frequency (RF) cell around the access point. If an eavesdropper in your parking lot cannot detect your network, your network is not susceptible to this kind of attack.

It may be tempting for network administrators to always use the maximum power output settings on all wireless LAN devices in an attempt to get maximum throughput and coverage, but such blind configuration will come at the expense of security. An access point has a cell size that can be controlled by the amount of power that the access point is emitting and the antenna gain of the antenna being used. If that cell is inappropriately large to an extent that a passerby can detect, listen to, or even gain access to the network, then the network is unnecessarily vulnerable to attack. A proper site survey, discussed in further reading, can determine the necessary and appropriate cell size. The proper cell size should be documented, along with the configuration of the access point or bridge for each particular area. It may be necessary to install two access points with smaller cell sizes to avoid possible security vulnerabilities in some instances.

Try to locate your access points towards the center of your house or building. This will minimize the signal leak outside of the intended range. If you are using external antennas, selecting the right type of antenna can be helpful in minimizing signal range. Turn off access points when they are not in use. This will minimize your exposure to potential hackers and lighten the network management burden.

User Authentication

Because user authentication is a wireless LAN's weakest link, and the 802.11 standard does not specify any method of user authentication, it is imperative that the administrator implement user-based authentication as soon as possible upon installing a wireless LAN infrastructure. User authentication should be based on device-independent schemes such as usernames and passwords, biometrics, smart cards, token-based systems, or some other type of secure means of identifying the user, not the hardware. The solution you implement should support bidirectional authentication between an authentication server (such as Remote Authentication Dial-In User Service [RADIUS]) and the wireless clients.

RADIUS is the de-facto standard in user authentication systems in most every information technology market. Access points send user authentication requests to a RADIUS server, which can either have a built-in (local) user database, or can pass the authentication request through to a domain controller, an NDS server, an Active Directory server, or even a Lightweight Directory Access Protocol (LDAP)-compliant database system.

A few RADIUS vendors have enhanced their RADIUS products to include support for the latest family of authentication protocols, such as the many types of EAP.

Administering a RADIUS server can be very simple or very complicated, depending on the implementation. Because wireless security solutions are very sensitive, care should be taken when choosing a RADIUS server solution to make sure that the wireless network administrator can administer it or can work effectively with the existing RADIUS administrator.

Remember that wireless security has many faces—man-in-the-middle attacks, eavesdropping, "free rides," and so forth—and you have to consider all of them when implementing user authentication. When supporting mobile users, one way to ensure the ongoing security of your network is to force users to reauthenticate every time their IP address or network attachment point changes.

Security Needs

Choose a security solution that fits your organization's needs and budget, both for today and tomorrow. Wireless LANs are quickly gaining popularity partly because of their ease of implementation. That means that a wireless LAN that began as an access point and five clients could quickly grow to 15 access points and

300 clients across a corporate campus. The same security mechanism that worked just fine for one access point will not be as acceptable, or as secure, for 300 users. An organization could waste money on security solutions that they will quickly outgrow as the wireless LAN expands. In many cases, organizations already have security, such as intrusion detection systems, firewalls, and RADIUS servers, in place. When deciding on a wireless LAN solution, leveraging existing equipment is an important factor in keeping costs down.

Use Additional Security Tools

Taking advantage of the technology that is available, such as virtual private networks (VPNs), firewalls, intrusion detection systems (IDS), standards and protocols (802.1x and EAP, for example), and client authentication with RADIUS, can help make wireless solutions secure above and beyond what the 802.11 standard requires. The cost and time to implement these solutions vary greatly from small office/home office (SOHO) solutions to large enterprise solutions.

Monitoring for Rogue Hardware

To discover rogue access points, regular access point discovery sessions should be scheduled, but not announced. Actively discovering and removing rogue access points will likely keep out hackers and allow an administrator to maintain network control and security. Regular security audits should be performed to locate incorrectly configured access points that could be security risks. As part of a regular security routine, this task can be done while monitoring the network for rogue access points. Present configurations should be compared to past configurations to see if users or hackers have reconfigured the access points. Access logs should be implemented and monitored for the purpose of finding any irregular access on the wireless segment. This type of monitoring can even help find lost or stolen wireless client devices.

Switches, Not Hubs

Another simple guideline to follow is always connecting access points to switches instead of hubs. Hubs are broadcast devices, so every packet received by a hub will be sent out on all of the hub's other ports. If access points are connected to hubs, every packet traversing the wired segment will also be broadcast across the wireless segment. This functionality gives hackers additional information, such as passwords and IP addresses.

Wireless DMZ

Another idea in implementing security for wireless LAN segments is to create a wireless demilitarized zone (WDMZ). Depending on the level of implementation, creating WDMZs using firewalls or routers can be costly. WDMZs are generally implemented in medium- and large-scale wireless LAN deployments. Because access points are basically insecure and untrusted devices, they should be separated from other network segments by a firewall device, as illustrated on the Wireless DMZ Diagram.

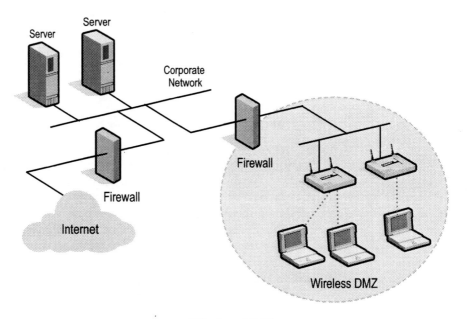

Wireless DMZ

Firmware and Software Updates

Update the firmware and drivers on your access points and wireless cards. It is always wise to use the latest firmware and drivers on your access points and wireless cards. Manufacturers commonly fix known issues, security holes, and enable new features with these updates.

Activities

1. In which two ways can you control cell sizes in your wireless network? (Choose two.)

   a. Locate APs near the center of the building.

   b. Use omnidirectional antennas whenever possible.

   c. Set the client devices to low power.

   d. Turn off APs when not in use.

2. How should you configure your WEP keys to help secure the network?

   a. Set them to 192-bit encryption

   b. Use a different key for each access point

   c. Do not relate them to the organization

   d. Match them to the SSID

3. On which of the following security schemes should wireless networks user authentication be based? (Choose three.)

   a. MAC filters

   b. Smart cards

   c. Biometrics

   d. RADIUS

4. Why would you want to place wireless APs on switches and not hubs?

   a. Hubs stop broadcast traffic, which can interfere with communications on the wireless network

   b. Switches implement application layer protocol filters to control network utilization

   c. Hubs don't pass layer 3 and above traffic

   d. Switches prevent the broadcasting of all packets to all network segments

5. A wireless DMZ is located on which network device?

   a. Firewall

   b. Switch

   c. Hub

   d. access point

Extended Activity

Design a wireless network located in a wireless DMZ. Show the necessary components. How would you configure the IP addressing scheme? Would you use a VPN for the wireless clients? Why or why not?

_____

_____

_____

_____

Summary

This unit explained the key to making a wireless LAN secure: educating those who implement and manage the wireless LAN about preventing security breaches. This unit discussed WEP, the much-maligned 802.11 security solution. You learned why WEP alone will not keep a hacker out of a wireless LAN, and how to use WEP with some level of effectiveness.

To prepare you to prevent security problems, this unit explained the various methods that can be used to attack a wireless LAN. Several emerging security solutions are available, but are not yet specified by any of the 802.11 standards. This unit also offered some recommendations for maintaining wireless LAN security and discussed corporate security policy as it pertains specifically to wireless LANs.

Unit 10 Quiz

1. According to the 802.11 standard, which one of the following is NOT one of the criteria for WEP implementation?

   a. Exportable

   b. Reasonably strong

   c. Self-synchronizing

   d. Computationally efficient

   e. Mandatory

2. Centralized encryption key servers should be used if possible. Which one of the following would NOT be a good reason to implement centralized encryption key servers?

   a. Centralized key generation

   b. Centralized key distribution

   c. Centralized key coding and encryption

   d. Ongoing key rotation

   e. Reduced key management overhead

3. Typical key rotation options implemented by various manufacturers for encryption key generation include which of the following? (Choose two.)

   a. Per-packet

   b. Per-session

   c. Per-user

   d. Per-broadcast

   e. Per-frame

4. What level of encryption is created by a WEP key using a 40-bit secret key concatenated with the initialization vector to form the WEP key?

   a. 24-bit

   b. 40-bit

   c. 64-bit

   d. 128-bit

5. Which piece of information on a wireless LAN is encrypted with WEP enabled?

    a. The data payload of the frame

    b. The MAC addresses of the frame

    c. Beacon management frames

    d. Shared Key challenge plaintext

6. AES uses which one of the following encryption algorithms?

    a. Fresnel

    b. NAV

    c. Rijndael

    d. Rinehart

7. What are the three types of filtering that can be performed on a wireless LAN? (Choose three.)

    a. SSID filtering

    b. MAC address filtering

    c. Protocol filtering

    d. 802.11 standard filtering

    e. Manufacturer hardware filtering

8. SSID filtering is a basic form of access control, and is not considered secure for which of the following reasons? (Choose two.)

    a. The SSID is broadcast in the clear in every access point beacon by default

    b. Using a sniffer, it is very simple to find out the SSID of a network

    c. The SSID of a wireless LAN client must match the SSID on the access point in order for the client to authenticate and associate to the access point

    d. SSID encryption is easy to break with freeware utilities

9. What can a network administrator use to reduce the time it takes to rotate WEP keys across an enterprise network?

    a. Distributed Encryption Key Server

    b. Centralized Encryption Key Server

    c. Router Access Control List

    d. Filter Application Server

10. MAC filtering is NOT susceptible to which one of the following intrusions?

    a. Theft of a PC card

    b. MAC address spoofing

    c. Sniffer collecting the MAC addresses of all wireless LAN clients

    d. MAC filter bypass equipment

11. Which of the following are types of wireless LAN attacks? (Choose two.)

    a. Passive attacks

    b. Antenna wind loading

    c. Access point flooding

    d. Active attacks

12. The statement "MAC addresses of wireless LAN clients are broadcast in the clear by access points and bridges, even when WEP is implemented" is which of the following?

    a. Always true

    b. Always false

    c. Dependent on the manufacturers WEP implementation

13. Which of the following is the best solution for a jamming attack?

    a. Use a spectrum analyzer to locate the RF source and then remove it

    b. Increase the power on the wireless LAN to overpower the jamming signal

    c. Shut down the wireless LAN segment and wait for the jamming signal to dissipate

    d. Arrange for the FCC to shut down the jamming signal's transmitter

14. Why should access points be connected to switches instead of hubs?

    a. Hubs are faster than switches and can handle high utilization networks.

    b. Hubs are full duplex and switches are only half duplex.

    c. Hubs are broadcast devices and pose an unnecessary security risk.

    d. Access points are not capable of full-duplex mode.

15. Which of the following protocols are network security tools above and beyond what is specified by the 802.11?
    (Choose two.)

    a. 802.1x and EAP

    b. 8011.g

    c. VPNs

    d. 802.11x and PAP

16. At what point on the wired network segment is an enterprise wireless gateway positioned?

    a. Between the access point(s) and the wired network upstream

    b. Between the access point(s) and the wireless network clients

    c. Between the switch and the router on the wireless network segment

    d. In place of a regular access point on the wireless LAN segment

17. Networks using the 802.1x protocol control network access on what basis?

    a. Per–user

    b. Per–port

    c. Per-session

    d. Per-MAC Address

    e. Per-SSID

18. Which of the following is NOT true regarding wireless LAN security?

    a. WEP cannot be relied upon to provide a complete security solution.

    b. A wireless environment protected with only WEP is not a secure environment.

    c. The 802.11 standard specifies user authentication methods.

    d. User authentication is a wireless LAN's weakest link.

19. Which of the following demonstrates the need for accurate RF cell sizing? (Choose three.)

    a. Co-located access points having overlapping cells

    b. A site survey utility can see ten or more access points from many points in the building.

    c. Users on the sidewalk passing by your building can see your wireless LAN.

    d. Users can attach to the network from their car parked in the facility's parking lot.

20. For maximum security, wireless LAN user authentication should be based on which one of the following?

    a. Device-independent schemes, such as user names and passwords

    b. Default authentication processes

    c. MAC addresses only

    d. SSID and MAC address

Unit 11
Site Survey Fundamentals

In this unit, we discuss the process of conducting a site survey, also known as a "facilities analysis." We discuss terms and concepts with which you are probably familiar if you have ever installed a wireless network from the ground up. If wireless is new to you, you might notice that some of the terms and concepts carry over from traditional wired networks. Concepts such as throughput needs, power accessibility, extendibility, application requirements, budget requirements, and signal range are all key components as you conduct a site survey. We further discuss the ramifications of a poor site survey and even no site survey at all. Our discussion covers a checklist of tasks that you need to accomplish and equipment you will use, and we will apply those checklists to several hypothetical examples.

Lessons

1. RF Site Surveys
2. Preparing for a Site Survey
3. Site Survey Equipment
4. Conducting a Site Survey
5. Site Survey Reporting

Terms

data rate—Data rate is the rate, in bits per second, that data traverses a network.

dead spot—A dead spot is a point in an RF signal's path where an obstacle blocks signal coverage.

distance wheel—A distance wheel is a handheld device with a wheel on one end and a handle on the other. It is used to roll across an area to be measured, and it represents the measurement in a specified unit.

Health Insurance Portability and Accountability Act of 1996 (HIPAA)—HIPAA added limited protections to families considering the availability of health insurance. HIPAA aims to reduce the chance of individuals losing existing coverage and provides avenues for individuals to purchase their own coverage if they lose their employer's group coverage. Visit the U.S. Department of Health and Human Services Web site at **http://www.hhs.gov** for more information.

interference—Interference is any energy that interferes with the clear reception of a signal. For example, if one person is speaking, the sound of a second person's voice interferes with the first. See noise.

link speed—Link speed is the data rate at which a network connection operates.

media converter—A media converter is a Physical Layer network device used to convert electrical signals from one physical media type to another. For example, you would use a media converter to convert Ethernet over copper to Ethernet over fiber.

Pocket PC—Pocket PC is the name Microsoft gave to its update of its Windows CE handheld computer operating system. It is also a term used to generically describe handheld computers running a version of Microsoft's Pocket PC operating system.

noise—Noise is any condition, such as electrical interference, that destroys signal integrity. Noise can be caused by many electromagnetic sources, such as radio transmissions, electrical cables, electric motors, lighting dimmers, or bad cable connections. See interference.

noise floor—Noise floor is the level of RF that is inherently present in the surrounding environment. This noise is generated by a number of sources and is typically between -70 and -100 dBm in most environments. For a data signal to be effectively communicated, it must be significantly higher than the noise floor, which is high enough for the receiver to clearly distinguish between the RF data signal and the background noise.

radio frequency (RF)—Radio antennas emit electromagnetic fields. These fields propagate at varying frequencies, depending on the application. These frequencies fall into a radiation spectrum called RF. The RF spectrum ranges from 3 KHz to over 300 GHz.

RF coverage—RF coverage is the area over which an RF signal must extend to support the network users.

shielded twisted-pair (STP)—STP is a type of copper wiring typically used for high-speed computer network transmission. A twisted pair consists of two thin copper wires, twisted around each other to cancel EMI and RFI. A flexible metal sheath encloses the wires to provide additional protection from interference.

signal strength—Signal strength is the power level of an RF signal.

site survey—Conducting a site survey is the act of surveying an area to determine the contours of RF coverage in order to ensure proper wireless LAN operation through appropriate wireless LAN hardware placement.

sniffer—A sniffer is a generic term used to describe a hardware or software device used to capture and display network packets and their contents. SNIFFER is a registered trademark of Network Associates, Inc.

spectrum analyzer—A spectrum analyzer is an instrument that identifies the amplitude of signals at various frequencies.

Windows CE—Windows CE is Microsoft's first operation system written for use on small, handheld computers.

Lesson 1—RF Site Surveys

A radio frequency (RF) site survey is a map to successfully implementing a wireless network. There is no hard and fast technical definition of a site survey. As a CWNA candidate, you must learn the process of conducting the best possible site survey for the client, whether that client is internal or external to your organization. The site survey is an involved task that can take days or even weeks, depending on the site being surveyed. The information provided by a quality site survey can be significantly helpful for a long time.

Note: By performing a thorough site survey, the wireless LAN, which is installed according to the site survey, is significantly more likely to work properly, preventing you or your client from spending thousands of dollars on hardware that does not do the intended job.

Objectives

At the end of this lesson you will be able to:

- Explain the importance of an RF site survey

- Identify the tasks involved in preparing to perform the site survey

- Gather information necessary to a successful RF site survey

 **Key Point**

An RF site survey is the most important step in implementing any wireless network.

What Is a Site Survey?

A site survey is a task-by-task process by which a surveyor discovers the RF behavior, coverage, interference, and determines proper hardware placement in a facility. The site survey's primary objective is to ensure that mobile workers (the wireless LAN's "clients") experience continually strong radio frequency (RF) signal strength as they move around their facility. At the same time, clients must remain connected to the host device or other mobile computing devices and their work applications. Employees who are using the wireless LAN should never have to think about the wireless LAN. Proper performance of the tasks listed in this section ensures a quality site survey and can help achieve a seamless operating environment every time you install a wireless network.

Site surveying involves analyzing a site from an RF perspective and discovering what kind of RF coverage a site needs in order to meet the business goals of customers. During the site survey process, the surveyor will ask many questions about a variety of topics, which are covered in this unit. These questions allow the surveyor to gather as much information as possible to make an informed recommendation about what the best options are for hardware, installation, configuration, and security of a wireless LAN.

A site survey is an attempt to define the contours of RF coverage from an RF source (an access point or bridge) in a particular facility. Many issues can arise that prevent the RF signal from reaching certain parts of the facility. For example, if an access point is placed in the center of a medium-size room, it is assumed that RF coverage is present throughout the room. This is not necessarily true due to the phenomena known as multipath. RF reflections may also create "holes" in the RF coverage pattern.

Although a surveyor may document the site survey results, another individual (possibly the RF design engineer) may perform the site survey analysis to determine the best type of hardware to be implemented. Therefore, all of the results of the entire survey must be documented. The surveyor and the designer may be the same person, or in larger organizations they may be different people. Organized and accurate documentation by the site surveyor results in a much better design and installation process.

A proper site survey provides detailed specifications addressing coverage, interference sources, equipment placement, power considerations, and wiring requirements. Furthermore, the site survey documentation serves as a guide for the network design and for installing and verifying the wireless communication infrastructure.

By performing a site survey, you can obtain knowledge of your clients' needs, determine the sources of interference, locate the "dead" spots (where no RF coverage exists), and find the best locations in which to install the access point(s). Using this information, you can also accurately inform your client how much the wireless LAN will cost to implement.

Finally, although performing RF site surveys is the only business that some firms conduct, a good site survey can be a network integration firm's best sales tool. Performing a quality site survey can, and many times should, enable your organization to perform the installation and integration of the wireless LAN for which the site survey was done.

Activities

1. Which one of the following is the primary objective of an RF site survey?

   a. To limit the installer's financial liability if the installation does not meet the customer's needs.

   b. To justify the installer's bid for the installation project.

   c. To ensure that mobile clients receive a good RF signal throughout the facility.

   d. To reduce the danger of hackers breaking into the wireless network.

2. A properly performed site survey will contain which of the following information? (Choose three.)

   a. Power considerations

   b. Security procedures

   c. Equipment placement

   d. RF coverage

3. Which interference sources could cause holes in the RF coverage pattern of an access point placed in the middle of a room?

   a. Bluetooth devices

   b. Multipath

   c. Stratification

   d. All band

4. Which statement best describes an RF site survey?

   a. Interviewing users to determine how well the network servers perform

   b. Sitting in the parking lot of a large corporation netstumbling for packets

   c. Evaluating the effectiveness of the network's security services

   d. Gathering information about coverage, interference, and equipment placement

Extended Activity

Many wireless device manufacturers include site survey tools with their wireless equipment. If you have access to a wireless access point that includes site survey software, install the software on a laptop or personal digital assistant (PDA) and familiarize yourself with the tool. What types of information does the software allow you to gather?

Lesson 2—Preparing for a Site Survey

Planning a wireless LAN involves collecting information and making decisions. The following list consists of the most basic questions that must be answered before the actual physical work of the site survey begins. These questions are purposely open-ended because each one results in more information being passed from the client to the surveyor, making the surveyor better prepared to go on site. Most, if not all, of these questions can be answered by means of phone, fax, or e-mail, assuming the people with the answers to the questions are available. Again, the more prepared one is before arriving at the site (with a site survey toolkit), the more valuable the time on site will be.

Objectives

At the end of this lesson you will be able to:

- Identify the tasks involved in preparing to perform the site survey

- Gather information necessary to create a successful RF site survey

 **Key Point**

You must know what the customer expects to ensure the survey meets their needs.

Presurvey Questions

This section describes some of the topics you may want to address to the network management before performing your site survey:

- Facilities Analysis

- Existing Networks

- Area Usage and Towers

- Purpose and Business Requirements

- Bandwidth and Roaming Requirements

- Available Resources

- Security Requirements

Facility Analysis

During the facility analysis we ask, "What kind of facility is it?" This question is very basic, but the answer can make a big impact on the site survey work for the next several days. Consider the obvious differences that would exist in conducting a site survey of a small office with one server and 20 clients, versus performing a site survey of a large international airport. Aside from the obvious size differences, you must consider the number of users, security requirements, bandwidth requirements, budget, and the kind of impact jet engines have on 802.11 RF signals, if any, and so forth.

All that and more comes from this one question. Your answers can come in the form of pictures, written descriptions, or blueprints whenever possible. The more you know before you get to the facility, the better prepared you will be when you actually arrive. Depending on the facility type, standard issues will need to be addressed. Knowing the facility type before arrival will save time on site.

To demonstrate the standard issues discussed above, we will consider two facility types. The first example is a hospital. Hospitals are subject to an act of Congress known as the Health Insurance Portability and Accountability Act (HIPAA). HIPPA mandates that hospitals (and other similar healthcare organizations) keep certain information private. This topic alone demonstrates that, when doing a site survey for a hospital, security planning must be of prime importance.

Hospitals also have radiology equipment, mesh metal glass windows, fire doors, very long hallways, elevators, mobile users (nurses and doctors), and X-ray rooms with lead-lined walls. This set of criteria shows the surveyor some obvious things to consider, such as roaming across large distances, a limited number of users on an access point due to mandated security (which means much security protocol overhead on the wireless LAN), and medical applications that are often connection-oriented between the client and server. To ensure only the necessary amount of coverage for certain areas, semidirectional antennas may be used instead of omni antennas. Semidirectional antennas tend to reduce multipath because the signal is being broadcast in fewer directions. Elevators are everywhere, and cause signal blockage and possibly RF interference. Elevators are basically "dead" RF zones. A hospital site survey is an effective training ground for individuals who want to immerse themselves in wireless LAN technology.

The second facility type is a real estate office with approximately 25 agents. In this environment, security is important, but not mandated by law; thus, rudimentary security measures might suffice. Coverage will likely be adequate with only one or two centrally located access points, and bandwidth requirements will be nominal because most of the access is Internet based or involves transferring small files back and forth to the file server.

These two scenarios are quite different, but both need site surveys. The amount of time that it will take to perform a site survey at each facility is also very different. The real estate office may not even take a full day, whereas the hospital, depending on size, might take a week or more. Many of the activities of the users in each facility, such as roaming, are very different. With nurses and doctors in a hospital, roaming is just part of the job. In the relatively small, multiroom facility of the real estate firm, users sit at their desks and access the wireless network from that one location; thus, roaming may not be necessary.

Existing Networks Analysis

The following questions must be addressed concerning any existing network:

Is a network (wired or wireless) already in place?

This question is very basic, but you must know if a client is starting from scratch, or if the wireless LAN will work with an existing infrastructure. Most of the time you will have to work with an existing infrastructure. You must know the contents of an existing infrastructure. You must consider documentation of existing wireless LAN hardware, frequencies being used, number of users, throughput, and so forth, so that you can make decisions about how the new equipment (if needed) will fit in. In some cases, the customer did the initial installation, and has since outgrown the initial installation. If the existing setup functions poorly, note this poor performance so the problems are not repeated.

A network administrator or manager is commonly asked to answer the following questions:

- What Network Operating Systems (NOSs) are in use?

- How many users (today and in the next two years) need simultaneous access to the wireless network?

- What is the bandwidth (per user) requirement on the wireless network?

- What protocols are in use over the wireless LAN?

- What channels and spread spectrum technologies are currently in use?

- What wireless LAN security measures are in place?

- Where are wired LAN connection points (wiring closets) located in the facility?

- What are the client's expectations of what a wireless LAN will bring to their organization?

- Is a naming convention in place for infrastructure devices, such as routers, switches, access points, and wireless bridges, as shown on the Naming Conventions Diagram? If not, who is responsible for creating one?

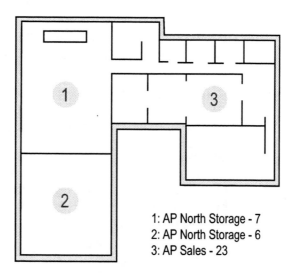

1: AP North Storage - 7
2: AP North Storage - 6
3: AP Sales - 23

Naming Conventions

Obtain a detailed network diagram (topology map) from the current network administrator. When one or more wireless LANs are already in place, the site survey will become all the more difficult, especially if the previous installations were not done properly. Without the cooperation of a network administrator, doing a site survey with an improperly functioning wireless LAN in place can be nearly impossible. Upgrades of existing wired infrastructure devices might also be necessary to enhance throughput and security on the wireless LAN.

Note: It may be necessary to sign a confidentiality agreement to obtain network diagrams or blueprints from your client.

Where are the network wiring closets located?

It is not uncommon to find that what seems like the most appropriate location for installing an access point is too far from a wiring closet to allow for upstream network connectivity over category 5 cabling. Knowing where these wiring closets are ahead of time will save time later. Locations of these wiring closets should be documented on the network topology map, blueprints, and any other facility maps. There are solutions for these problems, such as using repeaters, but this method of connectivity should be avoided when possible. Connecting bridges and access points directly into the wired distribution system is almost always favored. To circumvent this problem, fiber is often used between the access point or bridge and the wiring closet. This can be done with devices that accept fiber connections or with fiber-to-copper transceivers. However, if fiber is used, the ability to use PoE is lost.

Has a naming convention for access points and bridges been devised?

If a wireless LAN is not currently in place, a logical naming convention may need to be devised by the network manager. Using a logical naming convention for access points and bridges on the wireless network will make managing them much easier. For the site surveyor, having logical names in place for each access point and bridge will facilitate the task of documenting the placement of units in the RF Site Survey Report. In the same way, it is always beneficial to have an assigned IP subnet in place for the wireless LAN segment.

Area Usage and Towers Analysis

This next set of questions is used to determine where the wireless LAN needs to operate.

Is the wireless LAN going to be used indoors, outdoors, or both?

Outdoor usage of wireless LAN gear creates many situations and potential obstacles to installing and maintaining a wireless LAN. As we discussed in prior sections, a strong wind can move the antennas and eliminate the signal on a long-distance wireless link. If inclement weather, such as ice or strong rain is often present, radomes (a domelike shell transparent to RF radiation used to house RF antennas) might be considered for protecting outdoor antennas. Radomes should be used for sites with frequent hurricanes or tornadoes. If bridges or access points need to be mounted outdoors as well, a National Electrical Manufacturers'

Association (NEMA)-compliant weatherproof enclosure might be considered, as shown on the NEMA Enclosure Diagram.

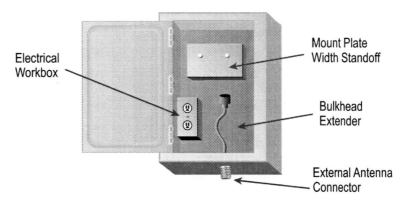

Electrical
Workbox

Mount Plate
Width Standoff

Bulkhead
Extender

External Antenna
Connector

NEMA Enclosure

Outdoor wireless connections are vulnerable to security attacks, because intruders do not have to be inside the building to get into the network. After it is determined that the survey is for indoors, outdoors, or both, obtain any and all property survey documents and diagrams that are available. Indoors, these documents show you the floor layout, firewalls, building structure information, wiring closets, and other valuable information. Outdoors, these documents will show how far the outdoor wireless LAN can safely extend without significant chance of intrusion. By accessing a directional antenna, wireless hackers can intrude upon a wireless LAN that has coverage intended only for indoor users. Hackers can use a directional antenna in this way if the access point is on a power setting that pushes its signal beyond the exterior walls of the building. If the wireless LAN is intended only for indoor use, care must be taken to locate access points to minimize the amount of signal that penetrates outside walls. When outdoors, look for RF signal obstructions, such as other buildings, trees, mountains, and so forth. Checking for other wireless LAN signals at the point where outdoor antennas will be installed is a good idea. If channel 1 in a direct-sequence spread spectrum (DSSS) system were to be used, and subsequently it was found that channel 1 is in use by a nearby outdoor system using an omnidirectional antenna, document in the report that a channel that does not overlap channel 1 should be used for this bridge link.

Is a tower required?

When performing a site survey, a 30-foot tower might be needed on top of a building to clear some trees that are in the direct signal path of an outdoor wireless link. If a tower is required, other questions that need to be asked might include:

- If the roof is to be used; if so, is it adequate to support a tower?
- Is a structural engineer required?
- Is a permit necessary?

A structural engineer may be required to determine if a tower can be placed on top of a building without safety risks to the occupants of the building. Permits may also be necessary to install a tower.

Note: Permits or government approval may be required to install a tower. For example, for towers that are more than 200 feet (61 meters) above ground level, the FCC requires that the FAA be notified prior to constructing or modifying an antenna structure (tower, pole, building, etc.). A 190-foot tall building with an 11-foot tall tower is in this category, for example, because the building (antenna structure) has been modified and exceeds 200 feet. Local municipalities must approve the building of any type of structure (antenna structures or otherwise); therefore, the installer/designer of such a structure should obtain proper permissions or licenses.

Purpose and Business Requirements Analysis

Questions asked during a purpose and business requirements analysis are, "What is the purpose of the wireless LAN? What are the business requirements?" From a temporary office to complete data connectivity for the Olympics, the answer to these questions drives many decisions. When contrasting the temporary office and the Olympics as an example, dozens of issues might surface, such as budget, number of users, outdoor connectivity, temporary network access, and security.

A survey recommending a high-speed 802.11a installation for an organization using only a few wireless PDAs reflects poor judgment and does not consider the needs of the organization's users. As much information as can be gathered is helpful in understanding how a wireless LAN will be used. This information gathering may require interviews with some network users, as well as network management.

Find out exactly what a client expects to do with the wireless LAN and what applications are going to be used over this new network. There might be several distinct and independent purposes for a wireless LAN. Thoroughly documenting the client's needs enables the network architect to design a solution that will meet all of the client's needs, and may also assist the client in their network management.

In order for a site surveyor, and subsequently a design engineer, to keep the business requirements as a main focus, the site surveyor needs a solid understanding of how the network will be used and for what purposes. By knowing how the wireless network affects the business goals of the organization, the site surveyor will be able to create a more effective RF Site Survey Report.

For example, at a ski resort, skiing instructors and ski instructor supervisors use wireless handheld PDAs to coordinate skiing classes running simultaneously across several slopes. Because these handhelds are used over a vast stretch of land, range is very important, but the small amount of data being carried over the wireless network means that many of these wireless PDAs can be used on a single access point at any given time without degraded performance. In contrast, a small workgroup of graphic designers in one room who need access to file servers (to which they transfer large images over the wireless network) need high-speed access, but minimal range. Only a small number of this type of high bandwidth users should be connected to an access point at any given time.

These scenarios show how uses of wireless LANs can vary significantly. Site surveyors must know the business needs of the organization in order to effectively perform a site survey.

Bandwidth and Roaming Requirements Analysis

Next, we ask questions concerning bandwidth and roaming needs:

What are the bandwidth and roaming requirements?

The answer to this question can determine the actual technology that will be implemented, and the technology to use when doing the site survey. For example, if the client is a warehouse facility and the only purpose that its wireless LAN will serve is scanning data from box labels and sending that data to a central server, the bandwidth requirements are very small. Most data collection devices, such as a computer on a forklift in a warehouse, require only 2 Mbps, but require seamless connectivity while moving. However, if a client requires that their wireless LAN serves 35 software developers who need high-speed access to application servers, test servers, and the Internet, consider using 802.11a equipment.

The necessary speed, range, and throughput per user must be determined so that when a site survey is given to an RF design engineer, the design engineer can create a solution that is cost effective and meets the needs of the users. The 2-Mbps Data Rate Diagram shows a survey diagram that will allow 2 Mbps per user, and the 5.5-Mbps Data Rate Diagram allows 5.5 Mbps per user. Most companies are broken into several departments, such as engineering, accounting, marketing, human resources, and so forth. Each department type may have different uses of the wireless LAN in their area.

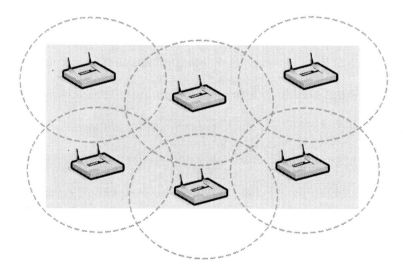

2-Mbps Data Rate

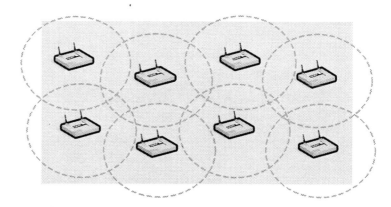

5.5-Mbps Data Rate

How many users are typically present in a given area?

An understanding of how many users will be located in a given area is required to calculate how much throughput each user is going to have. This information is also used to determine which technology, such as 802.11b or 802.11a, is best suited to the needs of the users. If a network manager is not able to provide this information, the person doing the site survey will need to interview the actual users to be able to make an informed decision. (Different departments within an organization have different numbers of users.) It is important to understand that the needs of one part of a facility might be different from the needs of another part of a facility.

What type of applications will be used over the wireless LAN?

Find out if the network is being used to transmit non-real-time data only, or time-sensitive data, such as voice or video. High bandwidth applications, such as voice or video, require more throughput per user than an application that makes infrequent network requests. Connection-oriented applications need to maintain connectivity while roaming. Analyzing and documenting these application requirements before conducting the site survey allows a site surveyor to make more informed decisions when testing areas for coverage.

Are there any nontypical times when network needs may change for a particular area?

A change in network needs could be something as simple as more users being on a particular shift or something as difficult to discover as seasonal changes. For example, if a building-to-building bridge link is surveyed in the winter, the trees lack leaves. In the spring, trees fill with leaves, which in turn fill with water, which could possibly cause problems with the wireless link.

What mobility or roaming coverage is necessary?

Users may want to roam indoors, outdoors, or both. Roaming may also have to incorporate crossing of router boundaries, maintaining virtual private network (VPN) connectivity, and other complex situations. In complex situations, it is important for a site surveyor to document these facts for the wireless network design engineer to have before presenting a solution to the customer. Some areas within or around a facility may require special connectivity solutions, due to blockage of RF coverage or special security requirements, in order to provide roaming.

Available Resources

Among topics to discuss with a network manager regarding available resources are a project's budget, the amount of time allotted for the project, and whether or not the organization has administrators trained on wireless networks. Thus, you would ask "What are the available resources?" If documentation of previous site surveys, current topology and facility maps, and current design plans are available, the site surveyor should request copies of these plans. It is possible that the network administrator may not allow you access to all of these resources, citing security reasons. If so, then the site survey may take additional time.

Another question asked during an available resources analysis is, "Are facility blueprints (electronic or printed) available?" Among the first items to request from a network manager are blueprints or some kind of map showing the layout of the facility, as shown in the Blueprints or Floor Plans Diagram. Without the official building or facility schematics, a diagram must be created that shows the dimensions of the areas, the offices, where the walls are located, network closets, power outlets, and so forth.

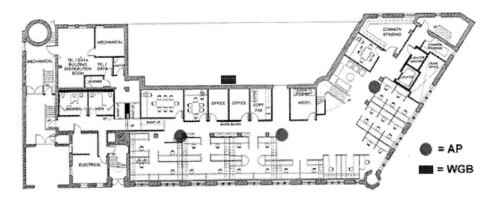

Blueprints or Floor Plans

Note: Creating a facility drawing can be a time-consuming task. If it is necessary to manually create such a document, simple things like notebook paper with grid lines are helpful in being efficient as the site survey is performed. This information can later be put into Visio, AutoCAD, or other such applications for professional presentation to the customer as part of the RF Site Survey Report.

Another question asked during an available resources analysis is, "Are any previous site survey reports available?" If a company has previously had a site survey performed, having that site survey report available can cut down on the time it takes for the new survey to be completed. Be sure that the previous report does not bias the decisions made regarding the current site survey.

Another question asked during an available resources analysis is, "Is a facilities escort or security badge required?" A security badge or an escort may be required to move freely throughout a facility. When performing a site survey, every square foot of the facility is usually covered in order to answer all of the questions needed to define the RF coverage.

Note: It has been said that RF site surveying is 90 percent walking, and 10 percent surveying. This is usually true; thus, one should wear comfortable shoes and make sure that an escort (if necessary) has plenty of time while the survey is being performed.

Another question asked during an available resources analysis is, "Is physical access to wiring closets and the roof available if needed?" Physical access to both the roof and to wiring closets may be needed to determine antenna placement and network connection points.

Security Requirements

One question asked during the security requirements analysis is "What level of network security is necessary?" Customers may have very strict demands for data security, or in some cases, no security may be required. It should be explained to the customer that WEP should not be the only wireless LAN security method used because WEP can be easily circumvented. Briefly educating the customer on available security options is an important step in getting started with a site survey. A discussion with the customer will provide them enough information to feel informed and will allow them to better understand the solutions likely to be presented by the design engineer. After this discussion, the customer may likely have several questions involving wireless network security that may aid the site surveyor in properly documenting the customer's business needs.

Another question asked during the security requirements analysis is, "What corporate policies are in place regarding wireless LAN security implementation and management?" An organization's network manager may not have any security policies in place. If the customer already has a wireless LAN in place, the existing security policies should be reviewed before the site survey is started. If corporate security policies relating to wireless LANs do not exist, ask questions about security requirements regarding installations of wireless LANs.

During the design phase (this phase is not part of the site survey) the RF design engineer can include a security report detailing security suggestions for a particular installation. The network administrator can then take this information and form a corporate policy based on the suggestions. Security policies may differ slightly between small, medium, and enterprise installations, and can sometimes be reused. There are general security practices that are common to all installations of wireless LANs. These policies may also include how to manage the wireless network once it is installed.

Preparation Exercises

As a thought-provoking exercise, consider some of the hypothetical examples mentioned earlier (small office wireless LAN, international airport wireless LAN, and a wireless LAN for connecting all the computers at the Olympics), and then ask the following questions:

- Are the users mobile within the facility (for example, do they have portable computers or desktops)?

- How far—inside or outside—will the users roam and still need connectivity?

- What level of access do the users need to sensitive data on the network? Is security required? How secure is "secure enough?"

- Will the users be able to take their laptop computers away from the wireless LAN where the wireless LAN cards can be stolen?

- Do these users use any bandwidth-intensive, time-sensitive, or connection-oriented applications?

- How often do the users change departments or locations?

- Will any or all of these users have Internet access, and what are the policies regarding e-mail and downloads?

- Does the users' office/work environment ever change for special events that could disrupt a wireless LAN?

- Who currently supports the users on the existing network, and are they qualified to support wireless users?

- If the users are mobile, what type of mobile computing device do they use (for example, PDA or Laptop)?

- How often and for how long will the users with laptops work without A/C power?

There are many specific questions to ask about the users of the wireless LAN and their needs, and this information is vital to a site survey. The more information that can be gathered about who will be using the wireless LAN and for what purpose, the easier it will be to conduct the site survey.

Preparation Checklist

Below is a general list of items that should be obtained from or scheduled with the client prior to visiting the site for the purpose of doing the site survey, if possible:

❑ Building blueprints (including power source documentation)

❑ Previous wireless LAN site survey documentation

❑ Current network diagram (topology map)

❑ A meeting with the network administrator

❑ A meeting with the building manager

❑ A meeting with the security officer

❑ Access to all areas of the facility to be affected by the wireless LAN

❑ Access to wiring closets

❑ Access to the roof (if outdoor antennas are anticipated)

❑ Future construction plans, if available

Now that all of these questions are answered and complete documentation of the facility has been made, you are ready to leave your office and go on site.

Activities

1. When preparing to perform the site survey, why is it important to ask the network manager how long users work on battery power?

   a. This determines the wireless technology used (802.11, 802.11b, or 802.11a)

   b. To determine the bandwidth each client requires

   c. To choose the correct channel frequency

   d. To choose between CAM or PSP capable client devices

2. Your site survey preparation interviews indicate that the customer's users will roam within the building. Which of the following situations should you consider as part of the site survey? (Choose two.)

   a. Router boundaries

   b. Client radio brands

   c. VPN connectivity

   d. access point radio channels

3. Your customer indicates that the new wireless network will support 30-40 computer engineers collaborating on large engineering diagrams across the network. The engineers are located in one "cubicle city" within the building. One or two APs are all they have funded. Given this information, which one of the wireless technologies listed should you consider?

   a. 802.11

   b. 802.11a

   c. 802.11b

   d. 802.11i

4. Your customer wants a wireless link connecting their two warehouses located 2.5 miles from the local airport. They want to mount the antennas on a tower to raise them above several tall trees and other obstacles. As part of your site survey, who will you need to notify?

   a. FAA

   b. FBI

   c. IEEE

   d. NSA

Extended Activity

If possible, obtain copies of your office building, floor, or school blueprints. On the blueprints, locate the network wiring closets, AC outlets, building entrance facilities, and so forth. Do your best to decide where you would locate access points and antennas to provide complete wireless coverage, and indicate these locations on the blueprints. Would you need to use Power over Ethernet (PoE) to power the access points? Will you have problems with the RF signal extending outside the building walls? Will you have access to the wiring closets and necessary AC outlets? Will the users be able to roam seamlessly?

_____

_____

_____

_____

Lesson 3—Site Survey Equipment

This lesson covers the wireless LAN equipment and tools required for a site survey. The type of equipment needed depends on the type of survey. You can assemble your own site survey kit, or buy one preassembled. Regardless of how big or small the survey is, be prepared to do a good deal of walking and writing.

Objectives

At the end of this lesson you will be able to:

- Choose the appropriate equipment and tools to use for a site survey

- Apply a site survey tool to a specific surveying task

 **Key Point**

To perform a good site survey, you will need a wide assortment of surveying tools and software.

Types of Site Survey Equipment

To perform a basic indoor site survey, you will need at least one access point, a variety of antennas, antenna cables and connectors, a laptop computer (or personal digital assistant [PDA]) with a wireless personal computer (PC) card, some site survey utility software, and lots of paper. Some minor things that can be added to your mobile toolkit, such as double-sided tape (for temporarily mounting antennas to the wall), a DC-to-AC converter and batteries (for powering the access point, which lacks a source of AC power), a digital camera for taking pictures of particular locations within a facility, a set of two-way radios if working in teams, and a secure case for the gear. Some manufacturers sell site survey kits already configured, but in many cases, the individual site surveyors prefer to select the tool kit and wireless LAN equipment piece by piece, to ensure that they get all of the pieces they need. A more comprehensive list of equipment required during a site survey is provided in a checklist at the end of this section.

Access Point

The access point used during a site survey should have variable output power and external antenna connectors. The variable output power feature allows for easy sizing of coverage cells during the site survey. This tool is particularly useful for situations involving long hallways, such as in a hospital.

Note: Very few manufacturers have a variable output power feature in an access point, but more vendors are expected to add this feature in the future. It is not hard to see how changing output power in software is more convenient than adding, mounting, and then dismounting and removing antennas with different amounts of gain.

Many experienced site survey professionals have an access point that operates on AC power connected to a DC-to-AC converter, which is connected to a battery pack. This configuration makes the access point mobile, and able to be placed anywhere the site surveyor needs to perform testing. This group of components can be tie-strapped together, or put into a single, portable enclosure. There are companies that have pieced together such a "kit" for the sole purpose of making site surveying easier. Many times the access point will be placed on a ladder or on top of the ceiling tiles while the antenna is temporarily mounted to a wall. Having completely portable gear with no need for AC power makes the site survey go much faster than it would otherwise.

Note: Mobile access points mounted to battery packs and DC-to-AC converters may resemble some sort of dangerous device, and may be confiscated at airports. Make sure you disclose to all security and airports personnel exactly what the configuration is, and what it is for. Placing such devices in a hard-shell travel case and checking the case is usually easier than traveling with these devices as carry-on items.

PC Card and Utilities

High quality wireless PC cards will come with site survey utility software, as shown on the Site Monitor Application Diagram. The site survey utilities from different manufacturers vary in their functionality, but most offer at least a link speed indicator and signal strength. These two tools provide general indications of coverage. To perform a quality site survey, the following actual quantitative measurements should be recorded:

- Signal strength (measured in dBm)
- Noise floor (measured in dBm)
- Signal-to-noise ratio (SNR) (measured in dB)
- Link speed

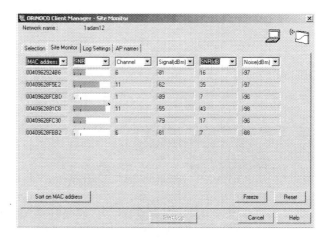

Site Monitor Application

Only a few vendors offer this complete set of tools in their client utility software. An additional tool that can be utilized is a spectrum analyzer, which is used for finding sources of RF interference. With quality site surveying software (whether using one or more wireless PC cards), site survey measurements can be efficiently completed with accuracy.

While walking around the intended coverage area, pay particular attention to the SNR measurement because this measurement shows the strength of the RF signal versus the background noise. This measurement shows the viability of the RF link, and is a good indicator of whether or not a client will connect and remain connected. Many experts agree that an SNR measurement of 22 dB or more is a viable RF link, but there is no hard and fast rule for this measurement. Whether a link is actually viable or not depends on factors other than just SNR, but as long as a link is stable and the access point provides the client with a level of RF power significantly above its sensitivity threshold, the link is considered viable.

A utility that can measure the signal strength, the SNR, and the background RF noise level (called the "noise floor"), such as that shown again on the Site Monitor Application Diagram, is very useful. Knowing the signal strength is useful for finding out if an obstacle is blocking the RF signal or if the access point is not putting out enough power. The SNR measurement lets the site surveyor know if the link is clean and clear enough to be considered viable. Knowing the noise level is useful in determining if RF interference is causing the link a problem or if the level of RF in the environment has changed from the time that a baseline was established. An engineer can use all three of these measurements to make design and troubleshooting determinations.

One function of a wireless PC card that is particularly useful is the ability to change the power output at the client station during the site survey. This feature is useful because a site surveyor should test for situations in which near/far or hidden node problems might exist. Not all site surveyors have the luxury of taking the time to do this sort of testing, but this feature is useful when time permits.

Third party utilities, such as Netstumbler, are valuable utilities during a site survey in which access points and bridges are already in place. These utilities enable the site surveyor to find all of these units quickly and record their information (such as media access control [MAC] address, service set identifier [SSID], Wired Equivalent Privacy [WEP] status, signal strength, SNR, noise, and so forth). These utilities can replace what the driver software and manufacturer utilities miss in many cases.

Link speed monitor utility software can be used to measure the wireless link speed. This information is useful when part of the site survey requirement is to size or shape the cells for 11 Mbps usage by clients. As we learned earlier, Dynamic Rate Shifting (DRS) allows a client to automatically downshift link speeds as range increases. If the business requirements are for all clients to maintain 11 Mbps connectivity while roaming, proper coverage patterns must be documented during the site survey.

Laptops and PDAs

A site surveyor uses a laptop computer or PDA unit to check for signal strength and coverage while roaming around the facility. Many site survey professionals have begun using PDAs, instead of laptop computers, to perform the site survey because of battery life and portability. PDAs can report the same information and connect to the network in the same way as a laptop, but without the 3 to 7 pounds of extra weight. Three to 7 pounds might not seem like much weight, but after carrying a laptop of this weight around a facility that measures over a million square feet, which is a common facility size, a PDA that supports the functionality you need to do your site survey may seem like a worthwhile purchase. Most manufacturers make Pocket PC and Windows CE drivers and utilities (including the site survey utilities) for their Personal Computer Memory Card International Association (PCMCIA) cards.

Miniature laptops that weigh as little as 1.5 pounds are on the market. They also serve the purpose of using a more portable unit for site surveying. However, an ultra-portable laptop tends to cost many times as much as a PDA.

Simple screen-capture software is also beneficial. For reporting purposes, screenshots show the actual results that the site monitoring software displayed. These screenshots will be presented to the customer as part of the RF Site Survey Report, which is why custom screen capture software is useful. Screen capture software packages are available for Windows, Pocket PC, and Linux operating systems.

Laptop batteries rarely last more than 3 hours, and a site survey might last 8-10 hours per day. Always having fresh batteries on hand will keep you productive while onsite. Without the luxury of extra laptop batteries, the only alternative is to charge the batteries during a break, which might not be a good alternative since many laptop batteries charge slowly. Another solution would be to find a very small, power-efficient laptop whose batteries are specified to last much longer than the typical 2-3 hours. As mentioned before, PDA batteries tend to last longer than do laptop batteries.

Paper

Both the surveyor and the network designer should make hard copy (paper) documentation of all findings in great detail for future reference. Digital photographs of a facility make finding a particular location within the facility much easier and serve as graphical information for the RF Site Survey Report as well. During most surveys scratch paper, grid paper, and copies of blueprints or floor plans are necessary. When added to the amount of equipment that will be carried around, this amount of paper and documentation tends to become a burden. For this reason, a sufficiently large mobile equipment cart that can contain all the necessary gear is quite useful while moving through a facility.

There are no industry standard forms for recording all the data that will be necessary during even the smallest site survey. However, it will prove very useful to create a set of forms that suits your style of work and recording, and to use these same forms on every site survey. Not only will this type of uniformity help you communicate your findings to the client, but it will also help maintain accurate and easy to understand records of past site surveys. These forms will be used during the creation of your site survey report as a reference for all readings taken during the site survey.

Outdoor Surveys

Outdoor site surveys will take more time, effort, and equipment than will indoor surveys, which is another reason that planning ahead will greatly improve productivity once on site. If a survey to create an outdoor wireless link is being done, obtain the appropriate antennas, amplifiers, connectors, cabling, and other appropriate equipment before arriving. Generally, the more experienced site surveying professionals do the outside site surveys because of the more complex and involved calculations and configuration scenarios that are necessary for outdoor wireless LANs.

Knowing characteristics of the wireless link (distance, link speed required, power output required, and so forth) beforehand will aid in determining whether just an omni antenna or an entire outdoor testing lab will be required. Remember that it takes <u>two or more</u> antennas to create a wireless link depending on the number of locations involved in the link. Binoculars, comfortable walking shoes, rain gear, different lengths of cables, different types of connectors, and some method of communicating with someone at the other end of the link (for example, a cell phone or walkie-talkie) will also make outdoor site surveys more efficient.

Spectrum Analyzer

Spectrum analyzers come in various types. The two main categories might be considered software and hardware spectrum analyzers. Hardware spectrum analyzers are made by many different manufacturers and may cost many thousands of dollars, depending on resolution, speed, frequency range, and other parameters.

There are companies in the wireless LAN industry who have created software capable of scanning the entire 2.4 GHz range and providing a graphical display of the results, as shown in the Spectrum Analyzer Screenshot Diagram. These products give a user the effective equivalent of a hardware spectrum analyzer, which, although it may not produce precisely accurate quantitative measurements, can give a user a general idea of what sources of RF are in use in the area.

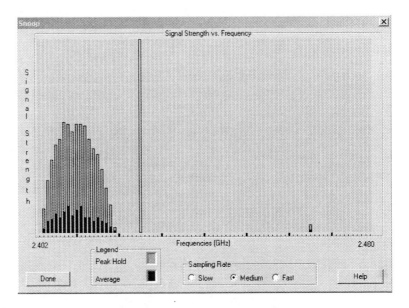

Spectrum Analyzer Screenshot

As part of the spectral analysis, have all the users turn their equipment off, if possible, so that any sources of background interference can be detected, such as low power sources of narrowband interference. Low power narrowband interference is easily located while there are no other sources of RF in use, but is quite difficult to locate when many sources of RF are in use. High power narrowband is easily located with the proper test equipment regardless of additional RF sources.

Part of a spectrum analysis should be to locate any 802.11b or 802.11a networks in use in the area around the implementation area of the proposed wireless LAN. If current or future plans involve installation of 802.11a products, it would be advantageous to both the site surveyor and the customer to know of any 5 GHz RF sources, especially if they are part of a wireless LAN.

Network Analyzer ("Sniffer")

After spectrum analysis is complete, a sniffer can be used to find other wireless LANs that are present in the area (perhaps on another floor of a building), which can affect the wireless LAN implementation. The sniffer will pick up any packets being transmitted by nearby wireless LANs and will provide detailed information on channels in use, distance, and signal strength, as shown on the Wireless Sniffer Screenshot Diagram.

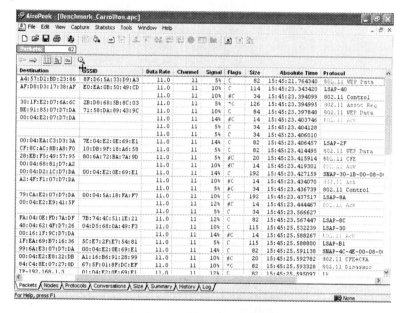

Wireless Sniffer Screenshot

Site Survey Kit Checklist

A complete site survey kit should include:

- ❑ Laptop and/or PDA
- ❑ Wireless PC card with driver and utility software
- ❑ Access points or bridges as needed
- ❑ Battery pack and DC-to-AC converter, as shown in the Access Point with Battery Pack Diagram
- ❑ Site survey utility software (loaded on laptop or PDA)
- ❑ Clipboard, pen, pencils, notebook paper, grid paper, and highlighter
- ❑ Blueprints and network diagrams
- ❑ Indoor and outdoor antennas
- ❑ Cables and connectors
- ❑ Binoculars and two-way radios
- ❑ Umbrella and/or rain suit
- ❑ Specialized software or hardware, such as a spectrum analyzer or sniffer
- ❑ Tools, double-sided tape, and other items for temporary hardware mountings
- ❑ Secure and padded equipment case for housing computers, tools, and secure documents during the survey and travel to and from the survey site
- ❑ Digital camera for taking pictures of particular locations within a facility
- ❑ Battery chargers
- ❑ Variable attenuator, as shown on the Variable Attenuator Diagram
- ❑ Measuring wheel, as shown on the Distance Wheel Diagram
- ❑ Appropriate cart or other mechanism for transporting equipment and documentation

Access Point with Battery Pack

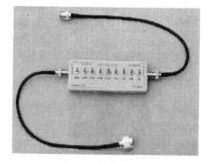

Variable Attenuator

Distance Wheel

If frequent site surveys are part of your business, create a toolkit with all this gear in it, so that you will always have the necessary site survey tools on hand. The last item in the above list—a cart—will become a valued possession after making a few dozen trips back and forth across a large facility moving the hardware and site survey support gear. The Site Survey Travel Case Diagram shows the type of cart that can be used to carry gear.

Site Survey Travel Case

Activities

1. How does using a variable power access point radio simplify the site survey process?

   a. It eliminates the need for a variable power client

   b. It allows you to white out other wireless networks

   c. It allows you to introduce RF interference in the surveyed area

   d. It may eliminate the need to carry multiple gain antennas

2. What does a low signal strength reading taken during a site survey indicate? (Choose two.)

   a. RF noise in the area

   b. Low access point power

   c. An obstacle in the signal path

   d. A low SNR

3. Using an adjustable power wireless client radio during a site survey is useful for measuring which one of the following conditions?

   a. Co-channel interference

   b. Noise

   c. Cell sizing

   d. Client battery usage

4. You are using your wireless client utilities to measure RF signal quality. The SNR measures 10 dB, although signal strength is good. What does this indicate about the RF signal?

   a. The received signal power is low.

   b. The RF link is not viable.

   c. The access point output power is low.

   d. The client antenna gain is low.

5. Why would you use a digital camera when performing a site survey?

   a. To obtain screen snapshots of RF signal levels

   b. To illustrate locations for wireless devices

   c. To prove that you performed the survey

   d. To eliminate the need to use facility blueprints

Extended Activity

As the text mentions, client utilities vary between wireless vendors. Home product utilities do not usually provide the utility features of enterprise-level products. If you have access to the following wireless products, you also have access to an appreciable set of site survey utilities, including: Lucent/Avaya/Agere/Proxim Orinoco wireless PC cards and Proxim RangeLAN2 wireless PC cards.

Additionally, Netstumbler will run on the Orinoco wireless cards.

If you have access to these devices, set up a test network and measure the signal levels, SNR, and noise floor in several areas of the room or building. Collect network information with Netstumbler. What other measurements can you make?

_____

_____

_____

_____

Lesson 4—Conducting a Site Survey

Once you are on site with a complete site survey toolkit, walking several miles throughout the client's facility is common. RF site surveying is 10 percent surveying and 90 percent walking, thus comfortable shoes should be worn when performing site surveys in large facilities. However, the general task of collecting and recording information has not changed. Beginning your site survey with the more general tasks of recording nonrelated information is usually the best course of action.

Objectives

At the end of this lesson you will be able to:

- Gather the appropriate information for an indoor and outdoor site survey

- Record collected information for later use in the site survey report

 **Key Point**

The more pertinent information collected, the better the survey results will be.

Indoor Surveys

For indoor surveys, locate and record the locations of the following items on a copy of the facility blueprints or a drawing of the facility:

- AC power outlets and grounding points

- Wired network connectivity points

- Ladders or lifts that will be needed for mounting access points

- Potential RF obstructions, such as fire doors, metal blinds, metal-mesh windows, and so forth.

- Potential RF sources, such as microwave ovens, elevator motors, baby monitors, 2.4 GHz cordless phones, and so forth. The 2.4-GHz DSSS Phone as Seen by a Spectrum Analyzer Diagram shows a spectrum analysis of a 2.4 GHz direct sequence spread spectrum (DSSS) phone.

- Cluttered areas, such as office cubical farms

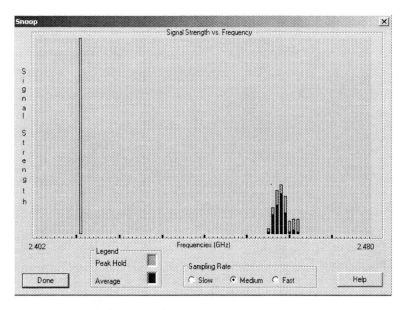

2.4-GHz DSSS Phone as Seen by a Spectrum Analyzer

Outdoor Surveys

For outdoor surveys, record the following items on a copy of a diagram or sketch of the property:

- Trees, buildings, lakes, or other obstructions between link sites

- In winter, identify trees that will grow leaves during other seasons that may interfere with the RF link

- Visual and RF line of sight between transmitter and receiver

- Link distance (if greater than 7 miles [11.7 km], calculate compensation for Earth bulge)

- Weather hazards (wind, rain, snow, lightning) common to the area

- Tower accessibility, height, or need for a new tower

- Roof accessibility, height

Before You Begin

After these preparatory items are checked and recorded, the next step is either to begin the RF site survey, or to obtain more information. Several sources from the above items could require further information from the client, including the following:

- Who will provide ladders and/or lifts for mounting access points on high ceilings?

- Is the client willing or able to remove trees that interfere with the Fresnel zone?

- If a new tower is needed, does the client have the necessary permits?

- Does the client have necessary permissions to install antennas on the roof, and will the roof support a tower if needed?

- Do the building codes require plenum-rated equipment to be used?

Weather hazards may be easier to compensate for if you also reside in the area because you may be familiar with the area's weather patterns. If you do not live there, gathering more detailed information about local weather patterns, such as winds, rain, hail, tornadoes, hurricanes, and other potentially severe weather may be necessary. Remember from the troubleshooting discussion that for the most part, only severe weather disrupts a wireless LAN's functions. However, you must be aware of, prepare, and compensate for these types of weather before the implementation of the wireless network.

You may need lifts and ladders for an area where a trade show or other similar function is going to take place. The event's location may have 40-foot ceilings, and the access points may need to be mounted in the ceiling for proper coverage. OSHA has many regulations regarding ladders and ladder safety.

If a facility such as a trade show is able to provide the personnel, ladders, and lifts to do the installation, let these individuals perform the work. These individuals are familiar with OSHA regulations and have processes in place to obtain the proper permits. The RF Site Survey Report needs to reference any lifts, ladders, or permits required for installation of the wireless LAN. In many cases, a sturdy 6-foot ladder for climbing into drop ceilings is all that is needed.

If an RF cable, Cat5 cable, access point, or any other device must be placed in the plenum (the space between the drop ceiling [false ceiling] and the hard-cap ceiling), the item must be rated to meet building codes, without being placed in a metal protective shell. This restriction also applies to wiring closets.

RF Information Gathering

The next task will be gathering and recording data on RF coverage patterns, coverage gaps (also called "holes" or "dead spots"), data rate capabilities, and other RF-related criteria for your RF Site Survey Report:

- Range and coverage patterns
- Data rate boundaries
- Documentation
- Throughput tests and capacity planning
- Interference sources
- Wired data connectivity and AC power requirements
- Outdoor antenna placement
- Spot checks

Gather and record data for each of these areas by slowly and systematically surveying and measuring the entire facility.

Range and Coverage Patterns

Start by placing an access point in what seems to be a logical location. You may move the access point many times before finding the proper location, as shown on the Access Point Coverage Testing Diagram. Generally speaking, starting in the center of an area is practical when using omni antennas. In contrast, when using semidirectional antennas, consider starting at one end of a stretch of intended coverage area.

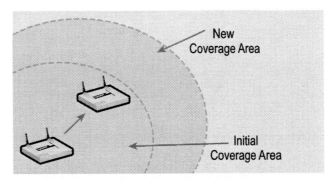

Access Point Coverage Testing

Mark the locations you chose for access points and bridges with bright-colored, easily removable tape. Take a digital picture of the location for use in the site survey report. Do not make location references in the report to objects, such as a temporary desk, table, or plant that may be moved and can no longer provide a reference for locating an access point. Be sure to note orientation of your antennas because not all wireless LAN installers are familiar with antennas.

Various types of antennas can be used for site survey testing, including highly directional, semidirectional, and omnidirectional. When using semidirectional antennas, be sure to take into account the side and back lobes both for coverage and security reasons. Sites may require the use of multiple antenna types to get the appropriate coverage. Long hallways may benefit from Yagi, patch, or panel antennas, while omnidirectional antennas more easily cover large rooms.

Opinions differ about where measuring coverage and data speeds should begin. Some experts recommend starting in a corner, while others say starting in the middle of the room is best. Measurements can start anywhere as long as every point in the room is measured during the survey and covered after installation. Pick a starting point in the room, and slowly walk with your laptop, PC card, and site survey utility software running. While walking, record the following data for every area of the room:

- Data rate (measured in megabits/second [Mbps])

- Signal strength (measured in dBm)

- Noise floor (measured in dBm)

- Signal-to-noise ratio (measured in dB)

Walking fast will speed up the survey process, but may cause you to miss dead spots or potential interference sources. Using a very simple example, the Marked Up Floor Plan Diagram illustrates what the recordings might look like on a floor plan or blueprint.

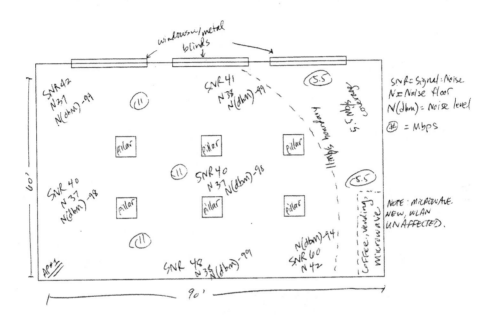

Marked Up Floor Plan

For outdoor coverage areas, be prepared to walk farther and record more. When planning an outdoor installation of an access point (for example, to cover areas between campus buildings), there are usually a very limited number of places where the access point may be mounted. For this reason, moving the access point around is rarely required. On top of a building is the most common location in such an installation. There are potentially many more sources of interference or blockage to a wireless LAN signal outdoors than indoors.

Site surveying is not an exact science, which is why thoroughness and attention to detail are required. Record the measurements for the general areas of the room, including measuring the farthest point from the access point, every corner of the room, and every point in the room at which no signal is present or the data rate either increases or decreases. The answers to the questions that were asked before you arrived on site to do the survey should determine points of measurement. Information such as where users will be seated in a room, where users will be able to roam, the types of users (heavy file transfer or bar-code scanning, for example), and locations of break rooms with microwave ovens all help determine for which points data rate and range should be recorded.

Data Rate Boundaries

Be sure to record the data rate boundaries. These boundaries are also known as the concentric zones around the access point. If you are using an 802.11b wireless LAN, for example, record where the data rate decreases from 11Mbps to 5.5Mbps to 2Mbps to 1Mbps, as shown on the Data Rate Boundaries Diagram. These boundaries should somewhat resemble concentric circles, with the slower data rate areas farther from the access point than the higher data rates. When a user roams out past the coffee machine to the mailroom, the client organization must be told that user will not get the highest possible throughput due to the data rate decrease because of the distance increase.

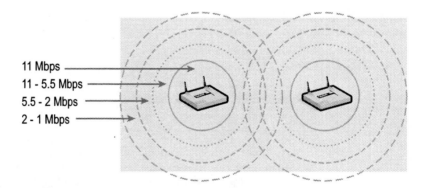

11 Mbps
11 - 5.5 Mbps
5.5 - 2 Mbps
2 - 1 Mbps

Data Rate Boundaries

Documentation

By this point, the copy (or copies) of the facility blueprint should be well marked, with circles, dead spots (if any), data rates, and signal strength measurements in key spots. Now another location within the facility can be documented, and the process begins again. When surveying a small office, and the entire office has facility-wide coverage with maximum throughput from the first testing location chosen, the process does not need to be repeated; the survey is finished. However, that will rarely be the case. Therefore, this lesson will prepare you for the worst-case scenario of site surveying.

Be prepared to repeatedly survey and move, until the optimum coverage pattern for a particular area has been determined. This repetition is the reason for making multiple copies of the facility blueprint or floor plan and bringing lots of paper.

The end result of this portion of the exercise should be a map of the range and coverage of the access point from various locations, with the best results and worst-case results noted. Certainly you can save a lot of time by documenting only the best possible coverage pattern. Thus, in the interest of efficiency, it is a recommended practice to quickly test until a "somewhat optimum" location for the access point is found, and then do the complete set of documentation (drawings, recording of data, and so forth.). Like anything else, it takes practice to become effective at site surveying. Because site surveying is a very time-consuming task, making decisions that affect the use of time is important.

Throughput Tests and Capacity Planning

Conducting throughput testing from various points throughout a facility is another type of measurement (outside of the typical SNR, noise, and signal strength discussed thus far) that can be performed by the site surveyor. Throughput testing will provide valuable information to the wireless network design engineer. The point of doing all of this coverage and data rate documentation is to understand and control what the user's experience will be on the wireless LAN. Doing live throughput tests, such as file transfers to and from a File Transfer Protocol (FTP) server gives the site surveyor a more thorough look at what the user might experience. Sometimes this test is not possible due to a lack of wired infrastructure connectivity, but it is a valuable option when it is available.

Planning for user capacity is very important if the user wants to make productive use of the wireless LAN. From the answers provided by the network manager or administrator, you will know to look for locations within the facility where there are different types of user groups present. For example, if one 50' x 50' area houses 20 people who work from desktop PCs using client/server applications, determine whether or not one access point can provide the necessary capacity, or if co-located access points are required to provide for these users' networking needs. In this scenario, it is likely that at least two access points would be required. In contrast, if 30 doctors are using wirelessly connected PDAs, all connecting through a single access point, co-located access points will probably not be needed due to the fact that a PDA cannot transmit large amounts of data across the network very quickly.

These pieces of information add to the markings on the blueprint in the form of specific data rates, throughput measurements, and capacity notes. With the 11 Mbps coverage circle around each access point (drawn to illustrate that particular coverage area), for example, you might determine that 10 people in that area need a minimum of 500 kbps (per person) throughput at all times. These measurements also determine equipment needs and expenses.

Interference Sources

In this phase of the site survey process, the surveyor will ask questions about potential sources of narrowband and spread spectrum RF interference.

The first question is, "Are there any existing wireless LANs in use in or near the facility?" Existing wireless LANs can cause hardship on a site-surveyor if permission is not provided to disable existing radios as needed. Disabling existing wireless LAN gear may not be possible due to production environments, or the surveyor may have to conduct the site survey during nonproduction hours.

Another question to be answered is, "Are there any plans for future wireless LAN installations other than the one in question?" Determine if there is another wireless LAN project that needs to be included in the analysis. These projects could affect implementation of the wireless LAN for which this site survey is being performed.

Other questions concern organizations near the client:

- If the client is in a multitenant building, do any other organizations within the building have wireless LANs or sources of RF?

- Are any other organizations planning wireless LAN implementations?

For multitenant buildings, it is possible that another organization within the same building is also planning to build a wireless LAN in the future that would impact the site survey, as shown on the Multitenant Office Buildings Diagram. Organizations within the same multitenant office building could have wireless LANs in place disrupting each others' communications. If the location is a high-rise building, try to find out if any of the neighboring high rises have wireless LANs.

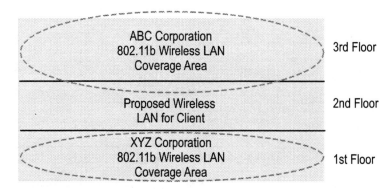

Multitenant Office Buildings

Another question concerns common sources of RF interference. "Are there any other common sources of RF interference in the 2.4-GHz band in use in the facility?" Microwave ovens, 2.4 GHz cordless phones, radiology equipment, and baby monitors are common sources of RF interference in the 2.4-GHz band. These potential interference sources need to be documented in the survey as potential problems with the installation. Microwave ovens can easily be replaced, though radiology equipment in a hospital installation may not be. 2.4 GHz phones running on the same channel as the wireless LAN can render a wireless LAN useless.

Finally, you would ask, "In case 802.11a networks are installed, are there any RF sources in the 5 GHz range?" If there are many other organizations in the area already using 802.11b, using 802.11a avoids the interference caused by trying to coexist with another 802.11b network. However, it should be noted whether other 802.11a networks exist in the area that could interfere with an 802.11a implementation.

Obstacle-Induced Signal Loss

The Signal Loss Table provides estimates on RF signal losses that occur for various objects. Using these values as a reference will save the surveyor from having to calculate these values. For example, if a signal must penetrate drywall, the range of the signal would be reduced by 50 percent. The loss is indicated in decibels, and the resulting range effect is shown.

Signal Loss

Obstruction	Additional Loss (dB)	Effective Range
Open Space	0	100%
Window (nonmetallic tint)	3	70
Window (metallic tint)	5-8	50
Light wall (dry wall)	5-8	50
Medium wall (wood)	10	30
Heavy wall (6" solid core)	15-20	15
Very heavy wall (12" solid core)	20-25	10
Floor/ceiling (solid core)	15-20	15
Floor/ceiling (heavy solid core)	20-25	10

Find and record all sources of interference as you map your range and coverage patterns, as shown on the RF Obstacles Diagram. When measuring the coverage in the break room, for example, measure both when the microwave is running and when it is off. In some cases, the microwave could impact the entire wireless LAN infrastructure if the microwave is an older model. If this is the case, advise the client to purchase a new microwave oven and not use the existing unit. The client and the users need to be aware of the potential interference and possible lack of connectivity from the break room (or wherever a microwave oven is operated).

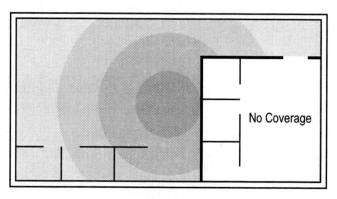

RF Obstacles

Other common sources of indoor interference to look for include metal-mesh cubicles, metal-mesh glass windows, metal blinds, inventory (what if the client manufactures metal blinds?), fire doors, cement walls, elevator motors, telemetry equipment, transformers, fluorescent lights, and metal studded walls (as opposed to wood studs). Piles of objects made of paper, cardboard, wood, and other similar products also serve to block RF signals.

There are standards for how a firewall (a physical fire barrier) may be penetrated. It is important to find firewalls during the site survey because they should be noted in the site survey report. When existing firewalls prevent Cat5 or RF cabling from being implemented in required areas, it should be documented. Firewalls can also hamper the RF signal. Some firewalls have fire doors directly underneath. Do the site survey with the doors closed because some locations require fire doors to remain shut at all times. Poured concrete walls and hard cap ceilings pose the same problems as firewalls.

In a multitenant office building, interference could be caused by a microwave oven belonging to a company located on the same floor or possibly on floors directly above or below you. This situation can pose a difficult problem because you have no jurisdiction over the microwave oven.

There are many outdoor interference sources, and some can change just by their nature. Seek out and record the effects of the following:

- Trees, buildings, lakes, or other obstructions or reflective objects

- Trees without leaves that will later have leaves or will grow to interfere with the Fresnel zone

- Automobile traffic (If you are linking two buildings at first-story height across a road, a large truck or bus could disable the link)

Record the interference source, its location, and its effect and potential effect on wireless LAN coverage, range, and throughput. This data should be recorded both on your copy of the blueprint as well as in a separate list for easy future reference. Taking pictures of interference sources that are permanent (for example, lakes and buildings) will serve as a visual reference to the client. Pictures of potential sources of interference such as young trees or future building sites will also help the client's decision making for the future.

Wired Data Connectivity and AC Power Requirements

While moving an access point around the site, indoors and out, you may not be able to locate the access point in the best positions. Rather, the location will be constrained to where AC power sources exist and network connectivity is within a given distance. Record on the blueprint or floor plan the locations of each AC power source and network connection point. These points will lead to the easier (not necessarily the best) locations for access points. Document and make recommendations for the best locations for all access points. Preferred access point locations may be a solid reason for the client to install new AC power sources as well as new network connectivity points. Remember that many brands of access points can utilize Power over Ethernet (PoE).

Some questions to consider when looking for the best place to install wireless LAN hardware are:

- **Is AC power available?**

  Without an available source of AC power, access points will not function. If AC power is not available in a particular location, an electrician's services may be required (added cost) or Power over Ethernet (PoE) can be used to power the unit.

- **Is grounding available?**

  Proper grounding for all wireless LAN equipment provides added protection against stray currents from lightning strikes or electrical surges.

- **Is wired network connectivity available?**

  If network connectivity is not available, a wireless bridge may be required, or an access point may need to operate in repeater mode to provide network connectivity. Using access points as repeaters is not a desirable scenario, and the network performance is much better if the access point can be wired to the network.

  If the distance between the access point and the network connection is more than 100 meters, shielded twisted-pair (STP) cabling or an access point that supports a fiber connection can be used. However, using an access point that has fiber network connectivity negates the use of PoE and requires a source of AC power nearby. Media converters can be used when fiber runs are necessary. These converters change Cat5 to fiber and vice versa. When using an access point that has only a Cat5 connector, and its nearest network connection is more than 100 meters away, a media converter can solve the problem. Remember that in this configuration, PoE cannot be used.

Cable lengths in the site survey report should be estimated, but never "as the crow flies." Rather, estimate RF connector cable lengths using straight runs with 90-degree turns. Try to keep RF cable runs under 300 feet (91.4 km), but remember to add an extra few feet of cable in case extra length is needed in the future to move the access point or bridge.

- **Are physical obstructions present?**

    Doorways, cement ceilings, walls, or other obstructions can result in some construction costs if they need to be altered to allow for power connections or to run power or data cabling to the access points or antennas.

Outdoor Antenna Placement

For outdoor antenna placement, record the location and availability of grounding points, towers, and potential mounting locations. Outdoor antennas require lightning arrestors, which require grounding. Grounding is an easy point to miss, and the client may not be aware of this necessity. Make notes of where antennas could best be mounted and whether any special mounting materials may be required.

Keep in mind that adding network connectivity outdoors will be a very new concept to most companies implementing wireless LANs. Specify exactly what is required to bring the network outside the building, including cables, power, weather protection, and protection from vandalism and theft.

Spot Checks

After a wireless LAN is installed, it might not work exactly as planned, although it may be close. Spot-checking by a site surveyor after installation is complete is most helpful in avoiding troubleshooting situations during production use of the network. Items that should be checked are:

- Coverage in perimeter areas
- Overlapping coverage for seamless roaming
- Co-channel and adjacent channel interference in all areas

Activities

1. Once a site survey is completed and the wireless LAN is installed, what site survey items should be spot checked to test for proper network operation? (Choose three.)

   a. The client and access point locations

   b. The perimeter area coverage

   c. Seamless roaming coverage

   d. Co-channel and adjacent channel interference

2. How might you compensate for access point distances farther than 100 meters from the wired network connection?

   a. Install PoE repeaters

   b. Install STP cable

   c. Install Cat5 cable

   d. Install fiber optic cable

3. What would likely result from estimating cable lengths "as the crow flies" in the site survey?

   a. Cable runs will be much shorter than estimated.

   b. Cable runs will be much longer than estimated.

   c. RF coverage will be smaller than estimated.

   d. A gain will be much greater than estimated.

4. Which of the following should you consider when deciding where to place antennas for outdoor wireless links? (Choose three.)

   a. Protection from vandalism

   b. Cable penetrations

   c. Aircraft radio traffic

   d. AC power availability

Extended Activities

You are going to install a wireless link between your house and your neighbor's house for the purpose of sharing your broadband Internet connection. The connection must meet the following requirements:

- The link will carry e-mail and Web traffic.

- It will not connect to your home-wired network; it will connect instead only to the Internet through your Internet gateway router.

- You do not want other neighbors to be able to access the link.

- You want to limit the RF coverage to as small an area as possible to prevent signal interception.

- No roaming is required.

- Your neighbor does not own an access point or a wireless client device.

- You will use no antenna towers.

- You do not know if other neighbors are running wireless networks.

List the tools you will need, and the measurements you will take to prepare the site survey. Are there any obstructions with which you should be concerned? What kind of signal loss can you expect if you pass the signal through walls and so forth? Is AC power available? Where will you locate the antenna, APs, and clients? Draw a diagram of your house and your neighbor's house, including potential obstacles.

Lesson 5—Site Survey Reporting

Now that you have thoroughly documented the client's facility, the necessary data is available to prepare a proper report for the client. The report will serve as the map for implementation of the wireless LAN and future reference documentation for the network's administrators and technicians.

Objectives

At the end of this lesson you will be able to:

- Prepare an RF site survey report
- Include the necessary information in the report to support your recommendations

 **Key Point**

A site survey report does more than document the results of the site survey; if properly prepared and presented, it is a valuable marketing tool.

Preparing the Report

The site survey report is the culmination of all the effort thus far, and might take days or even weeks to complete. It may be necessary to revisit the site to gather more data or to confirm some of the initial findings. Several more conversations may be needed with the decision makers and some of the people with whom you were unable to meet when you were on site.

Report Format

There is no body of standards or laws that define how a site survey report should look. The following are recommendations that will serve as a starting point and guideline:

- First, while preparing this report, remember that it is what the client will have after you leave. This work will represent both your knowledge and that of your company.
- Second, you may be doing the wireless LAN implementation, and if so, you will be working from your own documentation. If the report is accurate, the implementation will work as planned.

- Third, save every piece of data collected, and include everything with the report as an attachment, appendix, or another set of documentation. This information may be needed in the future.

After the site survey is delivered and reviewed by the client, ask the client to sign a simple form (the site survey report is your only deliverable) that states that the client has received, reviewed, and accepted the report. The client may ask for additional information before signing off.

Below are the main sections of documentation that should be provided to the client in a site survey report. Include graphics that may help illustrate the data when appropriate.

Purpose and Business Requirements

The site survey report should include all contact information for the site survey company and the client company. Both the site survey company and the customer receive copies of the report.

Restate the customer's wants, needs, and expectations, and provide details of how these wireless LAN expectations can be met (item-by-item) as a result of using the site survey as a roadmap for implementing the new wireless LAN. Supplement this section with graphical representations (either sketches, or copies of actual blueprints) to show the client the types of coverage and wireless connectivity they requested. This section may include an application analysis where the site surveyor has tested the client's application to ensure that the proper implementation of the new wireless LAN provides appropriate coverage and connectivity for wireless nodes.

Methodology

Discuss in detail the methodology for conducting the site survey. Tell the customer exactly what was done, how it was done, and why it was done.

RF Coverage Areas

Detail RF coverage patterns and ranges specific to the requirements that were collected. If the client said that he or she needed 5 Mbps for all users in one particular area, correlate the findings and suggestions against that particular requirement. The concentric circle drawings on the floor plan or blueprint will be the center of attention here. It may also be helpful at this point to detail access point placements that did not work. Document and explain any coverage gaps.

Throughput

Detail bandwidth and throughput findings, showing exactly where in the facility the greatest and the least of each will occur, using the drawings made on blueprint copies. Be sure to include screenshots of the actual numeric measurements that were recorded. These exact numbers help determine the proper solution.

Interference

Detail RF interference and obstruction findings by correlating them to the particular requirements that were collected during the network management interview. Include the location and other details, such as pictures, about each interference source. Include suggestions for removing RF interference sources where possible, and explain how the RF interference sources will affect the wireless LAN once it is installed.

Problem Areas

Discuss in depth the best possible solutions to the RF (and other networking) problems that were found and documented. The client may not be aware of problems that can surface in doing a thorough site survey. This section should include recommendations for which technologies and equipment types will best serve the customer's needs. There is rarely one solution to any technology situation. If possible, present two or three solutions. It is possible that while performing a site survey, you may find problems with the customer's wired LAN. Tactfully mention any problems you find to the network administrator, especially if those problems will directly affect implementation of the wireless LAN.

Drawings

Provide Visio, Computer Assisted Design (CAD), or other types of drawings and graphical illustrations of how the network should be configured, including a topology map. All of the survey findings should be documented in words and pictures. It will be much easier to present a range of coverage using a floor plan instead of only words. Provide floor plan drawings or marked-up blueprints to the customer to graphically show RF findings and recommendations. The Access Point Placement and Coverage Diagram illustrates where access points will be placed on a multifloor installation.

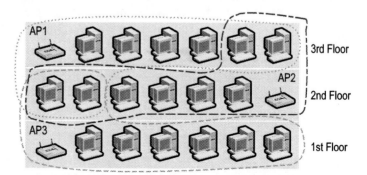

Access Point Placement and Coverage

Provide screenshots of the site monitor software and digital pictures outlining locations of access points and bridges.

As mentioned earlier in this section, the site survey report can take days or weeks, and may require return visits to the site. The site survey report should be a professional technical documentation of your investigation and findings of the client's site, which can serve as a technical reference for the wireless LAN design and future network implementations.

Hardware Placement and Configuration Information

The report should answer the following questions about hardware placement and configuration:

- What is the name of each manageable device?
- Where and how should each access point and bridge be placed or mounted for maximum effectiveness?
- What channels should each access point be on?
- How much output power should each access point deliver?

A list of facts about each access point to be installed (or already installed) should be included in the RF Site Survey Report. This list should include at least the following:

- Name of the device
- Location within facility
- Antenna type to be used
- Power output settings
- Connectors and cables to be used
- Antenna mount type to be used
- How power should be provided to unit
- How data should be provided to unit
- Picture of location where unit is to be installed

Additional Reporting

The site survey report should focus on informing the customer of the best coverage patterns available in the facility. Additional pieces of information that belong in the site survey report are interference findings, equipment types needed, and equipment placement suggestions.

A site survey report should not be turned into a consulting report for implementation and security. A wireless consulting firm should be able to come in, read the site survey report, and then be able to provide effective information on equipment purchasing (including vendor selection) and security solutions. The site survey report should be kept separate from implementation and security reports, which can be equally as involved as the site survey, and require as much time to complete. Often, a company that does quality work during the site survey is asked to return to perform the equipment recommendations, installation, security audits, and subsequent security solution implementations.

Consultants may charge additional fees for a report that includes information about one or more of the following:

- The manufacturers that make appropriate products for this environment and what those particular products are

- The security solution that makes sense for this environment and how to implement it

- Detailed diagrams and drawings that show how to implement the suggested solutions

- Cost and time involved to implement the suggested solutions

- Details of how each wireless LAN requirement listed in the RF Site Survey Report will be met (item-by-item) in the suggested solution.

Recommendations for equipment vendors are very important, and require:

- Knowing each vendor's specialty, strengths, and weaknesses

- The level of support that is available from a vendor and how easy it is to get replacement hardware

- The costs and part numbers of the appropriate hardware

When a customer reads the site survey report, he or she may determine that another vendor offers better or cheaper hardware that can provide the same functionality. Part of the recommendation should be to include justification for the decision in choosing a particular vendor's hardware. In creating a report for the purpose of equipment recommendations and installation, create a detailed equipment purchase list (bill of materials) that covers everything needed to implement a solution that meets the customer's requirements as stated in the site survey. If you recommend three solutions (inexpensive, moderate, and full featured, for example), three complete equipment lists should be provided. Do not omit anything, because it is better to overestimate the potential cost of a solution, and then provide ways to complete the job under budget.

Note: Some customers have contractual obligations to buy a particular brand of wireless LAN hardware. In order to identify this situation, the site surveyor may choose to ask this question as part of the network manager's interview. If not, then this fact should be disclosed during the implementation consultation.

One additional point to keep in mind is that the costs of wired and wireless installations (parts and labor combined) are roughly equivalent. Moving a wired user only once will drastically sway the cost advantage toward the wireless LAN.

Activities

1. Your customer asks you to prepare, as an additional component of your site survey report, a report recommending three equipment solutions. How many lists should you include in the equipment solution report?

   a. 1

   b. 2

   c. 3

   d. 4

2. Which statement is true concerning site survey reports?

   a. It is better to underestimate costs to get the business, and then adjust the project costs later.

   b. A best guess about vendor equipment capabilities is sufficient.

   c. Screen snapshots and drawings are needed to support findings and recommendations.

   d. Leave hardware placement for the implementation report.

3. What are some additional items of information you can offer for an additional fee as a report subsequent to the site survey report? (Choose two.)

   a. The manufacturers that make appropriate products for this environment and what those particular products are

   b. The security solution that makes sense for this environment and how to implement it

   c. Equipment names, locations, radio channel settings, and output power levels

   d. Detailed bandwidth and throughput information concerning existing equipment

4. Which of the following information concerning hardware should be included in the wireless site survey? (Choose two.)

   a. Manageable device names

   b. Manufacturer specifications

   c. Access point channel settings

   d. Client node make and model

5. Why is it important to prepare a good-quality site survey report?

_____

_____

_____

6. Why do you separate the site survey from implementation and security reports?

_____

_____

_____

_____

_____

_____

Extended Activities

Using the information gathered from the Lesson 4 Extended Activities, create a site survey report. Format the report as shown in the sample site survey report located at **ftp://telnet.westnetinc. com/pub/devinstown.pdf**.

Summary

This unit discussed the process of conducting a site survey, also known as a "facilities analysis," and provided a list of the most basic questions that must be answered before the actual physical work of the site survey begins. These questions are purposely open-ended because each one results in more information being passed from a client to the surveyor, making the surveyor better prepared to go on site. This unit also covered the wireless LAN equipment and tools required for a site survey. The type of equipment needed depends on the type of survey; you can assemble your own site survey kit or buy one preassembled. Concepts such as throughput needs, power accessibility, extendibility, application requirements, budget requirements, and signal range are all key components to consider as you conduct a site survey.

After documenting a client's facility, which involves approximately 10 percent surveying and 90 percent walking, the necessary data is available to prepare a proper report for the client. The report serves as the map for implementation of the wireless LAN and future reference documentation for the network's administrators and technicians. This unit also discussed the ramifications of a weak site survey and no site survey at all.

Unit 11 Quiz

1. Which of the following business requirements should be determined prior to beginning the site survey? (Choose two.)

   a. The location of RF coverage areas

   b. Where users will need to roam

   c. Whether or not users will run applications that require Quality of Service

   d. The location of dead spots

2. When determining the contours of RF coverage, site survey utilities should be used to measure which of the following? (Choose three).

   a. Obstructions in the Fresnel Zone

   b. Signal strength

   c. Signal-to-noise ratio

   d. Link speed

3. Which one of the following is true of an RF site survey?

   a. A site survey is not necessary to perform a successful wireless LAN implementation.

   b. A site survey should be performed every six months on all wireless LAN installations.

   c. A site survey is the most important step in implementing a wireless LAN.

   d. Anyone who is familiar with the facility can perform a site survey.

4. Which of the following does a site surveyor need to have before performing an indoor site survey? (Choose two.)

   a. Blueprints or floor plans of the facility

   b. Permission to access the roof and wiring closets

   c. A thorough working knowledge of the existing network infrastructure

   d. Advance notice of all future construction within five miles (8.35 km) of the facility

5. Why is a site survey a requirement for installing a successful wireless LAN?

   a. To determine if a wireless LAN is an appropriate solution for the problem or need

   b. Because RF equipment will not operate in accordance with the manufacturer's specifications without a site survey

   c. To ensure that the client's network managers are experts at RF technology

   d. To determine the range, coverage, and potential RF interference sources

6. Which one of the following should be done prior to conducting a site survey?

   a. Interviewing the network manager or administrator

   b. Preparing a thorough site survey report

   c. Installing temporary access points

   d. Walking the entire facility with a spectrum analyzer

7. Which one of the following measurements is important to record during a site survey?

   a. The signal-to-noise ratio in a particular area

   b. The average temperature of the facility

   c. The average population of people in a given workspace

   d. The humidity in a particular area

8. How long does an average site survey take to perform?

   a. Exactly one eight-hour day

   b. One to five hours

   c. It depends on the facility and client needs

   d. One week

9. Which of the following are pieces of information pertaining to the RF link and are gathered during a site survey? (Choose three.)

   a. Range and coverage pattern

   b. Data rate and throughput

   c. Interference sources

   d. Wired network connectivity and power requirements

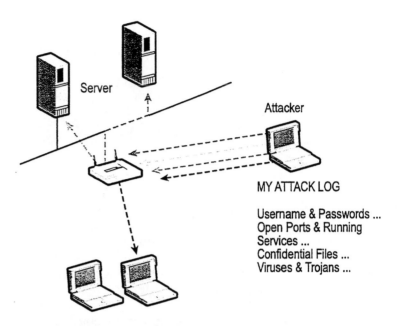

Server

Attacker

MY ATTACK LOG

Username & Passwords ...
Open Ports & Running
Services ...
Confidential Files ...
Viruses & Trojans ...

Active Attack Example

A drive-by spammer or a business competitor who wants access to your files may perpetrate an active attack. A spammer can queue e-mails in his or her laptop, and then connect to your home or business network through the wireless LAN. After obtaining an IP address from your DHCP server, the hacker can send tens of thousands of e-mails using your Internet connection and your Internet service provider (ISP)'s e-mail server without your knowledge. This kind of attack can cause your ISP to cut your connection for e-mail abuse.

A business competitor may try to get your customer list with contact information or perhaps your payroll information to better compete with you or steal your customers. These types of attacks happen regularly without the knowledge of the wireless LAN administrator.

A hacker who has a wireless connection to your network might as well be sitting in his or her own office with a wired connection, because the two scenarios are not much different. Wireless connections offer hackers plenty of speed and access to servers, wide area connections, Internet connections, and users' desktops and laptops. With a few simple tools, it is relatively simple to gather important information, impersonate a user, or even cause damage to the network through reconfiguration. The following harmful actions can be done by following the instructions in off-the-shelf hacker books: probing servers with port scans, creating null sessions to shares, and causing servers to dump passwords to hacking utilities and then logging into servers using existing accounts.

Jamming

Whereas a hacker uses passive and active attacks to gain valuable information from your network or to gain access to your network, jamming is a technique that is used to simply shut down your wireless network. Similar to saboteurs arranging an overwhelming denial of service (DoS) attack aimed at Web servers, an overwhelming RF signal can shut down a wireless LAN. That overwhelming RF signal can be intentional or unintentional, and the signal may be removable or nonremovable. When a hacker stages an intentional jamming attack, the hacker could use wireless LAN equipment, but more likely, the hacker would use a high-power RF signal generator or sweep generator. The Jamming Attack Example Diagram illustrates an example of jamming a wireless LAN.

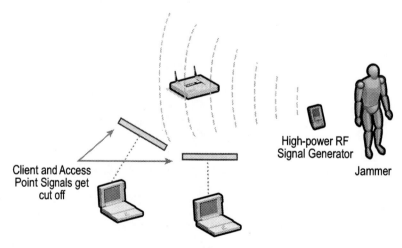

Jamming Attack Example

18. Which of the following are possible sources of RF interference to look for when performing a wireless site survey in a hospital? (Choose four.)

    a. Microwave ovens

    b. Elevator motors

    c. Baby monitors

    d. 2.4 GHz cordless phones

    e. Walkie-talkies

19. Which one of the following is NOT considered a potential RF obstruction?

    a. Fire doors

    b. A large crowd of users

    c. Metal blinds

    d. Metal-mesh windows

    e. Concrete walls

    f. Metal-framed office cubicles

COURSE QUIZ

1. Wireless links over 7 miles long will always experience which effect?

   a. reduced visual LOS

   b. decreased RF LOS

   c. decreased Earth bulge

   d. reduced fresnel zone size

2. You are performing a spectral analysis as part of a site survey. Which of the following actions should you have the users perform to aid you in detecting background noise sources?

   a. reduce their receiver gain

   b. turn off their client devices

   c. increase their transmitter gain

   d. remove any attached antennas

3. Your wireless network consists of two AP's, A and B, operating in root mode. Which statement best describes how the wireless devices communicate on the network?

   a. AP B wirelessly relays roaming client signals to AP A

   b. APs operating in root mode create a wireless backbone for connecting physically separated wired LANs

   c. APs A and B could be used to connect two buildings across a business campus

   d. APs A and B pass data between their respective associated wireless clients over the wired network

4. You need to connect two buildings located on each side of a 100-foot wide drainage canal, and are shopping patch antennas. The site survey indicates that the antennas must double the wireless bridge IR power. Which one of the following is the minimum antenna gain that will meet this requirement?

   a. 3dB

   b. 3dBi

   c. 10dBm

   d. 10dB

5. Which one of the following antenna types would typically provide the most narrowly focused horizontal and vertical beamwidths?

   a. parabolic dish

   b. yagi

   c. "rubber duck"

   d. omnidirectional

6. In which of the following instances will VSWR be a factor? (Choose two.)

   a. a 50 Ohm radio card connected to a 50 Ohm pigtail

   b. a 50 Ohm pigtail connecting to a 75 Ohm attenuator

   c. an unloaded 75 Ohm cable segment connected to a 75 Ohm radio

   d. a 75 Ohm pigtail connecting to a 75 Ohm radio

7. Which of the following determines an RF signal's freznel zone size? (Choose two.)

   a. earth bulge

   b. signal frequency

   c. visual LOS

   d. link distance

8. At the edge of the RF signal's coverage area your 802.11b network operates at 1 Mbps. Which modulation technology are the wireless links using?

   a. 2GFSK

   b. 4GFSK

   c. DBPSK

   d. DQPSK

9. Which one of the following IEEE standards uses OFDM to support bandwidths up to 54Mbps?

   a. 802.11

   b. 802.11b

   c. 802.11g

   d. 802.11h

10. Which type of antenna creates RF signal patterns that consist of a primary forward lobe as well as secondary side and back lobes?

    a. yagi

    b. grid

    c. dipole

    d. dish

11. You determine that your point-to-multipoint wireless bridge link exceeds the FCC stated maximum power output; the antenna's gain has resulted in an EIRP of 8 watts. What size attenuator will you need to insert in the RF signal path in order to comply with the FCC regulations?

    a. -3dB

    b. -3dBi

    c. -.5dB

    d. -10dBm

12. Which of the following is the lower UNII band's maximum allowable point-to-multipoint EIRP?

    a. 12.5mW

    b. 25mW

    c. 50mW

    d. 125mW

13. Within each of the UNII bands, what is the amount of FCC specified separation between channels?

    a. 1MHz

    b. 5MHz

    c. 20MHz

    d. 22MhZ

14. Given the following steps to shared key authentication:

    1. The access point decrypts the challenge text with its own WEP key, and returns an association response frame authenticating the client.

    2. The client makes a request to associate by sending an association request frame.

    3. The client responds to the access point by sending back the challenge text encrypted using the client's WEP key.

    4. The access point sends a clear text challenge to the client.

    Choose the option that lists the above steps in the correct order.

    a. 1, 2, 3, 4

    b. 2, 4, 1, 3

    c. 3, 4, 1, 2

    d. 2, 4, 3, 1

15. Which two of the following choices provide the most secure means of wireless client authentication? (Choose two.)

    a. 128-bit WEP shared key

    b. open system with 40-bit WEP

    c. 40-bit WEP shared key

    d. open system

16. Which factor does an AP use to determine the link speed between itself and a wireless client?

    a. SNR

    b. noise floor

    c. signal strength

    d. distance

17. Which two of the following service sets can use DCF mode? (Choose two.)

    a. EBSS

    b. BSS

    c. EISS

    d. IBSS

18. Which one of the following wireless technologies defines a slot time of 20us?

    a. DSSS

    b. FHSS

    c. Infrared

    d. 802.11a

19. The AP polls PCF mode stations for information during which superframe time period?

    a. contention period

    b. beacon free period

    c. contention free period

    d. PCF poll period

20. Which choice is the largest frame size that can traverse a wireless network segment without fragmentation?

    a. 576 bytes

    b. 1500 bytes

    c. 1518 bytes

    d. 2346 bytes

21. Your wireless link's received RF signal degrades significantly between the transmitter and receiver. Of which connectivity problem is this a symptom?

    a. multipath

    b. near/far

    c. antenna diversity

    d. hidden node

22. Which one of the following would be a source of wireless LAN spread spectrum interference?

    a. baby monitors

    b. microwave ovens

    c. plasma cutters

    d. bluetooth devices

23. Which two of the following might be sources of wireless LAN narrowband interference? (Choose two.)

    a. AM radio stations

    b. microwave ovens

    c. plasma cutters

    d. bluetooth devices

24. Why is the WEP implementation of the RC4 cipher stream considered weak?

    a. WEP only enables encryption up to 128-bit, while RC4 supports up to 192-bit encryption

    b. The IV is broadcast using only 24-bit encryption

    c. The WEP implementation uses only a 24-bit IV, while other implementations use a 128-bit IV

    d. Both 64- and 128-bit WEP transmit the IV in the clear

25. A wireless residential gateway is designed to support a maximum of how many wireless nodes?

    a. 10

    b. 25

    c. 50

    d. 100

26. A wireless residential gateway includes which of the following options? (Choose three.)

    a. network address translator

    b. internal hub or switch

    c. DHCP server and client

    d. modular radio cards

27. You are performing a wireless site survey, and find that the customer is currently operating a HomeRF 2.0 wireless LAN. At what maximum data rate can this network operate?

    a. 1 Mbps

    b. 2 Mbps

    c. 5.5 Mbps

    d. 10 Mbps

28. You are building a wireless network that will need to provide up to 35Mbps maximum throughput. Which of the following configurations will meet this requirement?

    a. three 802.11b APs operating on channels 1, 6 and 11 and three 802.11 APs

    b. 20 802.11 APs operating at the maximum bandwidth

    c. two 802.11b APs operating on channels 1 and 8, and a single 802.11a AP

    d. two 802.11 APs operating at 2Mbps and two 802.11b APs on channels 6 and 8

29. You are building a wireless network consisting of previously wired desktop Ethernet clients. Which of the following devices would allow you to quickly connect these devices to the wireless network without opening the PC cases?

    a. home wireless gateway

    b. wireless Ethernet converter

    c. PCMCIA wireless converter

    d. AP operating in repeater mode

30. You plan to convert 50 wired laptop and desktop PCs to wireless LAN clients. You want to purchase a single wireless client device that would work on both types of PCs. Which one of the following client devices is the best choice?

    a. USB device

    b. PCMCIA device

    c. PCI device

    d. CF device

31. How many channels must exist between two 802.11b frequency bands in order to avoid channel overlap?

    a. 2

    b. 3

    c. 4

    d. 5

32. An FHSS system is configured with a dwell time of 50ms per frequency. According to the FCC pre-8/31/00 rules, how many times must the wireless nodes hop through the entire frequency spectrum?

    a. 2

    b. 3

    c. 6

    d. 8

33. An FHSS system is configured according to FCC post-8/31/00 rules. If a device is currently transmitting at 2.456 GHz, its next hop must be at least to either of which two of the following frequencies? (Choose two.)

    a. 2.441 GHz

    b. 2.450 GHz

    c. 2.462GHz

    d. 2.471GHz

34. Which three of the following specifications would you consider when choosing an RF amplifier? (Choose three.)

    a. gain

    b. power

    c. data rate

    d. frequency range

35. You are choosing between four RF antennas for a building to building link. Based on the information listed below, which antenna is the best choice?

    • Antenna A: VSWR 1.4:1

    • Antenna B: VSWR 1.3:1

    • Antenna C: VSWR 1.1:1

    • Antenna D: VSWR 1.2:1

   a. Antenna A

   b. Antenna B

   c. Antenna C

   d. Antenna D

36. Why are pigtails often used to connect antennas to wireless devices?

   a. to extend the RF signal's coverage area

   b. to adapt one vendor's radio card to another vendor's AP

   c. to allow the client to move around freely within the RF coverage area

   d. to adapt proprietary connectors to industry standard antennas

37. Which of the following would be a connector type you might see used on an antenna cable? (Choose two.)

   a. N-type

   b. F

   c. ST

   d. SC

38. You are installing a single AP to service wireless clients on either side of a building firewall. Below the AP is a fire door that is normally closed. You need to ensure that wireless clients on each side of the wall are able to reliably connect to the AP. Without installing a second AP, which one of the following options best meets your requirements?

   a. install a second AP radio card, assign it a non-overlapping channel, and use PIFS

   b. increase the AP radio signal to "blast" through the firewall

   c. use RTS/CTS, install an RF splitter, and place antenna's on each side of the firewall

   d. use RTS/CTS and increase the client power on the side of the wall opposite the AP

39. You have configured an 802.11b wireless bridge link between buildings located several miles from each other. Though the RF signal leaves the antenna at the FCC allowed maximum EIRP, the received signal power is near the noise floor. What might you do to resolve this problem?

    a. Change from 802.11b to 802.11a

    b. Use a lower frequency link

    c. Use a lower frequency DSSS channel

    d. Use a higher frequency link

40. Which two of the following frequency bands does the FCC specify for use by wireless LANs? (Choose two.)

    a. 900MHz ISM

    b. 2.4GHz IR

    c. 2.4GHz ISM

    d. 5.8 GHz ISM

41. In which two of the following power classes do Bluetooth devices operate? (Choose two.)

    a. 1mW

    b. 50mW

    c. 100mW

    d. 125mW

42. The 802.11i working group proposes which encryption standard as a replacement for the RC4 algorithm used in WEP?

    a. AES

    b. EAP

    c. EAS

    d. DES

43. Which technique do most LAN administrators use to avoid requiring double-logins when using EAP?

    a. limit clients to only data link layer connections

    b. use the same user database for layer 2 and higher logons

    c. use WEP at layer 2, and EAP at the higher layers

    d. use NDS instead of NT authentication at the higher layers

44. Which portion of a wireless frame does a VPN tunnel secure?

    a. the data packet

    b. the WEP key

    c. the MAC address

    d. the SSID

45. Which term is another name for Lightweight Extensible Authentication Protocol (LEAP)?

    a. EAP-Cisco Wireless

    b. EAP-MD-5 Challenge

    c. EAP-Tunneled Transport Layer Security

    d. EAP-Secured Remote Password

46. Which statement describes how a basic service set (BSS) functions?

    a. clients pass packets back and forth directly

    b. clients pass packets back and forth via the AP

    c. clients roam seamlessly between APs

    d. clients pass packets to other service sets via gateways

47. Which statement is true concerning how the 802.11b standard addresses roaming on wireless LANs?

    a. it specifies protocols that enable APs to forward packets to the next AP to which the client is associated

    b. it includes utilities designed to resolve lost connection problems when DHCP is used on the network

    c. it leaves much of the details of how APs handle roaming clients up to the manufacturers

    d. it specifies interoperability standards between manufacturers' roaming solutions

48. A wireless client sends re-association frames in which one of the following circumstances?

    a. when roaming between APs

    b. when first joining the network

    c. when the first or subsequent attempts to join the network fail

    d. when shifting data rates

49. Which two of the following statements are true concerning the post-8/31/00 FHSS rules? (Choose two.)

    a. specifies a 15 hops per sequence minimum

    b. a point-to-multipoint system can output up to 1 watt IR

    c. the carrier frequency can be a maximum of 5MHz

    d. specifies 75 hops per sequence minimum

50. Which two of the following statements are true concerning 802.11b wireless LAN channels? (Choose two.)

    a. each channel is separated by 3MHz

    b. European wireless networks use 11 channels

    c. each channel is 25MHz wide

    d. each channel starts 5MHz after the previous

GLOSSARY

5-Unified Protocol (5-UP™)—5-UP is a standard proposed by Atheros Communications to enhance the features of 802.11a and HiperLAN/2 into one interoperable standard.

10BaseTX—10BaseTX is the IEEE standard for 10 Mbps baseband Ethernet over twisted-pair wire.

100BaseFX—100BaseFX is the IEEE standard for 100 Mbps baseband Ethernet over optical fiber.

100BaseT—The group of proposed IEEE 802.3 Physical Layer specifications for 100-Mbps Ethernet (fast Ethernet) over various wiring specifications is referred to as 100BaseT. Fast Ethernet and the 100BaseT standard are synonymous. 100BaseT is the specification for twisted pair wiring in a Fast Ethernet environment.

100BaseTX—100BaseTX is the IEEE standard for a 100 Mbps baseband Ethernet over twisted-pair wire.

802.1p—802.1p is the IEEE extension to the 802.1D media access control (MAC) bridges standard. IEEE 802.1p allows MAC layer frames on the network to be prioritized. IEEE 802.1p uses a portion of the 802.1Q VLAN tag to represent one of eight possible priority values, each mapped to one of eight traffic classes.

802.1Q—IEEE 802.1Q is a vendor-neutral standard for modifying a frame header to represent the frame's virtual local area network (VLAN) membership. This modified header is transferred between 802.1Q-capable switches and bridges, but is not passed to clients.

802.1x—IEEE 802.1x is a recently approved IEEE standard for port-based access control. It is used to control access to a network access device (switch, access point, etc.).

802.1x authentication server—An 802.1x authentication server is a network device that determines if a client is authorized to access the network. The authenticator contacts the authentication server to verify client credentials.

802.1x authenticator—An 802.1x authenticator is a network device that desires to authenticate a network client. The authenticator is the port with which the client, or supplicant, wishes to authenticate.

802.1x supplicant—An 802.1x supplicant is a client device that uses the services of the authenticator.

802.3af—IEEE 802.3af is a standard proposed by the Institute of Electrical and Electronic Engineers (IEEE) for powering Ethernet devices over twisted pair cabling. IEEE 802.3af is a legacy Ethernet-compatible, internationally standard power distribution technique.

802.5—See Token Ring.

802.11—802.11 is the IEEE standard that specifies medium access and Physical Layer specifications for 1 Mbps and 2 Mbps wireless connectivity between fixed, portable, and moving stations within a local area.

802.11a—802.11a, a revision to the IEEE standard, operates in the unlicensed 5 GHz band. Most 802.11a products have data rates up to 54 Mbps and must support 6, 12, and 24 Mbps.

802.11b—802.11b is a revision to the IEEE standard for direct sequence wireless LANs. Most 802.11b products have data rates of up to 11 Mbps, even though the standard does not specify the techniques for achieving these data rates.

802.11f—IEEE 802.11f is an IEEE draft specification that proposes a set of functions and protocols that will enable multi-vendor access points to support roaming on a wireless network. An Interaccess Point Protocol (IAPP) will map media access control (MAC) addresses to distributed system (access point) addresses, in order to support client reassociation as they move between APs.

802.11g—IEEE 802.1g is a proposed wireless network standard designed to provide the bandwidth of 802.11a networks while maintaining backward compatibility with 802.11b networks. 802.11g operates in the 2.4-GHz ISM band.

802.15 Bluetooth—Bluetooth is a close-range, frequency hopping technology that operates in the 2.4-GHz ISM band and hops at a rate of 1600 hops per second. Bluetooth devices create all-band interference with other 2.4-GHz ISM band devices. Bluetooth is considered Wireless Personal Area Network (WPAN) technology and does not directly compete against Wi-Fi devices in the market.

access layer—The access layer provides client devices access to the network in a three-layer hierarchy network design.

access point—An access point is a Layer 2 (Data Link Layer) device that serves as an interface between the wireless network and a wired network and can control medium access using RTS/CTS. Access points combined with a distribution system (Ethernet, for example) support the creation of multiple radio cells (also called basic service sets [BSSs]) that enable roaming throughout a facility.

acknowledgment (ACK)—In networking, an acknowledgement is an indication from the receiving device that information has been successfully received. In wireless LANs, an ACK frame indicates that the target device received the data frame.

ad hoc network—An ad hoc network is a wireless network composed of only stations and no access point.

adjacent channel interference—Adjacent channel interference is interference caused when a channel exceeds its assigned frequency band, and "spills over" into the band assigned to another channel.

Advanced Encryption Standard (AES)—AES is an encryption technique that improves upon the RC-4 algorithm used in WEP. AES uses the Rijndael algorithm and is considered uncrackable.

all-band interference—All-band interference is radio frequency (RF) interference that covers the entire usable RF spectrum of a certain wireless technology. For example, 802.15 Bluetooth creates interference across the entire 2.4-GHz ISM band.

alternating current (AC)—AC is the alternatively positive and negative polarity current supplied to homes and businesses by the local utility company. U.S. AC power changes polarity 60 times per second; each cycle is called a "hertz." Hence, U.S. AC current is known as 60-Hz power. Other countries in Europe and the Far East use 240-volt AC (VAC) at 50 Hz.

amplifier—An amplifier is used to increase signal strength between the transmitter/receiver and the antenna along the antenna cable.

amplitude—Amplitude is the height of a wave, or how far from the center it swings.

Announcement Traffic Information Message (ATIM)—ATIM is used in ad hoc mode to indicate to stations the presence of transmissions bound for a particular station. ATIM tells stations not to enter sleep mode before receiving their transmitted frames.

antenna diversity—Antenna diversity is the use of multiple antennas on wireless APs or client radios to allow the device to sample the received signals and choose the antenna with the best reception.

AppleTalk—AppleTalk is Apple's proprietary, seven-layer, peer-to-peer network communications protocol for MacIntosh networks. AppleTalk runs on Apple network topologies and over Ethernet and Token Ring networks.

association service—An association service is an IEEE 802.11 service that enables the mapping of a wireless station to the distribution system by means of an access point.

association table—An association table is a list of wireless client devices associated with the access point. The association table shows the client connection status, including the connection state.

Asymmetric Digital Subscriber Line (ADSL)—ADSL is a relatively new technology used to deliver high-speed digital communications across the local loop over standard local loop copper wire. ADSL data rates range from 128 Kbps to over 1.5 Mbps downstream, and 64 Kbps to over 640 Kbps upstream.

Asynchronous Transfer Mode (ATM)—ATM is connection-oriented cell relay technology based on (53-byte) cells. An ATM network consists of ATM switches that form multiple virtual circuits to carry groups of cells from source to destination. ATM can provides high-speed transport services for audio, data, and video.

authentication—Authentication is the process a station uses to announce its identity to another station. The IEEE 802.11 standard specifies two forms of authentication: open system and shared key.

authentication, authorization, and accounting (AAA)—AAA is the method by which users are authenticated, authorized, and tracked to gain access and move about inside a network.

automatic rate selection (ARS)—See Dynamic Rate Shifting.

bandwidth control unit (BCU)—A BCU is a network device installed between a wired network device, such as a switch or router, and an access point; it controls the amount of network bandwidth used by wireless users.

Barker code—Barker code is one of the spreading codes (a.k.a. chipping codes) used in 802.11- based wireless LANs.

basic service set (BSS)—BSS is a set of 802.11-compliant stations and an access point that operate as a fully connected wireless network.

basic service set identifier (BSSID)—A BSSID is a 6-byte address that distinguishes a particular access point from others.

beacon—See beacon management frame.

beacon management frame—Beacon management frames are short frames sent from the access point to the stations in infrastructure mode or from station-to-station in adhoc mode. They are used to organize and synchronize wireless LAN communications.

beamwidth—Beamwidth is the measure of the horizontal and vertical lobes of an antenna signal. An omnidirectional antenna has a 360-degree horizontal beamwidth, while a semidirectional antenna may only have a 30-degree beamwidth.

bidirectional amplifier—A bidirectional amplifier is an RF amplifier that boosts (adds gain) to both the transmitted and received signal.

Binary Phase Shift Keying (BPSK)—BPSK is a signal modulation technique that shifts the carrier frequency between two states to represent the transmitted data.

biometrics—Biometric identification techniques identify users by a physical feature, such as fingerprints, the blood vessel pattern in the retina, or voice characteristics.

bit error rate (BER)—BER is the number of erroneous bits divided by the total number of bits transmitted, received, or processed over some stipulated period.

BNC—Short for British Naval Connector (or Bayonet Nut Connector), BNC connectors are small devices used to connect computers to a thin coaxial cable bus (10Base2) or terminate the ends of a bus.

There are several different types of BNC connectors. A BNC barrel connector joins two Thinnet cables. A BNC terminator is used to terminate the end of a cable. It acts as a resistive load that absorbs the signal that reaches one end of the bus. (Two terminators are needed on each bus.) BNC adapters connect different types of cable, such as Thinnet to Thicknet. BNC connectors can also be used to connect some monitors, which increases the accuracy of the signals sent from the video adapter.

bridge mode—A bridge is a network component that provides internetworking functionality at the data link layer. A wireless access point operating in bridge mode serves to wirelessly bridge multiple wired segments.

broadcast—The term broadcast is used in several different ways in communications and networking. With respect to LANs, the term refers to information (frames) sent to all devices on the physical segment. For example, a bus topology, in which a common cable is used to connect devices, is considered a broadcast technology.

cable modem—A cable modem is a device located in a cable television subscriber's home that provides broadband Internet access over a cable television provider's network.

Canadian Department of Communications (DOC)—The DOC is the Canadian equivalent to the U.S. Federal Communications Commission (FCC) and is now called "Industry Canada."

Carrier Sense Multiple Access/Collision Avoidance (CSMA/CA)—CSMA/CA is a type of contention protocol. It is a set of rules determining use of the wireless medium, and it is used to prevent collisions in a wireless network. Use of this protocol means that all stations that want to transmit will listen for other transmissions in the air, and if there are transmissions, they will back off for a random period of time, and then try again. As soon as no transmissions are detected, the station will begin transmitting.

Carrier Sense Multiple Access/Collision Detection (CSMA/CD)—CSMA/CD is a type of contention protocol. It is a set of rules determining how network devices respond when two devices attempt to use a data channel simultaneously (called a collision). Standard Ethernet networks use CSMA/CD. This standard enables devices to detect a collision. After detecting a collision, a device waits a random delay time and then attempts to retransmit the message. If the device detects a collision again, it waits a longer period of time to attempt retransmission of the message. This is known as exponential back off.

Category 5 UTP data cable—Category 5 cabling is certified for data rates up to 100 Mbps, which facilitates 802.3 100BaseT (Ethernet) networks.

cell—In wireless networking terminology, a cell is the coverage area created by the radio signal transmitted by a single access point.

Challenge Handshake Authentication Protocol (CHAP)—CHAP is a protocol used to authenticate remote network access over Point-to-Point Protocol. CHAP initiates a three-way handshake between the remote access service client and the server. The server responds to the client authentication request with a randomly generated challenge value. The client requestor generates and sends to the server a one-way hashed response, which the server uses to verify the user's identity and access permissions.

channel—In wireless networks, a channel is a set of frequencies used between two or more communicating devices.

channel reuse—During channel reuse, a technique used in large wireless LANs, nonoverlapping channels alternatively provide multicell seamless roaming while avoiding co-channel and adjacent channel interference. Cells are arranged side-by-side to form a mesh of nonoverlapping channels.

chip—A chip is a component of a spread spectrum radio frequency (RF) signal that determines the frequency shift rate. The number of chips in the chipping code determines the amount of spreading that occurs; the number of chips per bit and the speed of the code determine the data rate.

chipping code—The chipping code represents how the data bits sent on a set of RF carrier frequencies are spread across the frequencies. The wider the spreading is, the higher the resistance to narrowband interference. Also, the wider the bit spreading is, the higher the processing gain.

chips—Chips are a set of bits used in wireless LANs to indicate a single bit of digital data. It may take 10 or 11 chips (0s or 1s) to equal one data bit.

cipher—Cipher is a generic term used to describe the algorithms an encryption technique uses to scramble data to protect it from interception.

co-channel interference—Co-channel interference is RF interference caused by wireless access points operating on the same channel in close proximity to each other.

Code Division Multiple Access (CDMA)—CDMA is a form of cellular communications that uses spread spectrum technologies.

co-location—Co-location is the arrangement of multiple access points (APs) within the same physical area. When co-located, APs can interfere with one another, or if properly configured, provide additional bandwidth, throughput, and failover capabilities.

Command Line Interface (CLI)—A CLI is a method of managing network devices from a terminal–like interface, where the administrator inputs commands in a textual format.

compact flash (CF)—CF is a small form factor (1.7" x 1.4" x .13" thick) expansion card, designed initially in 1994 by the SanDisk Corporation as nonvolatile storage. CF devices now provide input/output functionality (modems, networking) for palmtop PCs and personal digital devices (PDAs).

complementary code keying (CCK)—CCK is one of the spreading codes used in 802.11b wireless LANs operating at 5.5 and 11 Mbps. The spreading code determines how large a frequency range the signal covers.

contention—Contention in data communications networks occurs when two stations attempt to send data over a shared communications medium at the same time. The most common occurrence of this is found with the Ethernet protocol (CSMA/CD). When this occurs, the data on the bus is corrupted and each station must retransmit its data.

contention-free period—The contention-free period is the portion of the super-frame that the access point uses to poll those stations operating in PCF mode for data. During the contention-free period, DCF modes sense the medium as busy through Network Allocation Vector (NAV)

timers and clear channel assessments and wait to transmit.

contention period—The contention period is the portion of the superframe that allows DCF mode stations to contend for access to the medium. No polling of PCF stations occurs during the contention period.

core layer—In a three-layer hierarchy network design, the core layer provides access to external networks, and routes packets between distribution layers. The core layer should be fast, versatile, stable, and redundant.

coverage area—An RF signal's coverage area is the area around the access point where the radio signal is of sufficient strength and quality to provide acceptable throughput to wireless clients.

data encryption standard (DES)—DES is a cryptographic algorithm that protects unclassified computer data. DES is a National Institute of Standards and Technology (NIST) standard and is available for both public and government use. DES is a popular single-key encryption system that uses a 56-bit key. 3DES uses the DES algorithm to encrypt a message three times, using two 56-bit keys. It is considered a hardware solution to encryption because of the time necessary to encrypt and decrypt a message.

data rate—Data rate is the rate, in bits per second, that data traverses a network.

dead spot—A dead spot is a point in an RF signal's path where an obstacle blocks signal coverage.

decibel (dB)—A decibel is a logarithmic relational measure of a change in power in watts or milliwatts. Decibels allow us to represent very small or very large power levels in an easily read form. Power gain and loss (positive or negative changes) are measured in dBs.

decibels isotropic (dBi)—dBi is the unit of measure of an antenna's gain.

decibels referenced to one milliwatt (dBm)—A dBm is an absolute measure of signal power, defined as the relationship of the dB scale to the watt scale with a reference point of 1mW. On this scale, 1mW equates to 0dBm.

Differentiated Services (DiffServ)—DiffServ is an IETF recommended protocol used to provide IP traffic preferential treatment across a network. DiffServ uses the IP packet header priority bits to represent traffic forwarding classes (FCs). These forwarding classes tell network routers and switches how each is to handle the DiffServ marked packets. Packets needing QoS can be routed over high-bandwidth, low-delay paths, while routine data packets may be routed over busier, lower throughput links.

diffraction—Diffraction occurs when a surface with sharp irregularities or a rough surface obstructs an RF signal's path. The RF wavefront bends around the obstruction, changing the signal's path.

Direct Sequence Spread Spectrum (DSSS)—DSSS combines a data signal at the sending station with a higher data rate bit sequence, which many refer to as a chip sequence (directly related to processing gain). A high processing gain increases a signal's resistance to interference. The minimum processing gain that the FCC allows is 10, and most products operate under 20.

distance wheel—A distance wheel is a handheld device with a wheel on one end and a handle on the other. It is used to roll across an area to be measured, and it represents the measurement in a specified unit.

distributed coordinated function interframe space (DIFS)—DIFS is the longest 802.11 fixed interframe space used to control when DCF nodes can contend for the network medium.

distributed coordination function (DCF)—DCF mode is a mode during which all stations, including the access point, contend for access using the CSMA/CA protocol.

distribution layer—In a three-layer hierarchy network design, the distribution layer moves packets between the access layers, and passes information up to the core layer.

Domain Name System (DNS)—DNS is the online distributed database system used to map human-readable computer names into IP addresses. DNS servers throughout the connected Internet implement a hierarchical namespace that allows sites freedom in assigning computer names and addresses. In addition, DNS supports separate mappings between mail destinations and IP addresses.

downfade—Downfade is the reduction of the received RF signal amplitude as a result of multipath.

Drip loop—A drip loop is installed in a cable run to provide a path for moisture to run away from the connectors and entry facilities. Hence, the drip loop is installed below the cable entrance.

dwell time—The dwell time is the amount of time a frequency hopping device remains on a single carrier frequency.

Dynamic Host Configuration Protocol (DHCP)—DHCP issues IP addresses automatically within a specified range to devices such as PCs when they are first powered on. The device retains the use of the IP address for a specific license period that the system administrator can define. DHCP is available as part of many operating systems including Microsoft Windows, NT Server, and UNIX.

dynamic rate shifting—Dynamic rate shifting is a method by which wireless LAN clients will fall back to lower data rates when bit error rates exceed a predefined level due to interference or radio signal attenuation. Clients will shift to higher rates when signal attenuation or interference is no longer present.

EAP Tunneled Transport Layer Security (TTLS)—EAP-TTLS extends EAP-TLS by tunneling legacy, password-based authentication over the secure connection created during the TLS handshake. Therefore, less secure password-passing algorithms can still authenticate over an EAP-TLS secured communications channel.

EAPCisco Wireless (Cisco LEAP)—LEAP, developed by Cisco Systems, Inc., is an authentication algorithm that enhances WEP by supporting 802.1x port-level access control. LEAP requires mutual authentication between the user and the access point, ensuring that rogue APs cannot masquerade as authentic network APs. As with other EAP versions, LEAP uses authentication servers to perform the client authentication process.

EAP-Secure Remote Password (SRP)—EAP-SRP uses the authentication mechanism defined in RFC 2945 to eliminate the vulnerability of password-based authentication to interception and subsequent cracking. EAP-SRP uses hashing algorithms and secure-key exchanges between the client and the authenticator. The authenticator stores a verifier for each client, and uses this to ensure the client's password is not compromised.

EAP-Subscriber Identity Module (EAP-SIM [GSM])—EAP-SIM is an EAP authentication mechanism for use on GSM networks. EAP-SIM uses a challenge-response mechanism based on a 128-bit long random number (RAND) challenge generated by the SIM installed inside a wireless device. The calling client contacts the carrier network, which refers the caller to the EAP authenticator. The EAP authenticator requests the caller's identity, and the client responds with its unique identity. The authenticator then asks for the client's SIM packet, and the client responds with a 32-bit response and 64-bit key. The authenticator verifies the response and sends back a challenge. The client runs the authentication algorithm on the SIM, and responds to the challenge. Assuming all progressed as desired, and the client is authenticated, communications can commence.

EAP-Transport Layer Security (TLS)—EAP-TLS uses the TLS protocol to ensure private communications between two users over a public network. TLS protects client/server applications from eavesdropping, interception, and forgery by using two protocol layers: the Record Protocol and the Handshake Protocol. The Record Protocol ensures privacy through the use of data encryption and reliability with a message integrity check. The Handshake Protocol verifies peer entity identities, negotiates a secure shared secret, and verifies the integrity of the negotiation process.

Earth ground—Earth ground is a rod or grid driven into or buried in the Earth for the purpose of providing electrical signals a path to ground. Earth ground provides lightning and over-current protection and is often used as a zero-reference voltage point.

encoding—Encoding is the process of translating binary data (1s and 0s) into signals to be transmitted across a physical link. The most common signaling forms are electrical signals, light signals, and radio signals.

equivalent isotropically radiated power (EIRP)—EIRP is the power actually radiated by the antenna element. This concept is important because the FCC regulates EIRP, and EIRP is used in calculating whether or not a wireless link is viable. EIRP takes into account the gain of the antenna.

Ethernet—Ethernet technology, originally developed in the 1970s by Xerox Corporation in conjunction with Intel and DEC, is now the primary medium for LANs. The original Ethernet has 10-Mbps throughput and uses the CSMA/CD method to access the physical media. Fast Ethernet (100-Mbps Ethernet) and Gigabit Ethernet (1,000-Mbps Ethernet) are also used.

Ethernet switch—An Ethernet switch is a connectivity device that is more intelligent than a hub, having the ability to connect the sending station directly to the receiving station in a full duplex configuration. Additionally, it has filtering and learning capabilities.

European Telecommunications Standards Institute (ETSI)—ETSI is a nonprofit organization whose mission is to produce the telecommunications standards that will be used throughout Europe, including Hiper-LAN/1 and HiperLAN/2.

Extended Interframe Space (EIFS)—EIFS is a variable-length space used as a waiting period after a device receives a frame with a bad frame check sequence. EIFS is used in DCF mode to allow enough time for a node on the network to acknowledge the receipt of a frame that was received in error by another node. The EIFS allows the node that received the erred frame to resynchronize to the current state of the medium.

extended service set (ESS)—An ESS is a collection of basic service sets, tied together by means of a distribution system, that share a common network name (Service Set Identifier).

Extended SSID (ESSID)—See Service Set Identifier (SSID).

Extensible Authentication Protocol (EAP)—EAP is a general protocol for Point-to-Point Protocol (PPP) authentication that supports multiple authentication mechanisms. EAP does not select a specific authentication mechanism at link control phase, but rather postpones this step until the authentication phase. This allows the authenticator to request more information before determining the specific authentication mechanism. This also permits the use of a "back-end" server, which actually implements the various mechanisms while the PPP authenticator merely passes through the authentication exchange. EAP serves as a flexible replacement for CHAP and/or PAP.

F connector—A coaxial cable F connector is a screw-on connector of the type used for cable television connections and typically has a 75-ohm impedance.

failover routing—Failover routing is a feature built into network devices that allows them to fail over to an alternative link if the primary connection fails.

Federal Communications Commission (FCC)—The FCC is an independent U.S. government agency, directly responsible to Congress. The FCC was established by the Communications Act of 1934 and is charged with regulating interstate and international communications by radio, television, wire, satellite, and cable. The FCC's jurisdiction covers the 50 states, the District of Columbia, and U.S. possessions.

File Transfer Protocol (FTP)—FTP is a TCP/IP protocol for file transfer.

firewall—A firewall is a device that interfaces the network to the outside world and shields the network from unauthorized users. The firewall does this by blocking certain types of traffic. For example, some firewalls permit only electronic mail traffic to enter the network from elsewhere. This helps protect the network against attacks made on other network resources, such as sensitive files, databases, and applications.

fragmentation threshold—In a wireless LAN, the fragmentation threshold is the point at which the network divides large frames into smaller ones for transmission. Each smaller frame is sent on its own and requires its own acknowledgement.

frame relay—Frame relay is a packet switching technology designed to move data across a WAN. Frame relay normally operates at speeds of 56 Kbps to 45 Mbps.

free-space path loss—Free-space path loss refers to the loss incurred by an RF signal due largely to "signal dispersion," which is a natural broadening of the wave front. The wider a wave front is, the less power that can be induced into the receiving antenna. This loss of signal strength is a function of distance alone and becomes a very important factor when considering link viability.

frequency converter—A frequency converter is an RF device used to convert one frequency range to another. A frequency converter converts a wireless link from a congested Industrial Scientific Medical (ISM) band to one that is less congested.

Frequency Hopping Spread Spectrum (FHSS)—FHSS takes the data signal and modulates it with a carrier signal that hops from frequency to frequency as a function of time over a wide band of frequencies. For example, a frequency-hopping radio will hop on individual carrier frequencies over the 2.4-GHz Industrial Scientific Medical (ISM) band between 2.402 GHz and 2.480 GHz. A hopping sequence called a "channel" determines the frequencies on which it will transmit and in which order. To properly receive the signal, the receiver must be set to the same channel and listen to the incoming signal at the right time at the correct frequency.

Fresnel Zone—The Fresnel Zone is the conical area around an RF transmission path extending out from an antenna in the direction the signal is traveling.

gain—Gain or amplification is the ratio of the strength of an output signal to that of an input signal. The output signal strength will be greater than the input.

Gigahertz (GHz)—A GHz is one billion cycles per second (hertz).

Global Positioning System (GPS)—GPS is a system that determines a position on the Earth's surface by triangulating signals from several satellites through a receiver on Earth.

Global System for Mobile Communications (GSM)—GSM is a family of global cellular network services providing voice, data, and messaging in over 170 countries. GSM is nonproprietary, uses time division multiple access (TDMA) technologies, and performs digital voice encoding.

GSM Subscriber Identity Module (SIM)—A GSM SIM is a smartcard installed in a cell phone that stores cryptographic codes used to authenticate callers and bill them for services. The SIM stores a customer unique key used to authenticate the caller. The SIM runs an algorithm that generates random numbers used to respond to authenticator challenges.

Health Insurance Portability and Accountability Act of 1996 (HIPAA)—HIPAA added limited protections to families considering the availability of health insurance. HIPAA aims to reduce the chance of individuals losing existing coverage and provides avenues for individuals to purchase their own coverage if they lose their employer's group coverage. Visit the U.S. Department of Health and Human Services Web site at **http://www.hhs.gov** for more information.

hidden node—Hidden node occurs when two wireless clients cannot hear each other's transmissions, but the access point can hear both; it causes excessive collisions on a wireless LAN. RTS/CTS can reduce collisions that are due to hidden node.

highly directional antenna—A highly directional antenna is one that tightly focuses the horizontal and vertical RF beamwidths to maximize the distance the propagated wave can travel.

HiperLAN—HiperLAN is a wireless LAN protocol developed by ETSI (European Telecommunications Standards Institute) that provides a 23.5 Mbps data rate in the 5-GHz band.

HiperLAN/2—HiperLAN/2 is an extension to the HiperLAN protocol developed by ETSI that provides a 54 Mbps data rate in the 5-GHz band.

HomeRF—Founded in March 1998, this organization's charter is to establish the mass deployment of interoperable wireless networking access devices; products utilize the 2.4-GHz ISM band, FHSS technology, and a proprietary access protocol called Simple Workflow Access Protocol (SWAP) to achieve data rates of up to 10 Mbps.

hop time—The hop time is the amount of time it takes for a frequency hopping device to hop to a new frequency.

horizontal beamwidth—Horizontal beamwidth is the measure of an RF signal's focus as it travels parallel to the Earth's surface.

horizontal polarization—In reference to antennas, horizontal polarization is the electrical field that is parallel to the surface of the earth.

Hypertext Transfer Protocol (HTTP)—HTTP is the Application Layer protocol used to request and transmit HTML documents. HTTP is the underlying protocol of the World Wide Web.

Hypertext Transfer Protocol Secure (HTTPS)—HTTPS secures Internet connections using Secure Socket Layer (SSL) technology to encrypt the client/server transactions. Also see Secure Sockets Layer.

IEEE 1363 (Public Key Encryption)—Pubickey encryption is a cryptographic system that uses two mathematically related keys: one key is used to encrypt a message, and the other to decrypt it. People who need to receive encrypted messages distribute their public keys but keep their private keys secret.

IEEE 1394 (Firewire)—IEEE 1394, named Firewire by Apple Computer, is a high speed serial bus technology designed to support fast PC peripherals. IEEE 1394 supports such real-time, high-bandwidth applications as full-motion video and CD–quality audio. Current versions 1394a and 1394b are rated at 800Kbps and 1600 Mbps, respectively.

impedance—Impedance is a component's resistance to AC current flow.

independent basic service set (IBSS)—IBSS is an IEEE 802.11-based wireless network that has no backbone infrastructure and consists of at least two wireless stations. This type of network is often referred to as an ad hoc network because it can be constructed quickly, without much planning, and it has no access point with which to connect. Client stations connect directly to each other.

Industrial, Scientific, and Medical (ISM) bands—ISM bands are radio frequency bands that the Federal Communications Commission (FCC) authorized for wireless LANs. The ISM bands are located at 915+/-13 MHz, 2450+/-50 MHz, and 5800+/-75 MHz.

Industry Standard Architecture (ISA)—ISA is an older PC bus technology used in IBM XT and AT computers.

infrared light—Infrared light is composed of light waves that have wavelengths ranging from about 0.75 to 1,000 microns, which is longer (lower in frequency) than the spectral colors, but much shorter (higher in frequency) than radio waves. Therefore, under most lighting conditions, infrared light is invisible to the naked eye.

Infrastructure mode—Infrastructure mode is a wireless network operating mode that requires an access point through which all wireless traffic is passed. Client-to-client transmissions are not allowed in infrastructure mode.

Initialization vector (IV)—The IV is a 24-bit number used to start and track wireless frames moving between nodes. The IV is concatenated with (appended to) the secret key to yield the WEP key.

insertion loss—Insertion loss is the reduction in signal strength caused by connecting any RF-rated device into a transmission path between the transmitter and the antenna.

Institute of Electrical and Electronic Engineers (IEEE)—IEEE is a United States-based standards organization participating in the development of standards for data transmission systems. IEEE has made significant progress in the establishment of standards for LANs, in particular, the IEEE 802 series of standards.

Inter Access Point Protocol (IAPP)—Developed by several wireless product vendors, IAPP is a protocol designed to support roaming across multivendor APs. The protocol supports roaming both on single subnets and across subnet boundaries.

interference—Interference is any energy that interferes with the clear reception of a signal. For example, if one person is speaking, the sound of a second person's voice interferes with the first. See noise.

Internet Packet Exchange (IPX)—IPX is Novell's Network Layer protocol that is a derivative of the Xerox Network Systems Internet Datagram Protocol (XNS IDP) developed by Xerox. It is used in Novell NetWare networks.

Internet Protocol (IP)—IP is a Layer 3 protocol that assigns IP addresses to devices in a network for routing purposes.

Internet Protocol Security (IPSec)—The IETF has proposed IPSec as a set of protocols and procedures for securing IP packet traffic on publicly accessible IP networks. IPSec supports several cipher algorithms, and enables both payload authentication and encryption.

key server—A key server is a centralized device that dynamically generates WEP keys for each session or packet.

last mile—Last mile is a term used to describe the local loop. A local loop is the pair of copper wires that connects a customer's telephone to the telephone company's CO switching system.

LEAP—See EAPCisco Wireless.

Lightweight Directory Access Protocol (LDAP)—LDAP is a set of protocols for accessing information directories conforming to the X.500 standard.

link speed—Link speed is the data rate at which a network connection operates.

load balancing—Load balancing is the practice of spreading processing work or communications requests evenly across multiple devices, communication links, or agents. For example, large Web sites load balance among two or more identical Web servers. Contact centers use load balancing software to distribute work fairly among its agents.

lobes—Lobes are the electrical fields emitted by an antenna; also called beams.

logarithm—A logarithm is a mathematical function; it is the exponent that indicates the power to which a number is raised to produce a given number. For example, 10 squared = 100; thus, 10 raised to the second power equals 100.

loss—Loss is a ratio of the strength of an output signal to that of an input signal, where the output signal strength will be smaller than the input.

media access control layer (MAC Layer)—The MAC Layer, one of the two sublayers that make up the Data Link Layer of the Open Systems Interconnection (OSI) model, provides medium-access services for IEEE 802 LANs.

media converter—A media converter is a Physical Layer network device used to convert electrical signals from one physical media type to another. For example, you would use a media converter to convert Ethernet over copper to Ethernet over fiber.

megabits per second (Mbps)—Mbps identifies the rate at which information travels down a physical medium or through space (wireless). Mbps is equivalent to 1,000,000 bits per second. 1.544 Mbps is equivalent to 1,544,000 bits per second.

megahertz (MHz)—Radio signals are measured in cycles per second, or Hertz (Hz). One Hz is 1 cycle per second; 1,000 cycles per second is 1 kHz; 1 million cycles per second is 1 MHz; and 1 billion cycles per second is 1 GHz.

Message Digest 5 (MD5)—MD5 is a one-way hash algorithm that converts a message into a fixed string of digits called a "message digest." It is used to create digital signatures.

message integrity code (MIC)—A MIC is a cryptographic checksum appended to an encrypted packet used by the recipient to validate that the data was not tampered with in transit.

microsecond—A microsecond is one millionth of a second.

milliwatt—A milliwatt is one thousandth of a watt. It is used as a reference point for signal levels at a given point in a circuit.

Mobile Internet Protocol (IP)—Mobile IP is a protocol developed by the Internet Engineering Task Force (IETF) to enable users to roam to parts of the network associated with a different IP address than what is loaded in the user's appliance. It is an extension to IP that provides mobile clients a single IP address, no matter where they are connected to the home network. Mobile nodes connect to the local network by means of home agents, which are routers that track the mobile nodes' location; or if away, by means of foreign agents, which are routers on foreign networks that can relay packets from the home agent to the mobile node. Wherever located, the mobile keeps its home IP address and subnet, using a second IP address supplied by the foreign agent when on the foreign network.

modulation—Modulation is the process of modifying the form of a carrier wave (electrical signal) so that it can carry intelligent information on a communications medium.

multicast—A multicast is a frame addressed to a specific group of nodes. A unicast is a frame addressed to a single node. A broadcast is a frame destined for all nodes on a network.

multipath—Multipath refers to the routes taken by RF energy between a transmitter and a receiver. At a given transmitter, one signal is transmitted. However, after the signal hits many reflection points along the path from the transmitter to a receiver, many signals can result. Signals can cancel themselves out, decrease in amplitude, increase in amplitude, or becomes corrupted.

narrowband—Narrowband is a form of radio transmission that uses only a small portion of the RF spectrum. In the context of wireless LANs, a narrowband signal is one that uses only as much of the frequency spectrum as is needed to carry the data signal.

narrowband interference—Narrowband interference is RF interference that occurs over a small portion of the RF spectrum.

National Electrical Manufacturers Association (NEMA)—NEMA is an organization established in 1926 to "support the standardization of electrical equipment, enabling consumers to select a range of safe, effective, and compatible electrical products." Learn more about NEMA at **http://www.nema.org**.

National Institute of Standards and Technology (NIST)—NIST is a nonregulatory US federal agency whose mission is to "develop and promote measurements, standards, and technology to enhance productivity, facilitate trade, and improve the quality of life." See **http://www.nist.gov** for more information.

NetBIOS Extended User Interface (NetBEUI)—NetBEUI is a Network and Transport Layer protocol designed to work within a single physical LAN. (It does not provide packet routing between networks.) NetBEUI is typically integrated with NetBIOS.

Network Address Translation (NAT)—NAT is an Internet standard that enables a local-area network (LAN) to use one set of IP addresses for internal traffic and a second set of addresses for external traffic. The four types of IP addresses are: static, dynamic, overloading, and overlapping.

Network Allocation Vector (NAV)—The NAV is a virtual carrier sense mechanism used to predict future network traffic based on the time set in the RTS and CTS frames' NAV field. When the NAV equals a value of zero, the medium is assumed idle, while any other state indicates the medium is busy.

This carrier-sensing mechanism is considered virtual because nodes do not listen to the physical medium, but instead reference the timer state to determine when to access the medium.

Network Basic Input/Output System (NetBIOS)—NetBIOS is a software system developed by Sytek and IBM that has become the de facto standard for application interface to LANs. It operates at the Session Layer of the OSI protocol stack. Applications can call NetBIOS routines to carry out functions, such as data transfer, across a LAN.

noise—Noise is any condition, such as electrical interference, that destroys signal integrity. Noise can be caused by many electromagnetic sources, such as radio transmissions, electrical cables, electric motors, lighting dimmers, or bad cable connections. See interference.

noise floor—Noise floor is the level of RF that is inherently present in the surrounding environment. This noise is generated by a number of sources and is typically between -70 and -100 dBm in most environments. For a data signal to be effectively communicated, it must be significantly higher than the noise floor, which is high enough for the receiver to clearly distinguish between the RF data signal and the background noise.

Novell Directory Services (NDS)—NDS is Novell's global database that stores all information about network objects (resources) and user permissions, and provides secure access to those objects.

N-type connector—An N-type connector is a large, threaded connector used on many commercial antennas. The connector was named for Paul Neill of Bell Labs, its inventor. N-type connectors are rated at either 50 ohms or 75 ohms and come in an assortment of types, such as reverse polarity, reverse thread, and standard. NIST certifies these connectors to 18 GHz, but they are sometimes used in transmission circuits up to 26 GHz.

nulling—Nulling is the multipath condition that occurs when one or more reflected RF signals arrive at the receiver 180 degrees out-of-phase with the main wave, at such an amplitude that they cancel, or null, the main wave.

omnidirectional antenna—An omnidirectional (omni) antenna is one that has a 360-degree horizontal beamwidth and a variable vertical beamwidth. Omni antennas propagate the RF signal equally in all horizontal directions.

open system authentication—Open system authentication is the IEEE 802.11 default authentication method, which is a very simple, two-step process. First the station wanting to authenticate with another station sends an authentication management frame containing the sending station's identification. The receiving station then sends back a frame alerting whether it recognizes the identity of the authenticating station.

OpenAir—OpenAir is an FHSS standard, developed by the Wireless LAN Interoperability Forum, that specifies data rates of 800 Kbps or 1.6 Mbps.

Organization Unit Identifier (OUI)—The OUI is the company ID component of a MAC address assigned by the IEEE. The OUI is the first six hex characters (24 bits) of the MAC address.

Orthogonal Frequency Division Multiplexing (OFDM)—OFDM is a communications technique that divides a communications channel into a number of equally spaced frequency bands. A subcarrier carrying a portion of the user information is transmitted in each band. Each subcarrier is orthogonal with (independent of) every other subcarrier.

packet binary convolutional code (PBCC)—PBCC is a Texas Instruments-developed coding technology for wireless LANs designed to support data rates of 22 Mbps on 802.11b networks. Its current version is called PBCC-22.

packet queuing—A generic term used to describe the segregation of outbound packets at a network device's port, arranging them and putting them in line for transmission based on some Quality of Service (QoS) characteristic.

Password Authentication Protocol (PAP)—PAP is a method to identify and authenticate Point-to-Point (PPP) peers.

Peripheral Component Interconnect (PCI)—PCI is a local bus that provides a high-speed connection between peripherals and a CPU. It includes buffers that allow relatively slow peripherals to operate asynchronously and can be used with other buses such as ISA or EISA.

personal area network (PAN)—A PAN is a short-distance wireless network that connects a user's personal electronic devices, such as a cell phone, PDA, and headphones. It is also called a WPAN.

Personal Communications System (PCS)—PCS is a set of digital cellular services popular in the United States. PCS phones communicate digitally in the 1.9 GHz frequency band.

Personal Computer Memory Card International Association (PCMCIA)—The PCMCIA slot in a laptop was designed for PC memory expansion. Network interface cards (NICs) and modems can attach to a laptop through the PCMCIA slot.

personal digital assistant (PDA)—PDAs are small, handheld devices that provide a subset of the operations of a typical PC. They are used for scheduling, electronic notepads, and small database applications.

phase—RF signals cycle over a period of 360 degrees. A signal's phase refers to its relationship to its horizontal axis, typically represented on a graph as a horizontal line. A signal at its peak amplitude is considered at a phase of 90 degrees, while at its lowest amplitude its phase it 270 degrees. When a signal is phase modulated, each phase of the signal presents a certain digital bit pattern.

Physical Layer Convergence Protocol (PLCP)—PLCP is the Physical Layer convergence function through which the Physical Layer communicates with the Data Link Layer in 802.11 wireless networks. PLCP maps the MAC layer frames into a format suitable for the transmission of data (user and management) between wireless devices.

pigtail—Pigtails are used for adapting proprietary connectors on bridges and access points to standard connectors.

plaintext—Plaintext is unencrypted information.

Plug and play (PnP)—PnP is a standard that gives computers the ability to automatically recognize a newly installed device, without a complex process of user configuration.

Pocket PC—Pocket PC is the name Microsoft gave to its update of its Windows CE handheld computer operating system. It is also a term used to generically describe handheld computers running a version of Microsoft's Pocket PC operating system.

Point Coordination Function (PCF)—PCF is an IEEE 802.11 mode that enables contention-free frame transfer based on a priority mechanism; stations are polled for the need for frame transmission. It enables time-bounded services that support the transmission of voice and video.

Point Coordination Function Interframe Space (PIFS)—PIFS is used as interframe spacing on PCF mode networks to allow an access point to gain control of the medium before any DCF node.

point-to-multipoint (PtMP)—A PtMP connection connects a single point to multiple outlying points. Also known as hub-and-spoke, the hub is the focal point for communications between several adjacent networks. All communications center on the hub.

point-to-point (PtP)—A PtP connection provides dedicated communications between two, and only two, endpoints.

Point-to-Point Protocol over Ethernet (PPPoE)—RFC 2516 describes PPPoE as an extension to the PPP protocol for use over shared network connections. A service provider can assign login credentials to each user of the shared connection, require them to log in to the carrier network to use the connection, and thus bill each user individually.

Point-to-Point Tunneling Protocol (PPTP)—Microsoft developed PPTP for VPNs using Microsoft Windows 95/98 and Windows NT. PPTP can support tunneling of IP, IPX, NetBios, and NetBEUI protocols inside IP

packets. PPTP also works with Windows 2000, XP, Linux, and FreeBSD.

polling—Polling is sequential interrogation of devices for various purposes, such as avoiding contention, determining operational status, or determining readiness to send or receive data.

Port Address Translation (PAT)—PAT is a NAT technique where the local network host source address is converted by the NAT device to a single public address shared by many local hosts. This single source IP address and a unique source port address, again assigned by the NAT device, identify each outbound connection. This eliminates the need for the NAT device to maintain a one-to-one mapping of local host addresses to public host addresses.

portal—A portal is a logical point where MAC Service Data Units (MSDUs) from a nonIEEE 802.11 LAN enter the distribution system of an extended service set wireless network.

Power over Ethernet (PoE)—PoE is the method of injecting DC current over the unused pairs in Cat5 cabling to power access points in remote locations; it reduces difficulty in access point installation in terms of power installation.

Power Save Polling (PSP) mode—A wireless client operating in PSP mode can sleep for short time periods. This sleep mode conserves power on client nodes that operate on batteries, such as laptops and handhelds.

print serving—Print serving occurs when several network devices need to share a single printer, and a print server is used. A print server is a LAN-based computer or device that provides users on a network access to the shared printer.

probe frame—When a wireless station is actively scanning for access points, it sends a probe frame containing the SSID of the target network. The answering access points respond to the probe frame with a probe response frame that contains basically the same information as a beacon management frame.

probe request frame—Probe request frames are sent by a wireless client when actively scanning for access points to locate a network to join. The probe frame contains the desired network SSID, or a broadcast SSID, and indicates the need for the access point to respond with connectivity information.

processing gain—Processing gain is the ratio of the chip rate to the data rate of a direct sequence signal. A higher-processing gain is better and increases a signal's interference immunity. Also see chipping code.

profile—In general, a profile is a set of characteristics that identify a certain user, capability, or component. On a wireless device, a profile is used to identify a connection's characteristics, such as the encryption level, SSID, and so forth. By using profiles, one can easily change a client's configuration to match a particular network configuration.

pseudo-random number generator (PRNG)—A PRNG is a hardware device designed to generate a random number string for use in cryptography and other applications. A PRNG emulates a hardware random number generator in software.

Quadrature Phase Shift Keying (QPSK)—QPSK is a modulation technique that represents digital data with a four-phase shift in the radio frequency (RF) carrier frequency.

Quality of Service (QoS)—QoS defines the type of service a communications link can provide. QoS can specify factors such as delay, throughput, error rate, and loss.

radiation pattern—A radiation pattern is the pattern in which radio signals propagate from an antenna.

radio frequency (RF)—Radio antennas emit electromagnetic fields. These fields propagate at varying frequencies, depending on the application. These frequencies fall into a radiation spectrum called RF. The RF spectrum ranges from 3KHz to over 300 GHz.

Rate limiting—Rate limiting is a technique of controlling how much of the available link bandwidth each connection is supplied.

RC4—RC4 is an encryption cipher used in WEP to generate the encryption key for wireless node to wireless access point authentication.

reassociation service—Reassociation service enables an IEEE 802.11 station to change its association with different access points as the station moves throughout the facility without reauthentication.

Received Signal Strength Indicator (RSSI)—The RSSI is the indicator of the received RF signal energy at the network device. This is an optional parameter ranging from 0 to the maximum RSSI intended to be used as a relative measure of the received signal.

reflection—Reflection occurs when RF signals contact a large surface through which they cannot pass. The signal's path is modified from that of the main signal's, causing signal loss and scattering.

refraction—Refraction is the tendency of a light ray, or electromagnetic signal, to be deflected from a straight path when it passes obliquely from one medium into another medium that has a different index of refraction.

Remote Authentication Dial-In User Service (RADIUS)—RADIUS is an authentication service specified by the IETF that utilizes a computer-based database (RADIUS server) to compare usernames and passwords to allow access to a network.

repeater mode—When operating in repeater mode, an access point relays wireless signals between remote access points or access points and clients. This serves to extend the reach of a wireless network, but takes a toll on throughput.

Request to Send/Clear to Send (RTS/CTS)—RTS/CTS is a virtual carrier sense protocol used on WLANs. When RTS/CTS is enabled on a wireless LAN, a station wishing to communicate effectively reserves the medium for a period of time. All other stations then must wait for the communications to end before they can use the medium.

resistance—Resistance refers to the opposition of current flow in a conductor. Different conductors present different resistance characteristics.

Resource Reservation Setup Protocol (RSVP)—RSVP is a network protocol that allows a network node to reserve the transmission medium for a specified period of time for Quality of Service (QoS)-oriented applications, such as video.

reverse polarity N-type—A reverse polarity N-type is an N-type connector with the positive and negative contacts reversed.

reverse threaded N-type—A reverse threaded N-type is an N-type connector with the threads reversed.

RF attenuator—An RF attenuator is a component installed in the path of an RF sig-

nal for the purpose of introducing loss. The attenuator is placed between the radio output and the antenna input.

RF coverage—RF coverage is the area over which an RF signal must extend to support the network users.

RF line of sight (LOS)—RF LOS is the clear radio signal path from the transmitting node to the receiver. An RF device can see an RF LOS based on both the visual line of sight and a clear Fresnel Zone.

Rijndael—The Rijndael algorithm is used to generate the 128-bit, 192-bit, and 256-bit keys used in the AES encryption standard.

roaming—The process of moving from one access point to another without having to reauthenticate to the wireless network.

Role-based access control (RBAC)—RBAC allows a network administrator to assign a certain level of wireless network access to a person based on their role in the organization. This allows the administrator to control network resource usage while allowing easy user moves, adds, and changes.

root mode—When operating in root mode, an access point is connected to the host wired network segment, and is able to communicate with other root mode APs over the wired segment. Clients and APs operating in repeater mode connect over wireless links to a root mode access point.

Routing Information Protocol (RIP)—RIP is a common routing protocol. RIP bases its routing path on the distance (number of hops) to the destination. RIP maintains optimum routing paths by sending out routing update messages if the network topology changes. For example, if a router finds that a particular link is faulty, it will update its routing table and then send a copy of the modified table to each of its neighbors.

Routing Information Protocol (RIP) v2— RIPv2 is a distance vector routing protocol designed to improve on the original RIP by subnet mask information and provide some security to the routing table update messages.

scattering—Scattering is the diffusion of an RF signal caused by the signal coming in contact with uneven yet reflective surfaces or by travelling through a medium containing heavy particle content. The scattered signal is simultaneously dispersed in many directions; resulting signals do not have enough power to reach the intended receiver.

Secure Sockets Layer (SSL)—SSL is an application of both public-key and single-key encryption that secures an Internet connection between browser and server. Web-page URLs that use SSL begin with "https://."

semidirectional antenna—A semidirectional antenna is one where the antenna focuses most of the radio signal energy in one direction, while creating several smaller lobes around the edges of the major signal. Semidirectional antennas are well suited for short to medium range bridging between buildings, but can also be used indoors to better direct the radio signal down halls or around obstacles.

sensitivity threshold—A wireless radio's sensitivity threshold is the point at which the radio can clearly distinguish a signal from the background noise.

Service Set Identifier (SSID)—The SSID is a unique, case-sensitive, alphanumeric network name used to identify a wireless LAN. The SSID can be used to segment wireless networks, but is only a rudimentary security measure. Access points broadcast SSIDs in their beacon frames; therefore, SSIDs can be easily intercepted.

shared key authentication—Shared key authentication is a type of authentication that assumes each station has received a secret shared key through a secure channel that is independent from an 802.11 network. Stations authenticate through shared knowledge of the secret key. Use of shared key authentication requires implementation of the 802.11 Wireless Equivalent Privacy (WEP) algorithm.

Shared Wireless Access Protocol (SWAP)— SWAP is a wireless protocol used in Home-RF networks that combines CSMA and TDMA technologies for wireless voice and data networking.

shielded twisted-pair (STP)—STP is a type of copper wiring typically used for high-speed computer network transmission. A twisted pair consists of two thin copper wires, twisted around each other to cancel EMI and RFI. A flexible metal sheath encloses the wires to provide additional protection from interference.

Short Interframe Space (SIFS)—SIFS are the short interframe spaces between RTS, CTS, and ACK frames that are designed to give these frames priority over all others on the network. To enable a receiving station to formulate a response to the received frame, SIFSs are used as a time for processing or turn-around.

signal strength—Signal strength is the power level of an RF signal.

signal-to-noise ratio (SNR)—The signal-to-noise ratio is a measure of the useful information being communicated relative to anything else, including external noise or interference.

Simple Network Management Protocol (SNMP)—SNMP is a network management protocol that defines the transfer of information between Management Information

Bases (MIBs). Most high-end network monitoring stations require the implementation of SNMP on each of the components the organization wishes to monitor.

site survey—Conducting a site survey is the act of surveying an area to determine the contours of RF coverage in order to ensure proper wireless LAN operation through appropriate wireless LAN hardware placement.

small office/home office (SOHO)—SOHO is a term used to describe data and voice communications workers who either work from their home, or work in a small office of 50 or fewer workers.

smart card—Smart cards are plastic cards that contain embedded integrated circuit (IC) microprocessors and a standard magnetic strip. A user inserts a smart card into a chip-reading terminal, which reads the information stored on it. Smart cards can eliminate the need for users to remember (and frequently change) passwords and other authentication information.

sniffer—A sniffer is a generic term used to describe a hardware or software device used to capture and display network packets and their contents. SNIFFER is a registered trademark of Network Associates, Inc.

Spanning Tree Protocol (STP)—STP is a link management protocol that is part of the IEEE 802.1 standard (802.1d) for media access control bridges. Using the spanning tree algorithm, STP provides path redundancy while preventing undesirable loops in a network that are created by multiple active paths between stations. Loops occur when there are alternate routes between hosts. To establish path redundancy, STP creates a tree that spans all of the switches in an extended network, forcing redundant paths into a

standby, or blocked, state. STP allows only one active path at a time between any two network devices (this prevents the loops) but establishes the redundant links as a backup if the initial link should fail.

spectrum analyzer—A spectrum analyzer is an instrument that identifies the amplitude of signals at various frequencies.

stratification—Stratification occurs when air layers of different temperatures or densities are stacked one on top of the other. Stratification causes RF waves to bend as they pass through the layers.

subminiature type A (SMA) connector—An SMA connector is a small, threaded connector used on coaxial cables. The male component includes six flat lands to facilitate tightening the connector with a wrench. These connectors almost always have a 50-ohm impedance and are typically used up to 26 GHz.

superframe—A superframe is a special timeframe during which a network in Point Coordination Function (PCF) mode is allowed to alternatively have both a contention-free period and a contention period. This allows DCF and PCF mode clients to coexist on the same network at the same time. The superframe consists of a beacon, a contention-free period (CFP), and a contention period (CP).

Third Generation (3G)—3G is the latest Global System for Mobile Communications (GSM) cellular communications technology, which combines code division multiple access (CDMA) technologies with Internet Protocol (IP) services.

throughput—Throughput describes the overall capacity of a network to perform useful work. While bandwidth measurements focus on the raw number of bits a network can carry, throughput measurements express the actual or effective data rates of a network. Throughput is most often used to describe the overall performance of a network. It is measured in pulses per second (PPS) or bits per second (bps).

Time Division Multiple Access (TDMA)—TDMA is a technology for delivering digital wireless service using time division multiplexing (TDM). TDMA works by dividing a radio frequency into time slots, and then allocating slots to multiple calls. In this way, a single frequency can support multiple, simultaneous data channels. TDMA is used by HomeRF, HiperLAN/1 and /2, and cellular systems (GSM).

TNC connector—A TNC connector is a small, threaded connector, knurled around its circumference to facilitate finger tightening.

Token Ring—Token Ring is a network architecture that uses a ring topology and a token passing strategy to control network access. The IEEE 802.5 standard defines the token ring architecture and how it operates at the OSI model Physical and Data Link Layers. Each node on the ring acts as a repeater, passing the token from node to node as the token travels around the entire ring. Each node must wait its turn to transmit data and may only transmit when it controls the token.

transient current—A transient current is a momentary, additional, unintentional current introduced into a circuit by some external phenomena, such as a nearby lightning strike, high current device, or high voltage line.

unicast—A unicast is a transmission sent to a single network address. A unicast functions differently than a broadcast, which is sent to all network addresses simultaneously, and a multicast, which is sent to several addresses at once.

unidirectional amplifier—A unidirectional RF amplifier boosts the signal's power level in only one direction, typically on the radio's transmit side.

Universal Serial Bus (USB)—USB is an external bus that can transfer up to 12 Mbps. Up to 127 peripheral devices can be connected to a single USB port. A USB adapter is a PC expansion device that conforms to the USB standard. USB device examples include network interface cards (NICs), modems, scanners, and CD-ROM drives.

Unlicensed National Information Infrastructure (UNII) bands—A segment of RF frequencies allocated by the FCC for unlicensed data communications, used by IEEE 802.11a, 802.11h, and HyperLAN2 wireless LANs; the three bands are: 5.15 to 5.25 GHz, 5.25 to 5.35 GHz, and 5.725 to 5.825 GHz.

unused pair—Unused pairs become available in Ethernet UTP networks. Typical Ethernet unshielded twisted pair (UTP) networks only use two pairs of a 4-pair Category 5 cable for data transmission. The remaining unused pairs can be used for other purposes, such as supplying Power over Ethernet.

upfade—Upfade describes the condition when multipath causes an RF signal to gain strength.

User tracking—User tracking enables the network administrator to locate and track hosts on the network.

variable output—Variable output is a feature built into a wireless access point that allows the administrator to control the radio output by means of software, rather than inserting attenuators in the RF signal path.

vertical beamwidth—Vertical beamwidth is the measure of an RF signal's focus as it travels perpendicular to the Earth's surface.

vertical polarization—In reference to antennas, vertical polarization is the orientation or alignment of the electrical field perpendicular to the surface of the Earth.

Virtual Private Network (VPN)—A VPN is a connection over a shared network that behaves like a dedicated link. VPNs are created using a technique called "tunneling," which transmits data packets across a public network, such as the Internet or other commercially available network, in a private "tunnel" that simulates a point-to-point connection. The tunnels of a VPN can be encrypted for additional security.

virtual server—A wireless gateway can act as a virtual network server, accepting connection requests for a specific service, such as HTTP or FTP, and forwarding the request to a local host. To the requesting node, the connection appears to terminate at the gateway, when in fact the gateway forwards the request to the local server. The local server is not accessible directly from the outside network.

visual line of sight (LOS)—Visual LOS is the apparently "straight" line from the object in site to the observer's eye.

Voltage Standing Wave Ratio (VSWR)—VSWR is the ratio of forward RF signal power to the reverse power. Reverse power occurs when there is an impedance mismatch in the RF circuit.

war driving—War driving is a slang term that describes the practice of listening in on and capturing information from wireless LANs by intercepting RF signals emanating outside of a network coverage area. For example, an individual who parks in a company's parking lot, points a directional antenna at the building, and captures packets from RF signals "leaking" beyond the building's walls, is war driving.

watt—A watt is the unit of electricity consumption that represents the product of amperage and voltage. The power requirement of a device is listed in watts; thus, you can find the ampere requirement by dividing the wattage by the voltage (for example, 1,200 watts divided by 120 volts, equals 10 amps).

WEPv2—WEPv2, the latest iteration of the WEP protocol, was designed to add increased security by using technologies such as the AES algorithm to generate encryption keys of 192 bits and 256 bits. See Wired Equivalent Privacy.

wide area network (WAN)—WANs are essentially interconnected local area networks (LANs) or metropolitan area networks (MANs). They can be homogeneous, interconnecting similar networks, but are often heterogeneous, interconnecting LANs or MANs that have been built using different technologies. A WAN can span campuses, cities, states, or even continents.

Wi-Fi hot spot—A Wi-Fi hot spot location is a location considered likely to host many wireless users.

Windows CE—Windows CE is Microsoft's first operation system written for use on small, handheld computers.

Wired Equivalent Privacy (WEP)—WEP is an optional IEEE 802.11 function that offers frame transmission privacy similar to a wired network. WEP generates secret shared encryption keys that both source and destination stations can use to alter frame bits to avoid disclosure to eavesdroppers.

Wireless demilitarized zone (WDMZ)—A WDMZ is a security solution typically implemented in medium-scale and large-scale wireless LAN deployments. Using a firewall device, WDMZs separate access points, which are insecure devices, from other network segments.

Wireless Ethernet Compatibility Alliance (WECA)—WECA's mission is to certify interoperability of Wi-Fi™ (IEEE 802.11) products and to promote Wi-Fi as the global wireless LAN standard across all market segments.

Wireless Fidelity™ (Wi-Fi™)—Wi-Fi™ is the WECA certification standard signifying interoperability among 802.11b products.

Wireless Internet Service Provider (WISP)—A WISP is an Internet service provider (ISP) that provides customers with access to the Internet over wireless networks. WISPs often operate in rural areas where the wired infrastructure is inadequate for providing anything but dialup Internet access.

Wireless LAN Association (WLANA)—WLANA is a nonprofit educational trade association, comprised of the leaders and technology innovators in the local area wireless technology industry. Through sponsor and affiliate members' knowledge and experience, WLANA provides a clearinghouse of information about wireless local area applications, issues, and trends. In addition, WLANA serves as an industry resource regarding wireless LAN and PAN products, as well as to industry press and analysts.

wireless metropolitan area network (WMAN)—A wireless MAN provides communications links between buildings, avoiding the costly installation of cabling or leasing fees and the down time associated with system failures.

wireless personal area network (WPAN)—A wireless PAN uses RF technology to create a short range, personal communications network.

wireless wide area network (WWAN)—A wireless WAN is a wireless network that connects LANs across large geographic areas, such as between sites in different cities or states.

xDSL—xDSL is a generic term used to describe different types of Digital Subscriber Line services.

network 14
personal area network (See WPAN)
residential gateway 161 to 164
VPNs 477
wide area network (WWAN) 78
workgroup bridge 147 to 149
Wireless LAN 82
WISP 6
WLANA 255, 274
WLIF 281
WMAN 78, 84
WPAN 78, 83
WWAN 78

X

xDSL 6

Notes

Overall Course Evaluation Survey

Congratulations on completing this course! We hope you enjoyed your learning journey.

This survey will help us identify where we can focus our strengths and improve our weaknesses. As a token of our appreciation for your time in completing this, we will send you a Certificate of Appreciation (if you tell us who you are!).

Certified Wireless Network Administrator: Official Certification Guide

Course # (see book cover): _____

Location of course: _____

Instructor-led ☐   Self-paced ☐

Did you use the CD?   Yes ☐   No ☐   Comments: _____

Did you access the online course?   Yes ☐   No ☐   Comments: _____

Did you use the Web board for support?   Yes ☐   No ☐   Comments: _____

Did you visit the student Web site?   Yes ☐   No ☐   Comments: _____

What are this course's strengths? _____

What did you like best? _____

What are this course's weaknesses? _____

What did you like least? _____

Would you be interested in other titles from this publisher? _____

If so, what specific topics would you like to see addressed? _____

Optional (must provide this information if you would like a Certificate of Appreciation):

Name: _____

Occupation/Title: _____

Company: _____

Address: _____

City/State/ZIP: _____

Country (if outside USA): _____

E-mail address: _____

Gender: Male ☐   Female ☐

Age: Under 25 ☐   26-40 ☐   41-60 ☐   61+ ☐

Please return this survey to: WestNet Learning Technologies, Attn: Executive Vice President, 5420 Ward Rd., Suite 150, Arvada, CO 80002 USA

Or fax to: 303-432-2565